CONCEPTS AND INQUIRIES FOR TEACHING ELEMENTARY SCHOOL SCIENCE

Fifth Edition

Joseph M. Peters
The University of West Florida

David L. Stout
The University of West Florida

PEARSON

Merrill
Prentice Hall

Upper Saddle River, New Jersey
Columbus, Ohio

Library of Congress Cataloging in Publication Data

Peters, Joseph M.
    Concepts and inquiries for teaching elementary school science / Joseph M. Peters, David L. Stout. — 5th ed.
        p. cm.
    Rev. ed. of: Concepts and inquiries in elementary school science / Joseph M. Peters, Peter C. Gega. 4th ed. c2002.
    Includes bibliographical references and index.
    ISBN 0-13-171598-4
    1. Science—Study and teaching (Elementary) I. Stout, David L. II. Peters, Joseph M. Concepts and inquiries in elementary school science. III. Title.
    LB1585.G38 2006
    372.3'5044—dc22

2005040828

Vice President and Executive Publisher: Jeffery W. Johnston
Senior Editor: Linda Ashe Montgomery
Senior Editorial Assistant: Laura J. Weaver
Senior Development Editor: Hope Madden
Production Coordination: Jolynn Feller, Carlisle Publishers Services
Senior Production Editor: Linda Hillis Bayma
Design Coordinator: Diane C. Lorenzo
Photo Coordinator: Monica Merkel
Cover and Text Designer: Kristina Holmes
Cover photos: Nature Picture Library
Production Manager: Pamela D. Bennett
Director of Marketing: Ann Castel Davis
Marketing Manager: Darcy Betts Prybella
Marketing Coordinator: Brian Mounts

This book was set in Goudy by Carlisle Communications, Ltd. It was printed and bound by Courier Kendallville, Inc. The cover was printed by Phoenix Color Corp.

Photo Credits: Anthony Magnacca/Merrill: 4, 118, 152, 216, 264, 298, 330; Anne Vega/Merrill: 38, 182, 368; Irene Springer/ PH College: 62, 307; Cindy Charles/PhotoEdit: 66; Spencer Grant/Stock Boston: 84; Harold E. Edgerton/ USDA/NRCS/NCGC/ National Cartography and Geospatial Center: 85; Sybil Shelton/ PH College: 96; U.S. Department of Agriculture: 206, 313; Bruce Roberts/Photo Researchers: 207; National Institutes of Health: 227; Runk/Shoenburger–Grant Heilman Photography: 232, 251 (bottom); American Museum of Natural History: 233, 238; W.P. Taylor/ U.S. Department of the Interior: 234 (left); Modern Curriculum Press/Pearson Learning: 234 (right); Silver Burdett Ginn: 251 (top); USDA Soil Conservation Service: 312; U.S. Geological Survey/ U.S. Department of the Interior: 323(A, C), 324(E, H), 325(I, J, K, L); Richard M. Busch: 323(B); USGS/Courtesy James B. Stevens: 323(D); U.S. Geological Survey, Denver: 324(F, G); National Oceanic and Atmospheric Administration: 363(A, B, C); Courtesy of All Weather Inc., Sacramento, CA: 364.

Pearson Education Ltd.
Pearson Education Singapore Pte. Ltd.
Pearson Education Canada, Ltd.
Pearson Education—Japan

Pearson Education Australia Pty. Limited
Pearson Education North Asia Ltd.
Pearson Educación de Mexico, S.A. de C.V.
Pearson Education Malaysia Pte. Ltd.

10 9 8 7 6 5 4 3 2
ISBN 0-13-171598-4

CONCEPTS AND INQUIRIES FOR TEACHING ELEMENTARY SCHOOL SCIENCE

This book is dedicated to Darlene, Joseph B., and
Brenda Peters and Patty, Danny, and Kelly Stout
for their inspiration and support throughout this project.

PREFACE

Elementary and middle school teaching is a rewarding and exciting career. Your future as a professional educator includes the responsibility to help your students meet the demands and challenges of society, and the elementary and middle school classroom is where it all begins. It is your job to build the skills, content knowledge, and desire for inquiry that will allow your students to function in a society that will be highly scientific and technologically developed. This new edition of *Concepts and Inquiries for Teaching Elementary School Science* has been crafted to help you do just that.

The text focuses on inquiry activities and related conceptual information. Its 12 inquiry units utilize the constructivist learning model (Yager, 1991) and the learning cycle model—concept exploration, conception invention, and concept explanation (Barman, 1989) —to help model constructivist applications for science teaching and learning.

Each inquiry unit begins with a brief introduction, followed by sample benchmarks and standards, and inquiry activities grouped by topic. The inquiry investigations also offer chances for you and your students to inquire, as co-investigators if you wish, into open-ended problems and topics. The learning experiences use everyday, easy-to-get materials and can also enrich school science programs. Engaging in the inquiry activities can help you gain confidence in conceptual knowledge even as the concept explanations located at the end of each inquiry unit will help you solidify your science background knowledge. The scientific concepts that are tied to the inquiry experiences provide useful, everyday examples of scientific principles at work.

A Closer Look at the Text's Features

Addressing Today's Science Teaching Realities

Today's science teachers must be accountable to state and national standards as they ensure their teaching meets the needs of every learner in their classroom:

- *Benchmarks and Standards* features throughout inquiry units help you see how to integrate the *National Science Education Standards* in your own teaching.

- *Scaffolding for English Learners* features in the inquiry units help you adapt your instruction to benefit English learners.

- *Adapting for Students with Exceptionalities* features in the inquiry units help you adapt your inquiry lessons to better support students with exceptionalities.

Providing the Materials You Need

To truly prepare you for your classroom, we have created tools that will build your own understanding of inquiry science teaching and become meaningful tools for your own classroom.

- *Twelve Inquiry Units* model constructivist applications, build conceptual knowledge, and provide a bank of classroom-tested lessons to use in your own science classroom.

- *Teaching Tips* throughout inquiry units provide starting points, suggest activities, and consider safety to help you master constructivist science teaching.

Additional Titles of Interest

- *Science in Elementary Education: Methods, Concepts, and Inquiries,* Tenth Edition, 0-13-171601-8
- *Methods for Teaching Elementary School Science,* Fifth Edition, 0-13-171599-2

Acknowledgments

We thank the many people who helped with the fifth edition of *Concepts and Inquiries for Teaching Elementary School Science,* especially editors Linda Montgomery and Hope Madden of Merrill/Prentice Hall for their extensive editorial support, insight, encouragement, continued assistance, and constructive comments.

We also acknowledge the external reviewers of this text: Mary Margaret Capraro, Texas A&M; Huabin Chen, Saint Martin's College; Raymond W. Francis, Central Michigan University; Karen Ivers, California State University, Fullerton; Robbie V. McCarty, Southwestern Oklahoma State University; James T. McDonald, Central Michigan University; Leah M. Melber, California State University, Los Angeles; Michael Odell, University of Idaho; John Shimkanin, California University of Pennsylvania; Lori-Anne Stelmark, Teachers College Columbia University; and Rita K. Voltmer, Miami University, Oxford, Ohio.

References

Barman, C. R. (1989). A procedure for helping prospective elementary teachers integrate the learning cycle into science textbooks. *Journal of Science Teacher Education, 1*(2), 21–26.

Yager, R. (1991). The constructivist learning model. *The Science Teacher, 58*(6), 52–57.

DISCOVER THE COMPANION WEBSITE ACCOMPANYING THIS BOOK

The Prentice Hall Companion Website: A Virtual Learning Environment

Technology is a constantly growing and changing aspect of our field that is creating a need for content and resources. To address this emerging need, Prentice Hall has developed an online learning environment for students and professors alike—Companion Websites—to support our textbooks.

In creating a Companion Website, our goal is to build on and enhance what the textbook already offers. For this reason, the content for each user-friendly website is organized by chapter and provides the professor and student with a variety of meaningful resources.

For the Professor

Every Companion Website integrates **Syllabus Manager**™, an online syllabus creation and management utility.

- **Syllabus Manager**™ provides you, the instructor, with an easy, step-by-step process to create and revise syllabi, with direct links into Companion Website and other online content without having to learn HTML.

- Students may logon to your syllabus during any study session. All they need to know is the web address for the Companion Website and the password you've assigned to your syllabus.

- After you have created a syllabus using **Syllabus Manager**™, students may enter the syllabus for their course section from any point in the Companion Website.

- Clicking on a date, the student is shown the list of activities for the assignment. The activities for each assignment are linked directly to actual content, saving time for students.

- Adding assignments consists of clicking on the desired due date, then filling in the details of the assignment—name of the assignment, instructions, and whether it is a one-time or repeating assignment.

- In addition, links to other activities can be created easily. If the activity is online, a URL can be entered in the space provided, and it will be linked automatically in the final syllabus.

- Your completed syllabus is hosted on our servers, allowing convenient updates from any computer on the Internet. Changes you make to your syllabus are immediately available to your students at their next logon.

For the Student

- **Web Destinations**—links to www sites that relate to chapter content.

- **Learning Network**—the Pearson Learning Network offers a wealth of additional resources to aid in their understanding and application of content.

- **Message Board**—serves as a virtual bulletin board to post—or respond to—questions or comments to/from a national audience.

- **Chat**—real time chat with anyone who is using the text anywhere in the country—ideal for discussion and study groups, class projects, etc.

To take advantage of the many available resources, please visit the *Concepts and Inquiries for Teaching Elementary School Science* Companion Website at

www.prenhall.com/peters

EDUCATOR LEARNING CENTER: AN INVALUABLE ONLINE RESOURCE

Merrill Education and the Association for Supervision and Curriculum Development (ASCD) invite you to take advantage of a new online resource, one that provides access to the top research and proven strategies associated with ASCD and Merrill—the Educator Learning Center. At **www.educatorlearningcenter.com,** you will find resources that will enhance your students' understanding of course topics and of current educational issues, in addition to being invaluable for further research.

How the Educator Learning Center Will Help Your Students Become Better Teachers

With the combined resources of Merrill Education and ASCD, you and your students will find a wealth of tools and materials to better prepare them for the classroom.

Research

- More than 600 articles from the ASCD journal *Educational Leadership* discuss everyday issues faced by practicing teachers.
- A direct link on the site to Research Navigator™ gives students access to many of the leading education journals, as well as extensive content detailing the research process.
- Excerpts from Merrill Education texts give your students insights on important topics of instructional method diverse populations, assessment, classroom management, technology, and refining classroom practice.

Classroom Practice

- Hundreds of lesson plans and teaching strategies are categorized by content area and age range.
- Case studies and classroom video footage provide virtual field experience for student reflection.
- Computer simulations and other electronic tools keep your students abreast of today's classrooms and current technologies.

Look into the Value of Educator Learning Center Yourself

A four-month subscription to Educator Learning Center is $25 but is **FREE** when packaged with any Merrill Education text. In order for your students to have access to this site, you must use this special value-pack ISBN number **WHEN** placing your textbook order with the bookstore: 0-13-172888-1. Your students will then receive a copy of the text packaged with a free ASCD pincode. To preview the value of this website to you and your students, please go to **www.educatorlearningcenter.com** and click on "Demo."

CONTENTS

INQUIRY UNIT 1
Light Energy and Color   **INQ-4**

Pathways of Light Inquiry   INQ-6
*A Camera with a Surprise Inside • Me and My
Shadow • Shadows in the Sun • Making Money •
Mirror Reflections • Up Periscope • I Can See
Myself • The Real You • Light Relay Races •
Mirror Balance*
Pathways of Light Concepts   INQ-15
Shadows • Reflections • Mirrors • Symmetry
Light Refraction Inquiry   INQ-18
*Some Everyday Magnifiers • How Big Can
It Get?*
Light Refraction Concepts   INQ-19
Density and Light Speeds • Lenses
Color Inquiry   INQ-23
*How to Mix Colors • Color Mix-Ups • Colored
Comics • The Makeup of Colored Liquids • The
Colors of the Sun*
Color Concepts   INQ-26
*Mixing Colors • Color Pictures from Digital
Cameras*
Perception and the Eye Inquiry   INQ-30
*How Far Is That? • Your Side Vision and Color
• Tired Eyes*
Perception of the Eye Concepts   INQ-32
Iris • Retina • Lens • Eyeglasses • Perception

*References • Selected Trade Books: Light Energy
and Color • Resource Books*

INQUIRY UNIT 2
Heat Energy   **INQ-38**

Safety   INQ-39
Expansion and Contraction Inquiry   INQ-40
*A Hot Association • Water Thermometer •
Hot Air*
Expansion and Contraction Concepts   INQ-42
*Molecules • Water • Differences in Cohesion •
Plastics and Expansion and Contraction*

Changing States of Matter Inquiry   INQ-45
Melting Away • A Cold Drink
Changing States of Matter Concepts   INQ-46
*Temperature • What Pressure Does • Heat Loss
and Gain*
Temperature and Heat Energy Inquiry   INQ-49
*Heat Energy • The Mixing of Hot and
Cold Water*
Temperature and Heat Energy Concepts   INQ-52
*Heat Quantity • Heat Capacity • The Calorie
and the BTU • Heat Conservation • Thermal
Equilibrium • Thermodynamics*
Conduction, Convection, and Radiation
    Inquiry   INQ-54
*Warm Feelings • Bottle Currents • Warm Air •
Solar Energy and Colors • Staying Warm • Hot
Lights • How to Keep Heat In or Out*
Conduction, Convection, and Radiation
    Concepts   INQ-59
*Changing Forms of Energy • Conduction •
Convection • Radiation • From Solar to Heat
Energy • Solar Heating for Homes • Controlling
Heat Loss*

*References • Selected Trade Books: Heat Energy
• Resource Books*

INQUIRY UNIT 3
Sound Energy   **INQ-66**

Sound Vibrations Inquiry   INQ-68
*A Vocal Activity • Good Vibrations •
Mystery Sounds*
Sound Vibrations Concepts   INQ-70
*Molecules and Sounds • Loudness • Waves •
Forced Vibrations • Sympathetic Vibrations •
Properties of Objects and Vibrations*
How Sounds Travel Inquiry   INQ-74
*It Sounds Fast • Sound Travels • The Vibrations
of Metal Objects • A String Telephone •
Underwater Sounds*
How Sounds Travel Concepts   INQ-78
Speeds of Sound • Sonic Booms

Reflected and Absorbed Sounds Inquiry   INQ-80
    Sounds and Megaphones • Echoes • Materials
    That Quiet Sound
Reflected and Absorbed Sounds Concepts   INQ-83
    Sound Reflection • Echoes • Absorbed
    Sounds • Reverberation and Reflected and
    Absorbed Sounds
How Pitch Changes Inquiry   INQ-87
    Changing Pitches • How to Make a Rubber-
    Band Banjo • A Soda-Straw Oboe • A Bottle
    Xylophone
How Pitch Changes Concepts   INQ-90
    Stringed Instruments • Wind Instruments
    • Homemade Instruments • Mass and Noise
Hearing and Locating Sounds Inquiry   INQ-93
    Do You Hear What I Hear?
Hearing and Locating Sounds Concepts   INQ-93
    Hearing Ranges • Locating Sounds

    References • Selected Trade Books:
    Sound Energy • Resource Books

INQUIRY UNIT 4
Magnetic Interactions   INQ-96

Magnets and What They Attract Inquiry   INQ-98
    Objects Magnets Can Pull • Magnetic
    Separations • The Power of Magnets
Magnets and What They Attract Concepts   INQ-100
    What Magnets Attract • Lodestones
    • Manufactured Magnets
Making Magnets Inquiry   INQ-102
    How to Make Magnets • Long-Lasting Magnets
Making Magnets Concepts   INQ-104
    Temporary Magnets • Permanent Magnets
    • Making Superconducting Magnets
Fields of Force Inquiry   INQ-106
    Magnetic Fields • Does Magnetism Go
    Through Objects?
Fields of Force Concepts   INQ-108
    Inferring the Field • Magnetic Transparency
Magnetic Pole Inquiry   INQ-109
    Make Your Own Compass • Finding
    Directions
Magnetic Pole Concepts   INQ-110
    The Earth's Magnetism • Geographic Poles
Magnetic Theory and Care of Magnets Inquiry   INQ-113
    Lost Magnetism?
Magnetic Theory and Care of Magnets
    Concepts   INQ-114

    Magnetic Domains • Caring for Magnets

    References • Selected Trade Books: Magnetic
    Interactions • Resource Books

INQUIRY UNIT 5
Electrical Energy   INQ-118

Closed and Open Circuit Inquiry   INQ-120
    How to Make a Bulb Light • Switches
Closed and Open Circuit Concepts   INQ-123
    Switches • Batteries • Bulbs • Fahnestock
    (Wire) Clips • Wire • Connections • Two-,
    Three-, and Four-Way Switches
Series and Parallel Circuit Inquiry   INQ-126
    Series Circuits • Parallel Circuits • Hidden
    Parts of Electrical Circuits • Test Your Nerves •
    Blinking Signals
Series and Parallel Circuit Concepts   INQ-132
    Connecting Wires • Connecting Cells •
    Voltage
Electrical Flow Inquiry   INQ-135
    Materials That Conduct Electricity • How to
    Measure Bulb Brightness • Dimmer Switches
    • Fuses
Electrical Flow Concepts   INQ-138
    Conductors • Resistance • Circuit Hazards •
    Short Circuits • Overloaded Circuits •
    Fuses and Circuit Breakers
Electromagnet Inquiry   INQ-142
    Electromagnets
Electromagnet Concepts   INQ-143
    Electric Bell • The Telephone • Electric
    Motor • Relays
Generating Eletricity Inquiry   INQ-146
    Static Electricity • A Way to Generate
    Electricity
Generating Electricity Concepts   INQ-148
    Static Electricity • Current Electricity •
    Producing Electromagnetic Waves

    References • Selected Trade Books: Electrical
    Energy • Resource Books

INQUIRY UNIT 6
Simple Machines   INQ-152

Screws and Inclined Planes Inquiry   INQ-154
    Inclined Planes
Screws and Inclined Planes Concepts   INQ-155
    Inclined Planes • Wedges • Screws

Lever Inquiry INQ-158
Common Levers • Common Double Levers •
The Making of a Mobile
Lever Concepts INQ-162
Three Parts • Three Classes • Mobiles
• Archimedes and the Application of Levers
Wheel and Axle Inquiry INQ-165
Easier Work • Wheel–Belt Systems •
Gearing Up for Speed
Wheel and Axle Concepts INQ-168
Gears, Chains, and Belts
Pulley Inquiry INQ-170
How Pulleys Work
Pulley Concepts INQ-171
Fixed and Movable Pulleys • Block and
Tackle • Power Pulleys
Motion and Friction Inquiry INQ-174
Moving Parts • Pendulums • Friction
Motion and Friction Concepts INQ-178
Three Basic Motions • Friction

References • Selected Trade Books: Simple
Machines • Resource Books

INQUIRY UNIT 7
Plant Life INQ-182

Seed-Related Inquiry INQ-184
Seed Parts • The Growth of Seeds • Deep
Down Seeds • Where Are the Seeds?
Seed-Related Concepts INQ-187
Seed Parts • Growth Stages • Survival
Conditions • How Seeds Travel • Sprouting
Seeds • Soil
Vegetative Reproduction Inquiry INQ-190
New Plants from Old Plants • Sweet Potatoes •
Tapping into New Growth
Vegetative Reproduction Concepts INQ-191
Roots • Stems • Leaves • Why Vegetative
Reproduction?
Environmental Conditions Inquiry INQ-194
How Colored Light Affects Plant Growth •
How Saltwater and Other Liquids Affect Plants
Environmental Conditions Concepts INQ-196
Growth Conditions • Three Habitats •
Terrarium Investigations
Plant Part and Function Inquiry INQ-199
Plant Roots • How Water Rises in Plant
Stems • The Properties of Leaves • How
Leaves Lose Water • Leaf Rubbings •
A Budding Activity • Inside a Flower

Plant Part and Function Concepts INQ-205
Roots • Stems • Leaves • Flowers •
Pollination • Life Cycles
Adaptation and Survival Inquiry INQ-209
Plants and Gravity • Growing to the Light
Adaptation and Survival Concepts INQ-210
Adaptation • Tropisms • Survival and
Environment
Molds and Fungi Inquiry INQ-213
How Molds Grow
Molds and Fungi Concepts INQ-214

References • Selected Trade Books: Plant Life •
Resource Books

INQUIRY UNIT 8
Animal Life INQ-216

Classification of Animals Inquiry INQ-218
Animal Classification
Classification of Animals Concepts INQ-218
Animal Classification Extensions
Animals with Backbones Inquiry INQ-221
Bones • Tadpoles • How to Train Goldfish •
Changing Temperatures • Making Casts of
Animal Tracks
Animals with Backbones Concepts INQ-225
Mammals • Classroom Mammals • Birds •
Reptiles • Amphibians • Fishes • Setting Up
an Aquarium
Animals Without Backbones Inquiry INQ-241
Mealworms and What They Do • Crickets •
Brine Shrimp • Snails and What They Do
Animals Without Backbones Concepts INQ-246
Insects and Life Cycles • Crayfish and Brine
Shrimp • Snails • Earthworms
Ecological Inquiry INQ-253
Food Chains • How Color Protects Animals •
Ant Responses to Sweeteners • The Fright
Distances of Wild Animals • Bird Nests
Ecological Concepts INQ-257
Habitats and Their Dwellers • Biotic
Potential • Material Cycles

References • Selected Trade Books: Animal Life •
Resource Books

INQUIRY UNIT 9
The Human Body and Nutrition INQ-264

Skeletal and Muscle Systems Inquiry INQ-266
Soft Bones • All Thumbs • Tired Muscles

Skeletal and Muscle Systems Concepts   INQ-267
    Groups of Bones • Composition of Bones •
    Movable Joints • Muscles • Tendons •
    Makeup of Muscles
Nervous System Inquiry   INQ-271
    Eye Blinking • Your Reaction Time •
    How Practice Improves Learning • Your Sense
    of Touch • The Sensitivity of Your Skin • Your
    Sensitivity to Temperature
Nervous System Concepts   INQ-278
    The Nerves • Quick Reflexes • The Brain •
    Learning • The Senses
Circulatory and Respiratory Systems
    Inquiry   INQ-281
    People's Pulse Beats • The Volume of Air You
    Breathe • How Fast People Breathe
Circulatory and Respiratory Systems Concepts   INQ-285
    Circulatory System • Respiratory System •
    Breathing • The Cardiopulmonary System
    and Vital Signs
Digestive System Inquiry   INQ-288
    Sweet Crackers
Digestive System Concepts   INQ-288
    The Mouth • The Food Tube •
    The Stomach • The Intestines
Food and Nutrition Inquiry   INQ-290
    Starchy Foods • Fatty Foods • Some
    Properties of Powdered Foods
Food and Nutrition Concepts   INQ-292
    Carbohydrates • Fats • Proteins • Vitamins •
    Minerals • Water • Choosing a Healthful Diet

    References • Selected Trade Books: The Human
    Body and Nutrition • Resource Books

INQUIRY UNIT 10
The Earth's Changing Surface   **INQ-298**

Weathering and Erosion Inquiry   INQ-300
    Breaking Rocks • How Weathering Breaks
    Down Minerals • Cave Deposits • Freezing
    Water and Rocks • Changing Rocks • Soil
    Erosion • Wind Erosion • Glaciers
Weather and Erosion Concepts   INQ-306
    Plant Actions • Chemical Weathering •
    Expansion and Contraction • Running Water
    • Wind Erosion • Glacial Erosion •
    Interplanetary Weathering
Soil and Its Makeup Inquiry   INQ-310
    The Makeup of Soils • How Water Sinks into
    Different Soils

Soil and Its Makeup Concepts   INQ-312
    Soil Makeup • Soil Conservation
Building Up of the Land Inquiry   INQ-314
    The Earth's Changing Crust
Building Up of the Land Concepts   INQ-315
    Magma • Earthquakes and Faults • Plate
    Theory
How Rocks Are Formed Inquiry   INQ-318
    The Properties of Rocks • Growing Crystals
How Rocks Are Formed Concepts   INQ-321
    Sedimentary Rocks • Igneous Rocks •
    Metamorphic Rocks • Fossils • Rock Cycle

    References • Selected Trade Books: The
    Earth's Changing Surface • Resource Books

INQUIRY UNIT 11
Water, Air, and Weather   **INQ-330**

Water Inquiry   INQ-332
    How Water and Other Liquids Stick Together
    • How to Measure Volume with Water • Things
    That Float in Water • Water Pressure • High
    Water • The Filtering of Polluted Water
Water Concepts   INQ-338
    Water Properties • Clean, Adequate Water
Air and Its Properties Inquiry   INQ-342
    Where Air Can Be • Soap Bubbles • Parachutes
    • Air and Space • Balloon Buoyancy • Air
    Needed for Burning
Air and Its Properties Concepts   INQ-349
    The Atmosphere • Air Pressure • Makeup of
    Air • The Reality of Air • Origins of Our
    Atmosphere
Weather Inquiry   INQ-353
    Heating Soil and Water • Evaporation •
    Relative Humidity • Water Vapor • Air
    Pressure Changes
Weather Concepts   INQ-358
    Causes of Winds • Air Temperature •
    Evaporation and Humidity • Condensation •
    Air Masses and Cyclones • Measuring Pressure

    References • Selected Trade Books: Water, Air
    and Weather • Resource Books

INQUIRY UNIT 12
The Earth in Space   **INQ-368**

Time and the Seasons Inquiry   INQ-370
    The Way the Earth Rotates • A Shadow Clock
    • Direct Sun • Why the Earth Has Seasons

Time and the Seasons Concepts INQ-374
  Globe and Shadows • Rotation and Time •
  Time Zones • Seasons
Moon, Earth, and Sun Interaction Inquiry INQ-378
  Moon Phases • An Earth–Moon Model •
  Eclipses of the Sun and Moon
Moon, Earth, and Sun Interaction Concepts INQ-381
  Moon Phases • Tides • Eclipses • The Earth–
  Moon System • The Moon's Orbit • Solar Wind
Solar System and Beyond Inquiry INQ-387
  Size and Distance in the Solar System •
  Constellations
Solar System and Beyond Concepts INQ-389
  Planets • Comets, Meteors, and the Asteroid
  Belt • The Stars • Stellar Types and Evolution
Gravity and the Laws of Motion Inquiry INQ-395
  The Sun's Gravity • Rockets
Gravity and the Laws of Motion Concepts INQ-397
  Causes of Orbits • Zero Gravity • Rockets •
  Problems in Space Travel

  References • Selected Trade Books: The Earth
  in Space • Resource Books

APPENDICES

A: Professional Bibliography AP-1

B: Science Curriculum Projects AP-5

C: Commercial Science Suppliers AP-9

D: Environments and Nutrition for
  Classroom Animals AP-10

E: Summary of Children's Thinking AP-11

F: State Education Agencies AP-12

INDEX IN-1

NOTE: Every effort has been made to provide accurate and current Internet information in this book. However, the Internet and information posted on it are constantly changing, and it is inevitable that some of the Internet addresses listed in this textbook will change.

CONCEPTS AND INQUIRIES FOR TEACHING ELEMENTARY SCHOOL SCIENCE

INQ-1

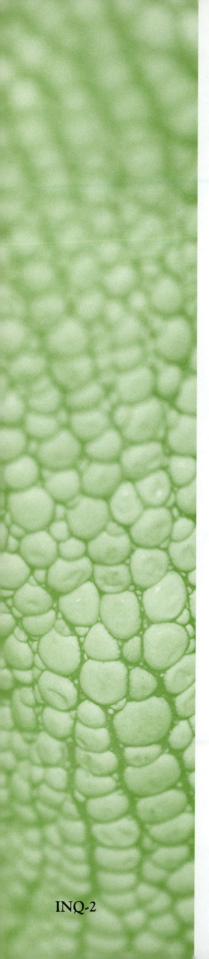

INQUIRY UNITS

The 12 inquiry units that follow help model constructivist applications for science teaching and learning. Each unit will help you reflect on the methodology and typical subject-matter areas found in children's textbooks, school district science guides, the *National Science Education Standards* (National Research Council [NRC], 1996), and the *Benchmarks for Science Literacy* (American Association for the Advancement of Science [AAAS], 1993). Each unit begins with a brief introduction, followed by sample benchmarks and standards. These are followed by inquiry activities grouped by topic. Finally, each group of activities is followed by concepts that apply to the activities provided.

As you scan through the inquiry activities, you will see that they generally follow both the constructivist learning model (Yager, 1991) and the learning cycle (Barman, 1989) model as follows:

Title

Invitation (modeled after the constructivist learning model "invitation" to inquiry)

Exploration (modeled after the constructivist learning model "exploration" part and the learning cycle "exploration" phase)

Concept Invention (modeled after the constructivist learning model "proposing explanations and solutions" part and the learning cycle "concept introduction" phase)

Concept Application (modeled after the constructivist learning model "taking action" part and the learning cycle "concept application" phase)

Specifically, the *invitation* is one or more questions or statements used to arouse children's interest and to tie in their former experiences. This sets the stage for further investigation in the next section; this section also includes the materials needed for the inquiry.

The *exploration* is the basic activity that children will use to study a scientific phenomenon or concept. This child-centered section includes teaching comments and applicable background knowledge you may need to facilitate that specific inquiry. (Note that more detailed information follows the activities in the concept invention section.)

The *concept invention* is an extension of the exploration and includes questions or extension activities or both. These will assist the children as they develop the applicable scientific concept.

Each inquiry ends with a *concept application* that challenges the children to test and apply their newly formed concepts. There is room here for the children to answer relevant questions and design extended activities.

REFERENCES

American Association for the Advancement of Science (AAAS). (1993). *Benchmarks for science literacy.* New York: Oxford University Press.

Barman, C. R. (1989). A procedure for helping prospective elementary teachers integrate the learning cycle into science textbooks. *Journal of Science Teacher Education, 1*(2), 21–26.

National Research Council (NRC). (1996). *National science education standards.* Washington, DC: National Academy Press.

Yager, R. (1991). The constructivist learning model. *The Science Teacher, 58*(6), 52–57.

LIGHT ENERGY AND COLOR

W hy does something look larger under a magnifying glass? What makes a rainbow? Why does writing appear backward in a mirror? Children want to know many things about the behavior of light. These and other phenomena become understandable when we learn how light travels, how light waves can be "bent," why light can be colored, and how we see light.

Benchmarks and Standards

Examples of standards in the area of light energy and color are guidelines related to how sunlight is made up of many colors; how light reflecting off objects allows us to see; and how light travels. Specific examples follow:

Sample Benchmarks (American Association for the Advancement of Science, 1993)

- Light from the sun is made up of a mixture of many different colors of light, even though to the eye the light looks almost white. Other things that give off or reflect light have a different mix of colors. (By Grades 6–8, p. 90)
- Something can be "seen" when light waves emitted or reflected by it enter the eye. (By Grades 6–8, p. 90)

Sample Standards (NRC 1996)

- Light travels in a straight line until it strikes an object. Light can be reflected by a mirror, refracted by a lens, or absorbed by an object. (By Grades K–4, p. 127)
- Light interacts with matter by transmission (including refraction) absorption, or scattering (including reflection). To see an object, light from that object—emitted by or scattered from it—must enter the eye. (By Grades 5–8, p. 155)

PATHWAYS OF LIGHT **Inquiry**

MATERIALS

- Salt or cereal box
- Sticky tape
- Pin
- Black paper
- Three rubber bands
- Waxed paper
- Scissors

A Camera with a Surprise Inside

Invitation

How can you make and use a pinhole camera? Have you ever used a pinhole camera like the one shown here? Light enters a tiny pinhole at one end, and travels to a waxed paper screen at the other end of the tube. You are able to observe an image of the object on the inside of the homemade camera. What you see may surprise you.

Exploration

1. Use a pin to punch a hole in the center of the box bottom.
2. Remove the box top. Put waxed paper over the box's open end to make the screen. Use a rubber band to hold it.
3. Point the camera at brightly lit objects inside or outside a dark room. What do you see on the waxed paper screen?
4. To use the camera in a lighted place, you must shield the screen from the light. Roll black paper into a large tube and fit it around the screen end of the box. Secure it with two rubber bands. Press your face against the paper shield's open end to see images on the screen.

Teaching Tips

Several kinds of boxes will serve for this activity, including milk cartons. If a black paper shield is used, it should be large. The observer's eyes will need to be about 30 centimeters (1 foot) away from the screen to see a sharp image.

Most children will be surprised to find that an upside-down image appears on the screen. You might sketch the pinhole camera on the chalkboard and invite students to think through what happens.

Scaffolding for English Learners

English learners may appear to have difficulty with concepts such as *smaller* and *larger* when, in fact, it is only due to their inability to associate the English word with the concept being taught. Teachers should be aware of the need to identify and develop key vocabulary words. (See Ovando, Collier, & Combs, 2003, for a discussion of the importance of vocabulary in science education.)

Concept Invention

1. How must you move the camera (a) to make the image move right? left? up? down? (b) to make the image get smaller? larger? What happens if the camera is still and the image moves (e.g., have a person walk from right to left)?
2. How can you make a brighter, sharper image appear on the screen? What will happen to the image if you (a) change the pinhole size? (b) line the inside of the box with black paper? white paper? (c) use a longer or larger box or a shoe box? (d) use paper other than waxed paper for the screen?
3. How can you make a pinhole camera with a larger paper cup? How can a second cup be used as a light shield?
4. What other ideas can you think of to try?

Concept Application

Describe how you will show someone else how light travels in straight lines.

Me and My Shadow

Invitation

What is a shadow? How can you make a shadow? How can you change the length and direction of a shadow?

Exploration

1. Put a nail, head down, on some white paper.
2. Shine the flashlight on the nail. What kind of a shadow do you see?

MATERIALS

- White sheet of paper
- Flashlight
- Pencil
- Small nail
- Partner

Concept Invention

1. How can you make a long shadow? a short shadow?
2. How can you make a shadow that points left? right?
3. Let your partner turn off the flashlight and point it at the nail. Where will the shadow be when your partner turns on the flashlight again? (The flashlight must be held still.) Draw a line on the paper where you think the shadow will be.
4. Can you tell how long a shadow will be?

Teaching Tips

In this investigation, children discover how to predict the lengths and directions of shadows. They learn how to make shadows dark and sharp and pale or fuzzy by changing the distance between an object and the light source. They also learn that this movement affects the shadow's size.

Concept Application

Describe how you can shine the light on the nail so that there is no shadow.

Shadows in the Sun ─────────

Invitation

What kinds of shadows can you make and see outdoors?

Exploration

1. Go outdoors into the sunshine.
2. Make some shadows on the ground like the example shown.

Concept Invention

1. Can you and a partner make your shadows shake hands without really touching each other's hands?
2. How can you make your shadow seem to stand on the shoulders of your partner's shadow?
3. How can you make a pale, fuzzy shadow darker and sharper?
4. How should you stand so that your shadow is in front of you? in back of you? to your left? to your right?
5. Draw a line where the shadow of some object is now. Where do you think the shadow will be in 1 hour? Draw a second line and then check to see later.
6. What are some other things you can try with shadows?

 Try determining the sizes of objects by their shadows with upper-elementary and middle grades students.

Concept Application

A shadow may be made when an object blocks some light; a shadow may be changed by moving the object or the light source in different ways. Can you think of ways to use the overhead projector to illustrate this concept?

Making Money ─────────

Invitation

How many pennies can you make with two mirrors?

Exploration

1. Fit two mirrors together like two walls joined to make a corner.
2. Place the penny between the mirrors. How many pennies do you see?
3. Change the mirror angle. Move the mirrors in other ways. Move the penny, too.

Concept Invention

1. What is the greatest number of pennies you can make? the fewest number?
2. Can you make more than one penny with only one mirror?

Adapting for Students with Exceptionalities

Exceptional students may have difficulty with following directions for this activity. Use classroom schedules so that students know when the activity will be taught so they can be prepared. Make sure you use a prearranged signal and have students' attention before you begin. Also make sure students are facing you when you give the directions. Use voice inflection to sustain attention and alert students to important instructions.

Concept Application

Where would the use of two or more mirrors be beneficial?

Mirror Reflections

Invitation

What are some things you can do with a mirror? Can you see someone else's eyes in a mirror without the other person seeing your eyes in the mirror? (Say the other person is also looking into the mirror.) How can you find out?

Exploration

1. Tape a mirror flat against a wall at your eye level.
2. Have your partner stand in back and to the right of the mirror.
3. Now you stand in back and to the left of the mirror.
4. Move around slowly until you see your partner's eyes in the mirror. Can your partner now see your eyes in the mirror?

MATERIALS
• Small mirror
• Sticky tape
• Partner

Most primary students should be able to do this exploration.

Concept Invention

1. What will happen if you or your partner moves farther to the side?
2. What will happen if you or your partner moves farther back?
3. Is there any spot where you can see your partner's eyes without your partner seeing your eyes?

Scaffolding for English Learners

Collaboration between students, as found in this mirror reflections activity, is an important strategy for assisting the English learner in constructing the content of science. (See Fathman, Quinn, & Kessler, 1992, for a discussion of the advantage of cooperative strategies with English learners.)

Concept Application

When would you want to be able to see someone without that person seeing you? Create an arrangement of mirrors you could use to make your observations.

Up Periscope

Invitation

How can you use two mirrors to see over objects taller than you?

Exploration

1. Push a piece of clay into the meterstick near each end.
2. Push a mirror sideways into each lump of clay, so that the mirror surfaces face each other.
3. Fix the mirrors so that they look like those illustrated here. When done, you will have a periscope.
4. Hold the periscope upright. Look in the bottom mirror. What can you see? You may have to move the mirrors a little to see clearly.
5. Over what tall objects can you see with your periscope?

MATERIALS

- Two small mirrors
- Soft clay
- Meterstick or yardstick

Concept Invention

1. How can you use your periscope to see around a corner?
2. How can you see around a corner with just one mirror on the stick?

Concept Application

Could you use three mirrors for your periscope? How would three mirrors need to be arranged in order to create a periscope?

 Teaching Tips When light strikes a mirror at an angle, it is reflected at the same angle in a different direction. That is why if you see someone else's image in a mirror, it is possible for that person to see yours. This also explains how periscopes work. Notice in the illustration that the two mirror angles are identical. For the same reason, a full-length mirror needs to be only about half as long as you are tall.

I Can See Myself

Invitation

Do you need a full-length mirror to see your feet and head at the same time?

Exploration

1. You can use two small mirrors instead of a large, full-length mirror. Have your partner stand at arm's length from the wall.
2. Tape one mirror flat against the wall at your partner's eye level.
3. Hold the second mirror flat against the wall below the first mirror.
4. Move the bottom mirror slowly down the wall. Have your partner say stop when she can see her shoes in the bottom mirror.
5. Tape the bottom mirror flat against the wall.
6. Now your partner should be able to see her head and feet. The top and bottom mirrors are like the top and bottom of a large, full-length mirror, as shown here.

MATERIALS

- Two small mirrors
- Meterstick or yardstick
- Sticky tape
- Partner

 Teaching Tips Check that the mirror is taped flat against the wall in the last two exploration steps. If it is not, you will likely have an error in measurement.

Concept Invention

1. How long is it from the top of one mirror to the bottom of the other mirror compared to your partner's height—half as long? three fourths as long? just as long as your partner is tall? Measure and find out.

2. Does moving back from the mirror make a difference in the size needed?
3. Does the mirror size needed depend on a person's height? How could you find out?
4. Can you predict the size of the shortest full-length mirror you'll need to see yourself? Switch with your partner and find out.

Concept Application

When light travels to a mirror at a slant, it is reflected at the same slant in another direction. Describe an everyday application of this concept.

The Real You —————

MATERIALS

• Two mirrors

Invitation

How can two mirrors show what you really look like?

Exploration

1. Look into one mirror. Think of your image as another person facing you.
2. Wink your left eye, then your right eye. Which eye does the image blink each time?
3. Fit two mirrors together in the way that two walls are joined. Move them slightly so that half of your face is seen in each mirror as shown.
4. Wink each eye. Touch your left ear. Tilt your head to the right. What happens each time?

Teaching Tips

Each mirror reflects half of the image onto the adjoining mirror. This puts it back to normal. A single mirror can only reflect an object backward. This is why our one-mirror image is not how we look to others.

Concept Invention

1. Study the illustration.
2. How can you explain why your right eye appears on the left, like that of a real person facing you?

Adapting for Students with Exceptionalities

Repeat directions as needed for students who are having difficulty with this activity. Try to have the students repeat the directions in their own words. (See Mercer & Mercer, 2005, for a discussion on accommodations involving interactive instruction.)

Concept Application

Why do car tires appear to be traveling "backward" in some movies?

Light Relay Races

Invitation

How can you relay light with mirrors?

Exploration

1. Hold a mirror in the light. Reflect the light onto a wall.
2. Pick a target on the wall. Reflect the light so that it shines on the target.
3. Reflect your light onto another mirror held by a partner. Have your partner try to hit the target.
4. With how many mirrors can you and some partners relay the light and hit a target?
5. Have a contest between two or more teams. Which team can hit a target fastest with light passed along from several mirrors? How can you make the contest fair?

MATERIALS
• Three or four small mirrors
• Sunshine or bright flashlight
• Partner

Teaching Tips

Caution: If using a laser, caution children not to look directly into the laser.

A fair contest will prevent one team from observing and profiting from the mistakes of the other. You can tell if every mirror in a relay is being used by shading each mirror in turn with your hand. The light shining on the target in each instance will disappear. Strong light is needed if more than two mirrors are used.

Concept Invention

How will you tell if light is being passed from every mirror?

Concept Application

Make a drawing that shows how the mirrors were held to hit the target as illustrated in this activity.

Mirror Balance

Invitation

Suppose you made a small, simple drawing. Then suppose you erased half of it. Could you hold a mirror on the drawing so that it would seem whole again? Would it depend on the drawing? In what way? Drawings that allow you to do this are said to have mirror balance, or symmetry. How can you find out what things have mirror balance?

MATERIALS
• Paper
• Pencil
• Small mirror
• Ruler

Teaching Tips

This is an introduction to mirror symmetry equivalent to the use of a Mira© in mathematics. Symmetry is the idea of balanced proportions in the shapes of objects.

Try to have available small rectangular mirrors with the trim removed from the edges. The trim may obscure part of the reflected drawing or letter.

Caution: If the mirror edges are sharp, cover them with strips of cellophane tape.

For early elementary children, find and mount mirror–sized magazine pictures of objects and patterns. Some should, and some should not, be symmetrical. On what place or places in each picture can children put a small mirror to see the whole object? Have them classify the pictures into two groups, such as those they can make whole again and those they cannot. Challenge children to use their mirrors to change each picture or pattern. Colored pictures in particular are fascinating for young children to explore.

Exploration

1. Put the edge of your mirror on line 1 of the butterfly. Can you see what seems like the whole butterfly? You can because the butterfly has side-by-side balance.

2. Now put the mirror on line 2. Can you see a whole butterfly now? You cannot because a butterfly's body is balanced only one way.

3. Some letters of the alphabet have balance, too. Put your mirror on line 1 of the capital letter A. Can you see what seems like a whole letter A? You can because capital letter A has side-by-side balance.

4. Now, put the mirror on line 2. Can you see a whole letter A? You cannot because this capital letter is balanced only one way.

5. Try your mirror both ways on capital B. Notice that you cannot see a whole letter on line 1, but you can on line 2. A capital B only has up-and-down balance.

6. Try your mirror both ways on capital H. Notice that you see a whole letter both ways. A capital H has both side-by-side and up-and-down balance.

7. Try your mirror both ways on capital F. Notice that you cannot see a whole letter either way. A capital F has no balance.

Concept Invention

1. Which capital letters of the alphabet do you think have side-by-side balance? up-and-down balance? both kinds? no balance? Arrange the letters into four groups. Then check each letter with your mirror to see if you put it into the right group.
2. Some words may be made up of only letters from one group. How many words can you think of whose letters have only side-by-side balance? only up-and-down balance? only letters with both kinds of balance?
3. Use what you know to write secret code words.

Concept Application

Some objects have evenly balanced or symmetrical shapes; a mirror may be used to explore an object's symmetry. Draw some common objects and show if they have side-to-side or up-and-down symmetry.

PATHWAYS OF LIGHT CONCEPTS

Imagine reaching for something that is visible in front of you and not finding it there, or shining a flashlight in the dark and having it illuminate only something in back of you. This, of course, is not likely to happen because light travels in straight lines.

It is true that a beam of light can "bend" under certain conditions, such as when going from air into water or glass, or the reverse. Scientists also know that light passing through space is attracted and curved by the gravitational fields of massive objects in space. Other than these exceptions, though, light does appear to travel in straight lines.

This property makes many interesting things take place. For example, look at the pinhole "camera" in INQ Figure 1–1. Light enters a narrow pinhole in the cereal box end from the candle flame. At the other end, an inverted image appears on waxed paper taped over the opening. Why? The numerals in the figure suggest an answer. If light travels in straight lines, the light going from spot 1 on the left can only go to spot 1 on the right, and vice versa.

Shadows

Because light travels in straight lines, it is easy to block it with objects. This is why we can identify an object from its shadow.

Only objects that we cannot see through, such as metal and wood, cast true shadows. These are called *opaque* objects. *Transparent* objects, such as clear glass and cellophane, do not cast a shadow because they block very little light. *Translucent* objects, such as frosted glass and waxed paper, allow only some light to pass through, but do not block enough light to produce a true shadow.

INQ Figure 1–1 **A pinhole "camera."**

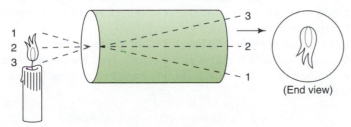

(End view)

Children can learn to make large or small shadows and clear or fuzzy shadows. They can do this by varying the distance from the light source to the opaque object and the place where the shadow falls. Shadow exploration is interesting to children of all ages. It can lay the foundation for understanding some important principles of physics in later grades.

Reflections

We can alter the pathways of light in several ways, some of them surprising. For instance, why do people powder their noses? Psychological reasons aside, they do it to scatter light reflections.

You know that a ball thrown straight down on smooth, level pavement bounces back up. Try it on rough gravel, however, and its return path is unpredictable. A smooth, shiny surface reflects light rays with very little scattering; but a rough or uneven surface may scatter the rays so thoroughly that reflections may be scarcely visible. What makes makeup powder so effective? Put some under a microscope. Greatly magnified, it resembles gravel!

Of course, even better reflections are possible with mirrors than with noses. Sprinkle some powder or chalk dust over half of the mirror and leave the remainder clear. Shine a flashlight on both sections of the mirror. Does the powder help reduce glare? Scattered light rays are called *diffused reflections*. Light rays that are not scattered are *regular reflections*.

The only time we can see something that doesn't glow by itself is when light reflects off it and travels to our eyes, such as light reflecting off the moon. Children generally do not think of light as reflecting off objects. Rather, they hold the misconception that they see all objects directly instead of the reflection of light that is cast from the objects.

Mirrors

When you deal with flat, or plane, reflectors, a special kind of regular reflection becomes possible. If you stand by a mirror and can see the eyes of another person, that person can also see your eyes. No matter from what position or angle you try it, the same results happen if you are close enough to the mirror to see a reflection. The angle at which light strikes a plane reflector (called the *angle of incidence*) always equals the angle at which it is reflected (called the *angle of reflection*).

Some explanations of convex and concave mirrors can be discussed at the elementary level. *Convex mirrors* have a bulging center that reduces a wide field to a small area. This is way they are used for rearview mirrors on some automobiles. *Concave mirrors* have a scooped-out center that magnifies images. They are useful for cosmetic work or shaving. Observing images with flexible plastic mirrors is a way to demonstrate how bending a mirror to change its plane will change an image.

If we could not look at photographs of ourselves or at our double reflections in two mirrors, we would never know how we appear to others. A mirror always produces a reversed image of the observer.

To learn why this is so, study INQ Figure 1–2. In a sense, a mirror image is an optical illusion. Light rays reflect off the mirror into the boy's eyes. He stares outward along the lines of the incoming rays. To him, his image appears to be just as far in back of the mirror as he is in front of it.

INQ Figure 1–2   Why a mirror image is reversed.

Image

Mirror

Object

INQ Figure 1–3 There is symmetry in letters of the alphabet. Dotted lines show how to hold a mirror to reconstruct the original letters.

Symmetry

Working with mirrors will enable you to introduce the concept of symmetry or the idea of balanced proportions in objects and geometric forms. The concept is of value in many fields, including biology, mathematics, and the arts. A butterfly, for example, has symmetry. If you draw an imaginary line down the middle of its body, the left half is a near duplicate of its right half. A starfish has another kind of symmetry. If you turn its body around on an imaginary axis, a rotational balance is evident.

Children will be surprised at the ways a mirror can reveal balanced proportions. They can learn to predict which letter shapes will reveal the property of symmetry. Notice that each letter in INQ Figure 1–3 is symmetrical. The left and right sides of A are opposite, but alike. The remaining letters are different in that the symmetry is vertical—that is, found in the tops and bottoms, but not laterally. A few letters, such as X, O, I, and H, have both lateral and vertical balance. Some, such as L, F, and J, have none at all.

LIGHT REFRACTION Inquiry

Some Everyday Magnifiers

Invitation

How can you make something seem larger? That is, how can you magnify it? What everyday objects can you use to magnify things?

Exploration

1. Place a piece of waxed paper on a printed page.
2. Dip a pencil tip into some water. Let a drop run off onto the waxed paper.
3. How does the print look through the water drop?

Concept Invention

1. Make water drops of different sizes. Which drops magnify the print more?
2. Put the waxed paper on a book. Make a row of drops, each drop bigger than the next. Hold up the book and paper to eye level. Look at the outline of the drops. Which are smaller and rounder? Which are larger and flatter? Which will magnify more?
3. Get two different-sized clear marbles. Which one do you think will magnify more? How much more? How will you find out?
4. Get a narrow jar of water. Put your pencil inside. Does your pencil look larger? Move your pencil to different places, inside and outside the jar. Where does it look the thickest?
5. Get another, wider jar of water. Will it magnify more or less than the narrow jar?
6. What other everyday things can you use as magnifiers?

Teaching Tips

Any clear, curved, transparent material acts like a lens; that is, light rays that pass through the material are bent. Objects viewed through the lens may appear to be magnified. Children will enjoy and learn from trials with additional examples of clear glass and plastic materials. Clear, narrow plastic pill vials become especially good magnifiers when filled with water and capped.

The magnifying power of a glass marble may be measured by placing it on narrow-lined paper. Count the number of lines seen inside the clear marble. The marble with the fewest visible lines has the greatest magnification.

Concept Application

A clear, curved object may appear to magnify things. The magnification produced by a clear, curved object increases as its diameter decreases. What type of object would be useful in making eyeglasses?

How Big Can It Get?

Invitation

How can you measure the magnifying power of a hand lens?

MATERIALS

- Hand lens
- Sheet of lined paper
- Ruler
- Pencil

Exploration

1. Draw two or three evenly spaced lines between each of the printed lines on your paper. A half sheet of extra lines should be enough.
2. Pencil a small **X** in the middle of the paper where you have drawn lines.
3. Center the **X** in the lens. Move the lens up and down until the **X** looks clearest.
4. Count all the lines you see inside the lens, as shown in the drawing.

Concept Invention

1. Count all the lines outside the lens that are between the first and last lines seen inside the lens.
2. Divide the number of lines you counted in step 1 by the number of lines you counted inside the lens. The answer is the power of the lens. For example, if the answer is 2, your lens makes things appear about twice as large as they are.

Teaching Tips

Thicker lenses usually magnify more than thinner lenses of the same diameter. The distance from the point of focus to the lens is the *focal length*. Because they have shorter focal lengths, thicker or curvier lenses must be held closer to the **X** to see it clearly.

Concept Application

What is the power of your lens? What is the power of other lenses you can try? How does the power of thicker lenses compare with that of thinner lenses? How far above the **X** must you hold different lenses to see it clearly?

LIGHT REFRACTION CONCEPTS

Have you ever jumped into the shallow part of a swimming pool, only to discover it was deeper than it seemed? Light travels more slowly in water than it does in air. This difference results in an optical illusion, even though we may be looking straight down into the water.

The topic of reflection and refraction lends itself to misconceptions. Illustrations in textbooks are often inadequate, and explanations are sometimes poor (Iona & Beaty, 1988). It is important to allow children plenty of time to discuss their constructions regarding these concepts.

Density and Light Speeds

The speed of light changes as it travels into or out of media of varying densities. The event is especially curious if the light beam enters or leaves a different medium at a slant. A change in speed may cause the beam to change direction of travel, or to *refract*.

Examples of refraction are all around us. A pencil placed partway into water looks bent. Distant images shimmer through unevenly heated air as we drive along a hot road. The scenery looks distorted through an inferior glass window because its thickness is uneven. Interestingly, the function of an automobile windshield wiper is to restore the rainy outside surface of a windshield to a plane surface. As water is wiped away, the light rays enter the glass at a uniform angle, rather than unevenly.

What happens when light enters or leaves water? Why does it bend? Let's look for a moment into the concept of density as it relates to this event. You know that anything in motion will slow down or stop when something is in the way. It is easy to dash across an empty room at top speed. Scatter some people around the room, and the runner will slow down, bumping head-on into some people and deflecting off others.

A similar thing happens with light as it travels through air, water, and glass. Water is denser than air. It has more matter in the same space. Therefore, glass is denser than water. When light enters a denser medium, it slows down. The reverse is also true: When light enters a less dense medium, it speeds up. What makes light bend can be understood through an analogy.

Notice INQ Figure 1–4. Part A explains why the coin in part B appears to be in front of its true location. In part A, the two wheels are rolling freely in the direction shown. But what happens when the leading wheel strikes the sand? The device moves on, but at a slightly different angle. To reverse this, if the device travels upward from the sand along the broken line, one wheel will hit the paved portion sooner. The direction will again change, but in an opposite way.

INQ Figure 1–4 Light "bends" and changes direction (B) in the same way the wheels change direction (A) when they hit a different surface.

In part B, light bends in a similar direction. As it leaves the water, the light bends slightly toward the horizontal. The observer sights along a stick toward where the coin seems to be. The line of sight seems to be a straight line from eye to coin, but it is not. If the stick is pushed into the water at the same angle at which it is poised (sliding it in the groove formed by a closed book cover may ensure this), it will overshoot the target.

Lenses

People have learned to control light refractions with lenses. Eyeglasses can correct certain vision problems. Magnifying glasses and optical instruments extend the power of sight far beyond that available to the naked eye.

INQ Figure 1–5 shows how light refracts when passing through a convex lens. In part A, the light rays enter the eye from two opposite slants. (It may help to think of the wheels–axle analogy again.) As the eye follows these slanted rays to the lens, they seem to continue outward, and so they form an enlarged image of the object.

How can we make the object appear even larger? Compare parts B and C. Notice that the two lenses differ in thickness, although their diameters are the same. Each will bring the sun's rays to a point or focus at a different distance. The distance from the point of focus to the lens is the *focal length*. Notice that the thicker lens has the shorter focal length. By extending the slanted rays outward, you can see why it magnifies more than the lens in part C.

A curious thing may happen when we observe a moving object through a convex lens. INQ Figure 1–6 shows the focal point of a small jar of water as light passes through it. (Although the jar is really a cylindrical lens, it acts as a convex lens in this example.) If a pencil is moved to the right *inside* the focal length of the lens, its image will also move to the right; but if it is moved to the right *outside* the focal length, its image will move to the left. The reason is apparent if we notice what happens beyond the focal point. The light rays cross and go to opposite sides.

INQ Figure 1–5 The shape of a convex lens is what determines how an image is magnified.

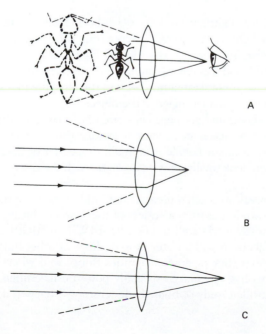

A

B

C

INQ Figure 1–6   When an object that is *inside* the focal length of a convex lens is moved right, its image also moves right. But if the object is *outside* the focal length when moved right, its image moves left.

INQ Figure 1–7   A concave lens makes objects appear smaller because the light rays diverge.

Convex lenses cause light rays to *converge*, or bring them together, as you have seen. Concave lenses cause light rays to *diverge*, or spread out; this causes objects viewed through them to appear smaller. You can see why in INQ Figure 1–7. The light from the object slants outward toward X and Y as it goes through the lens (remember the wheels–axle analogy). As the eye follows these slanted rays back to the lens, the rays seem to continue inward at a slant and form a smaller image of the object.

Thick drinking glasses and glass eye cups often have concave-shaped bases. The students can check whether images are smaller by looking through them. Perhaps the easiest concave lens to make is an air bubble in a small, capped jar of water. An object viewed through the bubble will look smaller, but if viewed through the convex part of the jar, it will appear larger.

Commercial lenses can teach a great deal. Children may learn even more, though, by fashioning their own lenses from a variety of transparent objects, containers, and fluids. A plastic soda bottle works well to bend light (Wilson, 1990). A clear-glass marble will also magnify objects, as will a water drop or drops of other fluids. A small drinking glass with vertical sides (not tapered) magnifies things well when filled with water or other fluids. Narrow olive jars make especially powerful magnifiers. However, the best possibilities for controlled study of homemade lenses will happen if you use clear, small plastic pill vials.

COLOR Inquiry

How to Mix Colors

Invitation

Suppose you have two different-colored crayons. How can you use the crayons to make three different colors? How can you make more than three colors with three different crayons?

Exploration

1. Rub three short, thick lines lightly across the white paper. Make one red, one yellow, and one blue.
2. Rub three thick up-and-down lines lightly on the white paper so that they cross the first three. Use the same three colors.
3. What colors do you see where the lines cross?

Concept Invention

1. How many colors did you make?
2. How many new colors can you make with crayons of other colors?

Concept Application

Draw pictures and color them.

MATERIALS

- White paper
- Crayons (red, yellow, and blue)
- Crayons of other colors

Teaching Tips

Children will get the best results when combining crayon colors if they rub lightly. When red, yellow, and blue paints or dyes are paired and mixed in the right proportions, we see green, orange, and purple.

Color Mix-Ups

Invitation

How can you make many colors by mixing water samples of several colors?

Exploration

1. Fill three small jars half full with water.
2. Put two drops of different food coloring in each jar.
3. Put a different straw into each jar and stir the colored water.
4. Mix a little colored water from two jars into a fourth jar. Use a straw to lift out the liquid from each jar as shown in the illustration on the next page.

MATERIALS

- Four baby-food jars
- Paper towel
- Water
- Three drinking straws
- Food coloring (red, yellow, and blue)

Concept Invention

1. How many new colors can you make by mixing two different colors each time? Use the same volume of each color when mixing colors. Keep a record.
2. What happens when you mix more of one color than another?
3. Mix a mystery color made from two colors. Use more of one color than another. Can someone else figure out how to match exactly your mystery color? Can you match someone else's mystery color? Try many different colors.

Adapting for Students with Exceptionalities

Students with physical impairments may have difficulty manipulating the straws in this activity. Try using eyedroppers.

Concept Application

When red, yellow, and blue dyes are paired and mixed, they produce green, orange, and purple. Mixing different proportions of the colors produces different shades. What other shades can you produce here?

Colored Comics ——————

MATERIALS

- Colored comic strips from different newspapers
- Strong hand lens

Invitation

How are the colors made in comic strips?

Exploration

1. Study different comic strip pictures with a hand lens.
2. Notice how many colors are made from only a few colors.
3. Notice that some dots may be printed side by side; or one colored dot may be printed partly over a dot of another color.
4. Observe how different shades are make by changing the distances between dots.

Teaching Tips | A dissecting microscope is ideal for analyzing colored comics.

Concept Invention

1. What side-by-side colored dots do you see?
2. What colors do they make?
3. What overprinted colors do you see?
4. What colors do they make?

Concept Application

In what ways are cartoon colors from different newspapers alike? different?

The Makeup of Colored Liquids ——————

Invitation

You know that mixing two or more colors can make a colored liquid. Most inks and dyes are made in that way. Some of the colors that are mixed to make another color are surprising. How can you find out the colors that make up a colored dye or ink?

Exploration

1. Cut some strips from a white paper towel. Make them about 10 centimeters by 2 centimeters (4 inches by 3/4 inch).
2. Put 1 drop of red food coloring and 1 drop of blue on waxed paper. Mix them.
3. Touch a toothpick to the coloring. Make a sizable dot on the middle of one strip.
4. Hold the strip in a small jar that is about half full of water. The colored dot should be just above the water level as shown.
5. What happens to the coloring as water is soaked up past the colored dot? (This may take a minute or longer.) How many colors appear as the colored dot spreads out?

MATERIALS

- Food coloring (red, blue, green, and yellow)
- Baby-food jar half full of water
- Scissors
- Waxed paper
- Four toothpicks
- White paper towel or coffee filters
- Ruler

The basic process of this investigation is called *paper chromatography*. The separate pigments that make up the color of a dye are absorbed by the paper at slightly different rates. This has the effect of spreading out the pigments, which makes them visible. Only washable (nonpermanent) dyes will work.

Concept Invention

1. What colors are in other food coloring samples? How are different brands of the same colors alike or different?
2. Try a game with a partner. Mix drops from several food colors, and then test them on strips. Keep a record. Remove the tested strips from the jar and let them

dry. Can your partner tell which food colors were mixed for each strip? Switch places with your partner. Can you tell which mixed colors were used for your partner's strips?

3. What colors make up some inks?
4. What other papers or filters can be used? How do they change the color separation?

Concept Application

The colors that make up a dye may be discovered through paper chromatography. Most dyes contain several blended colors. How do you think manufacturers produce colored cloth?

MATERIALS

- Cake pan about half filled with water
- Mirror
- Sunshine
- White paper

 This crude prism does an excellent job of refracting sunlight into its full spectrum of colors. Stirring the water mildly mixes the colors into white light again. The spectrum of a filmstrip projector's light will be similar but not identical to that of sunlight.

The Colors of the Sun ————

Invitation

What colors make up sunlight?

Exploration

1. Place the pan in the sun. Have the mirror face the sun.
2. Hold the mirror upright against the pan's inside rim.
3. Slowly tip back the mirror. Light must strike the mirror below the water's surface.
4. Point the mirror toward a white wall or large sheet of white paper.

Concept Invention

1. What colors do you see on the wall?
2. What happens to the colors if you stir the water lightly?

Concept Application

Try using the light from a filmstrip projector inside the classroom. How will these colors compare with those of sunlight?

COLOR CONCEPTS

When our ancestors saw a rainbow, they were probably inclined to give a magical or supernatural explanation to account for it. Later, people thought that the colors came from the rain droplets through which sunlight passes. Not until Isaac Newton (1642–1727) per-

INQ Figure 1–8   A prism separates white light into a spectrum of six colors.

formed experiments with prisms did people realize that these colors were the parts of visible sunlight itself. The six universally recognized colors in the visible spectrum of sunlight are red, orange, yellow, green, blue, and violet.

A prism separates white light into its components because each color has a different wavelength and rate of vibration. Red light has the longest wavelength, with about 1200 waves per millimeter (30,000 waves per inch). Violet light has the shortest wavelength, with about twice that number of waves per unit. As a light beam passes through a prism, the longer waves are refracted the least and the shorter waves the most (INQ Figure 1–8).

Differences in colors are often compared to pitch differences in sound. A low-pitched sound is a result of relatively slow vibrations; its visual counterpart is the color red. A high-pitched sound is a result of fast vibrations; its counterpart is violet.

Mixing Colors

We can mix colors in two basic ways: one with colored beams of light, and the other with paints or dyes. When light beams of only three primary colors (red, blue, and green) are added together in the right proportions on a white screen, different color combinations occur. These are shown in the overlapping sections of INQ Figure 1–9. When red, blue, and green are used as colored light beams, they are called the *additive colors*. Scientists have found that three certain-colored pigments can absorb these additive colors; that is, if you shine a red, blue, or green light on the right pigment, almost no color is reflected. The pigment looks black. Blue light is absorbed by a yellow pigment, and red light by a blue–green pigment called cyan. Green light is absorbed by a purple–red pigment called magenta.

If a white light beam shines on these colored pigments, each will absorb, or "subtract," the specific color mentioned above and reflect to our eyes what is not absorbed. We can mix these pigments to get various colors, but the results we get from mixing all three are the opposite from mixing the three light beams. This is shown in INQ Figure 1–10. In summary, when viewing an object, the color we see depends on (a) the color of light shining on the object and (b) the color reflected by the object to our eyes.

Children can do some experiments with colored construction paper and colored light beams to help them understand these ideas and their practical effects. With ordinary materials, it is difficult to predict the exact hues that will result from the many possible combinations. Another interesting activity is to use colored slides, a prism, and a slide projector to experiment with color (Dalby, 1991).

Don't be surprised if you find that several boys in your class are at least partly color-blind. One male in 12 has the deficiency, contrasted with only 1 in 200 females. Most com-

INQ Figure 1–9   The additive colors. When beams of red, blue, and green light are added together in the right proportions, the overlapping colors result. Color television is produced by an additive process.

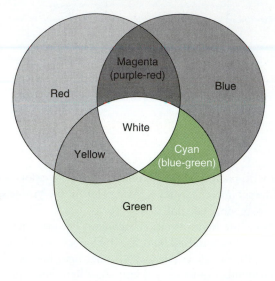

INQ Figure 1–10   The subtractive colors. Paints and dyes absorb, or "subtract," some colors from white light and reflect what is left. Note the overlapping colors when the three primary pigments are mixed in the right proportions.

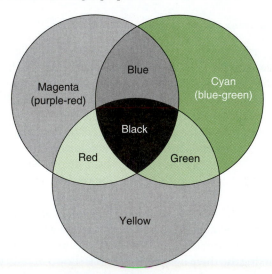

monly, reds and greens are seen in shades of gray; other colors are perceived normally. Rarely do color-blind people see all colors in black and white and shades of gray.

Color Pictures from Digital Cameras

A color digital picture begins when light, reflecting off of an image, passes through the lens of the camera. Then, instead of being focused on color photosensitive film as in a regular color camera, the image is focused on an *image sensor*. The image sensor is generally a fingernail-sized microchip called a charge-coupled device, or CCD. The CCD's surface contains an array of about 2 million or more photosensitive diodes that make up the discrete pixels of the image (*pix* for picture and *el* for elements).

Individual pixels create electrical impulses that are proportional to the intensity of the light they receive. These individual sensors are each covered with a different filter that is colored red, green, or blue (or alternatively cyan, magenta, and yellow). An analog-to-digital conversion process transforms the data for each pixel into a digital value. *Image enhancement* is then completed, as missing values are replaced through the use of software inside the camera. Using an interpolation process, the software adds information to the partially recorded image data processed by the pixels. These numbers are now used to reconstruct the image. Finally, the digital image is saved to the camera's storage.

PERCEPTION AND THE EYE Inquiry

How Far Is That?

Invitation

Suppose you had to see for a while with just one eye. How might this make a difference in telling how far something is from you? How can you test if two eyes let you tell distance better than one eye?

Exploration

1. Have a partner hold up a thumb at your eye level.
2. Hold a pencil upright, eraser end down, about 15 centimeters (6 inches) above the thumb. Using both eyes, try to touch the top of your partner's thumb with the eraser. Move the pencil down fairly quickly, but gently.
3. Have your partner slightly change the distance his thumb is from you.
4. Using one eye, try again to touch your partner's thumb. Move the pencil down fairly quickly, but gently.

When we see an object with two eyes, each eye views it from a slightly different angle. So, our perception of the object's distance is usually more accurate than if only one eye is used. With distant objects, the advantage decreases. We tend to use size, background, and other clues to estimate distance.

In this investigation, it is important for an object's position to be moved for each trial. Otherwise, muscle memory alone from a preceding trial may allow the child to touch the object. For the test to be valid, the child should not benefit from experience. Also, the pencil should be moved down with some speed, although gently. If done slowly, self-correction becomes too easy.

Concept Invention

1. In which trial was it easier to touch your partner's thumb?
2. Does which eye you close make any difference? How does using two eyes compare with using one? (Be sure your partner slightly changes his thumb position for each trial.)
3. Does which hand you use make any difference?
4. How else can you test if two eyes are better than one for telling distance?

Adapting for Students with Exceptionalities

Students with visual disabilities will have difficulty with these activities. Make students comfortable in asking for assistance or pair students to complete this activity as a team.

Concept Application

How can you show that two eyes are usually better than one for judging distance?

Your Side Vision and Color ————

Invitation

Suppose you notice an object from the corner of your eye while staring straight ahead. Can you notice it is there before you can tell its color? Or can you also tell the color at the same time? How far to the side can you tell different colors?

Exploration

1. Keep your eyes on some object across the room during this experiment.
2. Have a partner stand at your right side, about a step away.
3. Ask your partner to hold up a small colored square opposite your ear. (You should not know the color.)
4. Have your partner slowly move the square forward in a big circle as illustrated.
5. Say, "Stop," when you first notice the square at your side.
6. Then tell your partner the square's color if you can.
7. If you cannot, have your partner move the square forward until you can tell.

MATERIALS

- Four small (5-centimeter, or 2-inch) paper squares of different colors
- Four larger (10-centimeter, or 4-inch) paper squares of different colors
- Partner

Teaching Tips

The eye's inside lining, or retina, contains millions of cells sensitive to light intensity and color. Most of the eye's color-sensitive cells are clustered at the back of the eyeball near the optic nerve. To see color, some colored light must reach there. When light enters the eye at an angle, this area may not be stimulated. So, we can usually detect the presence of an object at our side before we can distinguish its color.

Be sure children keep their eyes fixed on some far object as they do this investigation so that they can properly test their side (peripheral) vision.

Start

Concept Invention

1. Was it as easy to notice the color as the object itself?
2. Will it make any difference if you try the test from your left side?
3. Will it make any difference if you try different colors? Can you identify some colors farther to the side than others?
4. Will it make any difference if you try the larger squares?
5. What results will you get if you test other people?

Concept Application

An object at one's side can be noticed before its color can be identified. What does this tell you about the structures in the eye?

Tired Eyes ─────────

MATERIALS

• Construction paper (blue, yellow, red, magenta, cyan, and yellow)

• Watch with second hand

• Scissors

• Pencil

• White paper

Invitation

Do you get tired seeing colors?

Exploration

1. Pencil an **X** in the center of the white paper.
2. Cut out one small (5-centimeter, or 2-inch) square each of blue, yellow, and red paper.
3. Put the blue square on the **X**. Look at it steadily for 30 seconds.
4. Remove the square and look at the **X**.
5. What color appears at the **X**?

Concept Invention

1. Rest your eyes for a minute or so. Then try the yellow and red squares in the same way.
2. What color appears after the yellow square? the red square?

Concept Application

Describe what you predict will happen with magenta, cyan, or yellow paper. Try out your prediction and describe the results.

PERCEPTION AND THE EYE CONCEPTS

In this section, we examine how the eye works and apply some ideas discussed previously. Although the eye has many parts, we concentrate on three parts directly involved in sight: iris, retina, and lens (see INQ Figure 1–11).

Iris ─────────────

The iris contains pigment that absorbs some colors and reflects others. Because the kind and amount of this coloring matter varies in individuals, eyes appear to be brown, hazel, or

INQ Figure 1–11   **An eye illustration.**

blue. Two sets of tiny muscles control the size of a small dot (pupil) in the iris. This ability regulates the amount of light entering the eye.

The pupils of cats' eyes can dilate far more than ours. This is one reason why their vision is better than humans in near darkness. A dramatic example of this capacity appears when the headlights of an automobile suddenly shine into the eyes of a cat on a dark night. The two shiny round spots we see are the headlight reflections from inside the cat's eyes.

Retina

Why is it difficult to see when we first walk into a darkened movie theater? Our eyes make a second important adjustment when light varies in brightness. The retina contains two kinds of light-sensitive cells: rods and cones. Cones are less sensitive than rods and are clustered near the back of the eyeball. They work best in strong light and enable us to see color. Rods are distributed in other parts of the retina and are sensitive to dim light.

Chemical changes sensitize either rods or cones under certain conditions. For example, when we walk into a dark theater on a sunny day, it takes several minutes before the rods work well. To achieve optimum sensitivity, up to a half hour may be required. It is thought that cones are most sensitive to three basic colors: red, green, and blue. According to this idea, we see many colors because the basic colors are seen in various combinations.

Lens

An eye lens is convex in shape and works like any other convex lens, with one important difference: A muscle permits it to change shape. If a large, nearby object appears before you, the lens thickens. This thicker lens refracts light rays entering the eye sharply enough for a focus to occur on the retina. Light rays from a small or distant object, however, enter the lens in a near parallel fashion. Only a small refraction is needed to bring the rays to a focus on the retina.

To experience this action, look at a distant object and then suddenly look at something 30 centimeters (1 foot) away. Do you feel the tug of your lens muscles pulling the lens? Do you find that the near object is fuzzy for the brief instant it takes for the muscles to adjust lens thickness? In a camera, of course, focusing is achieved by moving the lens back and forth.

Eyeglasses

The use of eyeglasses corrects two of the main vision problems in regard to image focus. In nearsightedness, the cornea or the lens may be thicker, or the eyeball longer, than normal. This causes an image to focus in front of the retina rather than on it. Notice in INQ Figure 1–12 how the problem is corrected. Part A shows a normal eyeball. Part B shows a longer-than-normal eyeball and a focal point in front of, rather than on, the retina. In part C, a concave eyeglass lens spreads out the incoming light rays. This lengthens the focal point just enough to fall on the retina.

In farsightedness, the cornea or the lens may be thinner, or the eyeball shorter, than normal. So, the focal point is at some imaginary distance beyond the retina. Part A of INQ Figure 1–13 shows this happening with a shorter-than-normal eyeball. In part B, a convex

INQ Figure 1–12   In nearsightedness, an abnormally shaped cornea or eyeball causes an image to focus in front of the retina rather than on it. A concave lens can correct the problem.

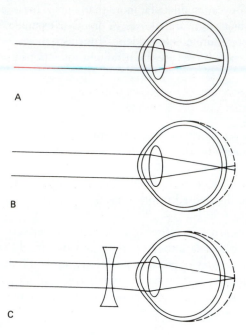

INQ Figure 1–13   In farsightedness, the image focuses at some imaginary point beyond the retina. A convex lens can correct the problem.

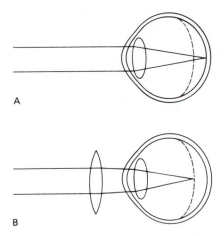

eyeglass lens corrects the defect by forcing the light rays to converge at a shorter focal point, which is on the retina.

Perception

An excellent example of how the brain and eyes work together takes place when we judge distance. Each eye sees an object from a different angle. The closer the object, the greater the difference in what each eye perceives. We actually see a tiny bit around the object. At the same time, we feel our eyes turn inward. With greater distances, the angle gets smaller. The brain interprets this accordingly.

Beyond about 46 meters (50 yards) we rely mainly on size to judge distance. A small telegraph pole looks far away mostly because we know that telephone poles are large. We also use other clues, such as increased haze and the surrounding scene.

A movie film flashes only still pictures on a screen. The apparent motion of a motion-picture projection results from persistence of vision. It takes about 1/16 of a second for an image to fade from our vision after it is withdrawn. By flashing 24 images per second on a screen, a projector creates the illusion of motion.

It took some experience before the current speed of projecting individual motion-picture frames was adopted. Early motion pictures were photographed and projected at much slower speeds. The short, unlighted pause between frames was noticeable. This is how the term *flickers* for movies originated.

It is easy to experience the persistence-of-vision effect with a pencil and a small pad of paper. For example, children can be guided to draw a cartoon with the pad of paper showing a pole that falls over. On the first page, children draw an upright pole on the bottom and center of the page. On each succeeding page, in the same spot, they draw the pole at successively lower angles, until it is horizontal. The number of pages used for this could total 20 pages, which is more than adequate. When the children rapidly flip the pad pages over, they see an animated sequence of a falling pole. Children enjoy making such flipbooks.

References

American Association for the Advancement of Science (AAAS). (1993). *Benchmarks for science literacy*. New York: Oxford University Press.

Dalby, D. K. (1991). Fine-tune your sense of color. *Science and Children*, 29(3), 24–26.

Fathman, A. K., Quinn, M. E., & Kessler, C. (1992). *Teaching science to English learners, grades 4–8*. Washington, DC: National Clearinghouse of Bilingual Education. Retrieved November 13, 2004, from *www.ncela.gwu.edu/pubs/pigs/pig11.htm*

Iona, M., & Beaty, W. (1988). Reflections on refraction. *Science and Children*, 25(8), 18–20.

Mercer, C. D., & Mercer, A. R. (2005). *Teaching students with learning problems* (7th ed.). Upper Saddle River, NJ: Merrill Prentice Hall.

National Research Council (NRC). (1996). *National science education standards*. Washington, DC: National Academy Press.

Ovando, C. J., Collier, V. P., & Combs, M. C. (2003). *Bilingual and ESL classrooms: Teaching in multicultural contexts*. Boston: McGraw-Hill.

Wilson, J. E. (1990). Bent on teaching refraction. *Science and Children*, 28(3), 28–30.

Selected Trade Books: Light Energy and Color

For Younger Children

Baines, R. (1985). *Light*. New York: Troll Associates.

Brockel, R. (1986). *Experiments with light*. New York: Childrens Press.

Carle, E. (1991). *My very first book of colors*. New York: HarperCollins.

Carle, E. (1995). *The very lonely firefly*. New York: G. P. Putnam.

Carroll, J. (1991). *The complete color book*. Parsippany, NJ: Good Apple.

Cole, J. (1997). *The magic school bus makes a rainbow: A book about color*. New York: Scholastic.

Cole, J. (1999). *The magic school bus gets a bright idea: A book about light*. New York: Scholastic.

Collins, D. (1983). *My big fun thinker book of colors and shapes*. Carson, CA: Educational Insights.

Crews, D. (1981). *Light*. New York: Greenwillow Books.

Ehlert, L. (1989). *Color zoo*. New York: HarperCollins.

Fowler, A. (1998). *All the colors of the rainbow*. Danbury, CT: Childrens Press.

Glover, D. (2002). *Sound and light*. New York: Kingfisher.

Gold-Dworkin, H. (2000). *Exploring light and color: A "hands-on" approach to learning*. New York: McGraw-Hill.

Goor, R., & Goor, N. (1981). *Shadows: Here, there, everywhere*. New York: Thomas Y. Crowell.

Hoban, T. (1995). *Colors everywhere*. New York: Greenwillow Books.

Hubbard, P. (1999). *My crayons talk*. New York: Henry Holt.

Livingston, M. (1992). *Light and shadow*. New York: Holiday House.

Macaulay, D. (1990). *Black and white*. Boston: Houghton Mifflin.

Martin, B., & Archambault, J. (1987). *Knots on a counting rope*. New York: Trumpet Club.

Moon, C., & Moon, B. (1992). *Look at a lamp.* Bothell, WA: Wright Group.

Munsch, R. (1992). *Purple, green, and yellow.* New York: Firefly Books.

Serfozo, M. (1988). *Who said red?* New York: Aladdin Picture Books.

Shepherd, D. (1995). *Light shows in the night sky: Auroras.* Danbury, CT: Watts.

Smith, K. B., & Crenson, V. (1987). *Seeing.* New York: Troll Associates.

Stinson, K. (1982). *Red is best.* Willowdale, Ontario: Annick Press.

Suess, Dr. (1996). *My many colored days.* New York: Knopf.

Taylor, B. (1990). *Bouncing and bending light.* Danbury, CT: Watts.

Taylor, B. (1991). *Color and light.* Danbury, CT: Watts.

Taylor, K. (1992). *Flying start science series: Water; light; action; structure.* New York: John Wiley.

Young, E. (1992). *Seven blind mice.* New York: Philomel Books.

For Older Children

Ardley, N. (1991). *Science book of color.* San Diego, CA: HarBrace.

Ardley, N. (1991). *Science book of light.* San Diego, CA: HarBrace.

Asimov, I. (1986). *How did we find out about the speed of light?* New York: Walker.

Berger, M. (1987). *Lights, lenses, and lasers.* New York: G. P. Putnam.

Catherall, E. (1982). *Sight.* Parsippany, NJ: Silver Burdett.

Challoner, J., & LeJars, D. (2001). *Sound and light.* United Kingdom, New York: Kingfisher.

Cooper, M. (1981). *Snap! Photography.* Parsippany, NJ: Julian Messner.

De Bruin, J. (1986). *Light and color.* Parsippany, NJ: Good Apple.

Dispezio, M., & Leary, C. (1999). *Awesome experiments in light & sound.* New York: Sterling Publications.

Dunham, M. (1987). *Colors: How do you say it?* New York: Lothrop, Lee & Shepard Books.

Farndon, J. (2000). *Light and optics (science experiments).* New York: Benchmark Books.

Fiarotta, P., & Fiarotta, N. (1999). *Great experiments with light.* New York: Sterling Publications.

Hecht, J. (1987). *Optics: Light for a new age.* New York: Macmillan.

Hill, J., & Hill, J. (1986). *Looking at light and color.* New York: David & Charles.

Jennings, T. (1992). *Sound and light.* New York: Smithmark.

Murata, M. (1993). *Science is all around you: Water and light.* Minneapolis: Lerner.

Nankivell-Aston, S., & Jackson, D. (2000). *Science experiments with light (science experiments).* London: Franklin Watts, Incorporated.

Searle, B., & Hewitt, S. (2002). *Light (fascinating science projects).* Sussex, England: Copper Beech Books.

Simon, H. (1981). *The magic of color.* New York: Lothrop, Lee & Shepard Books.

Simon, S. (1985). *Shadow magic.* New York: Lothrop, Lee & Shepard Books.

Simon, S. (1991). *Mirror magic.* New York: Lothrop, Lee & Shepard Books.

Walpole, B. (1987). *Light.* New York: Garrard.

Ward, A. (1991). *Experimenting with light and illusions.* Brookmall, PA: Chelsea House.

Whyman, K. (1986). *Light and lasers.* Danbury, CT: Watts.

Whyman, K. (1989). *Rainbows to lasers.* Danbury, CT: Watts.

Wilkins, M. J. (1991). *Air, light, and water.* New York: Random House.

Resource Books

AIMS Educational Foundation. (2000). *Ray's reflections.* Fresno, CA: Author. (mirror activities)

Bartch, M. (1992). *Literature activities across the curriculum.* West Nyack, NY: Simon & Schuster. (science topics on pp. 158–194)

Butzow, C. M., & Butzow, J. W. (1989). *Science through children's literature: An integrated approach.* Englewood, CO: Teacher Ideas Press. (eye, vision, and optics topics on pp. 169–173; shadows and light topics on pp. 174–177)

Gertz, S., Portman, D., & Sraquis, M. (1996). *Teaching physical science through children's literature.* Middletown, OH: Terrific Science Press.

Hillen, J., Mercier, S., Hoover, E., & Cordel, B. (1994). *Primarily physics: Investigations in sound, light, heat, and energy.* Fresno, CA: AIMS Education Foundation.

Russell, C. (1993). *Thematic unit: Color.* Huntington Beach, CA: Teacher Created Materials.

Shaw, D. G., & Dybdahl, C. S. (1996). *Integrating science and language arts.* Boston: Allyn & Bacon. (color topics on pp. 1–52)

Sneider, C. I., Gould, A., & Hawthorne, C. (2002). *Color analyzers.* Berkeley, CA: Great Explorations in Math and Science. (light and color activities)

Tolman, M., & Morton, J. (1986). *Physical science activities for grades 2–8.* West Nyack, NY: Parker.

HEAT ENERGY

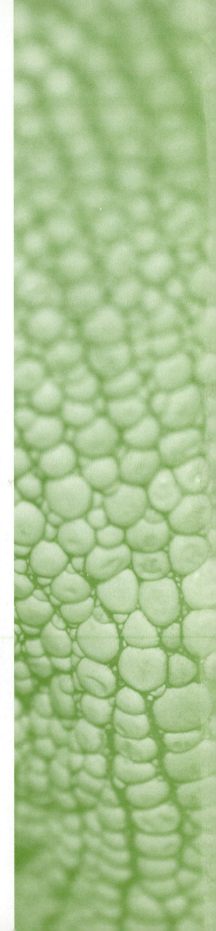

T he rising cost of fuels has made more people realize that knowing about heat energy has both economic and scientific value. Energy affects many aspects of our lives. This chapter considers what happens when materials are heated and cooled, how materials change state, how heat and temperature differ, and how heat travels.

SAFETY

Some experiences require use of a lighted candle. Supervise these occasions closely. We advise that you handle any burning candle yourself; if you choose to allow children to work with fire, make sure they wear safety goggles. Never allow a child with long hair or loose, trailing apparel to work by an open flame. Always use a metal tray or other fireproof material to contain a burning or hot substance. Develop standards about not touching a hot plate or other materials at random.

Benchmarks and Standards

Students in early grades should develop an understanding that materials can exist in liquid, gas, or solid form. Experimentation with water can be effective in introducing them to the states of matter and how heat affects the movement of molecules and the state of a substance. Specific benchmarks and standards are as follows:

Sample Benchmarks (AAAS, 1993)

- Heating and cooling cause changes in the properties of materials. Many kinds of changes occur faster under hotter conditions. (By Grades 3–5, p. 77)
- Some materials conduct heat much better than others. Poor conductors can reduce heat loss. (By Grades 3–5, p. 84)

Sample Standards (NRC, 1996)

- Materials can exist in different states—solid, liquid, and gas. Some common materials, such as water, can be changed from one state to another by heating and cooling. (By Grades K–4, p. 127)
- Heat moves in predictable ways, flowing from warmer objects to cooler ones until all reach the same temperature. (By Grades 5–8, p. 155)

EXPANSION AND CONTRACTION Inquiry

A Hot Association ———

MATERIALS

- Brass screw and screw eye (each screwed into the eraser end of a separate pencil as shown)
- Small dish and candle
- Matches
- Safety goggles

Invitation

How does heat affect a solid?

Exploration

1. Put on safety goggles. Light the candle and fix it to the dish.
2. Try to pass the screw through the screw eye as shown. This should not be possible until heat is applied.
3. Heat the screw eye in the flame for a minute or so.
4. Try step 2 again. Does the screw head pass through the heated screw eye? If not, try step 3 again. If so, keep passing the screw head through the eye. How many seconds go by before you cannot do it?

Concept Invention

What will happen if you heat the screw but not the screw eye? What will happen if you heat both screw and screw eye?

MATERIALS

- Small soda bottle
- Water
- Paper towel
- Soft clay
- Refrigerator
- Small card
- Plastic straw
- Sticky tape
- Crayon
- Red food coloring
- Pencil
- Regular thermometer
- Ruler

Adapting for Students with Exceptionalities

Take extra precautions to ensure the safety of exceptional students when facilitating this activity. Always stabilize equipment and maintain sufficient space for easy access and mobility.

Concept Application

Explain what happened in this activity.

Water Thermometer ———

Invitation

Many thermometers use mercury or red-colored alcohol in a closed tube. What happens to these liquids as they get warmer? cooler? How can you make a water thermometer that works in much the same way?

Exploration

1. Fill the bottle almost full with water.
2. Add some food coloring to the water so that it is easy to see.
3. Dry the bottle opening with a paper towel. Then put the straw about halfway into the bottle opening.
4. Use clay to stopper the bottle opening around the straw. Try to get a tight fit without getting the clay wet.
5. The water should rise about halfway up the straw beyond the clay. If it does not, move the straw up or down. Then press the clay down tightly again.
6. Put the bottle in the sun. After an hour, lightly mark the water level on the straw with crayon. Then put the bottle in a refrigerator for an hour and mark the water level.
7. Measure the distance between the two marks. On a card, mark two dots the same distance apart and draw evenly spaced lines between. Give each line a number, with the highest on top. Put the column of numbers on the right side of the card.
8. Tape the card to the straw so that the top and bottom numbers are even with the two marks on the straw as shown.
9. Use your water thermometer to take daily temperatures for a week. Record the temperatures. You might use a table like this one:

Clay

Water Thermometer Readings

Time	M	T	W	Th	F
9:30 A.M.	4	5			
Noon	6	7			
2:30 P.M.	7	7			

Concept Invention

1. At what time of day is it coolest? warmest?
2. During the week, what was the coolest morning? noon? afternoon?
3. How closely can you predict the noon temperature from the 9:30 A.M. temperature? How closely can you predict the 2:30 P.M. temperature from the noon temperature? Try this for a few days.
4. Ask a partner to make another water thermometer. Keep two separate records. How closely do your readings agree with your partner's? If they do not agree, can you figure out why?
5. Get a regular thermometer. Measure the temperature with both it and your water thermometer. Write the actual temperatures on the left side of the straw card. After a few days, use only your water thermometer to predict the real temperature. Then check the regular thermometer each time. How accurate is your water thermometer? How could you make it more accurate?

Teaching Tips

A one-hole rubber stopper and glass tube are more reliable than clay and a straw. Wet the tube and stopper before inserting the tube. Hold the tube with a thickly folded paper towel to guard against breakage, and use a twisting motion.

Water, especially with this large volume, takes considerable time to gain and lose heat, so readings should be hours apart. Rubbing alcohol responds more quickly to heat and may be substituted.

Concept Application

How does this activity show that liquids expand when heated and contract when cooled?

Hot Air ——————

MATERIALS

- Empty soda bottle (cool)
- Round balloon
- Partner

Invitation

How does heat affect air?

Exploration

1. Snap the balloon opening over the bottle opening.
2. Wrap both hands around the bottle to warm it. Let a partner help, too.
3. What happens to the balloon? What seems to be happening to the air inside the bottle?
4. What will happen to the balloon when the bottle cools? Why?

Teaching Tips

A partly filled balloon may be placed in sunlight. A string may be wrapped around it to compare before and after sizes. A round, moderately sized balloon inflates more easily than the small, tubular kind.

Concept Invention

How else can you warm the bottle air? cool the bottle air?

Concept Application

Explain how you could use only a balloon and string to find out if heated air expands.

EXPANSION AND CONTRACTION CONCEPTS

Question: How tall is the tallest building in the United States? Answer: I don't know; its height keeps changing. Although questions and answers like this seldom come up in conversation, it is a good example of the expansion and contraction concept. The height of a tall structure may vary 15 centimeters (6 inches) or more, depending on temperature differences when the measurements are taken. Likewise, a steel bridge may change more than 30 centimeters (12 inches) in length, and a ship's captain may stride a slightly longer deck in southern waters than in northern waters.

Molecules ——————

The molecular theory of matter offers an interesting explanation for these and many other events. To understand molecules, let's look for a moment at a drop of water. If we could subdivide it with an imaginary dropper, eventually we would get to a point where one more subdivision would produce two atoms of hydrogen and one of oxygen. Both are gases and, of course, look nothing like water. From this, we can say that a molecule is the smallest particle of a substance that can exist by itself and have the properties of that substance when interacting with other molecules.

Strictly speaking, only some gases are exclusively made up of molecules. Some liquids and many solids are composed of electrically charged atoms or groups of atoms called *ions*. But as nearly all ionic particles have physical properties very similar to molecules, it is convenient to treat them as such. Is there any direct proof that molecules exist? Yes, pictures of molecules have been taken through electron microscopes. It is a remarkable tribute to the brainpower of earlier scientists that they were able to forge a molecular theory from their secondhand observations.

Many early experiments may be duplicated today. A unit of alcohol added to a unit of water results in slightly less than two units of liquid. When gold and lead bars are clamped together for a long period, a slight intermingling of these elements occurs. Solid sugar crystals disappear when stirred into a liquid.

Atoms are formed from protons, neutrons, and electrons. Atoms combine to form the molecules that make up matter. Molecules have an attractive force (cohesion) between them. There is space between molecules. In a solid material, the molecules are very close together and are relatively fixed in place because their cohesion is greater than that of gases or liquids. The molecules of most liquids are slightly farther apart; their weaker cohesion permits them to slide about and take the shape of a container. Gas molecules are widest apart and have almost no cohesive attraction. Therefore, they can conform to a container's shape or escape from an uncovered container.

Molecules are always in motion, but they come almost to a standstill at absolute zero (−460°F or −273°C). Above this temperature, molecules of solids vibrate in place, whereas liquid and gas molecules move faster and more freely. With increased temperature, motion increases and the molecules move farther apart. The reverse happens when temperature is decreased. This is why most matter expands when heated and contracts when cooled.

Water

If liquids contract when cooled, why do some water pipes burst in freezing weather? Although molecular theory states that liquids contract when cooled, we note an interesting exception when water temperature drops toward freezing. Water does contract in volume with decreased temperature until about 4°C (39°F). Then its molecules begin to assemble into a crystalline form that becomes ice at 32°F (0°C). The latticelike arrangement of these crystals takes up more space, about 4% more, than an equal number of free-moving water molecules. This is why water pipes and engine blocks of water-cooled automobiles may burst in winter if the water inside them freezes.

It also explains why a lake freezes from the top down, rather than the reverse. At 4°C (39°F), water is densest and sinks to the bottom of the lake. Colder water, being less dense, floats to the surface. It freezes into surface ice and traps the heat energy in the slightly warmer water below. Unless the air temperature is extremely cold, this trapped energy is enough to keep the pond from freezing completely.

The importance of this phenomenon to living things can hardly be overestimated. Although it is clear that aquatic life is saved, consider what would happen to the world's climate if bodies of water froze from the bottom up. Because the heat trapped by ice would escape, ice formation would increase. Gradually, the earth's climate would become colder and would eventually become fatal to most life forms.

Differences in Cohesion

Different materials vary in their rates of expansion and contraction because their cohesive forces vary. It is easier to tear a paper sheet apart than an equally thin steel sheet because steel molecules attract one another with much greater force. A cohesive disparity is likewise true of alcohol and water. Notice in INQ Figure 2–1 how water bulges above the glass rim when it is overfilled.

INQ Figure 2–1   **Surface tension in alcohol and water.**

Water   Alcohol

The cohesive force of water molecules is greater than that of alcohol. This explains why equal amounts of heat energy cause alcohol to expand more than water; it is easier to overcome the weaker cohesive force. It also tells us why alcohol evaporates faster than water.

Expansion, contraction, and changes of state from solids to liquids and gases are the results of a constant tug of war between heat energy and cohesive force. Which side wins depends on which force is stronger.

Plastics and Expansion and Contraction

One way to introduce the effects of temperature on matter is to have children work with shrinkable polystyrene. Gertz, Portman, and Sraquis (1996) suggest a "Shrinky Plastic" activity incorporating the children's book *George Shrinks* (Joyce, 1998). The idea for this activity is for children to observe and compare polystyrene images of George before and after the heat source shrinks his polystyrene representation.

As an extension, children can also see which types of plastic shrink by heating a variety of plastic materials in a 325°F oven while placed on a brown paper bag inside of a disposable pie pan.

- Soda bottles (polyethylene terephthalate or PET)
- Milk jugs and detergent containers (high density polyethylene)
- Cooking oil containers (vinyl/polyvinyl chloride or PVC)
- Bread, produce, and garment bags (low density polyethylene)
- Yogurt containers and other storage containers (polypropylene)
- Foam cups, egg cartons, and meat trays (polystyrene)

When looking for shrinkable polystyrene plastic, check for recycle code 6 or the letters PS. For more information on shrinkable polystyrene, refer to *The Shrinkly Dinks Book* (Haab, 1999).

CHANGING STATES OF MATTER Inquiry

Melting Away ————

Invitation

Suppose you have a glass of water. It has the same temperature as the air. Would an ice cube melt faster in the water or the air? How can you find out if water or air will melt an ice cube faster?

Exploration

1. Use a thermometer to measure the air temperature inside one glass.
2. Also measure the temperature inside a glass of water. It should be about the same as the air temperature. If not, let the water stand awhile.
3. Find two ice cubes that are the same size.
4. Put one ice cube into the empty glass. Put the other into the glass of water.
5. Compare how fast the ice cubes melt.

> **MATERIALS**
> - Thermometer
> - Small plastic bag
> - Water
> - Salt
> - Ice cubes
> - Spoon
> - Two matched glasses

Concept Invention

1. How can you make an ice cube melt faster in water? Will stirring the water make a difference? Will an ice cube melt faster in warmer water? Does breaking or crushing the cube make a difference? Does changing the volume of water make a difference?
2. How fast will ice cubes melt in other liquids? Will an ice cube melt faster in saltwater? Does the amount of salt make a difference? What other liquids can you try? Can you predict the melting order of ice cubes in them?

Teaching Tips — The first activity of this investigation requires water of room temperature. Blend warm and cold tap water, or simply let a glass of water stand for a while.

Concept Application

Design another experiment that shows the melting time of an ice cube changes with conditions.

A Cold Drink ————

Invitation

What happens to the temperature of an iced drink as the ice melts?

> **MATERIALS**
> - Two ice cubes
> - Cup of water
> - Thermometer
> - Clock with a second hand

Exploration

1. Put the ice cubes into the cup of water.
2. Take the water temperature once a minute throughout this activity. Stir the water a bit each time.
3. Repeat step 2 until you get the same reading twice.

<table>
<tr><td>Teaching Tips</td><td>The ice melting process can be speeded up by heating a metal cup on a hot plate turned to low. Similar results should happen.</td></tr>
</table>

Concept Invention

1. What will happen to the temperature as the ice keeps melting?
2. When does the water temperature rise again?

Concept Application

Create a graph for the data in this activity.

CHANGING STATES OF MATTER CONCEPTS

Sometimes we get so used to our environment that it is difficult to imagine the things around us in new ways. Almost everyone knows that air is a mixture of gases. Yet, a favorite stunt of science demonstrators at high school assemblies is to pour liquid air grandly from one container to another. Many persons know that carbon dioxide is a gas. Yet, it is possible to trip over some or drop it on your toe when it is in the form of dry ice. Steel is certainly a durable solid, but tests conducted at high temperatures for possible spaceship uses turn the metal into vapor.

Temperature ───────

The state of matter at any given moment depends on its temperature and pressure. Temperature is a measure of the average speed of molecular movements. When increased heat energy is applied to a solid, its molecules vibrate faster. If the motion is great enough to overcome the molecules' cohesive forces, the molecules move farther away, and the solid becomes a liquid. If further energy is applied, the molecules move even faster and farther apart to become a gas. With loss of heat energy, the opposite occurs. The decreased speed of molecules enables cohesive force to be reasserted, which creates a liquid, and then a solid when enough heat is lost.

Does a solid become a liquid before it becomes a gas, or does a gas become a liquid before it becomes a solid? Usually, but a mothball changes to a gas directly, as does dry ice. Frost is an example of vapor freezing directly into a solid state. These phenomena are examples of *sublimation*.

Different substances change state at different temperatures. Adding salt to fresh water lowers the water's freezing point. Seawater, for example, freezes at 28.5°F (22°C) instead of 32°F (0°C). Unless the temperature is very low, sprinkling rock salt on an icy sidewalk melts the ice. We add an antifreeze liquid to our automobile radiators to prevent freezing. A heavy salt solution would be even more effective, except for its unfortunate tendency to corrode metal.

What Pressure Does ───────

Pressure also has an interesting effect on changes of state. As a liquid warms, some of its molecules move so fast that they bounce off into the air. We recognize this as evaporation.

The same thing happens with boiling, except the process is faster. To leave the surface of a liquid, though, molecules must overcome not only the cohesive pull of nearby molecules but also the pressure of air molecules immediately above.

At sea level, a 6.45 square centimeter (1-square-inch) column of air extending to outer space weighs 6.6 kilograms (14.7 pounds). At the top of a tall mountain, much less air, and therefore less weight, is pressing down. With less pressure, it is easier for liquid molecules to escape into vapor form. So, at 27,000 meters (90,000 feet), water boils at room temperature. Astronauts or pilots of high-altitude airplanes wear pressure suits, or are enclosed in a pressurized cabin, to keep their blood from boiling.

Because we usually associate boiling with a temperature of about 212°F, it is important to realize another practical effect of decreased pressure. Boiling-point temperature decreases about 1°F for each 550-foot increase in altitude. At a high location, it is difficult to cook foods satisfactorily in an open container because of the low temperature at which boiling occurs. A pressure cooker is almost a necessity.

Heat Loss and Gain ——————

Why is it possible to skate on ice, when we cannot on other smooth surfaces? The answer is that we do not skate directly on the ice. We skate on a thin film of water that may be caused by the leading edge of a blade striking the ice and causing enough friction energy to melt a trail for the rest of the blade. This furnishes a water-lubricated surface on which we slide. As the temperature drops, however, it takes increasing pressure to melt the ice. It may be difficult to skate at all.

Does an iced drink start warming up after the ice has half melted? A change of state always results in the absorption or release of heat energy. It requires energy for the fixed, jiggling molecules of a solid, like ice, to acquire a more freely moving liquid state. Interestingly, until an ice cube melts completely in a container of water, there is no appreciable increase in water temperature. The heat energy absorbed first changes the state of the frozen water and then raises the water temperature once the cube has melted. The next time you have an iced drink, try stirring the liquid until the last bit of ice has melted. You should sense no rise in temperature until after the frozen cubes have completely changed state.

Additional energy is required for liquid molecules to move fast enough and far enough apart to become a gas. Heat is absorbed from whatever accessible substance is warmer than the changing material.

So, if you hold an ice cube in your hand, it removes heat from your body. More heat is required as the liquid evaporates. This is why evaporation has a cooling effect. As the speed of evaporation increases, so does cooling. This is why rubbing alcohol cools your skin more effectively than water. Ethyl chloride evaporates so quickly that it is used by physicians to numb flesh for painless surgery.

Conversely, heat energy is released when a gas condenses to a liquid or a liquid freezes to a solid state. The energy is released because molecular motion continually decreases with each event. It used to be common in rural homes to place tubs of water near vegetable bins in the basement. As the water froze, enough heat was given off to prevent the vegetables from freezing.

Heat is absorbed in evaporation and released through condensation. This principle is applied in electric refrigeration. A liquid refrigerant moves at low pressure into the freezing unit. There it flashes into a vaporous state, cools rapidly, and absorbs heat. As the now slightly warmed vapor leaves the unit, a motor-driven pump compresses the vapor until it has changed to a hot liquid under high pressure. The liquid next circulates in tubes attached to the back of the refrigerator that radiate the heat into the air. The cycle then repeats itself.

A heat pump is a device that warms or cools a home by transferring heat from one area to another. A heat pump works on the same principle as electric refrigeration. In its cooling cycle, it transfers hot air from inside the house to the outside. You can feel the hot air over the condenser fan motor outside the house. When the refrigerant cycle is reversed in the heating mode, the heat is transferred from outside to inside the house. The outside unit will feel cool and could even freeze in colder temperatures, if the cycle is not intermittently reversed to reheat the outside unit. If the temperature is too cool (below 40°F or 4°C), heat pumps do not work very well, and electric heat strips in the inside unit will activate to assist in heating the house.

TEMPERATURE AND HEAT ENERGY Inquiry

Heat Energy

Invitation

Suppose you have two iron nails, one large and one small. Both are heated to the same temperature over a candle flame. Which nail do you think would have more heat energy in it? Or, would both nails have the same heat energy? How can you compare the amount of heat energy in heated nails?

Exploration

1. Put on safety goggles. Stick the candle upright in the middle of the pan. You can melt a little wax to hold the candle in place or use clay or glue as needed to support the candle.
2. Fill both cans with enough water to cover the nails when they are dropped in later. Check to be sure the water levels and temperatures are the same in the cans.
3. Light the candle. Use tongs or pliers to hold both nails in the flame for 3 minutes.
4. Drop one nail into each can. Wait 1 minute. Then stir the water in each can lightly with a thermometer and check the temperatures.

Concept Invention

1. Which can of water is warmer? Which nail had more heat energy in it?
2. Maybe one nail was just cooler than the other. Suppose you heated both nails longer to be sure they were the same temperature. Would you still get uneven results?
3. How can you give the small nail more heat energy than the larger one?
4. Suppose you heated together a large aluminum nail and a large iron nail. Which, if either, do you think would have more energy?

Teaching Tips

Supervise this investigation closely for safety.
   Caution: Children should handle heated material only with tongs or pliers. Also, you might prefer to light and extinguish the candles. A hot plate can be used to heat more objects at a time than is possible with a candle. Make sure that you and the students wear safety goggles when working with fire.

> ### Adapting for Students with Exceptionalities
>
> Be flexible with the level of participation of students with behavioral difficulties or severe or multiple disabilities in activities such as this where there are safety considerations. (See Turnbull, Turnbull, Shank, & Smith, 2004, for a discussion on adapting instruction through partial participation.)

Concept Application

If the amount of heat energy in the same materials depends on their mass as well as their temperature, can you show what happens to water temperature for each minute you heat a nail? Construct a graph similar to this one to show your results.

Minutes Nail Is Heated Versus Water Temperature

	25
Water temperature (°C)	20

          1   2   3   4   5   6

          Minutes nail is heated

The Mixing of Hot and Cold Water ———

MATERIALS

- Large container of hot water
- Large container of cold water
- Two small foam cups
- Half-gallon milk carton with top cut off
- Two thermometers
- Paper and pencil

Invitation

Have you ever added cold water to cool down hot bath water? Have you added hot water to heat up cool bath water? You can learn to predict the temperatures of a water mixture. How can you predict the temperature of two mixed samples of water?

Exploration

1. Fill one small cup with hot water. Take the temperature of the water with one thermometer and record it.
2. Fill another small cup with cold water. Take the temperature of the water with the other thermometer and record it.
3. Pour both cups of water into the large carton. Take the temperature of the mixed water and record it.
4. Study your records. Let's say your recorded temperatures are like these:

Hot Water	Cold Water	Mixture
60°C	20°C	40°C

5. Notice that the temperature of the mixture is halfway between the hot and cold temperatures (60 + 20 = 80, 40 is half of 80). Look at the temperature of your mixture. Is it about halfway between the hot and cold temperatures?

Concept Invention

1. Suppose you mix 2 cups of hot water and 2 cups of cold water. How hot do you predict the mixture will be?
2. Suppose you mix 2 cups of only hot water. How hot do you predict the mixture will be?
3. Suppose you mix 2 cups of cold water with 1 cup of hot water. Will the mixture be hotter or colder than halfway between the two temperatures? How closely can you predict the temperature of the mixture?

Teaching Tips

The temperature of mixed water depends on the temperature and the volume of each water sample mixed. When the volumes of water samples are equal, the mixture temperature is the average of the sample temperatures; but if the volumes are different, this has to be considered when figuring the average. For example, if one water sample is twice the volume of another, it will have twice the influence on the mixture temperature.

Caution: Never heat the water beyond the point that someone can comfortably touch it.

Scaffolding for English Learners

Concepts such as heat quantity, heat capacity, thermal equilibrium, calories, and thermodynamics are especially difficult for English learners. By taking the extra time to allow students to work with materials, they begin to learn the appropriate language to explain the concepts that they are developing. Inquiry approaches are naturally inclusive and allow the English learner to use verbal interaction with peers to promote concept development. (See Hampton & Rodriguez, 2001, for a discussion of the importance of inquiry with English learners.)

Concept Application

The temperature of mixed water samples depends on the temperature and volume of each sample. The mixture temperature is always somewhere between the high and low sample temperatures. Have a classmate provide two volumes of water and corresponding temperatures. Can you determine what the resultant temperature will be when they are mixed?

TEMPERATURE AND HEAT ENERGY CONCEPTS

You have seen before that the temperature of a material depends on the speed of its molecules. So, molecules of a cold substance move more slowly than those of a hotter substance.

Heat Quantity

Although many children understand the concept of temperature, quantity of heat is a subtler idea. Consider a white-hot horseshoe just removed from a blacksmith's forge and a large bathtub of warm water. Which contains more heat? It is probably the water. The amount of heat a material contains depends on how many molecules it has, as well as on how fast they are moving. This is why the owner of a large house pays larger winter heating bills than the owner of a small house, although the same air temperature may be maintained. The concept also explains why it takes about half as long to bring 1 liter (1 quart) of water to a boil as 2 liters (2 quarts). There are half as many molecules to move.

Heat Capacity

Different materials have different capacities for heat energy. For example, it takes more heat for iron to reach a given temperature than an equal weight of lead. More energy is required to heat water to a given temperature than any other common material, liquid or solid, and water retains this heat longer.

The most important effect of water's high heat capacity is found in weather and climate. Because the earth's oceans and lakes gain and lose heat more slowly than the land, they moderate changes in air temperature throughout the world. The most noticeable effects are found in coastal regions; summers are cooler and winters warmer there than they are inland.

The Calorie and the BTU

Two measures are commonly used to tell heat capacity: the calorie and the British thermal unit (BTU). A *calorie* is the quantity of heat needed to raise the temperature of 1 gram (about 1/28 ounce) of water 1°C. The caloric value of a food is found simply by burning a dry sample of known weight in a special chamber of a carefully insulated container of pure water. The temperature rise is multiplied by the weight of water in the container. For example, suppose 50 grams of water rises 20°C. $50 \times 20 = 1000$ calories.

To make calculations less cumbersome, a "large calorie" is used in finding the heat value of foods. Equivalent to 1000 small calories, the large calorie, or kilocalorie, abbreviated C, is what you see published in diet lists.

The *British thermal unit,* or the quantity of heat needed to raise 1 pound of water 1°F, is used widely by engineers. It is found by multiplying the mass of water by the temperature increase. So, to raise the temperature of 5 pounds of water 30°F requires 150 BTU.

Of course, this information is more for you than for the students at this level. Yet, it is not too early for many children to grasp the general idea of heat quantity. For this reason, we included the inquiry activity in which children heat different-sized nails, put them in water, and measure the increases in water temperature.

Heat Conservation

Heat energy is conserved when liquids are mixed—that is, not lost but transferred in proportion to the original amount. One liter (1 quart) of warm water has half the heat energy of 2 liters (2 quarts) of water at the same temperature. Also, if two equal volumes of water at different temperatures are mixed, the resulting temperature is halfway between that of the two samples.

Thermal Equilibrium

In some elementary science curricula, the concept of equilibrium is introduced. For example, when water is brought to a boil, its temperature stays at 212°F or 100°C (at sea level) until all the water has evaporated. Because water loses heat energy as fast as it gains heat energy, we see a state of dynamic equilibrium or a stable condition that remains until the water disappears.

A second example is seen when something cools. You know that when a jar of hot water is left standing long enough, it loses heat energy to the surrounding air and surface on which it rests. Eventually, the water temperature becomes stable when it reaches thermal equilibrium with these interacting objects. The air, of course, is the chief interacting object that influences the water's final temperature.

Thermodynamics

Thermodynamics is the branch of physics that involves heat and how heat is transformed to and from other forms of energy. A thermodynamic system involves temperature, pressure, volume, and chemical composition. There are many examples of changes from one form of energy to another.

One common instance of chemical energy producing heat energy is when you eat a hot pepper. A chemical substance called *capsaicin* produces heat on your tongue. Burning a log in the fireplace is another example of chemical energy producing heat energy because the wood is combining with oxygen to make the fire.

Electrical energy can produce heat in an electric heater, hairdryer, or similar appliance. The reverse is also true. A *thermocouple* is made from two different types of wires joined together at one end. When heat is applied, a small amount of electricity is produced. The electricity can even be measured to provide an indication of temperature.

Heat energy can be produced through mechanical means as you find when you rub your hands together. A large truck needs to use lower gears going downhill because the truck's brakes would burn up if applied while descending a steep hill. Likewise, heat energy can produce mechanical energy as in the Stirling engine. These engines use a variety of fuels that provide heat used to produce mechanical energy.

CONDUCTION, CONVECTION, AND RADIATION Inquiry

Warm Feelings

Invitation

What makes some things feel colder even when they have the same temperature?

Exploration

1. Hold the bulb of a thermometer against any metal object, such as scissors.
2. Find its temperature.
3. Do the same with a piece of wood and a folded newspaper. They should all be the same temperature. If not, keep them together and wait an hour or so.

Concept Invention

1. Touch a metal object with one hand and some wood with the other. Compare the metal and newspaper, too.
2. Which one felt coolest? warmest? Some materials conduct heat well, and some poorly. Good conductors take away heat quickly from our warm skin, so they feel cool. Poor conductors take away heat slowly; they seem warm because less heat is lost from our skin.

Concept Application

Compare other materials you find at school and home. Make a record of what you find. Share your record with others who test heat conductors.

MATERIALS

- Metal object
- Newspaper
- Piece of wood

Teaching Tips It is assumed in this activity that the temperatures of tested materials will be lower than body temperature. If your students seem capable, invite them to attempt an explanation and withhold, for a time, the explanation given.

MATERIALS

- Two matched clear soda bottles
- Red food coloring
- Small card
- White paper
- Cake pan or tray
- Hot and cold tap water
- Sheet of white paper

Bottle Currents

Invitation

How do warm and cold water form a current?

Exploration

1. Fill one bottle with cold tap water and the other with hot tap water.
2. Add 3 or 4 drops of red coloring to the hot water bottle. Put this bottle on the pan.
3. Hold a card tightly over the opening of the cold water bottle. Turn the bottle upside down and place it carefully on top of the hot water bottle as illustrated.

Concept Invention

What do you think will happen if you remove the card? Try it and see. Be careful not to tip over the bottle. Hold white paper behind the bottle to see the activity better.

Adapting for Students with Exceptionalities

A discrepant event is an occurrence during which things behave differently than expected. Discrepant event activities such as this may provide students with cognitive conflict because the results are unexpected. Keep in mind that situations may not be easily predictable or explainable for the students at first. Allow additional time and feedback to assist students in resolving the conflict.

Concept Application

Empty the bottles and do Exploration steps 1, 2, and 3 again, but this time put the hot water bottle on top. What do you think will happen now when you remove the card? How can you explain the results?

Warm Air

Invitation

Where does warmed air go?

Exploration

1. Stick a thumbtack into the middle of the stick near the edge. Tie string to the tack.
2. Hang the stick from the top of a wide table. Use another tack to fasten the loose string end there.
3. Fasten a string to each bag bottom with sticky tape.
4. Cut out the bottom of the bag.
5. Hang the bags from the stick ends. Use a tiny bit of clay to balance the stick if needed, as shown.
6. Place a cold, unplugged hot plate under one bag. (**Caution:** The bag should be at least 30 centimeters [1 foot] above the hot plate because it is flammable.)
7. Plug in the hot plate.

MATERIALS

- Yardstick or substitute
- String
- Scissors
- Two thumbtacks
- Two matched paper bags
- Bit of clay
- Sticky tape
- Hot plate

Clay balancer

Concept Invention

What do you think will happen to the bag over the hot plate when you turn on the hot plate?

Concept Application

What will happen to that bag when you turn off the hot plate?

Solar Energy and Colors

MATERIALS

• Four sheets of different-colored construction paper (such as blue, red, green, white)

• Four thermometers

• Four paper clips

• Sunshine

• Partner

Invitation

Have you ever felt extra warm when wearing a colored shirt in sunlight? When a colored shirt soaks up sunlight, it does get warmer. But how does the kind of color affect how warm it gets? How can you compare how warm different colors get in sunlight?

Exploration

1. Fold the four colored sheets in half. Clip together the open sides.
2. Push a thermometer all the way into each folded, clipped sheet as illustrated.
3. Place the sheets in a row where it is sunny.
4. Wait 5 minutes. Then check the thermometer temperatures. (Before you check, what do you think the warmest to coolest colors will be?)

Concept Invention

1. Try colored sheets such as orange, yellow, and black. What are the warmest to coolest colors?
2. How well can you feel the difference in heat among the colors? Close your eyes. Let a partner help you place your hands on the sheets. Can you feel the hottest and coolest sheets?
3. Will a large colored sheet get warmer than a small one?

Concept Application

Absorbed sunlight changes to heat energy; darker colors get warmer than lighter colors. Suppose you placed all the colored sheets in the shade. Would some colors still get warmer than others?

Staying Warm ———

Invitation

How do greenhouses and closed automobiles get warm?

Exploration

1. Place each jar on its side. Put a piece of cloth into each jar. Place a thermometer on each cloth. Cap only one jar.
2. Place the jars in a sunny area. Turn the jars so that their tops face away from the sun.
3. Watch the thermometers. Keep a record of any changes each minute. Remove a thermometer before it gets close to its highest temperature, because it can break.

Concept Invention

In which jar does the temperature climb faster? How much faster? A graph will help you answer these questions.

Concept Application

How much, if any, difference in jar temperature will there be on a cloudy day?

MATERIALS

- Two matched glass jars
- One jar cap
- Two thermometers
- Two equal-sized pieces of dark cloth
- Sunshine
- Clock

Hot Lights ———

Invitation

Where is it hottest around a lighted lamp?

Exploration

1. Check the room temperature with your thermometer. Then switch on the lamp.
2. Hold the bulb end of the thermometer toward the lamplight. Try the three places illustrated. Keep the thermometer the same distance from the light each time, and hold it there for the same amount of time. Wait for the thermometer to reach room temperature before trying a new place.

MATERIALS

- Table or gooseneck lamp (shade removed)
- Ruler
- Small pane of glass
- Thermometer
- Watch

Concept Invention

1. How hot does the thermometer get in each place?
2. Turn the lamp upside down. Again, hold the thermometer bulb toward the light.
3. How hot does the thermometer get? How can you explain your results?

Concept Application

Set the lamp upright again. Hold a piece of transparent glass between the light and the thermometer. Hold the thermometer in all four places again. What are your findings now? How can you explain them?

How to Keep Heat In or Out ————

Teaching Tips

Tape the edges of the glass shield with masking tape to avoid nicked fingers. A transparent shield of plastic kitchen wrap will also work. The temperature above an unshielded bulb should be highest because both convection and radiation occur. Heat produced by convection is blocked by a transparent shield, so the temperature above a shielded bulb should be like that found in other positions around the bulb.

Invitation

Most houses have an inside and outside wall. Packed between the double walls of many houses is insulation. This is a light, fluffy material that helps keep heat in or out. You can work with cans of water and different materials to learn about insulation. What can you do to see how insulation works?

Exploration

1. Pour the same amount of hot water into each small can.
2. Cover each small can with the same size piece of foil. Use a rubber band to hold each cover tight.
3. Wrap one small can with cloth.
4. Put this can into one large can and cap it.
5. Put the other small can into the second large can and cap it.
6. After 20 minutes, remove the four can covers. Dip a finger into each small can of water. Which is warmer?

MATERIALS

- Two small tin cans
- Hot water
- Two large tin cans with lids
- Piece of cloth
- Two equal-sized pieces of aluminum foil
- Different insulation materials
- Two rubber bands
- Ice cubes
- Thermometer
- Clock

Concept Invention

1. How much warmer is one can of water than the other? How can you use a thermometer to find out?
2. How hot can you keep a small can of water? Have a contest with a friend. Try different materials, such as sawdust, cotton, wool, puffed rice, or torn paper. Or try your own secret mix of materials. Put the materials between the larger and smaller can walls. Whoever has the warmer can of water after 30 minutes (or longer) wins.
3. Can you figure out which single material is the best insulator? the worst insulator? Does how tightly it is packed make a difference?

Teaching Tips

Use matched 1-pound coffee cans with lids for the larger cans. Small, identical juice cans fit nicely into the coffee cans. Identical pieces of foil may be used to cap the small cans so that insulating materials do not fall inside. Either hot or warm water from the tap will do for this activity.

4. In summer, you want your home to stay cool. Does insulation keep heat out as well as in? Find out. How cool can you keep a small can with an ice cube inside? Have a contest with a friend. Whoever has the larger ice cube after 1 hour (or longer) wins.
5. Are the best materials for keeping the can warm also best for keeping the can cold? If not, which are best?

Scaffolding for English Learners

This activity lends itself to a cultural perspective. Discuss how homes are heated and warmed in other cultures. Which cultures use insulation? Which cultures could benefit from insulation use? What materials are natural insulators used by cultures? What natural materials could be used to insulate that are not already in use by cultures? Test the materials you discuss with this activity. (See Laplante, 1997, for the importance of cultural perspectives with English learners.)

Concept Application

Describe how insulating materials may be used to slow the movement of heat energy in your home.

CONDUCTION, CONVECTION, AND RADIATION CONCEPTS

Until, the 19th century, it was generally thought that heat was a fluidlike substance (*caloric*) that could be poured from one material to another. Scientists now realize that heat is a form of energy, with *energy* being defined as the capacity to do work.

Changing Forms of Energy

Many experiments have shown that energy can be changed from one form to another. Our practical experience also shows that this is so. Electrical energy changes to heat in toasters and hot plates; chemical energy yields heat through fires and explosives; mechanical energy (motion) provides the force needed to overcome friction, and in the process heat is released. Heat, in turn, changes to other forms of energy. Hot fuel turns a generator to produce electricity, or gasoline is burned in automobile engines to produce mechanical energy.

If you put a pan of hot water in a cool room, after a while the water cools to room temperature. Place a pan of cool water in a hot oven, however, and the water warms to oven temperature. In moving toward thermal equilibrium, as we saw before, heat energy always travels from a place of higher temperature to one of lower temperature.

A misconception of what heat is may interfere with understanding how it travels. Instead of viewing cold as a lesser degree of heat, many students think that cold is distinctly different and the opposite of heat. So, it's logical for them to think that "cold" leaves the ice cube in a drink and goes into the liquid, rather than that heat goes from the liquid into the ice cube, making it melt (Erickson, 1979).

Because heat is felt rather than seen, it may also affect children's understanding of how it travels. By about age 8, they begin to think of heat as something that travels from a source to another place. Before then, children are more likely to view a hot stove or fire, for example, as something that instantly makes them warm (Albert, 1978).

In moving from one location to another, heat energy may travel in one or more of three ways: conduction, convection, and radiation. Let's consider these ways one at a time.

Conduction ───────────

If you grasp the metal handle of a hot frying pan, you quickly let go. How is it possible for the heat energy to go from the hot stove grid to the handle? Molecular *conduction* is responsible. As heat energy enters the pan bottom, the pan's molecules begin to vibrate faster. This motion is passed along, molecule by molecule, up the pan's sides to its handle. Eventually, all the particles are vibrating faster, and you feel the heat.

Of all solids, metals are the best conductors. Their molecules are very close together and transmit heat energy quickly. But each type of metal varies somewhat in conductivity. Copper is the best common conductor, followed by aluminum, steel, and iron. Other solids are comparatively poor conductors, including ceramic materials. This is one reason for using ceramic containers for heated beverages and microwavable food.

Because molecules of liquids are farther apart than solids, it is reasonable to expect that they do not conduct heat as efficiently as molecules of solids. Our ordinary experiences with bathwater help confirm this thought. When hot water is added to cooler water, the heat takes a long time to reach all portions of the tub. For this reason, we stir the water a bit to hasten the process.

Gases are the poorest conductors of all. Their molecules are spread so far apart that they do not collide often and regularly enough to pass on increased energy to any appreciable extent. This is why it is possible for the horizontal freezers in supermarkets to be left uncovered. Very little heat energy is conducted downward from the warmer air above the freezers.

Convection ───────────

Although liquids and gases conduct heat poorly, it is easy to heat a pan of water quickly to boiling temperature or to roast a frankfurter quickly in the hot air over a campfire. These examples indicate another, more efficient method of heat transfer in liquids and gases than conduction. To identify it, examine what happens when air is warmed.

Watch the smoke from burning material. Why does it rise? Is it unaffected by gravity? A clue to its behavior is found when smoke is pumped into an airless vacuum chamber. The smoke particles fall like lead weights. Therefore, smoke does not just "rise"; something must push it up.

When the glowing part of burning material warms the adjacent air, the increased energy agitates the air molecules to increased speeds and they spread farther apart. Because fewer air molecules take up a given volume of space, the hot air is lighter than an equal volume of the surrounding air. The hotter, lighter air is pushed up with the smoke particles as it is replaced by colder, heavier air. As the mass of lighter air rises, it carries increased energy with it. This is why air near the ceiling is warmer than air near the floor.

A *convection current* is set up when a room has an opening for warm air to escape and cool air to enter. This is what happens when we open a window at both the top and bottom to freshen the air in a room. It is also the primary cause of winds in the atmosphere.

Similar convection currents are set up in heated liquids. Warmed, expanded water in a pan rises as it is continuously replaced by cooler, heavier water until the same temperature is reached in the entire container. An example is a hot water tank. Convection currents take heated water away from the heating unit and circulate the water throughout the tank. Adding color to the liquid will help children see this effect for themselves (Rubino & Duerling, 1991).

Convection also has global effects. Warm water at the equator is continuously being replaced by cold water flowing from the polar regions; this movement sets up convective ocean currents. Likewise, air convection currents, along with the earth's rotation, form winds that contribute to weather patterns.

Radiation

A common example of the third method of heat transfer, *radiation*, is found in a fireplace. This is especially noticeable when the air temperature is low. As you warm yourself in front of the fire, only the portion of your body that faces the fire feels warm. Conduction is poor because air is the conducting medium. Convection is negligible because most of the hot air escapes up the chimney. Heat reaches you primarily by radiation.

All vibrating molecules release a certain amount of energy through invisible heat rays called *infrared waves*. These waves largely pass through transparent materials like air and glass but are absorbed by opaque objects, which become warmer as a result. We are aware of radiant energy only when the emitting source is warmer than body temperature. The sun is by far our most important source of radiant energy. In its rays are found visible light, invisible infrared waves, and other forms of radiant energy.

From Solar to Heat Energy

An air traveler who goes from a cold climate to a tropical climate quickly notices many differences in the new surroundings. Among the most impressive are house colors, which are largely light pastels and dazzling white. Similar differences can be noted in clothing colors. Dark-colored materials absorb more sunlight than light-colored materials. INQ Figure 2–2 reveals why persons in tropical countries find a greater need for lighter colors than those in countries farther away from the equator. Light is most intense when it is received from directly overhead. If the same amount of light is spread out over a larger area, any part of that area receives less light and so less heat.

The changing of solar energy to heat energy is most noticeable when there is an effective way of preventing the heat from escaping.

INQ Figure 2–2   **When light is projected directly overhead, it is most intense. This explains why people in tropical climates find a greater need for light-colored clothing and buildings than people in other climates.**

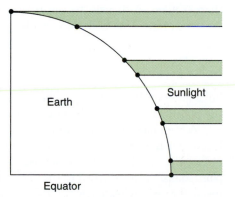

A common example is the temperature rise within a tightly closed automobile parked in sunlight. The rapidly vibrating short waves of sunlight can pass through the windows. When they strike the upholstery, they are absorbed and then reradiated as longer, slower vibrating heat waves. The longer waves are largely unable to penetrate glass, so most of the heat stays inside, building up in intensity as sunlight continues to stream in. Because the same thing happens in greenhouses, this phenomenon is aptly called the *greenhouse effect*.

INQ Figure 2–3   A flat-plate solar energy collector.

Our atmosphere is also warmed largely by reradiated heat waves. The atmosphere is like a giant glass cover that traps the longer, reradiated heat waves. This analogy is not perfect, however. Fortunately for us, the atmosphere is far less efficient than glass. A substantial amount of reradiated heat escapes into space. Were this not so, the earth's air temperature would become so hot that it would be intolerable to life.

Because of the greenhouse effect, air temperatures get warmest in the afternoon rather than at noon. Although the sun is most nearly overhead at midday, the buildup of heat continues for several hours afterward.

Solar Heating for Homes ────────

Solar energy is becoming a popular way to heat water and even entire homes, especially in the South and Southwest. Let's examine one way this is done.

A flat-plate collector is attached to, or built into, the house roof. Its purpose is to collect as much solar energy as possible. The collector, made of metal and glass, is positioned to face the sun. The glass is mounted just over a blackened metal plate. Water pipes, also painted black, are attached to the plate. As the plate and pipes absorb sunlight, the water inside the pipes is heated by conduction. The glass cover contributes to the buildup of heat by trapping the absorbed light energy (INQ Figure 2–3).

The heated water is stored in a large tank. Pipes circulate it throughout the house as needed. Other pipes are connected to hot water faucets in the house.

Notice the three conditions that affect the efficiency of the solar collector: The collector plate and pipes are painted black to absorb sunlight; a clear glass cover admits sunlight but prevents most of the absorbed energy from escaping; and the collector is mounted on a slope that faces the sun.

Controlling Heat Loss ───────

Knowing how heat travels permits us to control it. We use insulation to prevent or retard heat energy transfer. For example, to retard conduction, we use poor conductors. Because air is a poor conductor, materials with air spaces, such as wood and wool, make excellent insulators.

In homes, using hollow walls designed to trap the air reduces convection and conduction. Because some convection takes place anyway, many homeowners fill the walls with a light, fluffy material, such as fiberglass or cellulose insulation. An excellent way to insulate for radiation is to reflect it away because it behaves like light as it travels. This is why insulating materials in the home may use a shiny foil exterior, particularly in the attic. It also explains why silver paint is used on large gasoline storage tanks.

References

Albert, E. (1978). Development of the concept of heat in children. *Science Education, 62*(3), 389–399.

American Association for the Advancement of Science (AAAS). (1993). *Benchmarks for science literacy.* New York: Oxford University Press.

Erickson, G. L. (1979). Children's conceptions of heat and temperature. *Science Education, 63*(1), 83–93.

Gertz, S., Portman, D., & Sraquis, M. (1996). *Teaching physical science through children's literature.* Middletown, OH: Terrific Science Press.

Haab, S. (1999). *The Shrinky Dinks Book.* Palo Alto, CA: Klutz, Inc.

Hampton, E., & Rodriguez, R. (2001). Inquiry science in bilingual classrooms. *Bilingual Research Journal, 25*(4), 417–434. Retrieved November 13, 2004, from *http://brj.asu.edu/content/vol25no4/pdf/ar4.pdf*

Joyce, W. (1998). *George shrinks.* New York: HarperCollins.

Laplante, B. (1997). Teaching science to language minority students in elementary classrooms. *Journal of the New York State Association for Bilingual Education, 12,* 62–83. Retrieved November 13, 2004, from *www.ncela.gwu.edu/pubs/nysabe/vol12/nysabe124.pdf*

National Research Council (NRC). (1996). *National science education standards.* Washington, DC: National Academy Press.

Rubino, A. M., & Duerling, C. K. (1991). Around the world in science class. *Science and Children, 28*(7), 37–39.

Turnbull, R., Turnbull, A., Shank, M., & Smith, S. J. (2004). *Exceptional lives: Special education in today's schools* (4th ed.). Upper Saddle River, NJ: Merrill/Prentice Hall.

Selected Trade Books: Heat Energy

For Younger Children

Ardley, N. (1983). *Hot and cold.* Danbury, CT: Watts.

Cole, J. (1998). *The magic school bus in the arctic: A book about heat.* New York: Scholastic.

Daley, M. J. (1997). *Amazing sun fun activities.* New York: McGraw-Hill Professional Publishing.

Fowler, A. (1998). *Energy from the sun.* Danbury, CT: Childrens Press.

Hillerman, A. (1983). *Done in the sun.* Santa Fe, NM: Sunstone Press.

Ketteman, H. (2000). *Heat wave.* New York: Walker & Co.

Kim, S., & Melton, L. (2000). *Transforming energy: All about heat, work and energy (the activity learning books).* New York: Science Kids.

Llewellyn, C. (1991). *First look at keeping warm.* Milwaukee, WI: Gareth Stevens.

Maestro, B., & Maestro, G. (1990). *Temperature and you.* New York: Lodestar Books.

Oleksy, W. (1986). *Experiments with heat.* Danbury, CT: Childrens Press.

Petersen, D. (1985). *Solar energy at work.* Danbury, CT: Childrens Press.

Santrey, L. (1985). *Heat.* New York: Troll Associates.

Stille, D. R. (1990). *The greenhouse effect.* Danbury, CT: Childrens Press.

Wade, H. (1979). *Heat.* Austin, TX: Raintree.

For Older Children

Bendick, J. (1974). *Heat and temperature.* Danbury, CT: Watts.

Cobb, V. (1973). *Heat.* Danbury, CT: Watts.

George, J. C. (1983). *One day in the desert.* New York: Thomas Y. Crowell.

Kaplan, S. (1983). *Solar energy.* Austin, TX: Raintree.

Knapp, B. (1990). *Fire.* Austin, TX: Steck-Vaughn.

Langley, A. (1986). *Energy.* Danbury, CT: Watts.

Mebane, R. C., & Rybolt, T. R. (1987). *Adventures with atoms and molecules*. Springfield, NJ: Enslow.

Scott, J. M. (1973). *Heat and fire*. Springfield, NJ: Enslow.

Searle, B. (2001). *Heat and energy (fascinating science projects)*. Brookfield, CT: Copper Beech Books.

Whyman, K. (1987). *Heat and energy*. Danbury, CT: Watts.

Wood, R. (1996). *Heat fundamentals: Funtastic science experiments for kids*. New York: McGraw-Hill.

Yount, L. (1981). *Too hot, too cold, or just right*. New York: Walker.

Resource Books

Bartch, M. (1992). *Literature activities across the curriculum*. West Nyack, NY: Simon & Schuster. (science topics, pp. 158–194)

Butzow, C. M., & Butzow, J. W. (1989). *Science through children's literature: An integrated approach*. Englewood, CO: Teacher Ideas Press. (states of matter topics, pp. 200–205)

Gertz, S., Portman, D., & Sraquis, M. (1996). *Teaching physical science through children's literature*. Middletown, OH: Terrific Science Press.

Hillen, J., Mercier, S., Hoover, E., & Cordel, B. (1994). *Primarily physics: Investigations in sound, light, heat, and energy*. Fresno, CA: AIMS Education Foundation.

Tolman, M., & Morton, J. (1986). *Physical science activities for grades 2–8*. West Nyack, NY: Parker.

SOUND ENERGY

Play a radio loudly, and the windows rattle. Watch a parade at a distance, and the marchers seem to be out of time with the music. Sing in the shower, and suddenly your voice takes on new dimensions. Hold a seashell to your ear and the soft, ambient sounds are resonated and amplified by the shape of the seashell's cavity. Blow a dog whistle and you cannot hear it, but your pet comes running to you. The sound of a passing train changes as it approaches and retreats. Bats and dolphins use echolocation, or reflections of their own sounds, to move about. Caterpillars hear with hairs all over their body, and you use the hairs in your cochlea to hear.

Few topics present so many accessible materials and interesting things to explore as sound energy. Sound is produced by mechanical radiation, or the movement of energy from one place to another through a medium such as air or water (sound cannot be produced in a vacuum). Vibrations from an object moving back and forth cause molecules in the surrounding medium to begin vibrating and radiating waves of sound energy. We hear these regular, pleasant sounds as music and the irregular vibrations, or unpleasant sounds, as noise.

In this chapter, we consider how sound vibrations are made; how sounds travel in air, water, and solids; how sounds are reflected and absorbed; how the pitch of sounds may change; and how we hear.

Benchmarks and Standards

Children in the early grades have trouble associating the characteristics of sounds with the properties of the sound's source. Experiences with activities involving the making and hearing of sounds will provide students opportunities to make these associations. Additionally, children will begin to understand that sounds are vibrations and travel in waves. Some specific benchmarks and standards are as follows:

Sample Benchmarks (AAAS, 1993)

- Things that make sound vibrate. (By Grades K–2, p. 89)
- Vibrations in materials set up wavelike disturbances that spread away from the source. Sound and earthquake waves are examples. These and other waves move at different speeds in different materials. (By Grades 6–8, p. 90)

Sample Standards (NRC, 1996)

- Sound is produced by vibrating objects. The pitch of the sound can be varied by changing the rate of vibration. (By Grades K–4, p. 127)

SOUND VIBRATIONS Inquiry

A Vocal Activity

MATERIALS

- No materials are needed

Invitation

What makes your vocal cords work?

Exploration

1. Hum softly and feel your throat. Feel your voice box vibrate.
2. Hum with tightly closed lips. Then pinch your nose.
3. What happens? Why?

 Teaching Tips Air is needed in all these cases to make the vocal cords vibrate. It is difficult to speak while breathing in because the normal way humans make sounds is by breathing out.

Concept Invention

1. Breathe out as much air as you can from your lungs. Try to say something without taking in air.
2. What happens? Why?

Concept Application

Try to say your name the way a cat or cow makes sounds—while breathing air in. What happens? Why is this hard to do?

MATERIALS

- Tuning fork
- Two matched large soda bottles
- One small soda bottle

Good Vibrations

Invitation

How can one vibrating object make another vibrate?

Exploration

 Teaching Tips The first part of the exploration is an example of forced vibrations. If a tuning fork is unavailable, a sturdy, stiff rubber comb may be used instead. Run a finger down the teeth ends while holding the comb against a surface. The second part of the exploration is an example of sympathetic vibrations. If you vibrate one object, a second object may also vibrate if it has the same natural rate of vibrations as the first. No actual touching is necessary. The transfer of energy occurs in the air.
    Caution: If the bottles are used by more than one student, sterilize the bottle openings between uses. Dampen a paper towel with rubbing alcohol, wipe the bottle openings well, and then rinse the alcohol off well with running water. Dry with a clean paper towel.

1. Strike a tuning fork against a rubber heel (never against something hard).
2. As the sound dies, place the handle end against a tabletop. Notice how the sound gets louder as the tabletop is also made to vibrate.
3. Try holding the vibrating tuning fork against many different objects.
4. From which object can you get the loudest sound?
5. Which object allows you to hear the tuning fork when it has almost stopped vibrating?
6. Blow over the top of one large bottle to make a sound. Blow short, strong tones.
7. Hold the opening of a second large bottle close to your ear, but not touching. Blow short sounds again with the first large bottle.
8. Do you hear the same note from the second bottle? If you are not sure, have someone else blow short notes on one bottle while you listen with the second bottle.

Concept Invention

Repeat Exploration steps 6 and 7, but this time listen with the small bottle.

Concept Application

Do you hear the same note from the small bottle? Do you hear any note?

Mystery Sounds ──────────

Invitation

Can you hear something make a sound and tell what it is without looking? How can you find out if you can identify something by sound?

Exploration

1. Place one object from each pair of rolling objects on your desk.
2. Give the other rolling objects to your partner. He should put these where you cannot see them.
3. Have your partner put one of his objects in the shoe box. You should not know which one it is. Have your partner put the lid on the shoe box.
4. Slowly tip the covered shoe box back and forth. Listen to the sound.
5. Look at the objects on your desk. Which one may be the same as the one in the box? Point to a desk object so that your partner knows which one you picked.
6. Look inside the shoe box. Does the object inside match the desk object you picked?

Concept Invention

1. How many of the rolling objects can you identify? Which object is easiest to tell? the hardest to tell?
2. Suppose your partner holds and tips the box. Can you tell each rolling object just as easily?
3. How many of the sliding objects can you identify? Which object is easiest to tell? the hardest to tell?

MATERIALS

- Pairs of small objects that roll (crayons, table tennis balls, marbles, pencils, BBs, small pill vials)

- Pairs of small objects that slide (buttons, paper clips, checkers, dominoes, bottle caps, safety pins)

- Shoe box with lid

- Partner

Teaching Tips

This investigation mainly calls for children to make inferences by interpreting data. Try to use objects of about the same weight. This will eliminate weight as a clue. Children will focus on the sounds they hear or the vibrations they feel in their fingers as they handle the shoe box.

Older students can be challenged by increasing the number and similarity of paired objects to select from.

Adapting for Students with Exceptionalities

When working with students with hearing impairments, try prerecording sounds and playing them back at a higher than normal volume.

Concept Application

Describe how an object may be identified by the sounds it makes when interacting with another object.

SOUND VIBRATIONS CONCEPTS

Every so often in science fiction, a scientist will invent a machine that can collect and play back all the sounds that have ever been made. Plots usually reveal that at first the scientist uses the machine to help historians, but that soon after he offers the enemy military secrets discussed at the Pentagon.

Molecules and Sounds

Of course, all signs show that such a machine could never be invented. Sounds are simply waves of compressed molecules pulsating outward in all directions and planes from a vibrating source.

Consider the air around you. It is composed of tiny, individual molecules of different gases mixed similarly throughout the lower atmosphere. These molecules are rapidly and randomly moving about. A fast-vibrating source, such as a hummingbird's beating wings, a struck bell, a plucked guitar string, or a "twanged" ruler held on the edge of a desk, compresses billions of these molecules with each back-and-forth movement because the molecules are in the way. Because air molecules are elastic, they quickly assume their original shape after moving out of the vibrating object's path. Before this happens, however, they transfer energy to other molecules over a distance.

Note that it is the wave of energy, rather than the molecules, that may travel a great distance. Each molecule may move less than a millionth of a hair's width, but this is enough to bump the next randomly moving molecule and pass on the outward movement. INQ Figure 3–1 shows a wave motion resulting from a compression and rarefaction effect on molecules pushed by a vibrating ruler.

A sound fades away when energy behind the original vibrations is used in the transmitting process. As one molecule bumps another, it uses a tiny amount of energy. As more molecules are bumped, less energy is available. The sound stops when energy of the randomly moving molecules exceeds the wave's energy. The molecules simply resume their normal helter-skelter movements.

Loudness

How is loudness explained? First, for the moment, let's call it *intensity*; "loudness" is what we actually hear. If our ears are working poorly, a very intense sound may be barely heard. So, loudness is a matter of individual perception. Intensity, in contrast, can be consistently and accu-

INQ Figure 3–1 These frames illustrate a vibrating ruler producing sound waves. In part 1, the ruler pushes the air molecules together (compression). Notice the thinned-out space below it (rarefaction). Part 2 shows the opposite happening, with the first part of the sound wave now moving away. Parts 3 and 4 show other sound waves being produced. The wave moves outward as the molecules push others in the way, which in turn squeeze other molecules.

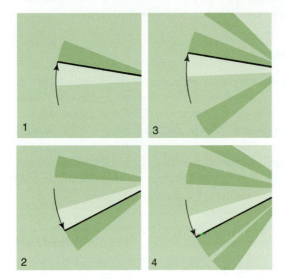

rately recorded by a sensitive sound detector in terms of the *decibel*, a unit of measurement in sound. The distinction between loudness and intensity may be too subtle for most children.

You know that shouting requires more energy than whispering. A boost in energy forces any vibrating medium to vibrate to and fro more widely than usual, but in the same amount of time. This movement compresses molecules more forcefully, so the greater energy is able to move more molecules.

Of course, distance is also a factor in sound intensity. The farther away we are from the source, the weaker the sound that gets to us. Molecules are pushed less because progressively less energy is available.

Interestingly, the same mathematical relationship is found in sound loss as in other forms of energy, such as light, magnetism, and electricity. Intensity fades as the distance between any sound source and the listener increases. In fact, the mathematical relationship used to compare sound intensity for two listeners standing at different distances from the sound source is the ratio of the square of the shorter distance to the square of the longer distance. For example, at 6 meters (20 feet), a sound has only one fourth of the intensity it exhibits at 3 meters (10 feet) from the source ($3^2 = 9$; $6^2 = 36$; $9/36 = 1/4$).

Waves

Sometimes the analogy of a water wave is used to teach how sound travels. A pebble is dropped into water, and a circular series of ripples spreads out on the water's surface. This example may be useful to show to your class, but it contains two main defects. First, water waves are up-and-down motions that travel at right angles to the line of the waves. These are called *transverse waves*. Sound waves come from back-and-forth motions that make *longitudinal waves*. This is the kind of wave you see when a row of dominoes falls, each one striking the next in order. Second, water waves move only horizontally, whereas sound waves travel outward in all planes. Many science teachers ask their students to imagine sound waves as they would a series of rapidly blown soap bubbles, each enveloped within another that is slightly larger, all quickly expanding.

The wave idea is useful to distinguish between sounds and noises. A *sound* consists of regularly pulsating vibrations; the time interval between each compression and rarefaction is the same. *Noise* is heard when irregular vibrations are passed on.

Forced Vibrations

If you place the handle of a vibrating tuning fork against a tabletop; the sound suddenly gets louder. The vibrating fork forces the tabletop to vibrate with equal speed. This sets in motion many more air molecules than would the fork alone. Try putting a vibrating tuning fork against other objects. Almost any hard object can be forced to vibrate at the fork's natural frequency.

A peculiar example of forced vibrations can occur when a group of soldiers marches over a bridge. If enough persons are marching in step, the entire structure can be forced to vibrate in time to the step, and the bridge may weaken or collapse. For this reason, soldiers do not stay in step when crossing a bridge.

Thomas Edison used his knowledge of forced vibrations when inventing the phonograph. He attached a sharp needle to a thin diaphragm that vibrated when sound waves struck it. The needle was placed against a cylinder wrapped with soft metal foil. As he spoke, he slowly cranked the cylinder around and around. The vibrating needle cut a series of impressions into the metal. To play back his sounds, he placed the needle in the impression first scratched and cranked the cylinder. As it followed the impressions, the needle was forced to vibrate, thus causing the diaphragm to vibrate. Edison could hear his recorded voice!

Sympathetic Vibrations

Have you ever heard windows vibrate in their frames as a low-flying airplane passes overhead? Or noticed dishes faintly rattle occasionally as a loud radio is played? To see why this happens, consider two identical tuning forks. If one vibrates and is held near the other, the second one also begins to vibrate; but with two tuning forks of different pitches, only the struck one vibrates.

When tuning forks are of identical pitch, sound waves arrive at the proper time to set the still fork in motion. Each additional air compression pushes a prong as it starts to bend in from a previous one. Each rarefaction arrives as the prong starts to bend back out. The steady, timed, push-pause-push-pause rhythm sets the fork vibrating in almost the same way as you would push someone on a swing.

When tuning forks are of different pitch, the timing is wrong for this process to happen. For example, a prong may bend inward properly with a compression, but as it starts to bend back, another air compression may strike it prematurely and slow or stop it. The same thing would happen with a moving swing that is pushed while only partway back on a downswing.

Every solid object has a natural frequency of vibration. If sound waves of that frequency push against an object, it may start resonating—vibrating sympathetically.

Remember that objects vibrate sympathetically only when they have the same natural pitch as the initial sound maker. In contrast, objects forced to vibrate always do so at the frequency of the vibrating object placed against them, regardless of their own natural frequency.

You may have learned that a very loud note sung or played into a thin drinking glass can shatter it through violent sympathetic vibrations; such vibrations have the natural pitch of the glass. It is not true, however, that seashore sounds may be detected in shell souvenirs. This is only true when listening through them at the beach. Otherwise, only sympathetic reflections of nearby sounds are heard through the shell.

Properties of Objects and Vibrations

Suppose someone hands you two closed shoe boxes. Inside one is a marble. Inside the other is a small ruler. Could you tell which box contains which object by tipping them back and forth and listening to the sounds? Of course, you may say. But what allows you to do this?

Every object has certain physical properties that produce "appropriate" vibrations. We expect a round (cylindrical) pencil to roll smoothly and a six-sided pencil to roll roughly. We assume that a short pencil lying crosswise in a box takes longer to slide and bump against the side than a longer pencil, if the box is tipped from side to side.

HOW SOUNDS TRAVEL Inquiry

It Sounds Fast

MATERIALS

- Large outdoor space
- Partner
- Hammer
- Thick piece of wood

Invitation

How fast does sound travel?

Exploration

1. Go outdoors to a large, open space.
2. Place a thick piece of wood on the ground. Walk a few steps away.
3. Watch a partner sharply hit the wood once with a hammer.
4. Do you hear the sound at about the same time the hammer hits?

Concept Invention

1. Move farther away. Have your partner hit the wood again. Repeat this moving-and-listening pattern several times until you are far away.
2. When do you hear each sound now—at the same time the hammer hits? Or does each sound appear later and later, after each hit?

Teaching Tips To ensure enough space for this activity, we suggest two widely separated, familiar reference points at least the length of a football field apart.

Concept Application

Why do you think that thunder and lightning occur at the same time when they are near but you hear thunder a few seconds later if it is farther away?

Sound Travels

MATERIALS

- Meterstick or yardstick
- Partner
- Wristwatch (one that ticks; used watches can often be found at yard sales or donation centers; other sound sources can be used)

Invitation

Does sound travel farther in air or in wood?

Exploration

1. Hold a ticking wristwatch or other sound source tightly against the end of a meterstick.
2. Touch the other end of the stick to your partner's ear. Only you should hold the stick, as shown.
3. Can your partner hear the ticking through the wood? If not, move the watch forward on the stick until the ticking is heard.
4. Measure the distance between the watch and the ear when the ticking is heard.

Concept Invention

1. Next, do not use the meterstick. Hold the watch in the air at ear level the same distance you found in the Exploration.

2. Can your partner hear the ticking now? (If you think your partner is just guessing, remove and then return the watch a few times. Each time, ask if the watch can be heard.)
3. From how far away can you hear a ticking watch through wood? Try a broomstick, a window pole, a long narrow board, and other wooden objects around you.

Adapting for Students with Exceptionalities

For students who have hearing disabilities, substitute a device that makes a louder noise when facilitating this activity. Also try to eliminate all other sounds in the classroom. (See Mastropieri & Scruggs, 2004, chapter on science and social studies for a discussion on adapting science activities involving sound.)

Concept Application

Predict how sound will travel through other materials, such as metals or water. Design an experiment to test your predictions.

The Vibrations of Metal Objects

Invitation

Many everyday objects made of metal make beautiful sounds when they vibrate. A metal coat hanger is one example. These objects sound much better when you hear them through a solid material than through the air. String is one such solid material. How can you hear the sounds of a metal hanger through a string?

Exploration

1. Cut a piece of string about 60 centimeters (2 feet) long.
2. Loop the middle of the string once around the hanger hook.
3. Wrap several turns of string end around the tip of each forefinger.
4. Gently put the tip of each wrapped finger into an ear, as illustrated on page INQ-76.
5. Bend from the waist so that the hanger hangs free. Ask your partner to strike a pencil and other objects gently against the metal. You can also make the hanger vibrate by yourself. Sway back and forth until the hanger swings. Then have it hit something that is hard, such as a table leg.

Concept Invention

1. How can you describe the sounds you hear?
2. What happens to the sound if your partner holds one of the strings? holds both strings?
3. What kind of string will give the clearest, loudest sound? Cut off equal lengths of different kinds of string and yarn. Test them in pairs. Tie one string end to the hook of one hanger. Tie another to a second matched hanger. Put one string end

MATERIALS

- **Two matched metal hangers**
- **Scissors**
- **Yarn**
- **Different metal objects**
- **Several kinds of string**
- **Partner**

Teaching Tips Oven cooling racks, barbecue grills, and other gridlike objects of metal make particularly strange, even eerie, sounds. These sounds come from the overtones produced when the many parts of the object vibrate differently.

into each ear. Have a partner first strike one hanger, then the other. When you find the best string, try it with both ears.

4. Does the length of a string affect the loudness? If so, in which kind of string do you notice it most? (You can test pairs of strings.)

5. What sounds do other metal objects make? Test such objects as old spoons, forks, cooling racks, oven racks, and different-sized cans.

Adapting for Students with Exceptionalities

This will be an excellent activity for students with severe hearing loss because they should feel the vibrations.

Concept Application

The sounds of a vibrating object may be heard more loudly and clearly through a solid than through air because solid materials help to channel the sounds. How many everyday applications of this concept can you find (for example, a mechanic would put her ear to a metal rod held against a running engine to hear sounds that the engine is making)?

A String Telephone

Invitation

Have you ever used a "string telephone"? It's a handy way to talk to someone far across a large room without shouting. How can you make a string telephone?

Exploration

1. Use a nail to punch a hole into the bottom center of each cup.
2. Put one end of a string into each hole.

MATERIALS

- Two sturdy paper cups
- Two paper clips
- Strong string (about 8 meters, or 26 feet, long)
- Partner
- Nail

3. Tie each string end to a paper clip. This will keep the string from slipping out of each hole.
4. Stretch the string tightly between you and your partner.
5. You speak into one cup while your partner listens with the other cup.

Concept Invention

1. Can you hear better through the string telephone than through the air? Whisper softly through the phone. Do it a little louder until your partner hears you. Then whisper to her at the same loudness without the telephone.
2. How can you stop a sound from reaching you on the string telephone?
3. Suppose two other children have a string telephone. How can you make a "party line"?
4. What can you do to make your phone work better? Try containers of different sizes and materials. Try different kinds of string and waxing the string with candle wax.

Teaching Tips

Holding the string or letting it sag will dampen or stop sounds, as will touching the vibrating cup bottom. For a party line, cross and loop around once the lines of two sets of phones.

Cylindrical cereal boxes (e.g., oatmeal containers) and table salt containers work well for string telephones. Metal can bottoms are too thick and rigid to vibrate well. Hard string or waxed string is superior to softly woven string.

Concept Application

Sound vibrations can travel through string and other solid materials. Can you describe some materials that sound will travel through?

Underwater Sounds

Invitation

What are underwater sounds like?

Exploration

1. Press an ear against the tank above the water level. Listen.
2. Have your partner repeatedly hit two spoons together inside the tank, but above the water.

MATERIALS

- Half-filled aquarium tank or large glass bowl
- Partner
- Two spoons

3. Again, press your ear against the tank but below the water level. Listen.
4. Now have your partner hit the spoons together below the water level, as shown here.

Concept Invention

How can you describe the difference between the two sets of sounds?

Concept Application

Does sound seem to travel better in water or in air?

HOW SOUNDS TRAVEL CONCEPTS

Watch a parade from afar, and band members seem to be out of step with the music they are playing. See a carpenter hammering a nail on a distant rooftop, and you hear the sound as the hammer is lifted instead of when the nail is struck.

Speeds of Sound

The speed at which sound waves travel lies behind each of the events mentioned. Light travels so fast (about 297,000 kilometers [186,000 miles] per second) that it seems instantaneous to our eyes. But sound is another matter. At sea level and 6.5°C (42°F), sound waves move about 330 meters (1100 feet) per second in the air, only as fast as a low-power rifle bullet. Sound also travels in liquids and solids. It moves about 5 times faster in water than it does in air; in steel, sound may travel 15 times faster than it does in air.

Three conditions affect the speed of sound: density, the elasticity or "springiness" of the molecules conducting the sound, and temperature. Density by itself does not increase the speed of sound. In fact, the speed of sound may decrease with density; but often associated with density is greatly increased elasticity of molecules. When highly elastic, close-together molecules of a solid transmit sound, the sound travels much faster than in either air or water.

Sounds travel faster when the temperature goes up. In fact, it is about 1 foot per second faster in air for every 1 degree Fahrenheit. Have you ever wondered why sounds carry such large distances on certain days? On a cold winter day with snow on the ground, for example, air next to the ground is often colder than the air far above the ground. Instead of a sound wave spreading out uniformly and then rapidly dying out, the temperature difference causes parts of the wave to travel at different speeds.

Given the same medium and temperature, all sounds travel at the same speed. If this were not so, it would be difficult or impossible to conduct concerts in large auditoriums. The reedy sound of an oboe and the brassy timbre of a trombone always reach your ears at the same time, if they are begun at the same time.

Sonic Booms

When children live where sonic booms often occur, one of the children may ask what happens when an airplane "breaks the sound barrier." We know that a sound-producing object sends out sound waves in all directions. When the object is set in motion, it continues to send out waves in all directions. But let's continue to increase this object's speed. As it goes faster, it is more difficult for waves to travel outward in front of it. When an airplane reaches a certain speed (about 1200 kilometers [750 miles], per hour, but varies greatly with altitude and temperature), air compressions of these sound waves pile up into a dense area of compressed air. This can subject the airplane to severe stresses.

A powerful engine and proper design enable an airplane to wedge through the dense air; but what happens to the compressed air? The tremendous energy is passed on, molecule to molecule, until it hits the earth as a booming shock wave. The shock wave continues on the ground in a wide strip that traces the airplane's flight path. It stops only when the pilot slows the aircraft to less than the speed of sound. Sonic booms that cause the least damage start at very high altitudes. By the time energy in the original area of compressed air is passed on to the ground, much of it has dissipated.

An explosion forms similar shock waves, except they may move out equidistantly in all directions. Very rapid expansion of gases in an explosion compresses the surrounding air. As the shock wave of compressed air moves outward, it may flatten almost anything in its path until the pressure finally dissipates over a distance.

REFLECTED AND ABSORBED SOUNDS Inquiry

Sounds and Megaphones

Invitation

What do you do when you want your voice to project farther? Do you cup your hands to your mouth? Doing this helps to keep the sound from spreading out, so it travels farther. There's another way to do this. You can make a megaphone. How can you make and use a megaphone?

Exploration

1. Roll up one sheet of heavy paper from one corner to make a cone. The small opening should be large enough to speak into.
2. Fasten the two ends and middle with sticky tape as illustrated.
3. Have a partner stand across the room from you.
4. Point the megaphone toward your partner. Whisper some numbers.
5. Have your partner walk toward you until he hears you and then stop walking.

Concept Invention

1. Can your partner hear you without the megaphone? Have him stay where he stopped. Whisper numbers just as before. How can you tell if your partner hears you?
2. Can you send a message to someone without another person hearing? Have a second partner stand to one side of you. She should be as far from you as your first partner. Point the megaphone toward your first partner and whisper numbers. How can you tell if only your first partner hears you?
3. How close must someone be to your first partner to hear you whisper?

Concept Application

How can a megaphone help us to hear something better? Put the clock on a table. Stand where you cannot hear the clock. Put the megaphone to your ear. Point it toward the clock. Slowly move toward the clock until you hear it. Then stop. Can you hear the clock without the megaphone at that distance? How much closer will you need to be to hear it? Will different-sized megaphones make a difference in how far the sound travels? How can you find out? How does this activity show that a megaphone reflects sounds in one direction or that a megaphone may be used to increase our speaking or hearing range?

MATERIALS

- One sheet of heavy paper
- Sticky tape
- Two partners
- Windup clock
- Meterstick or yardstick

 Teaching Tips

A megaphone tends to conserve sound energy by reflecting it in a specific direction. This allows sound to travel farther than when it spreads out in all directions. The effect also happens in reverse. The large end of a megaphone can gather sound and reflect it inward, like the old ear trumpets that were used before electronic hearing aids were invented. If we listen at the small end, the sound is louder than without the megaphone. More sound energy reaches the ear.

Echoes

Invitation

You probably know that smooth, hard walls reflect sounds well. A reflected sound that you hear is called an *echo*. Sound vibrations take time to travel to a wall and then back to you. When you are at the right distance, you hear the returning sound as a separate sound. How can you make an echo happen?

Exploration

1. Find a big wall outdoors in a large area. Try to locate a wall that has no buildings opposite it.
2. Measure a distance of about 25 meters (82 feet) from the wall. (You might cut a 5-meter string to speed up measuring.)
3. Hit a piece of wood once sharply with a hammer. Listen for an echo. If you hear more than one echo, try to find another place.

MATERIALS

- Meterstick or yardstick
- Scissors
- String
- Piece of wood
- Large outdoor wall
- Hammer

Concept Invention

1. How close can you be to the wall and still hear an echo?
2. How far away from the wall can you hear an echo? As you move farther away, does it take less or more time to hear the echo?
3. Try another wall. How do the results compare with the wall you already used?

Concept Application

How many echoes will there be with two reflecting walls? Try to find two facing, widely separated walls. Stand at different distances between them and bang the hammer. How do these results compare with those from a single wall? How does doing this illustrate that sounds are reflected over a distance?

MATERIALS

- Shoe box with lid
- Newspaper
- Pencil and paper
- Aluminum foil
- Windup alarm clock
- Different kinds of cloth
- Meterstick or yardstick
- Insulation materials of your choice

Materials That Quiet Sound

Invitation

Many people today are trying to cut down unwanted noise. They are putting materials around them that soak up sounds. These materials are called *sound insulators*. Some materials are better insulators than others. How can you find out which materials are good sound insulators?

Exploration

1. Wind up an alarm clock. Set the clock to ring within a few minutes.
2. Put the clock inside a shoe box and put on the lid.
3. Wait until the alarm rings. Measure how far away you can hear the ringing.
4. Record the distance.

Concept Invention

1. Suppose you wrap a sheet of newspaper around the clock. From how far away can you hear the sound now? Record and compare this distance with the first one.
2. What will happen if you wrap the clock in cloth? Record and compare this distance with the other distances.
3. What insulation materials will work best? Is it possible not to hear any ringing at all? Arrange your materials any way you want. All should fit inside the shoe box. How will you know whether the alarm has gone off?

 Teaching Tips Loosely woven, soft, fluffy materials absorb sounds well. Hard surfaces reflect sounds. This is why a formerly empty room seems quieter after carpeting, drapes, and upholstered furniture are put in. Many younger children will be unable to measure the hearing distance with a meterstick. Let them measure with different lengths of string or the number of footsteps between them and the clock.

Scaffolding for English Learners

One method of increasing the scientific literacy of English learners is to increase the relevancy of the science lesson to the student's everyday life. In this lesson, take the time to expand on the concept of *unwanted sounds*. Most likely, there will be cultural differences that can be integrated into this lesson as students brainstorm possible sound insulators. Think about what other items could be placed in the shoe box instead of an alarm clock. (See Fathman, Quinn, & Kessler, 1992, for a discussion of relevancy and science.)

Concept Application

What is another way to show that loosely woven, fluffy materials are good sound insulators?

REFLECTED AND ABSORBED SOUNDS CONCEPTS

Sound Reflection

One reason why singing in the shower is so popular has to do with the nature of sound reflections. As a sound hits the smooth shower walls, it bounces back and forth, seeming louder and prolonging the notes a little. This is pleasing to the ear. The smoother the reflecting surface, the better sound reflects. On a very smooth wall, sound reflections bounce off like light reflections from a mirror. The angle of reflection equals the angle of incidence.

Because sound can be reflected, we can direct or channel it in certain directions by using different devices. Open-air theaters often have large shell-like structures surrounding

INQ Figure 3–2   Open-air theaters often have shell-like structures to reflect sounds to the audience.

the stages (see INQ Figure 3–2). This shape enables sounds to be directed toward an audience with reduced energy loss. The same principle is used with cheerleaders' megaphones.

An even more efficient way to conserve sound energy is to enclose it within a tube. Because the sound is kept from spreading out by continual reflections within the encircling wall, such concentrated sound loses energy slowly and may travel a long way. Sometimes children use garden hoses as speaking tubes because these work well at surprising distances.

A reverse application of this reflection principle is found in the old-fashioned ear trumpet and in the ears of animals such as rabbits and donkeys. In these cases, sounds are "gathered," or reflected inward. Besides large ears, many animals have the additional advantage of being able to cock them separately in different directions.

Echoes

Because sound takes time to travel and can be reflected, it stands to reason that at a certain distance you should be able to hear a distinctly separate reflection of an original sound, an echo. Most persons need an interval of at least 0.10 second to distinguish between two sounds. If the interval is shorter than this, they hear one sound, much like the way the brain interprets separate frames of a motion picture as continuous motion.

If we assume that a sound wave travels at a speed of 330 meters (1100 feet) per second, in 0.10 second it travels 33 meters (110 feet). To hear an echo, or a distinguishable, separate sound, we must stand far enough away from a reflecting surface for the sound wave to travel a total distance of 33 meters (110 feet). Because the sound travels to the reflecting surface and back to our ears, a distance of 16.5 meters (55 feet) from the surface is adequate to hear an echo. Remember, this distance varies a bit with temperature variations.

INQ Figure 3–3   A bat's ears are well suited for echolocation.

Sometimes the combination of a loud sound and many distant reflecting surfaces produces multiple echoes, or *reverberations*. A common example is thunder, which may reverberate back and forth from cloud to earth and among air layers of varying densities.

An interesting application of echo detection is found in a U.S. Navy device called *sonar*. (The term is an acronym for SOund NAvigation and Ranging.) This apparatus sends a sound wave through the water and detects reflections from any direction. The time between an initial sound and its received echo enables a sonar operator to know the distance of a reflector, whether a submarine or an underwater obstruction. Similar devices are used on fishing vessels to detect schools of fish.

The use of sound reflections is found in nature in bats, dolphins, and porpoises. By listening to reflections of its cries, for example, a bat flying in total darkness avoids collisions and catches insects in midair. This ability to use sound reflections is referred to as *echolocation* (see INQ Figure 3–3).

Absorbed Sounds

Have you ever noticed how different the sounds seem in a room before and after furnishings are installed? Rugs, draperies, and cloth-covered furniture absorb more sound waves than we commonly realize. But even a furnished room may have a "hollow" sound if the walls and ceilings are hard and smooth. Porous acoustical tile on ceilings and rough, porous plaster blown on with a compressed-air applicator can reduce sound reflections. Besides absorbing some sound waves, a rough surface interferes with the wave reflection, just as light is diffused when it hits an irregular surface.

Sometimes older children ask, "What happens to a sound when it goes into a porous material?" It appears that sound energy is changed to heat energy. The regular pulsating movements of a wave are broken up into the normal, irregular motions of individual mol-ecules. As this happens, any energy passed into the porous substance is transmitted to other air molecules, slightly raising the temperature.

Reverberation and Reflected and Absorbed Sounds ——————

A reverberation was defined earlier as a multiple echo. After being produced, sound waves travel through the air in all directions. In a room, the various surfaces and materials absorb sound. The sound waves slowly lose a small amount of energy that is absorbed with each reflection until the waves gradually diminish and become inaudible.

The *reverberation time* is the number of seconds that a sound's average loudness can be heard, before it becomes completely inaudible under quiet conditions. This time depends on the ability of the room to reflect sound and may vary from about 1 second in a so-called dead room to 10 seconds in a highly reverberant room. Classrooms are designed to rever-berate for less than 1 second, since the maximum reverberation time for understanding speech is about 2 seconds. Music halls are designed for reverberation times between 1.5 and 2 seconds, the ideal reverberation time for orchestral music.

HOW PITCH CHANGES Inquiry

Changing Pitches

Invitation

What happens to pitch as the speed of vibrations changes?

Exploration

1. Hold a comb in one hand and a card in the other.
2. Pull the card tip across the teeth of the comb slowly and steadily. Listen to the pitch of the sound (how high or low it is).
3. Repeat step 2, but faster this time. Listen again.
4. Try many different speeds. Listen each time.

Concept Invention

1. What is the pitch like when the vibrations are slow?
2. What happens to the pitch as the vibrations move faster?

Concept Application

Turn a bicycle upside down. Crank a pedal around slowly to move the rear wheel. Hold the tip of a card against the spokes as the wheel slowly turns. Listen to the pitch as the card vibrates. Crank the wheel faster and faster. Listen again to the pitch as the card vibrates faster and faster. What is the pitch like when the vibrations are slow? What happens to the pitch as the vibrations move faster?

> **MATERIALS**
> - Comb
> - Small card
> - Bicycle

Teaching Tips | **Caution:** For safety, be sure that fingers holding the card are well away from the spinning bicycle wheel in the Concept Application.

How to Make a Rubber-Band Banjo

Invitation

What kinds of stringed instruments have you seen? How are they played? How can you make a rubber-band banjo?

Exploration

1. Write the numbers 1 through 8 on the inside of the lid. Use a ruler to space them evenly across the whole lid.
2. Put four thick rubber bands around half of the lid. Space them from numbers 1 through 4.
3. Put four thinner bands around the other half of the lid. Space them from numbers 5 through 8.

> **MATERIALS**
> - Stiff shoe box lid or topless cigar box
> - Ruler
> - Eight rubber bands (four thick, four thinner)
> - Pencil and paper

Teaching Tips

The tightness, thickness, and length of a rubber band (or string) all affect its pitch. Sounds are higher with taut, thin, short strings; they are lower with looser, thicker, or longer strings on any stringed instrument.

The tension of each rubber band may be adjusted by pulling up or down at the side of the lid. Friction between the band and the lid will hold the band in place for a while. However, the band will need to be strummed or plucked gently. A sturdy lid is preferable to a flimsy one that bows in the middle.

Concept Invention

1. Pluck one of the rubber bands. How can you make a soft sound? How can you make a loud sound?
2. Which bands—thick or thin—make the higher sounds? (The highness or lowness of a sound is its pitch.)
3. What happens to the pitch when a band is shortened? Press down a rubber band halfway across the lid. Pluck the band half nearest you.

Can you design another musical instrument that shows that length, tension, and thickness affect the pitch of a vibrating string?

A Soda-Straw Oboe

MATERIALS

- Paper or plastic straws (one should be smaller to fit inside a larger one)
- Straight pin
- Cellophane tape
- Scissors
- Small paper cup

Invitation

Have you ever seen an oboe? It is a reed instrument. When the player blows on the mouthpiece, two flat, thin reeds vibrate. This makes the air inside the oboe vibrate. By opening and closing holes, the player makes different amounts of air vibrate. The different amounts change the pitch of the notes played. You can make an instrument like this from a soda straw. How can you make a soda-straw oboe?

Exploration

1. Pinch the end of one straw between your thumb and forefinger to flatten it.
2. Snip off the flattened corners with scissors, as illustrated. If you have a plastic straw, cut to make a point.
3. Put about 3 centimeters (1 inch) of the cut straw end into your mouth. Keep your lips closed but a little loose. Blow hard into the straw. If no sound is made, blow less hard until a sound is made.

Concept Invention

1. What happens if you change the length of the straw? Join another straw of the same size to the first straw. To do so, slightly pinch the end of the second straw. Then gently push the pinched end into the first straw. Try adding a third straw in the same way.

2. What happens if you change the length another way? Try to fit a smaller straw into the larger one. If it is too loose, wrap some cellophane tape around the end of the smaller straw. Slide the second straw up and down as you blow.

3. What do you think will happen if you snip off pieces of a single straw while blowing? Try it and see.

Concept Application

How can eight people with different-sized straws play a song?
Does this demonstrate that changing the length of the vibrating air column inside changes the pitch of a wind instrument?

Teaching Tips

Paper straws typically work more easily than plastic straws in this activity. If students find it difficult or impossible to produce a sound, often the cut "reed" is to blame. It may help to press down gently with the lips on the straw just below the flattened part. This will open up the reed slightly and let it vibrate more easily when blown. A plastic-straw reed should be pointed for best results.

A "bell" for the instrument can be made by punching a small hole in the bottom of a paper cup and inserting the straw end into it. It should noticeably increase the loudness of the instrument.

A Bottle Xylophone

Invitation

Do you know what a xylophone looks like? This instrument has a row of different-sized blocks of wood. The player makes sounds by striking the blocks with two special sticks. You can easily make an instrument that works like a xylophone, but instead of wood, you can use bottles of water. How can you make a bottle xylophone?

Exploration

1. Put different levels of water in each bottle.
2. Line the bottles in a row in any order.
3. Tap each of the bottles lightly with a pencil. Notice how high or low each sound is. This highness or lowness is called *pitch*.

MATERIALS

- Eight matched soda bottles
- Pencil and paper
- Water

Teaching Tips

Bottles made of plain glass make clearer, purer sounds than those made of rippled glass. If you or one of your students can play the piano, the class may enjoy playing this eight-note xylophone either as an accompanying or as a leading instrument. The students may also enjoy singing with the instrument.

Teaching Tips

Caution: If the bottles are used by more than one student in the Concept Application, sterilize the bottle openings between uses. Dampen a paper towel with rubbing alcohol, wipe the bottle openings well, and then rinse the alcohol off well with running water. Dry with a clean paper towel.

Concept Invention

1. How much water is in the bottle of highest pitch? lowest pitch?
2. Can you put the bottles in order from lowest to highest pitch?
3. What must you do with the bottles to make an eight-note scale?
4. Can you play a simple song? Put paper slips in front of the bottles. Number them from 1 to 8 for an eight-note scale. Notice the numbers of the notes you play.
5. Can you write a song so that someone else can play it correctly? Write on paper the numbers of the notes to be played. Use your own made-up song or a known song. Observe how well the song is played.
6. How can you improve the way you wrote your song?

Concept Application

An instrument's pitch depends on how much mass vibrates. As mass increases, pitch lowers. With less mass, the pitch gets higher. Suppose you blew over each bottle top. Now the air inside would vibrate rather than the water. How do you think that would affect each pitch? Try it and see and then record the results.

HOW PITCH CHANGES CONCEPTS

Many pilots of crop-dusting airplanes actually rely on sound to gauge the safeness of their air speed. While flying low, it is difficult to watch both an air-speed indicator in the cockpit and ground obstructions. Flying speed is therefore estimated by listening to the pitch of sound made by the vibration of the airplane's struts and wires as the wind rushes past. Some seasoned pilots can judge their margin of safety to within narrow limits by this method.

Sometimes children fasten small cards against the spokes of their bicycle wheels to simulate a motor sound while riding. As the spokes go around and hit the card, it vibrates and makes a sound. The pitch rises with increased speed of vibrations and lowers with decreased speed of vibrations.

Stringed Instruments

In a stringed instrument, pitch depends on the length, tightness, and thickness of the strings. Shortening a string causes faster vibrations, raising the pitch. Lengthening a string has the opposite effect. Tightening a string also increases pitch, whereas loosening a string decreases pitch. A thick string vibrates more slowly than a thin one and so produces a lower-pitched sound.

Why do different instruments—a violin and a cello, for instance—play a note at the same pitch and yet sound different? The quality of tone (*timbre*) produced by these instruments is different. Most vibrations include more than just simple, back-and-forth movements along a string's entire length. Although a fundamental vibration governs the basic pitch, other parts of the string vibrate at faster frequencies. The combinations of vibrations are different with each string and with various stringed instruments. Together they produce tones of distinctly recognizable qualities.

Wind Instruments

In wind instruments, a vibrating column of air makes the sound. The vibrations may be started by a player's lips, as with trumpets and tubas, or by blowing past a reed, as with the saxophone and clarinet.

Pitch is regulated by changing the length of the air column vibrating within the instrument. In a wind instrument such as the saxophone, opening and closing valves with the fingers changes air-column length. In a trombone, air-column length is changed by pulling or pushing a long, closed double tube called the *slide*.

The property of timbre is also present in wind instruments. In this case, it is caused by the combinations of additional air vibrations set up within each instrument. Quality of voices is produced in much the same way. This is regulated by the size and shape of air cavities in the mouth and nose.

Homemade Instruments

An interesting way for children to learn about pitch and tonal quality is for them to make their own stringed and wind instruments. Rubber bands of different sizes make pleasant sounds when placed around topless cigar boxes or sturdy shoe box lids. Strong nylon fishing line fastened on pieces of wood with nails and screw eyes also works well (see INQ Figure 3–4).

INQ Figure 3–4   Children can experiment with pitch and tone by making their own instruments.

When the line is fastened to a screw eye, its tension can be adjusted by turning the eye in the appropriate direction. Tuned properly, nylon fishing line sounds somewhat like the string on a regular instrument. Simple tunes can be composed and played on the stringed instruments that children fashion.

Soda straws and bottles make acceptable wind instruments. Interestingly, opposite results in pitch occur with partly filled soda bottles, depending on whether they are used as wind or percussion instruments. That is, if you blow over the tops of soda bottles containing varying volumes of water, the scale may go from low to high, left to right. If you strike those same bottles sharply with a pencil, however, the opposite happens; the scale will go from high to low, left to right. With blowing, the bottle's air mainly vibrates; when striking the bottle, the water and glass mainly vibrate.

Mass and Noise

When a noise is made, the amount of mass in the vibrating object usually determines the pitch. A large, dropped wooden block sounds lower than a dropped smaller one. When thick paper is torn, it sounds lower than a torn thin paper. A dropped nickel sounds lower than a dropped dime. Both young and older children show interest in this phenomenon.

HEARING AND LOCATING SOUNDS Inquiry

Do You Hear What I Hear?

Invitation

How do you locate sounds with your ears?

Exploration

1. Have your partners sit in a large circle about half the width of the classroom.
2. Sit in the center of the circle. Keep your eyes tightly closed. Listen with both ears.
3. Let each partner, in random order, lightly tap two pencils together once.
4. Can you tell from which direction the sound comes? Point to the spot each time. Have someone record how often you are right or wrong.

Concept Invention

1. Now try Exploration steps 2 and 3 again, but this time listen with only one ear. Hold a hand tightly over the other ear.
2. Can you locate the sounds as well as before?

Concept Application

Will you get the same results with your other ear?

HEARING AND LOCATING SOUNDS CONCEPTS

The ear must be ranked among the body's most remarkable organs. In our hearing, sound waves are channeled into the ear canal by the outer ear, which acts as a megaphone in reverse. As sound waves collide with the eardrum, this thin membrane of stretched skin begins vibrating at the same frequency as the waves.

Just inside the eardrum are three tiny connected bones: the hammer, anvil, and stirrup (see INQ Figure 3–5). A vibrating eardrum starts the attached hammer shaking, and this movement is transmitted through the connected bones to the cochlea, or inner ear.

INQ Figure 3 –5   **The human ear.**

This snail-shaped apparatus is filled with a watery fluid and lined with sensitive nerve endings that trail off to the auditory nerve and brain. The transmitted vibrations pass through the fluid and excite the nerve endings. These excitations are converted into electrical impulses that zip to the brain.

Children should learn some reasonable rules for ear care and safety. A sharp object jabbed into the ear may cause a punctured eardrum. A puncture greatly impairs or prevents eardrum vibrations and results in hearing loss in the affected ear. Children should also beware of a sharp blow against the outer ear. This compresses air within the air canal and may cause a ruptured eardrum. Blowing the nose forces air up through the eustachian tube. If a person is suffering from a cold, hard blowing may force germs up the tube and infect the middle ear.

Hearing Ranges

Although our ears are sensitive to a wide range of pitches, there are limits to what we can hear. Almost no one can detect a sound that vibrates less than about 16 times per second or one that vibrates more than 20,000 times per second. As we grow older, this range is gradually narrowed.

Hearing ranges in animals often exceed those of humans. A bat may detect sounds that vary between 10 vibrations to 100,000 vibrations per second. A dog's hearing begins at only several vibrations per second and goes to 40,000 vibrations per second; this is why it is possible to use a "silent" whistle for calling a dog: The pitch is simply too high for humans to hear. A cat's hearing is even more remarkable; it can detect sounds up to 50,000 vibrations per second. Elephants can communicate with each other by producing rumblings too low pitched for us to hear; the elephants' huge outer ears act as giant funnels for channeling these rumblings to the ear canals. Sounds that are inaudible to us are called *infrasonic* when they vibrate too slowly and *ultrasonic* when they vibrate too quickly.

Locating Sounds

Most people can tell the direction from which a sound comes, even when blindfolded. With two ears, a sound usually reaches one ear just before the other. The slight difference is enough to let the brain interpret the information.

A person with only one functioning ear can receive similar signals by quickly turning the head slightly on hearing the first sound. When the sound is very short, this may not be possible.

References

American Association for the Advancement of Science (AAAS). (1993). *Benchmarks for science literacy.* New York: Oxford University Press.

Fathman, A. K., Quinn, M. E., & Kessler, C. (1992). *Teaching science to English learners, grades 4–8.* Washington, DC: National Clearinghouse of Bilingual Education. Retrieved November 13, 2004, from www.ncela.gwu.edu/pubs/pigs/pig11.htm

Laplante, B. (1997). Teaching science to language minority students in elementary classrooms. *Journal of the New York State Association for Bilingual Education, 12,* 62–83. Retrieved November 13, 2004, from www.ncela.gwu.edu/pubs/nysabe/vol12/ nysable124.pdf

Mastropieri, M., & Scruggs, T. E. (2004). *The inclusive classroom: Strategies for effective instruction* (4th ed.). Upper Saddle River, NJ: Merrill/Prentice Hall.

National Research Council (NRC). (1996). *National science education standards.* Washington, DC: National Academy Press.

Ovando, C. J., Collier, V. P., & Combs, M. C. (2003). *Bilingual and ESL classrooms: Teaching in multicultural contexts.* Boston: McGraw-Hill.

Selected Trade Books: Sound Energy

For Younger Children

Allington, R. L., & Cowles, K. (1980). *Hearing*. Austin, TX: Raintree.

Ardley, N. (1991). *The science book of sound*. Chicago: Harcourt Brace Jovanovich.

Barrett, S. (1980). *The sound of the week*. New York: Good Apple.

Berger, M. (1992). *Sound, heat & light: Energy at work*. New York: Scholastic.

Broekel, R. (1983). *Sound experiments*. Danbury, CT: Childrens Press.

Carle, E. (1997). *The very quiet cricket*. New York: G. P. Putnam.

Cole, J. (1995). *The magic school bus in the haunted museum: A book about sound*. New York: Scholastic.

Davis, K. (2000). *Who hoots?* Orlando: Harcourt.

Diller, H. (1996). *Big band sound*. Honesdale, PA: Boyds Mills Press.

Friedman, J. T. (1981). *Sounds all around*. New York: G. P. Putnam.

Gibson, G. (1995). *Hearing sounds (science for fun)*. Providence, RI: Copper Beech Books.

Hughes, A. E. (1979). *A book of sounds*. Austin, TX: Raintree.

Jennings, T. (1990). *Making sounds*. Danbury, CT: Watts.

Kaner, E. (1991). *Sound science*. Reading, MA: Addison-Wesley Publishing Company.

Lee, J. D. (1985). *Sounds!* Milwaukee, WI: Gareth Stevens.

Moncure, J. B. (1982). *Sounds all around*. Danbury, CT: Childrens Press.

Oliver, S. (1991). *Noises*. New York: Random House.

Parnall, P. (1989). *Quiet*. New York: Morrow Junior Books.

Pfeiffer, W. (1999). *Sounds all around*. New York: HarperCollins.

Ramsay, H. (1998). *Sound*. Danbury, CT: Childrens Press.

Richardson, J. (1986). *What happens when we listen?* Milwaukee, WI: Gareth Stevens.

Rowan, J., & Perham, M. (1993). *Making sounds*. Chicago: Childrens Press.

Spier, P. (1990). *Crash! Bang! Boom!* New York: Doubleday.

Wade, H. (1979). *Sound*. Austin, TX: Raintree.

Webb, A. (1988). *Sound*. Danbury, CT: Watts.

Wood, N., & Rye, J. (1991). *Listen: What do you hear*. New York: Troll Associates.

Wyler, R. (1987). *Science fun with drums, bells, and whistles*. Parsippany, NJ: Julian Messner.

For Older Children

Ardley, N. (1991). *Sound waves to music: Projects with sound*. Danbury, CT: Watts.

Birch, B., & Corfield, B. (1995). *Marconi's battle for radio*. Hauppauge, NY: Barron's.

Brandt, K. (1985). *Sounds*. New York: Troll Associates.

Catherall, E. (1982). *Hearing*. Parsippany, NJ: Silver Burdett.

Cobb, V. (2000). *Bangs and twangs: Science fun with sound*. Brookfield, CT: Millbrook Press.

Fleischman, P. (1988). *Joyful noise: Poems for two voices*. New York: HarperTrophy.

Grimshaw, C. (1999). *Invisible journeys: Sound*. Chicago: World Book.

Guthridge, S. (1986). *Thomas A. Edison: Young inventor*. New York: Aladdin Paperbacks.

Kettlekamp, L. (1982). *The magic of sound*. New York: Morrow.

Knight, D. C. (1980). *Silent sound: The world of ultrasonics*. New York: Morrow.

Knight, D. C. (1983). *All about sound*. New York: Troll Associates.

Kohn, B. (1979). *Echoes*. New York: Dandelion.

Mathers, D. (1992). *Ears*. Mahwah: NJ: Troll Associates.

Morgan, S., & Morgan, A. (1994). *Using sound*. New York: Facts on File.

Newman, F. R. (1983). *Zounds! The kid's guide to sound making*. New York: Random House.

Pettigrew, M. (1987). *Music and sound*. Danbury, CT: Watts.

Riley, P. (1987). *Light and sound*. New York: David & Charles.

Simon, S. (2003). *Eyes and ears*. New York: HarperCollins.

Taylor, B. (1991). *Sound and music*. Danbury, CT: Watts.

Ward, A. (1991). *Experimenting with sound*. Brookmall, PA: Chelsea House.

Ward, B. (1981). *The ear and hearing*. Danbury, CT: Watts.

Wood, R. W. (1997). *Sound fundamentals: Funtastic science activities for kids*. Philadelphia Chelsea House Publishers.

Resource Books

Butzow, C. M., & Butzow, J. W. (1989). *Science through children's literature: An integrated approach*. Englewood, CO: Teacher Ideas Press. (sound and hearing topics, pp. 112–118)

Cordel, B., & Hillen, J. (Eds.). (1994). *Sense-able science: Exploring and discovering our five senses*. Fresno, CA: AIMS Education Foundation. (hearing topics, pp. 120–137)

Hillen, J., Mercier, S., Hoover, E., & Cordel, B. (1994). *Primarily physics: Investigations in sound, light, heat, and energy*. Fresno, CA: AIMS Education Foundation. (sound activities pp. 2–39)

LeCroy, B., & Holder, B. (1994). *Bookwebs: A brainstorm of ideas for the primary classroom*. Englewood, CO: Teacher Ideas Press. (sound activities, pp. 57–63)

Sullivan, E. P. (1990). *Starting with books: An activities approach to children's literature*. Englewood, CO: Teacher Ideas Press. (hearing impairment topics, pp. 23–25)

Tolman, M., & Morton, J. (1986). *Physical science activities for grades 2–8*. West Nyack, NY: Parker. (over 180 hands-on activities including sound activities)

MAGNETIC INTERACTIONS

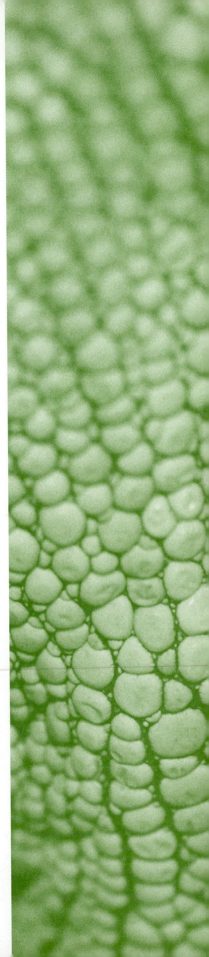

The use of magnets dates back more than 3000 years. Ancient Greeks, Romans, and Chinese discovered that the type of rock we now know as magnetite attracted bits of iron. This finding later became very important to sailors when they discovered that a floating piece of magnetite, or lodestone (meaning "lead" stone), would align with north–south direction. Sailors no longer had to rely on land sightings or star-filled skies to navigate their ships. Children today can magnetize a steel needle and float the needle on a small bit of cork, or suspend a bar magnet from a string, to repeat this discovery. One question often asked with this activity is, "Why isn't the steel needle already magnetized like the magnetite?" The answer is in how the steel and magnetite were formed.

Magnetite is a mineral containing a large amount of iron. The magnetite we find today was formed during the slow hardening of the earth's crust. As it cooled, the magnetite was either magnetized by the earth's magnetic field or possibly subjected to lightning strikes. Because of this, the magnetite developed a north-seeking and a south-seeking pole. The iron and steel we make today do not develop poles because these materials harden too fast to be affected by the earth's magnetism.

At the primary level, magnets may be studied more than any other science topic. It is common for young children to have their own magnets and magnetic toys. Let's consider several kinds of magnets and what they attract, how to make magnets, the field of force that surrounds a magnet, magnetic poles, and the theory and care of magnets.

Benchmarks and Standards

Magnets are commonly studied in the primary grades. Children should complete activities designed to observe and classify magnetic and nonmagnetic objects. Early activities will also lay the groundwork for future study of forces. Specific examples of benchmarks and standards are as follows:

Sample Benchmarks (AAAS, 1993)

- Magnets can be used to make some things move without being touched. (By Grades K–2, p. 94)
- Without touching them, a magnet pulls on all things made of iron and either pushes or pulls on other magnets. (By Grades 3–5, p. 94)

Sample Standard (NRC, 1996)

- Magnets attract and repel each other and certain kinds of other materials. (By Grades K–4, p. 127)

MAGNETS AND WHAT THEY ATTRACT Inquiry

Objects Magnets Can Pull

MATERIALS

- Two bags of small objects
- Magnet

Invitation

Have you ever played with a magnet? If so, what were you able to do with it? How can you find out which objects magnets can pull?

Exploration

1. Take out the objects from only one bag now.
2. Touch your magnet to each object.
3. Which objects are pulled by the magnet? Put these in a group.
4. Which objects are not pulled by the magnet? Put those in another group.

Teaching Tips

Try to get a variety of attractable and nonattractable small objects for both bags of test materials. Following are common objects and their chief metals or metal alloys.

Object	Metal
Nail	Iron
Wire	Copper (if reddish color; wires of other colors are other metals)
Safety pin	Steel (or brass)
Screw	Brass (or iron or aluminum)
Hair curler	Aluminum
Penny	Bronze

Give children the names of metals as needed to help them generalize about their experience.

Concept Invention

1. How are the objects in the pulled group alike?
2. Can you make a rule about which objects your magnet pulls? Put the objects back into the bag. Put the bag away.
3. Take out the objects from the second bag. Which do you think your magnet will pull? Which will it not pull? Put the objects into two groups. Now use your magnet on the objects in each group. Was every object in the correct group?
4. Which objects around the room will your magnet pull? Record your prediction and verify.

Concept Application

What other magnets can you try? Will they pull the same objects your first magnet pulled? How does this show that a magnet pulls objects made of iron or steel?

Magnetic Separations ───────

Invitation

How can a magnet separate mixed materials?

Exploration

1. Put two spoonfuls each of filings and salt into the jar.
2. Cap the jar and shake it to mix the two materials.
3. Pour the mixture onto a white paper "tray."
4. Try using the spoon to separate the filings and salt.

Concept Invention

1. Cover the magnet's poles with kitchen plastic wrap. Now try using the covered magnet to separate the filings and salt.
2. To remove the filings from the magnet, remove the kitchen wrap.
3. Which was an easier way to separate the filings and salt, using the spoon or using the magnet?

Concept Application

Many bits of iron may be found in sands and soils. Cover the magnet's poles again with wrap. Poke the magnet around in a sandbox or loose soil. How many iron bits do you find?

MATERIALS

- Magnet
- Plastic spoon
- Salt
- Small jar with lid
- Kitchen plastic wrap
- White paper with turned-up edges
- Iron filings
- Sandbox or loose soil

The Power of Magnets ───────

Invitation

Some people say they can tell how strong a magnet is just by looking at it. What do you think? How can you find out the power of a magnet?

Exploration

1. Put a paper clip on two pieces of soda straw, placed on a sheet of lined paper.
2. Make a pencil mark at the front of the clip.
3. Line up an end (pole) of a magnet with the clip as shown.
4. Slowly bring the magnet near the paper clip.
5. Stop moving the magnet when the clip moves.
6. Count the lines between the pencil mark and magnet.

MATERIALS

- Several different kinds of magnets
- Two small pieces cut from a straw
- Pencil
- Sheet of lined paper
- Paper clips

A magnet attracts objects most strongly at the ends, or poles. The attractive power gradually weakens toward the center of the magnet. The center has very little or no magnetic attraction.

Concept Invention

1. Test several magnets. Which is the most powerful? Can you put them in order from weakest to strongest?
2. Are both ends (poles) of a magnet equally powerful? How can you find out?
3. Do all parts of a magnet pull the clip? Which part of a magnet is strongest? Which is the weakest?

Concept Application

Magnets vary in power; magnets attract objects most strongly at their poles. What are some other ways to test a magnet's power? Do you get the same results?

MAGNETS AND WHAT THEY ATTRACT CONCEPTS

There are many magnets around the home and classroom for us to use as examples in teaching. In kitchens, cloth potholders containing magnets are placed on the sides of stoves. Automatic can openers have magnets to hold opened can lids. Cabinet doors remain closed because of magnets. Some people wear magnetic earrings. Toy stores have many toys that in some way use magnetism. At school, speakers, magnetic paper holders, and some games also have magnets.

What Magnets Attract ⸺⸺⸺

In nearly all these cases, the metals attracted to a magnet are iron and steel. Less well-known magnetic metals are cobalt and nickel. Among the more common metals not attracted by magnets are brass, aluminum, tin, silver, stainless steel, copper, bronze, and gold.

It will help you to know several facts that can clear up some common misunderstandings your students may have. For example, a question may arise about the attractable property of so-called tin cans. These are made of thin sheet steel and coated lightly with tin. Although tin is not attractable, steel is. Confusion may also result if some straight pins are attracted by a magnet and other identical-appearing pins are not because they are made of brass. Also, the U.S. 5¢ piece is largely composed of copper and so should not be used as an example.

Lodestones ⸺⸺⸺

Natural magnets are sometimes called lodestones, or "leading stones," because ancient mariners used them as crude compasses to point to the lodestar or leading star (the North Star), which is how they acquired their name. The lodestar is also known as the pole star, or North Star, presently Polaris. Lodestones are made of magnetite, an iron ore found in different locations on the earth's crust.

Only some of these ore deposits are magnetized, and scientists have developed theories to explain this phenomenon. One such theory holds that lightning may have been responsible. It is thought that electricity discharged into the ore may have arranged many atoms within the ore in a manner like that found in magnets.

INQ Figure 4–1   Magnets (A) bar; (B) V; (C) U; (D) horseshoe; (E) cylindrical; and (F) lodestone.

Traces of magnetite are common in soils. A magnet dragged along the ground or in a playground sandbox may attract many particles. These particles can be an effective substitute in activities in which iron filings are used.

Manufactured Magnets

Artificial magnets are often made of steel and magnetized by electricity. Named for their shapes, there are bar, **V**, **U**, horseshoe, and cylindrical magnets, to name the more familiar varieties (INQ Figure 4–1). Each of these magnets attracts substances most strongly at the ends, or poles. The **U**, **V**, and horseshoe magnets are more powerful than the others when all other factors except shape are equal; they are bent, so two poles attract instead of one.

Powerful alnico magnets are available from scientific supply houses and in commercial kits. These are made from aluminum, cobalt, nickel, and iron. Alnico magnets are used for home and commercial purposes.

MAKING MAGNETS Inquiry

How to Make Magnets

Invitation

Suppose you have an iron nail and a magnet. With these materials, you can make another magnet. How can you make a magnet?

Exploration

1. Get a large iron nail. Touch it to some steel pins to see if it attracts them.
2. Put one end of the magnet on the nail near the head.
3. Stroke the whole nail with the magnet 20 times. Stroke in one direction only, as illustrated.
4. Touch the nail again to some pins. How many pins does the nail attract? Record this number.

Teaching Tips
An iron or steel object may be magnetized by stroking it with a magnet. A soft iron object that is magnetized, such as a nail, weakens after several minutes. A steel object, such as the shank of a screwdriver, retains its magnetism. However, steel is more difficult to magnetize. Only a strong magnet is likely to produce significant results. Stroking an object both ways with a magnet is less effective than stroking it in one direction. Use steel straight pins to test the strength of whatever magnets are made.

Concept Invention

1. How much stronger can you make your nail magnet? How many pins does it attract after 30 strokes? 40 strokes? Record how many pins are attracted each time you test it.
2. How strong is the nail magnet after 10 minutes? Compare.
3. Test the other nail to see if it attracts pins. If it does not, stroke this nail back and forth, instead of just one way. How strong is the magnet after 20 strokes? 30 strokes? 40 strokes?
4. Suppose you stroke a small steel screwdriver one way with a magnet. How many pins will it attract after 20 strokes? 30 strokes? 40 strokes? Record and compare your findings with those for the nail.
5. Suppose you stroke a large steel screwdriver one way with a magnet. Will you get the same results?
6. How strong do you think both screwdrivers will be after 10 minutes?

Adapting for Students with Exceptionalities

For students experiencing difficulty with the directions, try highlighting the significant parts (e.g., the number of strokes). (See Mercer & Mercer, 2005, for a discussion on accommodations involving instructional materials.)

Concept Application

Iron and steel may be magnetized by a magnet; steel holds its magnetism longer than iron. What other objects can you make into magnets? How strong can you make each one?

Long-Lasting Magnets

Invitation

How can you make long-lasting magnets with electricity?

Exploration

1. Tightly roll a small file card around a pencil. Fasten it with sticky tape.
2. Tightly wind about 80 turns of thin copper wire in one direction around the tube. Leave 30 centimeters (1 foot) of wire free at each end. Tape the coil ends so that the wires stay tightly wound.
3. Use scissors to strip the insulation from the wire ends.
4. Remove the pencil from the tube. Put a straightened bobby pin inside.
5. Put three flashlight batteries together as pictured.
6. Touch the stripped ends of the wire to opposite ends of the batteries. Do this for no more than 5 seconds.
7. Remove the bobby pin and touch it to some tacks.
8. How many tacks does the bobby pin pick up?

> **MATERIALS**
> - Thin (number 26 or 28) insulated copper wire
> - Magnet
> - Three D-size batteries
> - Pencil
> - 3-by-5-inch file card
> - Scissors
> - Two steel bobby pins
> - Tacks
> - Sticky tape

Concept Invention

1. Suppose you made a second bobby-pin magnet by stroking it with a regular magnet. Could you make it as strong as or stronger than the "electrocuted" bobby pin?
2. If you think you can, how many times would the bobby pin need to be stroked? Find out.

Adapting for Students with Exceptionalities

This activity can result in overheating of the wires if students are not careful. Be sure to warn students to let go of the wires or batteries if they get warm. Also, as with any activity involving a safety issue, be sure to list rules, explain them, and enforce them during the experiment. Be sure to employ behavior management techniques to keep students safe and on task.

Concept Application

Magnetize with electricity other things that will fit into the tube. Which objects can be magnetized? Which will hold most of their magnetism over a week or more? Which will not?

MAKING MAGNETS CONCEPTS

Magnets made from a relatively soft material, such as iron, usually hold their magnetism only a short time, so they are called *temporary magnets*. Those made from a harder material, such as steel, retain their magnetism far longer, so they are called *permanent magnets*. You can make either kind from common materials. Let's see how.

Temporary Magnets

A magnet can be made from an iron nail by stroking the nail in one direction with one pole of a permanent magnet. The nail's magnetic power increases with the number of strokes you apply. Be sure to lift the magnet clear at the end of each stroke before beginning another. Merely rubbing it back and forth will usually bring poor results. Within a few minutes after making this magnet, you will notice a marked loss in its power, regardless of how many strokes it has received.

A second way to make a temporary magnet is by holding a permanent magnet very close to any attractable object. For example, if you hold a magnet near the head of a small nail, you may be able to pick up a few tacks or a paper clip with the nail. Move the magnet farther away from the nail head, and the objects typically will fall off the nail. This kind of magnetism is called *induced magnetism*.

You can also make a temporary magnet by wrapping an insulated wire around a nail and connecting the two wire ends to a battery. This is an *electromagnet*. Any wire that carries an electric current generates a weak magnetic field around it. Wrapping the wire around the nail core concentrates the field into the core. Disconnect the wire from the battery, and the nail is no longer an effective magnet.

Permanent Magnets

It takes longer to magnetize a steel object by stroking it with a magnet than it does an iron one. However, steel may hold its magnetism for years.

A more efficient way to make permanent magnets is by electricity. The steel object is placed into a tube wrapped in wire and attached to a battery or other electrical source. Current is applied for a few seconds to magnetize the object.

Making Superconducting Magnets

Superconducting magnets are electromagnets made from special alloys such as niobium-tin or niobium-titanium. A coil of superconducting wire is wrapped around a bobbin to make the magnet. These magnets are then cooled with liquid helium to reach a very low temperature while they are being used. At this very low temperature, almost all resistance to the flow of electricity has been eliminated. This lack of resistance prevents the electrons that are traveling through the magnet from burning the wires up due to friction.

Superconducting magnets can be very large, as in the case of the 6.7 meters (22 feet) long, 181 ton (200 short ton) superconducting dipole magnet built by Argonne National Laboratory. Superconducting magnets are also very powerful. The Superconducting Magnet Group at the Lawrence Berkeley National Laboratory developed a 1 meter (3.3 feet) long superconducting electromagnet that has coils made of 22.5 kilometers (14 miles) of niobium-tin wire. This magnet reached the field strength of 13.5 tesla. Tesla is the SI unit of flux density, or field intensity, for magnetic fields and is also called magnetic induction. One tesla is defined as the field intensity generating one newton of force per ampere of current per meter of conductor. The cost to build this prototype magnet was about $1 million.

The superconducting magnets built today will be used in future particle accelerators, devices that can accelerate electrons or other particles to high energies. The highest-energy particle accelerator in use today is the Tevatron. It is 6.4 kilometers (4 miles) in circumference and has 1000 superconducting magnets that are cooled by liquid helium to $-450°F$ ($-268°C$).

For more information on superconducting magnets, check the Superconducting Magnet Group at the Lawrence Berkeley National Laboratory (http://supercon.lbl.gov/), the Argonne National Laboratory (http://www.anl.gov/), or the Superconducting Magnets site of the National High Magnetic Field Laboratory in Tallahassee, Florida (http://www.magnet.fsu.edu/). To find out more about accelerators, check the Fermi National Accelerator Laboratory (http://www.fnal.gov/).

FIELDS OF FORCE Inquiry

Magnetic Fields

MATERIALS

- Container of iron filings
- Four matched bar magnets
- Four matched horseshoe or **U** magnets
- Two sheets of stiff white paper with turned-up edges
- Partner

Invitation

Have you found that some objects can be attracted to a magnet even when the magnet does not touch them? That is because around every magnet is an invisible field of force. The magnet pulls on any attractable object within its field. Although the field is invisible, there are ways to tell where it is. How can you find out about a magnet's field of force?

Exploration

1. Place a bar magnet on a table. Lay a sheet of white paper with turned-up edges over it.
2. Sprinkle some iron filings on this paper tray. Do this over and around where you think the magnet is.
3. Observe closely how the filings line up and where they are thick and thin.

Teaching Tips

Students should learn that iron filings only crudely show a magnet's field of force. The field extends much beyond where the filings stop. Permanent inference sheets of magnetic fields can be made easily. These will allow individual students to do the activity by trying to match the sheets. To make a permanent record of a field, use plastic spray to fix the filings on a stiff sheet of paper. Hold the spray can far enough away from the sheet that the filings are not blown away. For best results, use fine, powderlike filings and sprinkle lightly. Let the spray dry before removing the sheet from the underlying magnets.

You may also use a magnetic field detector available from scientific supply companies. These show the lines of force more accurately and work very well with refrigerator magnets.

Concept Invention

1. Ask your partner to observe your magnetic field, but do not reveal how you arranged your magnet or what kind it is. Can your partner make one just like it?
2. Have your partner make a magnetic field for you. Can you match it?

Concept Application

Here are more fields for you and your partner to try: How will two bar magnets look with like poles close together? How will they look with unlike poles close together? How will horseshoe or **U** magnets look with like and unlike poles close together? First, draw what you predict. What fields can you make with different combinations of magnets, positions, and distances apart? A field of force surrounds a magnet; it is most powerful near the ends or poles. What were the easiest fields of force for you and your partner to figure out? What were the hardest fields to figure out?

Does Magnetism Go Through Objects?

Invitation

Do you think magnetism can be blocked by some materials? If so, which ones? Do you think it can pass through other materials? If so, which ones? How can you find out if magnetism can go through materials?

Exploration

1. Set up your objects as illustrated. Be sure that the clip does not touch the magnet.
2. Make the space between the clip and magnet as big as possible, but do not let the clip fall. Slowly pull the thread end to widen the space.
3. Test one of your thin, flat materials. Put it in the space between the clip and the magnet without touching them.
4. Does the clip stay up? Then magnetism can go through the material. Does the clip fall? Then magnetism cannot go through the material.

MATERIALS

- Ruler
- Strong **U** or horseshoe magnet
- Books
- Small paper clip
- Thread
- Small thin materials to test

Concept Invention

1. Which of your materials do you think magnetism will go through? Which will magnetism not go through? Put the materials in two piles, and then test them to find out.
2. Will magnetism go through two materials put together? Test the materials to find out. (Be sure the two materials can fit between the magnet and the paper clip.)

> **Teaching Tips**
>
> In the exploration, try to provide materials thin enough to pass between the paper clip and magnet.

Concept Application

Magnetism goes through many objects, but not those made from iron or steel. Do you think magnetism will go through water? How can you find out? What are other ways to test if magnetism can go through your objects?

FIELDS OF FORCE CONCEPTS

As children explore with magnets, they can observe that a magnet can attract from a distance. For example, a small nail or paper clip will "jump" to a nearby magnet. They will also see that the attractive force is strongest at the poles. This gives us the chance to introduce the field of force surrounding a magnet.

Inferring the Field ——————

Although we cannot see a magnet's field directly, its presence may be inferred. Sprinkle iron filings on a sheet of stiff white paper placed over a magnet, and you will see the filings distribute in an orderly way. Their greatest concentration will be at the poles. Theoretically, a magnetic field extends outward to an indefinite distance. For practical purposes, the field ends when we can no longer detect it.

Magnetic Transparency ——————

If you hold a powerful magnet against the back of your hand, it can attract through your hand and move a paper clip in the palm of your hand. A magnetic field can also go through many other materials without any apparent loss of power. It seems as if these materials are "transparent" to the field's lines of force. This property makes it possible for people to wear magnetic earrings and for plumbers to locate iron pipes in closed walls.

Note that computer disks and other media, televisions, and wristwatches may be affected by magnets. Materials of iron or steel are considered "opaque" to this force. When a magnet touches them, the force passes inside them and back into the magnet.

MAGNETIC POLE Inquiry

Make Your Own Compass

Invitation

How can you make a needle compass?

Exploration

1. Place a glass on a paper towel. Fill it to the brim with water.
2. Magnetize a sewing needle. To do this, stroke it 10 times, from thick end to point, with the magnet's S pole.
3. Scratch a narrow groove in the sliced cork top. Lay the needle in the groove. (This will keep it from rolling off.)
4. Carefully float the cork and needle on the water surface, as shown.
5. In what direction does the needle point?

Concept Invention

1. Move the needle gently so that it points somewhere else. Wait a few seconds. What happens?
2. Use your magnet. How can you push away either end of the needle with it?
3. How can you pull either end of the needle with the magnet?

Teaching Tips A glass filled to the brim with water keeps a floating cork centered. With less water, the cork will drift against the sides of the glass.

> **MATERIALS**
> * Two sewing needles
> * Magnet
> * Cork top (thin slice or Styrofoam chip)
> * Water
> * Drinking glass
> * Paper towel

Scaffolding for English Learners

Students often construct different views as to what causes the needle compass to work, yet compasses have been used by various cultures for many years. Discuss how explorers in other cultures used compasses. Would they have constructed the same concept for how the needle compass works? Explain your views. (See Laplante, 1997, for a discussion on English learners and constructivism.)

Concept Application

Replace the magnetized needle with one that has not been magnetized. Float the cork and needle on the water as before. What do you think will happen if you repeat Concept Invention steps 1 through 3? Find out.

Finding Directions ————

Invitation

How can you use a compass to tell directions?

MATERIALS

- Topless cardboard box (large)
- Partner
- Large open area outdoors
- Magnetic compass

Exploration

1. Go to a large, open space outdoors. Study the compass. Notice how the needle points. Turn the compass so that the part marked "north" is under the pointing needle.
2. Walk 20 steps toward the north and observe the needle. While walking, try to keep the needle exactly on north.
3. Stop and then turn completely around. Look at the compass. Now "north" is behind you and "south" is straight ahead. The other end of the needle should point south. Walk 20 steps toward the south while watching the needle. Keep it exactly on south. If you do so, you should return to where you started.

 Teaching Tips "North" as shown on a compass may vary slightly from true north because of regional magnetic variation. For the purpose of this activity, such variation may be ignored.

Concept Invention

1. Can you use your compass well enough to walk somewhere and find your way back? How close will you get? Mark the spot where you are. Put something over your head so that you cannot see around you. Looking at only your compass, walk 300 steps north and then 300 steps south. Have a partner watch out for you.
2. How well can you do in step 1 without a compass?

Adapting for Students with Exceptionalities

It may be difficult for students who are mentally challenged to use a compass. Alter the content to allow these students to learn relevant skills. You may want to avoid tracking the number of steps. Have the students look at a GPS device that will display the direction of travel as they walk in nonspecified directions in the open space. (See Turnbull, Turnbull, Shank, & Smith, 2004, for a discussion on altering the curriculum.)

Concept Application

How can you use your compass to walk east or west? Practice these directions as you did in the Concept Invention.

MAGNETIC POLE CONCEPTS

Suspend a bar magnet from a string anywhere in North America, and a curious thing happens: It points toward the north magnetic pole. Do the same in South America, and the magnet points toward the south magnetic pole. (This result assumes no interference from nearby metals.) A magnetized needle placed horizontally on a floating slice of cork or foam plastic chip also points toward a magnetic pole.

To see why this is so, consider the poles of a magnet. When another magnet or magnetized object is held near a suspended or floating magnet, the like poles (north–north or south–south) repel each other. The opposite poles (north–south or south–north) attract each other.

The Earth's Magnetism

The earth itself acts like a giant magnet. No one knows why, but scientists have proposed some theories. One explanation holds that several parts of the earth's interior rotate at different speeds. The resulting friction strips electric particles from atoms, causing an electric current to be generated that creates a magnetic field. Because the earth's core is supposedly made of nickel-iron, the effect is that of a huge electromagnet buried within the earth.

Recall the earlier discussion about magnetic fields of force. When iron filings are sprinkled on paper placed over a bar magnet, they reveal lines of force looping from one pole to another and concentrating at both poles. On a gigantic scale, a similar kind of magnetic field happens with the earth's magnetism (see INQ Figure 4–2).

Lines of force from the earth's magnetism run roughly north and south far into space and then loop down to concentrate at the north and south magnetic poles. Therefore, a freely swinging magnet—bar, horseshoe, or any other type with dominant poles—aligns itself parallel to these lines of force. Because lines of force end at the magnetic poles, properly following a compass in the Northern Hemisphere eventually results in your arrival at the north magnetic pole. This is located above the upper Hudson Bay region of Canada. If you follow a compass south, your trip will end near Wilkes Land, a part of Antarctica.

Geographic Poles

The north and south magnetic poles should not be confused with the north and south geographic poles. The geographic and magnetic poles are about 1600 kilometers (1000 miles) apart in the north and 2400 kilometers (1500 miles) apart in the south. In other words, when a compass points north, it does not point true north, or toward the North Star.

INQ Figure 4–2   **The earth has a magnetic field that is concentrated at both poles.**

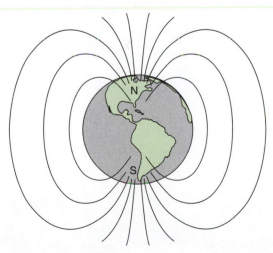

INQ Figure 4–3   Note in A, B, and C an angle between the meridian on which the compass is located and the direction toward which the needle points. These differences must be added to or subtracted from a compass heading to determine true north. For example, true headings for A, B, and C should all be 0°, or north. Actual readings are 35°, 5°, and 315°. A chart would show the need to subtract 35° from A, 5° from B, and the need to add 45° to C.

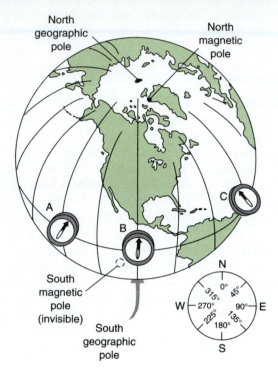

Charts made for navigators must show the angular variation between true north and the direction toward which a compass points. These charts must be periodically updated, as the magnetic poles are slowly but continually shifting (see INQ Figure 4–3).

MAGNETIC THEORY AND CARE OF MAGNETS Inquiry

Lost Magnetism?

Invitation

What are some ways a magnet can lose its magnetism?

Exploration

1. Test to see how dropping a magnet affects its magnetism. (Use magnetized nails so that regular magnets will not be destroyed.) To do this, follow these steps.
2. Magnetize two nails. Stroke the length of each nail 30 times with one pole of a magnet.
3. Test to see if each of the nail magnets attracts the same number of tacks. If they do not, stroke the weaker magnet until it is equally strong.
4. Hold one nail high and drop it on a hard surface, such as a concrete sidewalk. Do this 20 times.
5. Test each nail again. You might record what you find in this way:

	Dropped Magnet	Other Magnet
Before	6 tacks	6 tacks
After	2 tacks	5 tacks

6. How did dropping the nail magnet affect it?
7. What will happen if you drop the second nail magnet?

Concept Invention

1. Test to see how heating affects magnetism. Repeat the steps above to magnetize two nails.
2. Put on safety goggles. Light the candle in the dish. Use tongs or pliers to hold one magnetized nail upright in the candle flame for 3 minutes.
3. Before testing, dip the nail in water to cool it.
4. Test the two nails. Record your findings.
5. How did heating the nail magnet affect it? What will happen if you heat the second nail magnet?

MATERIALS

- Magnet
- Concrete sidewalk
- Two large matched nails
- Tacks or paper clips
- Small dish and candle
- Match
- Safety goggles
- Glass of water
- Tongs or pliers
- Clock

 Teaching Tips Iron nails do not retain magnetism very long. So, it is possible that the second magnet, too, will be weaker during the posttest; but this change should be slight.
Caution: Supervise the candle activity closely for safety.

Scaffolding for English Learners

One way to assist English learners in this activity is to write their questions on the chalkboard or markerboard with small illustrations when appropriate. Key vocabulary are also identified, and written and illustrated if possible. This assists the English learners with visual and linguistic cues so that they can share their knowledge constructions with others in the class. (See Amaral, Garrison, & Klentschy, 2002, for a discussion of the importance of visual and linguistic cues.)

Concept Application

What are other ways to lose magnetism? Test your theories and record the results.

MAGNETIC THEORY AND CARE OF MAGNETS CONCEPTS

Although magnetism has been known and used for many centuries, science cannot fully explain it. One theory, when simply explained, can be understood by children. It is based on observations they can make for themselves: Heating or repeatedly dropping a magnet will cause it to lose its magnetic properties. And, although a magnet may be broken into smaller and smaller pieces, each fragment continues to have a north and south pole. To find out why, you need to understand domains.

Magnetic Domains

Scientists believe that many tiny clusters of atoms, called *domains*, are contained within potentially magnetic objects. The clusters are usually randomly arranged; but when an object is stroked in one direction, or otherwise magnetized, the domains line up in a single direction. Notice that in part A of INQ Figure 4–4, the bar magnet could be broken into many pieces, yet each piece would continue to have opposite poles. Heating a magnet forces the domains into violent motion, and so they are likely to be disarranged, as in part B. As a magnet is repeatedly dropped, the tiny clusters of atoms or domains are jarred out of line, therefore causing the same result as if the magnet was heated.

Caring for Magnets

Magnets can keep much of their power for years when properly cared for and stored. Storing magnets improperly in the classroom is probably the chief reason why they quickly become weak. A small metal bar, called a keeper, should be placed across the poles of a magnet before it is stored. If the regular keeper has been lost, a nail can be substituted. Placing opposite poles of magnets together is another effective way to store them. Children can also learn not to drop magnets, which is another common reason why magnets become weaker.

INQ Figure 4–4   A magnetized steel bar (A) with the domains aligned and an unmagnetized steel bar. (B) with randomly arranged domains due to heat or violent action.

A

B

INQ Figure 4–5 **Sample charts to help children remember how to handle magnets.**

A   B

INQ Figure 4–5 shows two charts that provide guidance to help children remember some rules when handling magnets. Chart A is for primary children; chart B is suitable for older children.

References

Amaral, O. M., Garrison, L., & Klentschy, M. (2002). Helping English learners increase achievement through inquiry-based science instruction. *Bilingual Research Journal, 26*(2), 213–239. Retrieved November 13, 2004, from http://brj.asu.edu/content/vol26 no2/pdf/ART2.PDF

American Association for the Advancement of Science (AAAS). (1993). *Benchmarks for science literacy.* New York: Oxford University Press.

Laplante, B. (1997). Teaching science to language minority students in elementary classrooms. *Journal of the New York State Association for Bilingual Education, 12,* 62–83. Retrieved November 13, 2004, from www.ncela.gwu.edu/pubs/nysabe/vol12/nysabe124.pdf

Mercer, C. D., & Mercer, A. R. (2005). *Teaching students with learning problems* (7th ed.). Upper Saddle River, NJ: Merrill/Prentice Hall.

National Research Council (NRC). (1996). *National science education standards.* Washington, DC: National Academy Press.

Turnbull, R., Turnbull, A., Shank, M., & Smith, S. J. (2004). *Exceptional lives: Special education in today's schools* (4th ed.). Upper Saddle River, NJ: Merrill/Prentice Hall.

Selected Trade Books: Magnetic Interactions

For Younger Children

Borton, P., & Cave, V. (1994). *The Usborne book of batteries and magnets.* London, England: Usborne Publishing Ltd.

Branley, F. (1999). *What makes a magnet?* Topeka, KS: Econo-Clad Books.

Challand, H. J. (1996). *Experiments with magnets: A new true book.* Chicago: Childrens Press.

Fowler, A. (1995). *What magnets can do.* Danbury, CT: Childrens Press.

Freeman, M. (1980). *The real magnet books.* New York: Scholastic.

Gibson, G. (1995). *Playing with magnets.* Brookfield, CT: Copper Beech Books.

Glover, D. (1993). *Batteries, bulbs, and wires.* New York: Kingfisher Books.

Jennings, T. (1990). *Magnets.* Danbury, CT: Watts.

Kirkpatrick, R. K. (1985). *Look at magnets.* Austin, TX: Raintree.

Knight, D. C. (1967). *Let's find out about magnets.* Danbury, CT: Watts.

Podendorf, I. (1971). *Magnets.* Danbury, CT: Childrens Press.

Schneider, H., & Schneider, N. (1979). *Secret magnets.* New York: Scholastic.

Wade, H. (1979). *The magnet.* Austin, TX: Raintree.

Ward, A. (1992). *Magnets and electricity.* New York: Franklin Watts.

Whalley, M. (1993). *Experiment with magnets and electricity.* Minneapolis: Lerner.

Wood, R. W. (1990). *Physics for kids: 49 easy experiments with electricity and magnetism.* Blue Ridge Summit, PA: Tab Books.

For Older Children

Adamsczyk, P., & Frances-Law, P. (1993). *Electricity and magnetism.* London, England: Usborne Publishing Ltd.

Adler, D. (1983). *Amazing magnets.* New York: Troll Associates.

Adler, I., & Adler, R. (1966). *Magnets.* New York: Day.

Catherall, E. A., & Holt, P. N. (1969). *Working with magnets.* Lebanon, NH: Whitman.

Fitzpatrick, J. (1987). *Magnets.* Parsippany, NJ: Silver Burdett.

Freeman, M. B. (1968). *The book of magnets.* Portland, OR: Four Winds.

Friedhoffer, R. (1992). *Magnetism and electricity.* Chicago: Franklin Watts.

Levine, S., & Johnstone, L. (1997). *The magnet book.* New York: Sterling.

Santrey, L. (1985). *Magnets.* New York: Troll Associates.

Sootin, H. (1968). *Experiments with magnetism.* New York: Norton.

Victor, E. (1967). *Exploring and understanding magnets and electromagnets.* New York: Benefic.

Ward, A. (1991). *Experimenting with magnetism.* Broomall, PA: Chelsea House.

Wood, R. W. (1997). *Electricity and magnetism fundamentals.* New York: McGraw-Hill.

Woodruff, J. (1998). *Magetism.* London, England: Hodder Wayland.

Resource Books

Shaw, D. G., & Dybdahl, C. S. (1996). *Integrating science and language arts: A sourcebook for K–6 teachers.* Boston: Allyn & Bacon. (physical cycles including magnetism, pp. 93–110)

Tolman, M., & Morton, J. (1986). *Physical science activities for grades 2–8.* West Nyack, NY: Parker. (magnetism activities pp. 189–209)

Winkleman, G. (Ed.). (1994). *Mostly magnets.* Fresno, CA: AIMS Education Foundation. (27 complete magnetism activities and a resource section)

ELECTRICAL ENERGY

Can children learn to appreciate the advantages of a ready source of electricity? One good beginning is for them to count the number of electrical devices we use and then try to devise nonelectrical substitutes for them. By doing such activities in this chapter, children should also begin to appreciate some things that make electrical energy available and the principles that make them work.

We consider how electrical circuits are closed and opened, conditions that affect the flow of electricity, electromagnets, and ways to produce electricity.

CLOSED AND OPEN CIRCUIT Inquiry

How to Make a Bulb Light

MATERIALS

- D-size battery
- Two wires (15 centimeters, or 6 inches, long)
- Scissors or wire strippers
- Two flashlight bulbs
- Paper and pencil

Invitation

Have you ever used a flashlight? The electricity to light the bulb comes from one or more batteries. You don't need a flashlight to make the bulb light. You can do it with a single wire and a battery. How can you light a flashlight bulb with a wire and a battery?

Exploration

1. Use scissors or wire strippers to remove the insulation from the wire ends.
2. Put the bulb bottom on the raised button end of the battery as shown.
3. Touch one wire end to the metal part of the bulb.
4. Touch the other end of that wire to the battery bottom.

Teaching Tips Use number 22 or 24 bell wire, available at Radio Shack or most hardware or electrical supply stores. Be sure the students strip the insulation from both ends of the wires to ensure good contact.
  Caution: Advise students to notice quickly, and to discontinue trying a connection, if the wire they use to connect the bulb and battery begins to get warm. Heating occurs when the bulb (resistor) is bypassed and the wire ends touch only the battery terminals—a type of short circuit.

Concept Invention

1. How many other ways can you light the bulb? Keep a record of what you do. Make drawings of the circuits.
2. Study each of the drawings shown. Which ways will light the bulb? Which will not? Record your predictions and then test them.

Scaffolding for English Learners

This activity is one that often surprises even preservice teachers as they discover how electricity must flow in order to light the bulb. Often, the teacher must provide verbal clues to assist students. This *linguistic scaffolding* helps the students light the bulb. It is especially important to use an array of verbal gestural, written, and graphic forms of communication to facilitate success with English learners. (See Hart & Lee, 2003, for a discussion of linguistic scaffolding.)

Concept Application

Electricity flows when a circuit is complete; there are several ways to light a bulb. How many ways can you light a bulb with two wires? (Use one battery.) Record your observations. How many ways can you light two bulbs with two wires? (Use one battery.) Record your observations.

Switches

Invitation

How can you make some paper clip switches?

MATERIALS

- Flashlight bulb
- Two paper clips
- Sticky tape
- Cardboard
- Bulb holder
- Six paper fasteners
- Scissors
- Five small wires
- D–size battery

Teaching Tips | For the light to work properly, all connections need to be tight. Be sure the paper fasteners are securely seated and the wires are stripped of insulation where contact is made.

Exploration

1. Cut a small piece of cardboard. Punch two holes in it and put in two paper fasteners as shown in the illustration.
2. Use scissors to strip the insulation off the wire ends. Assemble the rest of the materials as shown. Bend a paper clip for the switch.
3. What happens when you move the switch on and off the paper fastener? How does this switch work in the circuit?

Concept Invention

1. Suppose you have a stairway light. You need to control it from both upstairs and downstairs. Make a pair of switches to control a single light (a "three-way" switch). Do it as illustrated here.
2. What happens when you move each switch from one paper fastener head to another? What would happen if only a single wire was between the two switches? How do these switches work?

Adapting for Students with Exceptionalities

Some students with exceptionalities are impulsive, not reflective. Monitor activities involving electricity to be sure students do not try to plug wires or paper clips into outlets. Keep them away from classroom wiring, outlets, lights, switches, and devices.

Concept Application

Would it be possible to control a light from three different locations (a "four-way" switch)?

CLOSED AND OPEN CIRCUIT CONCEPTS

Each time we push a button or flip a switch that "turns on" electricity, there is a continuous flow of electrical energy in wires connected from the generating plant to our appliance and back again to the plant. On a smaller scale, much the same thing happens when a battery is connected to a miniature bulb. If the connection between the source of electricity and the appliance or device using it is continuous, lights go on, bells ring, or motors spin. This continuous connection is called a *closed circuit*. Anytime a break or gap occurs in the circuit, the flow of electricity stops. This incomplete connection is called an *open circuit*.

Switches

Regardless of their shape, size, or method of operation, electric switches serve only to open or close circuits. They offer a safe and convenient way of supplying the flow of electricity when we want it by providing a linkage through which the energy can flow to the connecting wires.

Batteries

Much of the work in this chapter calls for the use of dry cells (children are more familiar with the term *batteries*), copper wire, and flashlight bulbs. D-size dry cells or number 6 dry cells should be used because they are safe, fairly long lasting, and relatively inexpensive. When fresh, they deliver 1 1/2 volts of electricity, as contrasted with 110 to 120 volts or so supplied in the home. **Caution:** House current is dangerous for electrical investigations, and children should be reminded never to use household electric current for investigations.

Bulbs

It will be helpful to be familiar with using miniature bulbs properly, since they are a requirement for many of the experiments in this chapter. Miniature bulbs are designed to be used with a loosely specified number of 1 1/2-volt dry cells. Therefore, there are one-cell, two-cell, or multicell bulbs. One-cell bulbs are sometimes marked "1.2V," two-cell bulbs "2.5V," and so forth.

INQ Figure 5–1   A number 6 dry cell (center) and two D-size cells connected in complete circuits.

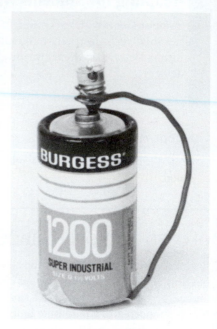

If three dry cells are connected to a one-cell bulb, it is likely that the thin tungsten filament inside will burn out quickly. Be careful to match the bulb with the number of cells used. Too many cells will cause the bulb to burn out quickly; too few will cause it to glow feebly, if at all.

Fahnestock (Wire) Clips

Many unit activities call for the use of commercial-type miniature bulbs and sockets. Several substitutes are possible, but most of these are cumbersome and less useful. For maximum ease in using miniature sockets, a Fahnestock clip should be fastened to each side of the socket with the screw found there (see INQ Figure 5–1 for an example). To connect a wire, simply press down on the springy, open end of the clip and insert the wire end into the exposed half loop. The wire stays in place when you release the pressure on the clip.

Wire

The wire you use should also be selected with an eye to convenience. Number 22 wire is excellent for almost every activity. Get plastic-covered solid copper wire, rather than cotton-covered wire consisting of many small, twisted strands. These strands become unraveled at the ends, and cotton insulation is harder to strip off than a plastic covering.

Insulation can be removed quickly with a wire stripper (INQ Figure 5–2). This device also cuts wires efficiently. With the wire suggested here, scissors may serve almost as well. In fact, the activities call for students to use scissors to strip off the insulation from the wire ends.

INQ Figure 5–2   A wire stripper.

Connections ───────

There are several easy ways to connect cells and bulbs, depending on the kinds of materials you have. INQ Figure 5–1 shows how a D-size cell and a number 6 dry cell can be connected to form a closed or complete circuit. Tape or a wide rubber band will hold the stripped wire ends snugly against the D-cell terminals. The center terminal (positive), recognizable by the bump, corresponds to the center terminal on a large cell. The opposite terminal (negative) is equivalent to the rim-mounted terminal on the large cell. The third arrangement needs only a single wire, with one end touching the negative terminal and the other wrapped around the bulb base. The base touches the positive terminal to complete the circuit. Notice that the wire end wrapped around the bulb base also serves as a bulb holder.

Two-, Three-, and Four-Way Switches ───────

Students are challenged to explore three-way switches in the Concept Invention section of the Switches inquiry on page INQ-122. The term *three-way switch* may be confusing, since there are only two switches pictured. Historically, the term *three way* evolved because electricians had to make three "drops," or installations. Electricians installed two switches and one "load," which was often a light fixture. Therefore, a "two-way" switch would be one switch and one load, and a "four-way" switch would be three switches and one load.

A three-way switch works because it can be on in either the up or down position, depending on the position of the other switch. A three-way switch requires an extra wire between the two switches as compared to a two-way switch. In other words, a two-way switch only switches the black "power" or "hot" wire on and off. A three-way switch has an additional red traveler, or switch wire, between the two switches, as well as a load connection on one switch and a power connection on the other. For more information, you may want to refer to the How Things Work website (http://www.howthingswork.com/three-way1.htm).

SERIES AND PARALLEL CIRCUIT **Inquiry**

Series Circuits

MATERIALS
• Three flashlight bulbs
• Four wires
• Three bulb holders
• Two D–size batteries

Invitation

What does the word *series* mean to you? Here, it means placing electric bulbs in order, with one ahead or behind the next one. How can you set up a series circuit?

Exploration

1. Use scissors to remove the insulation from the wire ends.
2. Use two bulbs and bulb holders, two batteries, and three wires. Set up the circuit as shown.
3. Suppose you remove light A. What will happen to light B? If you remove light B, what will happen to light A?

In a series circuit, if any wire or bulb is disconnected, all the bulbs go out. This occurs because all the electricity flows through each connected part. For the same reason, adding more bulbs to the circuit causes all the lighted bulbs to dim. Each resistor cuts down the available flow of electricity.

Concept Invention

1. Suppose you disconnect the wire at place 1. What do you think will happen to light A? light B?
2. Suppose you disconnect the wire at place 2. What will happen to light A? light B?
3. Add another bulb to the series. Use one more wire, bulb, and bulb holder. What, if anything, happens to the lights?

Adapting for Students with Exceptionalities

Encourage students with exceptionalities to work with other students in small groups to develop graphic organizers to assist in organizing the conceptual material such as series and parallel circuits. (See Mercer & Mercer, 2005, for a discussion on accommodations involving student performance.)

Concept Application

Does the fact that in a series circuit all the electricity flows through each connected part explain the results you found above? How does electricity seem to flow in a series circuit?

Parallel Circuits ──────────

Invitation

What does the word *parallel* mean to you? Here, it means placing electric wires side by side in a parallel circuit. How can you set up a parallel circuit?

MATERIALS

- Scissors
- Three flashlight bulbs
- Six wires
- Three bulb holders
- Two D-size batteries

Exploration

1. Use scissors to remove the insulation from the wire ends.
2. Use two batteries, two bulbs and bulb holders, and four wires. Set up the circuit as shown.

Concept Invention

1. Suppose you remove light A. What will happen to light B? If you remove light B, what will happen to light A?
2. Suppose you disconnect the wire at place 1. What do you think will happen to light A? light B?
3. Suppose you disconnect the wire at place 2. What will happen to light A? light B?
4. Add another bulb to the circuit. Use two more wires and another bulb and bulb holder. What, if anything, happens to the brightness of the lights?

In a parallel circuit, the wires are arranged to bypass a burned-out or missing bulb. Therefore, adding more bulbs to the circuit does not noticeably affect bulb brightness. Each bulb beyond receives the same flow of electricity (but all bulbs must have the same resistance in order to burn with equal brightness).

Concept Application

Does the fact that in a parallel circuit the electricity flows both to and around each connected bulb explain the results you found above? How does electricity seem to flow in a parallel circuit?

Hidden Parts of Electrical Circuits ———

MATERIALS

- Paper punch
- Ruler
- D–size battery
- Pencil
- Manila folder
- Scissors
- Aluminum foil
- Two wires (30 centimeters, or 12 inches, long)
- Sticky tape
- Flashlight bulb

Invitation

Suppose you have a folder like the one shown. Notice the four holes on the front cover. Each hole has aluminum foil underneath, so each looks the same. Now, look at the back of the front cover. A foil strip goes from hole 1 to hole 3. It conducts electricity like a wire. However, only small pieces cover holes 2 and 4. Suppose you do not know where the strip is and you cannot open the folder. How can you test for and find the hidden strip?

Front

Back

Exploration

1. First, prepare your own folder. Cut a regular-size manila folder in half the short way. (Save the other half for later use.)

2. Use a paper punch to punch four holes. Cover them with foil as shown in the first illustration. Fasten the foil with sticky tape. Number the holes on the cover.

3. Now prepare your tester as shown next. Use scissors to bare the ends of two wires. Tape the ends to a D-size battery. Bend one of the opposite wire ends into a loop. Wrap the other end around the bulb base and twist it to hold it fast.

4. Touch the bulb bottom to the looped end of the other wire. If the bulb lights, you are ready to test your folder.

5. Press the bulb bottom into one hole. Press the wire loop into another hole. Test these pairs of holes; see which completes the circuit and lights the bulb:

1—2	2—3	3—4
1—3	2—4	
1—4		

Teaching Tips

In this case, the foil strip conductor is hidden and stretches between two holes. Touching the bulb bottom and the free wire end to the strip completes the circuit, allowing electricity to flow. The free wire end is bent into a loop to avoid gouging the foil.

Concept Invention

1. Suppose you tested another folder with the following results:

Paired Holes	Bulb Lights
1—2	Yes
1—3	No
1—4	Yes
2—3	No
2—4	Yes
3—4	No

2. Let's say there are two strips connecting holes. How do you think they are arranged? Is more than one way possible? Make drawings of your ideas. Then prepare a folder and test your ideas.

Scaffolding for English Learners

An extension of this activity would be to have groups of students pair English and Spanish words with the foil. Students who choose correct English and Spanish pairs will light the tester.

Concept Application

Parts of an electrical circuit may be inferred from tests if the wires are hidden. Can you test and find out how different folders are "wired"? Have others prepare hidden circuits for you. (You can do the same for them.) Keep a record of your results and what you observe. Then open each folder to check your observations.

Test Your Nerves ———

Invitation

How can you make an electric "nerve tester" game?

MATERIALS

- Bare copper bell wire (60 centimeters, or 2 feet, long)
- Sticky tape
- Number 22 or 24 insulated wire
- Bulb holder
- Clay
- Pencil
- Heavy cardboard
- D-size battery
- Flashlight bulb
- Scissors

Exploration

1. Put two lumps of clay on some cardboard, as shown.

Teaching Tips

Any single-strand, somewhat stiff wire will serve for the heavier bare wire. Even a piece cut from a wire coat hanger will work if the paint is sanded off. To make the bulb light more brightly when the wire is touched, use two D-size batteries in series.

2. Bend the heavy bare copper wire as shown and stick each end into a clay lump.
3. Cut three pieces of the lighter, insulated wire as shown. Use scissors to bare the ends.
4. Put the bulb in the bulb holder. Attach the three wires to the bulb holder and the D-size battery. Attach the free end of the battery wire to the end of the heavy bare wire. Twist it around and push the twisted wires slightly into the clay.
5. Bend the free end of the bulb-holder wire around a pencil to make a slightly open loop. Touch the loop end to the heavy bare wire. See if the light goes on.
6. To play the game, carefully place the open loop over the heavy bare wire so that the wire is inside the loop. Move the loop from one end to the other and back without touching the heavy bare wire. If it touches, the light will go on. The person who lights the bulb least often wins.

Concept Invention

1. Predict and observe the following:
   • Who has the steadiest nerves in the class?
   • How does practice help?
2. Is your left hand shakier than your right hand?

Concept Application

How could you test if people's hands are shakier before or after lunch? What else might affect how shaky people's hands are? How is this "nerve tester" different from a "lie detector" used by police?

Blinking Signals ———————

Invitation

How can you make a two-way blinker system?

MATERIALS

- Two flashlight bulbs and holders
- Scissors
- Ruler
- Four large tacks
- Sticky tape
- Two small wooden blocks
- Wire (6 meters, or 7 yards)
- Hammer
- D-size battery
- Thin aluminum pie pan
- Partner

Exploration

1. Cut three short pieces of wire and two equally long wires, as shown. Use scissors to bare the ends of all five wires.
2. Cut two strips 10 centimeters (4 inches) long from the pie pan. Attach the strips, wires, and battery. Use tape to fasten wires to the battery. Use a hammer to pound the tacks into the wooden blocks.
3. Test your signal blinker.

Concept Invention

1. Could you use this device to send dot–dash signals?
2. Press the "key" (the pie pan strip) a short or longer time. Your partner must hold down the second key while you are sending a message. Both bulbs will flash on and off as signals are sent.

 Teaching Tips If both bulbs are dim, add a second battery in series; if only one bulb is dim, replace it with another that matches the bright bulb.

Adapting for Students with Exceptionalities

Substituting a doorbell or buzzer for the light bulb in this activity makes it readily adaptable for students who are visually impaired or blind.

Concept Application

Try using the International Morse Code to send signals, as follows:

A	B	C	D
.—	—...	—.—.	—..
E	F	G	H
.	..—.	——.	....
I	J	K	L
..	.———	—.—	.—..
M	N	O	P
——	—.	———	.——.
Q	R	S	T
——.—	.—.	...	—
U	V	W	X
..—	...—	.——	—..—
Y	Z		
—.——	——..		

What messages can you send and receive? How can you send clearer messages?

SERIES AND PARALLEL CIRCUIT CONCEPTS

Electrical devices in a circuit can be connected in only two basic ways: series or parallel wiring (INQ Figure 5–3).

Connecting Wires ———————

In series wiring (INQ Figure 5–3A), all the usable electricity flows through each bulb or appliance. A chief disadvantage of this circuit is obvious to anyone who has had a bulb burn out in an old-fashioned, series-type string of Christmas-tree lights. When one bulb burns out, the circuit is broken and all the lights go out. All the bulbs must then be tested to discover which one needs to be replaced.

To avoid the troubles of series circuits, most wiring for home and commercial use is parallel wiring. In this kind, electricity flows through a main wire and through branching wires connected to it as well, as shown in INQ Figure 5–3B. (In this figure, the Fahne-stock clips represent the branching wires.) If a bulb or other fixture should burn out, no other bulb or fixture is affected. Bulbs receive electricity regardless if the others are in use. When children make parallel circuits, they will notice no change in bulb brightness as bulbs are added.

Connecting Cells ———————

Cells can also be arranged in series and parallel as shown in INQ Figure 5–4. A wide rubber band can serve to affix wires to flashlight batteries, but the lined-up batteries will buckle where they join unless they are enclosed in a plastic sheath or other holder. A sheet of rolled, stiff paper can be used for this purpose. Pairing students up will preclude the use of holders, since four hands will be able to hold everything together.

INQ Figure 5–3   Two contrasting circuits: (A) lights in series and (B) lights in parallel.

(Others added as needed)

A

(Others added as needed)

B

Note that in the series examples, negative terminals (−) join to positive (+) terminals. In the parallel examples, positives are joined to positives and negatives are joined to negatives.

Voltage

Hooking up cells in series increases the voltage, or pressure, behind the flow of electricity. In contrast, arranging several or more cells in parallel makes available a longer lasting supply of current without increasing the voltage. For example, a bulb connected to two cells in series will burn about twice as brightly as when the cells are connected in parallel. However, the bulb will burn about two times longer with the parallel arrangement.

An analogy, as shown in INQ Figure 5–5, can clarify why these differences take place. Cells in series are like connected tanks of water, one mounted higher than the other. The force of the water flow is directly related to how many higher tanks are used. In contrast, cells in parallel are like water tanks mounted on the same level. The water flows at about the same rate as it would with one tank. So, in this case, the water supply lasts about twice as long as in the other setup (see Fife, 1996).

Voltage is an electromotive force. It can be thought of as the energy source in a circuit that produces the force that causes electrons to flow. Voltage is measured in volts. Current is the actual flow of the electrons, and it is measured in amps (amperes). Resistance, measured in ohms, is the opposition to the flow of electrons in a circuit or the ability to resist, or slow down, the flow of electric current. To again use the water analogy, consider a garden

INQ Figure 5–4   Cells arranged in series (A) and parallel (B).

A   B

INQ Figure 5–5   **A is twice as forceful as B, but B will flow twice as long.**

Series
circuit

A

Parallel circuit

B

hose. Water pressure is the voltage, the diameter of the hose sets the resistance, and the amount of water actually coming out of the hose is the current.

Voltage, current, and resistance are related through Ohm's law. This law states that the voltage needed to force a given amount of current through a circuit is equal to the product of the current and the resistance of the circuit. Another way to state this is that the amount of current in a circuit is equal to the voltage applied to the circuit divided by the resistance of the circuit. Finally, the resistance of a circuit is equal to the voltage applied to the circuit divided by the amount of current in the circuit. Symbolically, we could state this as follows: Voltage = E, Current = I, and Resistance = R; then $E = IR$, $I = E/R$, $R = E/I$.

In studying circuits, children have many interesting chances to make predictions about which bulbs will light and to make inferences about hidden wires.

ELECTRICAL FLOW Inquiry

Materials That Conduct Electricity

Invitation

You know that electricity can travel through a wire, but how about other materials? How can you find out which materials conduct electricity?

Exploration

1. Arrange your materials as shown, except for the key. Use scissors to bare both ends of each wire. Be sure the wire is wrapped tightly around the bulb base by twisting the end.
2. Touch the bulb bottom to the end of the other wire. If the bulb lights, you are ready to test materials.
3. Get some objects to test, such as a key. Touch the bulb bottom to one part. Touch the end of the other wire to another part. If the bulb lights, the object is a conductor of electricity. If it does not light, the object is a nonconductor of electricity.

MATERIALS
• Small wooden objects
• Small rubber objects
• Small metal objects
• Sticky tape
• Pencil
• Small plastic objects
• Small glass objects
• Flashlight bulb
• D–size battery
• Scissors
• Two wires (30 centimeters, or 12 inches, long)

Concept Invention

1. What, if any, rubber objects are conductors? plastic objects? metal objects? wooden objects? glass objects? Make a chart like the following to record your findings.

Teaching Tips If the bulb is to operate properly, the wire wrapped around the bulb base should be twisted tightly for good contact.

Object	Made From	Conductor	Nonconductor
Key	Metal	X	
Others			

2. Some objects are made of several materials. With a pencil, you can test wood, paint, metal, rubber, and graphite. Which of these will conduct electricity?

Concept Application

Metals are usually good conductors of electricity. Most other solid materials are nonconductors or poor conductors. Look around the room. What other objects can you test? Make your conductor tester more powerful. Use two batteries end to end. Test some materials again. How do these results compare with your first results?

How to Measure Bulb Brightness ————

Invitation

Have you noticed that a bulb burns less brightly as a battery wears down? A bulb's brightness can help you know how fresh a battery is. How can you measure the brightness of a lit flashlight bulb?

Exploration

1. Have a partner light a bulb with one battery and wire (make sure the wire ends are bare).
2. Tear a small piece from a sheet of paper.
3. Hold it tightly against the bulb. Can you see the glow through the paper, as illustrated?
4. Tear off another piece of paper. Hold both pieces together tightly against the bulb. Can you still see the glow through the double thickness?
5. Keep adding pieces until you cannot see the bulb's glow.
6. Record the largest number of pieces through which you saw the bulb glow.

MATERIALS

- Two sheets of paper
- Partner
- Flashlight bulbs
- D-size battery
- Scissors
- Sticky tape
- Several batteries of the same size
- Wire (30 centimeters, or 12 inches, long)
- Pencil

 Teaching Tips | Most fresh D-size batteries can be interchanged and a given bulb will glow with no noticeable difference in brightness. As batteries wear down unevenly, however, the brightness is affected.

Concept Invention

1. Get some batteries of the same size. How can you compare how strong each is? Can you put them in order from weakest to strongest? Record your findings.
2. How many times brighter will the bulb be with two batteries? with three batteries? Add batteries end to end. (The raised button end of each battery should face the same way.) Record your findings.

Concept Application

The brightness of a flashlight bulb may vary because of its resistance to electricity and the power of the battery. Try different flashlight bulbs. How can you compare how brightly each burns? Can you put them in order from dimmest to brightest? Record your findings. Will someone else get the same results?

Dimmer Switches ———

Invitation

How can you make a dimmer switch?

Exploration

1. Tape each end of the graphite to a tabletop.
2. Touch the bulb base of the tester to the graphite. Touch the wire end just next to it. The bulb should light.
3. Slowly, move the wire end of the tester along the graphite. Move it first away from the bulb, then back again, as shown.

MATERIALS

- Graphite (pencil "lead" about 7 centimeters, or 3 inches, long)
- Circuit tester
- Sticky tape
- Tabletop

Concept Invention

1. What happens to the bulb brightness as the graphite connection gets longer?
2. What happens to the bulb brightness as the graphite connection gets shorter?

Teaching Tips

Graphite from either a mechanical or cut-apart wooden pencil may be used. Graphite is resistant to electricity. If the tester bulb does not light, try adding one or two more batteries in series.

Concept Application

Where have you used dimmer switches at home or elsewhere?

Fuses

Invitation

How does a fuse work?

Exploration

1. Prepare the fuse. Cut a piece from the gum wrapper about 4 centimeters (1 and 6/10 inches) long and 0.5 centimeter (2/10 inch) wide. Leave the paper attached to the foil. Cut a V-shaped nick in the middle of the piece so that barely any foil is left.
2. Use scissors to bare the ends of the three wires. Also bare a small section in the middle of two of those wires.
3. Set up the materials as shown.
4. Holding the insulated part of the wire, touch one bare wire part with the other. This makes a short circuit.

Fuse (4 cm x .5 cm)

Concept Invention

1. What happens to the fuse?
2. What happens to the wires?
3. What happens to the bulb?

Concept Application

Why do you think it is important to have a fuse in a house current?

MATERIALS

- Three D–size batteries
- Small piece of heavy cardboard
- Three short insulated wires
- Two all-metal tacks
- Flashlight bulb and holder
- Foil from a gum wrapper
- Scissors
- Ruler

ELECTRICAL FLOW CONCEPTS

Conductors

The term *conductor* is usually given to any substance that permits an easy flow of electricity. Metals are by far the best conductors of electricity, and so they are commonly used for wires. Although several of the precious metals are better conductors, copper is most often used, as it is comparable in efficiency and yet inexpensive enough to use in quantity. We often hear the term *nonconductor* for materials such as rubber, glass, plastic, cloth, and other nonmetallic substances. This term is misleading, as almost anything will conduct electricity if given enough voltage. These materials are better called *poor conductors* or *insulators*.

The concept of insulators is the reason electricians may wear rubber gloves, and electric wires are covered with cloth, plastic, or rubber. It also explains why appliance plugs are covered with rubber or plastic, and glass separators are used on power line poles to keep apart high-voltage lines.

Some poor conductors become good conductors when wet. Pure, or distilled, water is a poor electrical conductor, but when dissolved minerals are added to it, the resultant mixture becomes a fairly good one. Wet human skin is a far better electrical conductor than dry skin. For this reason, it is safer to turn appliances on and off with dry hands.

Resistance

Although metals are better electrical conductors than nonmetals, metal wire still has some resistance to the flow of electrons. The length of the wire has a direct relationship to the amount of resistance; the longer the wire, the greater the resistance.

You may have experienced the gradual dimming of lights in a theater or adjusted the brightness of dashboard lights in an automobile. In both cases, the change may have been caused by a *rheostat*, or dimmer switch. One kind of rheostat increases or decreases the length of wire through which electric current flows, thereby increasing or decreasing the wire's resistance. A simple model is shown in INQ Figure 5–6. Some metals have so much resistance to the flow of electricity that they glow brightly when enough electrical pressure, or voltage, forces a relatively large quantity of electricity to flow in them. Unfortunately, most metals melt or evaporate within a short period of time when hot enough to give off light.

This unfortunate property of most metals necessitated a long search by Thomas Edison for materials to use as bulb filaments before he found reasonable success. Some of the materials he tried reveal the exhaustive character of the search: Bamboo slivers, sewing thread, and even human hair were carbonized and then tested.

Tungsten, sometimes called wolfram, is the metal used in incandescent bulbs today. (Any bulb that gives light from a very hot filament is called an incandescent bulb.) With a melting point of almost 3400°C (6200°F), tungsten is well able to withstand the temperature caused by the movement of electricity through its highly resistant structure. An inactive gas, such as argon, is pumped into the bulbs to help prevent the burning away of the filament. Still, some of the tungsten evaporates eventually, and the filament separates, breaking the circuit. The ever-darkening appearance of the portion of the bulb next to the filament shows the deposition of the evaporating tungsten. Electric heaters also have wires of highly resistant metal. Most heaters today use Nichrome wire, a combination of nickel and chromium.

So far, you have seen that length and composition of wire affect resistance to the flow of electricity. Another factor is the diameter of the wire. An analogy here will help explain why wire size affects resistance. Imagine part of a large crowd in a sports stadium converging into a narrow passageway. As some of the people begin to enter the passageway, the

INQ Figure 5–6   **A simple rheostat, or dimmer switch.**

Sliding contact

Coil of wire

forward speed of the crowd slackens. At the end of the passageway, the forward pace again picks up.

A thick wire presents a broad pathway for the flow of electricity. A narrow wire constricts the flow. In the "effort" of electrons to crowd through the narrow pathway, much friction is created, and the wire gets hot. If the wire is thin enough and made of material like tungsten, it can also produce much light as it heats.

Circuit Hazards

You have seen that when bulbs or appliances are wired into a circuit, they show resistance to the flow of electrical energy. At the place where the energy enters these resistors, a change of energy takes place. Some of the electrical energy changes into heat (as in a heater), or light (as in a bulb), or sound (as in a radio), or motion (as in a motor). In other words, a significant amount of electrical energy is "used up," or changed.

Suppose, though, there is no resistor connected within the circuit. Because the copper wire has relatively low resistance, a great surge of electricity flows through the wire. The wire now heats up rapidly even though it usually offers little resistance to a current.

Short Circuits

In residential and commercial circuits, intense heating of the wires may come from a "short circuit." This may happen when two bare wires touch each other, preventing the main supply of current from flowing through the resistor. Because the resistor is largely bypassed, a huge amount of electricity flows.

A common cause of short circuits is an appliance cord placed under a heavily traveled rug. If the insulation between the two internal wires wears away, they may touch and a short may develop. A circuit is not necessarily shortened in length for a "short" circuit to occur. The essential thing is that the resistor is bypassed.

Overloaded Circuits

Overloading a circuit is perhaps an even more frequent cause of wires overheating. Many older houses, for example, were wired when only a few of today's common appliances were widely used. Small-diameter, lightly insulated wires were adequate then; but as more and more of today's appliances are added to circuits, intense heating occurs and poses a potential threat of fire.

Fuses and Circuit Breakers

Fuses and circuit breakers protect us from electrical fire hazard. In some older houses, a screw-in type of fuse contains a narrow metal strip that melts at a fairly low temperature. When a fuse is placed in a circuit, the electricity must travel through the strip. If the wire heats up to a dangerously high temperature, then the strip melts and the circuit opens, thereby shutting off the current.

A bimetallic strip circuit breaker is used instead of a fuse in many houses. It consists of two thin metal ribbons fused together. The ribbons are made of two different metals. When placed in a circuit and heated, the bimetallic strip bends away from one of the contact points, opening the circuit. The bending is the result of different expansion rates of the metals. Another modern type of circuit breaker works because any wire containing electric current generates some magnetism. Increasing the supply of current has the effect of increasing the magnetism. When a movable steel rod is enclosed in a coil of wire placed in a circuit, it may be pulled upward as the current (and so magnetism) increases. If the rod is connected to a contact point, its upward movement will result in the circuit being opened. A spring catch that can be reset by hand prevents the rod from dropping down again. An electromagnetic device that operates in this way is called a *solenoid*.

ELECTROMAGNET Inquiry

MATERIALS

- Pencil
- Partner
- Box of paper clips
- Large iron nail
- Aluminum rod
- Wire (one piece should be 2 meters, or about 6 feet, long)
- Scissors
- Two D–size batteries

Electromagnets

Invitation

Suppose you have some wire, a large nail, and a flashlight battery. With these materials you can make a magnet or an electromagnet. How can you make an electromagnet?

Exploration

1. Get a large nail. Touch it to a paper clip to test the nail for magnetism. The nail should be free of magnetism at the start.
2. Use scissors to bare the wire ends. Wrap the 2-meter-long wire tightly around the nail. Leave about 0.5 meter (1.5 feet) of wire free at both ends.
3. Have your partner touch the bare wire ends to a battery. Touch the nail end to some paper clips. How many paper clips does your electromagnet pick up?
4. Have your partner move one wire away from the battery. What happens? *Note:* Do not leave the battery connected for more than 10 seconds each time.

 Teaching Tips

Use number 22 or 24 bell wire insulated with plastic. Strip off some insulation at both ends so that good contact can be made with the battery. A regular D-size battery works well. Be sure to advise children that the wires should be held to the battery no more than about 10 seconds without interruption. Otherwise, its power will be drained quickly. A 3- to 4-inch iron nail should be adequate for the core of the electromagnet. If possible, get a similar-sized rod of aluminum. It will present an interesting contrast if used in place of the nail.

Most of the materials attracted to an electromagnet fall when the electromagnet is disconnected from the battery. One paper clip or other light item may remain. This shows that some magnetism is left in the nail.

Concept Invention

1. Which end of your electromagnet will pick up more clips?
2. How can you change the strength of your electromagnet? Make a record of what you try and the results.
3. What will happen if you wrap more wire around the nail?
4. What will happen if you take away the iron nail?
5. What will happen if you switch a pencil for the nail?
6. What will happen if you use an aluminum rod instead of the nail?

Concept Application

Electricity flowing through a wire acts like a magnet; its magnetic power can be increased in several ways. Can an electromagnet attract anything a regular magnet cannot attract? What will happen if you use two batteries end to end?

ELECTROMAGNET CONCEPTS

In 1820, a professor of physics in Copenhagen made a discovery that opened for development one of the most useful devices ever conceived: the electromagnet. Hans Christian Oersted had believed for years that a relationship existed between magnetism and electricity. Despite much research, Oersted had not succeeded in discovering a useful connection between these two phenomena. One day, while lecturing to a class, he noticed that a wire carrying electric current was deflecting a nearby compass needle. Oersted realized immediately that the wire was generating a magnetic field. His later experiments, writings, and lectures helped spread the new concept of electromagnetism to the world.

The telephone, the electric motor, and many other tools of modern living had their origin in Oersted's work and related discoveries. We consider some of these devices here.

Electric Bell —————

An electric bell or a buzzer operates because its electric current is "interrupted," or continually turned off and on. INQ Figure 5–7 shows how this happens. Follow the current as it moves from the battery into the bell. When the current flows around into the two electromagnets, they pull the metal clapper, which rings the bell. The act of moving the clapper breaks the circuit at the contact point, and the electricity stops flowing. The clapper then springs back into place and current flows again to repeat the cycle.

The Telephone —————

INQ Figure 5–8 shows how the telephone works. Notice the complete, or closed, circuit between the transmitter and the receiver. When we speak into the transmitter, a very thin metal diaphragm vibrates from the sounds we make. The diaphragm variably squeezes the

INQ Figure 5–7   An electric bell or buzzer.

Circuit broken here

INQ Figure 5–8   A telephone circuit.

carbon granules behind it. Loud sounds, for example, squeeze the granules more tightly than soft sounds. This makes the granules conduct variable electrical pulses rather than a steady current.

The electrical impulses, rather than the voice itself, are transmitted in the wire. So, they are able to travel to the other telephone's receiver almost instantly, rather than at the much slower speed of sound. As the variable electric current reaches the receiver, it also causes the electromagnets to pull the diaphragm in a variable way. This pulling sets the diaphragm vibrating in the same manner as the first one, and sounds are created.

To summarize, sound energy is used to vary electrical energy at one end, which is then used to make sound energy at the other end. Students can experiment with old telephones and batteries to see how this works.

Electric Motor

You may know that it is possible to rotate a suspended bar magnet with a second bar magnet. You can do this because unlike poles attract each other, and like poles repel each other. The suspended magnet is rotated by alternately attracting and repelling each pole. To do this, you twist the bar magnet you are holding so that the poles are attracted at first and then repelled. If timed properly, the suspended magnet will rotate smoothly.

You can demonstrate a similar technique with an electromagnet; however, you will not need to twist it to make the suspended magnet rotate. INQ Figure 5–9 shows how to proceed. First, find the pole on the electromagnet that is the opposite of the bar magnet's nearer pole. It will attract the bar magnet. Next, reverse the way you touch the terminals on the battery. This will also reverse the poles on the electromagnet. The nearer pole of the bar magnet will now be repelled. Rotate the suspended magnet smoothly by touching the battery terminals first one way and then the opposite way. A child can hold the electromagnet in one fixed position while you do this.

In an electric motor, the electromagnet spins. A device reverses the current automatically, which continually reverses the poles of the electromagnet. The electromagnet spins because it is first attracted to, and then repelled by, another magnet inside. An electric motor is really a spinning electromagnet.

Relays

Another example of the use of an electromagnet is a relay. A relay is a simple electromechanical switch that is activated by an electrical signal. A relay consists of an electromagnet, an armature (moveable "arm") that can be attracted by the electromagnet, a

INQ Figure 5–9   You can get a bar magnet to spin by alternately reversing the way you touch the wire ends of an electromagnet to a battery's terminals.

spring (to return the armature back when no longer attracted by the electromagnet), and a set of contact points (to connect the armature to the main circuit). The electromagnet functions to open or close the contact between main terminals. This allows one circuit to control another completely independent circuit.

A relay uses a small amount of power, consisting of a few volts at extremely low milliamperage, to turn an electromagnet on and off. The electromagnet, in turn, will allow the armature and contacts to switch on and off a much larger current such as the 120 volts or 240 volts of current that you might need to run a large appliance in your house. For example, a relay might control the compressor of a refrigerator, a dehumidifier, or an air conditioner. Another place a relay is found is in your car's engine. A relay uses a small amount of current to control the starter motor, since this motor uses a large amount of current that would shock you if you made the contact directly. Relays are used so extensively that challenging students to find relay examples is a good extension activity to the electromagnetic inquiry.

GENERATING ELECTRICITY Inquiry

Static Electricity

MATERIALS

- Plastic spoon and fork
- Piece of wool and piece of nylon
- Paper and pencil
- Sticky tape
- Heavy string
- Plastic bag
- Rubber comb

Invitation

When you comb your hair on a dry day, does it crackle and stick to the comb? Have you felt a shock when you touched something after crossing a carpet? These are examples of static electricity. You can get static electricity by rubbing different objects together. What objects can you rub together to produce static electricity?

Exploration

1. Use sticky tape to attach string to the spoon. Attach it where the spoon balances. Hang the spoon from a table edge. Tape the string end to the table.
2. Hold the fork backward. Bring the fork handle near the hanging spoon handle, but do not touch it, as illustrated. Notice that probably nothing happens. So far, there is no static electricity.

Teaching Tips

Almost any plastic items may be substituted for the fork and spoon. The use of a heavy string will keep the suspended object from spinning too freely. Students will find that using an unlike material in the Exploration will change their findings. Postpone this activity on rainy or especially humid days, as results will be less noticeable.

3. Rub each handle with wool. Bring the fork handle near the spoon again. Watch what happens.
4. Rub one handle again with wool but the other with nylon. Watch what happens. (Static electricity may have either a positive [+] or a negative [–] charge. When two objects have the same charge, positive or negative, they repel, or push each other away. When each has a different charge, they attract each other.)

Concept Invention

1. Did the objects in Exploration step 3 have the same charge, or did they have different charges? How about in Exploration step 4?
2. What happens when you rub the handles with different materials?
3. Which combinations make the handles repel?

4. Which combinations make the handles attract? Keep a careful record. To do so, you might set up a chart like this:

	Spoon Rubbed with Wool	Spoon Rubbed with Plastic Bag	Spoon Rubbed with Nylon
Fork Rubbed with Wool	Repel		
Fork Rubbed with Plastic Bag			
Fork Rubbed with Nylon			

5. After you complete the first column, can you predict the remaining results?

Concept Application

Rubbing different materials together may produce static electricity. Like charges repel each other, and unlike charges attract each other. What results will you get if you substitute other objects for the plastic fork? For example, what happens if you rub a rubber comb with each material?

A Way to Generate Electricity

Invitation

Have you ever seen an electric generator in a power plant? Usually, a magnetic field produces an electric current in a coil of wire. You can even produce a current by moving a small magnet in and out of a small coil of wire. But the current will not be enough to light a bulb. To tell that a current is present, you need a current detector, or galvanometer. How can you generate electricity and tell it is being produced?

Exploration

1. Use scissors to bare the wire ends.
2. Coil 50 turns of wire around your hand. Slip off the coil and fasten it in three places with sticky tape. This will keep the coil tight.
3. Wrap 20 turns of wire narrowly around the compass. This will be your galvanometer.
4. Twist the bare ends of the wire together to close the circuit.
5. Push a magnet end into the coil. See how the compass needle moves. Pull the magnet out of the coil. Watch again how the needle moves. The needle moving shows you have generated a current each time. The farther the needle moves, the stronger the current. (However, be sure the magnet is far enough from the compass so that it does not directly affect it. You want the electricity in the wires to move the needle.)

> **MATERIALS**
> - Insulated wire (12 meters, or 13 yards, long)
> - Magnetic compass
> - Two strong magnets (one stronger)
> - Scissors
> - Sticky tape

Concept Invention

1. Does it make any difference if the coil or the magnet moves?
2. What happens to the needle if you move the magnet more quickly?
3. What happens to the needle if you move the magnet more slowly?
4. What difference does it make if you move the magnet's other end?
5. How does using a stronger or weaker magnet affect the compass needle?
6. How does changing the number of turns in the coil affect the needle?

Teaching Tips

By moving the magnet alternately in two directions, the current that is produced also alternates directions. This is shown by the compass needle moving first one way and then the other. The mechanical energy used to move the magnet comes, in this case, from the students. The teaching strategy of the discovery sequence is to provide the type of experience that encourages students to experiment on their own.

Concept Application

An electric current may be generated when a magnet and a wire coil interact. A galvanometer may be used to detect the current. What is the strongest current you can generate? That is, how far can you make the compass needle move? Describe how you made the strongest current.

GENERATING ELECTRICITY CONCEPTS

Electricity can be generated in several ways. First we consider how to produce static electricity, then current electricity, and last, electromagnetic waves that can be sent to various places without wires.

Static Electricity ───────

Not all electricity is useful. Almost everyone has experienced some form of static electricity. You may have heard the crackling sound of hair when it is combed after having been washed and dried, or you may have felt a slight shock from a metal doorknob when you touch it after you've scuffed across a rug. You may also have heard the flash of lightning that briefly illuminates a darkened sky. In each case, an electric charge appears to build up on an object and then stay there (hence, the name *static*) until a conductor provides a route through which the charge can escape. Although forms of static electricity vary considerably, their causes are similar. To understand these causes, it will be helpful for us to peer briefly into the makeup of molecules and atoms.

We know that most matter is made up of molecules. A *molecule* is the smallest bit of any substance that retains the chemical properties of that substance. If we subdivide the molecule further, it no longer resembles the original substance. In this case, we have arrived at the atomic level.

Only two of the particles that make up an atom need concern us here: electrons and protons. Each of these particles has a tiny electric charge. The electron has a negative charge; the proton has a positive charge.

In their "normal" state, atoms have as many electrons as protons. Because these charged particles attract each other with equal force, they balance, or neutralize, each other. The atom is said to be neutral, or uncharged. But electrons are easily dislodged or torn away from atoms by rubbing and other means. When two neutral, unlike materials are rubbed together, one of the materials has a tendency to lose electrons to the other. For example, when a hard rubber rod is rubbed with a wool material, the wool loses some of its electrons to the rod. This gives the wool a positive charge and the rod a negative charge. When a glass rod is rubbed with silk, however, some electrons leave the glass and go onto the silk. This gives the silk a negative charge and the glass a positive charge.

The basic law of static electricity is "like charges repel each other and unlike charges attract each other." Children may discover that identical objects rubbed with the same material will repel each other. If the objects are rubbed with different materials, they will usually attract each other. What causes lightning? It is produced by friction. A cloud contains varying amounts of dust particles, raindrops, air (gas) molecules, and sometimes ice crystals. When violent currents occur in clouds, these substances rub together in various combinations. If a huge electric charge builds up, an oppositely charged cloud or the ground may attract it. When this happens, we see lightning. (Thunder results when the air through which lightning passes quickly heats up and cools. The rapid expansion and contraction of the air forces air molecules to smash together, which causes loud sounds.)

Current Electricity ───────────

Static electricity is both unreliable and difficult to manage, so we use current electricity to meet our needs. This electricity generally comes from two sources: batteries (both wet cells and dry cells) and power plants.

Batteries

Children are curious about how a battery can "make" electricity. Some think it is stored, as water is stored in a tank. What really happens is that chemical energy changes into electrical energy.

Here is how an automobile battery (a wet cell) works. When strips of two different metals (e.g., zinc and copper) are placed into an acid, both strips begin to dissolve slowly. However, the zinc dissolves more quickly than the copper. A surplus of electrons from the dissolving parts of the zinc strip builds up on the rest of the strip, giving it a strong negative charge. Some electrons are also released at the slower-dissolving copper strip, but these go into the acid, leaving the copper strip with a positive charge. If we connect the end of the zinc strip to the end of the copper strip with a wire, a continuous circuit is set up. Electrons flow from the zinc strip through the wire to the copper strip. If we connect a bulb in this circuit, it lights; if we connect a starter in this circuit, it starts an automobile engine. Many pairs of dissimilar metal strips, or *electrodes*, can be used to get this effect, and other liquids besides acid can work to release and hold electrons. Such liquids are called *electrolytes*.

A dry cell or flashlight battery works in a way similar to the wet cell as described. A moist, pastelike electrolyte is used in place of a liquid. The electrodes are most commonly a carbon rod (found in the center of the cell) and a zinc cylinder (which surrounds the paste and rod).

Dry cells are convenient, but they are too weak and expensive for widespread residential or commercial use. Mechanical energy, the energy of motion, is by far the main method for generating electricity. Today, most electricity is produced by changing the energy in fuels and falling water.

Power Plants

In hydroelectric power plants, water falls on the blades of huge wheels, causing them to revolve. Other power plants may use oil, coal, natural gas, or atomic energy to heat water into steam. The steam or falling water forces giant turbines to whirl. A wire coil is spun inside an electromagnetic field, causing electrons to flow into the wire.

Producing Electromagnetic Waves

You know that a steady electric current produces a weak magnetic field around a wire. This is why we can make an electromagnet. Long ago, scientists learned that by rapidly varying the electric current in a wire they could change the magnetic field. Instead of a steady field, rapidly vibrating energy waves were given off by the wire. These are called *radio waves*.

At a radio station, music or voice vibrations are changed into a variable electric current. The method is like that used in a telephone transmitter. The vibrating current is strengthened until strong radio waves are given off by the wire carrying the current. The waves are beamed off in all directions from a tall tower. Some of the waves strike a radio antenna. A weak current begins vibrating in the antenna, and the current is picked up and strengthened in the radio. A connected loudspeaker vibrates and produces sound energy much like a telephone receiver.

References

American Association for the Advancement of Science (AAAS). (1993). *Benchmarks for science literacy*. New York: Oxford University Press.

Fife, J. (1996). *Watered-down electricity: Using water to explain electricity*. Huntington, WV: University Editions.

Hart, J. E., & Lee, O. (2003). Teacher professional development to improve the science and literacy achievement of English language learners. *Bilingual Research Journal, 27*(3), 475–501. Retrieved November 13, 2004, from http://brj.asu.edu/content/vol27 no3/art6.pdf

Mercer, C. D., & Mercer, A. R. (2005). *Teaching students with learning problems* (7th ed.). Upper Saddle River, NJ: Merrill/Prentice Hall.

National Research Council (NRC). (1996). *National science education standards*. Washington, DC: National Academy Press.

Selected Trade Books: Electrical Energy

For Younger Children

Bailey, M. W. (1978). *Electricity*. Austin, TX: Raintree.

Bains, R. (1981). *Discovering electricity*. New York: Troll Associates.

Berger, M. (1990). *Switch on, switch off*. New York: HarperCollins.

Challand, H. (1986). *Experiments with electricity*. New York: Childrens Press.

Cole, J. (1997). *The magic school bus and the electric field trip*. New York: Scholastic.

Curren, P. (1977). *I know an electrician*. New York: G. P. Putnam.

Lawson, R. (1988). *Ben and me: An astonishing life of Benjamin Franklin*. Boston: Little, Brown.

Lillegard, D., & Stoker, W. (1986). *I can be an electrician*. Danbury, CT: Childrens Press.

Taylor, B. (1991). *Batteries and magnets*. Danbury, CT: Watts.

Wade, H. (1979). *Electricity*. Austin, TX: Raintree.

Wood, Robert W. (1990). *Physics for kids: 49 easy experiments with electricity and magnetism*. Blue Ridge Summit, PA: Tab Books.

For Older Children

Adamsczyk, P., & Frances-Law, P. (1993). *Electricity and magnetism*. London, England: Usborne Publishing Ltd.

Ardley, N. (1984). *Discovering electricity*. Danbury, CT: Watts.

Bains, R. (1982). *Discovering electricity*. New Jersey: Troll Associates.

Birch, B., & Corfield, R. B. (1995). *Benjamin Franklin's adventures with electricity*. New York: Barron's Juveniles.

Brandt, K. (1985). *Electricity*. New York: Troll Associates.

Clemence, J., & Clemence J. (1991). *Electricity*. Ada, OK: Garrett Educational Corp.

Cobb, V. (1986). *More power to you!* Boston: Little, Brown.

De Bruin, J. (1985). *Young scientist explores electricity and magnetism*. Torrance, CA: Good Apple.

Friedhoffer, R. (1992). *Magnetism and electricity*. Chicago: Franklin Watts.

Fritz, J. (1982). *What's the big idea, Ben Franklin?* New York: Coward-McCann.

Glover, D. (1993). *Batteries, bulbs, and wires*. New York: Kingfisher Books.

Gutnik, M. J. (1986). *Electricity: From Faraday to solar generators*. Danbury, CT: Watts.

Mackie, D. (1986). *Electricity*. Cincinnati: Penworthy.

Math, I. (1981). *Wires and watts*. New York: Scribner.

Parker, S. (1992). *Electricity*. New York: Dorling Kindersly.

Seifer, M. (1991). *Nikola Tesla: The man that harnessed Niagara Falls*. Kingston, RI: MetaScience.

Taylor, B. (1990). *Electricity and magnets*. Danbury, CT: Watts.

Vogt, G. (1985). *Electricity and magnetism*. Danbury, CT: Watts.

Vogt, G. (1986). *Generating electricity*. Danbury, CT: Watts.

Ward, A. (1986). *Experimenting with batteries, bulbs, and wires*. New York: David & Charles.

Ward, Alan. (1992). *Magnets and electricity*. New York: Franklin Watts.

Whyman, K. (1986). *Electricity and magnetism*. Danbury, CT: Watts.

Wilcox, C. (1996). *Powerhouse: Inside a nuclear power plant*. Minneapolis: Carolrhoda Books.

Wood, R. W. (1997). *Electricity and magnetism fundamentals*. New York: McGraw Hill.

Zubrowski, B. (1991). *Blinkers and buzzers*. New York: Morrow.

Resource Books

Butzow, C. M., & Butzow, J. W. (1989). *Science through children's literature: An integrated approach*. Englewood, CO: Teacher Ideas Press. (batteries and electrical circuit topics, pp. 226–231)

Erickson, J., & Beals, K. (2002). *Electric circuits: Inventive physical science activities*. Berkeley, CA: Great Explorations in Math and Science. (electical activities)

Gosnell, K. (1994). *Thematic unit: Electricity*. Huntington Beach, CA: Teacher Created Materials. (thematic electrical activities)

Shaw, D. G., & Dybdahl, C. S. (1996). *Integrating science and language arts: A sourcebook for K–6 teachers*. Boston: Allyn & Bacon. (electrical circuit topics, pp. 102–103)

Summers, M., Kruger, C., & Mant, J. (1997). *Teaching electricity effectively: A research-based guide for primary science*. Hatfield, Herts., UK: Association for Science Education. (research-base electrical activities)

Tolman, M., & Morton, J. (1986). *Physical science activities for grades 2–8*. West Nyack, NY: Parker. (static and current electricity activities pp. 211–259)

Winkleman, G., & Youngs, D. (Eds.). (1991). *Electrical connections*. Fresno, CA: AIMS Education Foundation. (30 electrical activities)

SIMPLE MACHINES

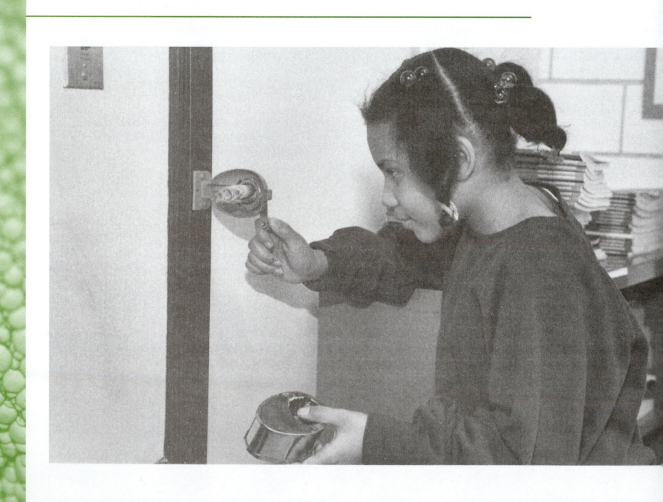

Imagine a parade of the world's machines including airplanes, tweezers, bulldozers, baby carriages, computers, and egg beaters—an almost endless line of inventions without which we would fare far less well. But perhaps the most remarkable thing about these inventions lies in their construction. All machines, no matter how complex, are variations of just six simple machines: inclined plane (ramp), wedge, screw, lever, wheel and axle (windlass), and pulley. Let's take a closer look at these machines and the effects of motion and friction on them.

Benchmarks and Standards

Practical examples of the uses of simple machines will help reinforce the types of simple machines and how they can be used in combination with each other. Forces and motion related to the use of simple machines are common themes, as evidenced in the following sample benchmarks and standards.

Sample Benchmarks (AAAS, 1993)

- The way to change how something is moving is to give it a push or a pull. (By Grades K–2, p. 89)
- Something that is moving may move steadily or change its direction. The greater the force is, the greater the change in motion will be. The more massive an object is, the less effect a given force will have. (By Grades 3–5, p. 89)

Sample Standards (NRC, 1996)

- The position and motion of objects can be changed by pushing or pulling. The size of the change is related to the strength of the push or pull. (By Grades K–4, p. 127)
- The motion of an object can be described by its position, direction of motion, and speed. That motion can be measured and represented on a graph. (By Grades 5–8, p. 154)

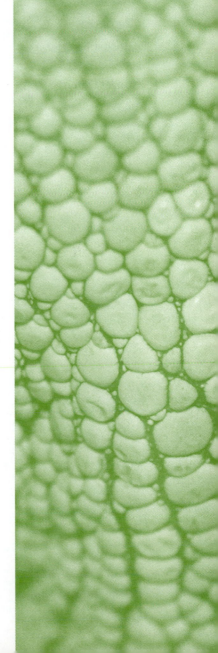

SCREWS AND INCLINED PLANES **Inquiry**

Inclined Planes ———————

Invitation

Is it easier to walk up a steep hill or a low hill? Suppose both hills were the same height, but one was twice as long. Which would be easier then? A hill is a kind of inclined plane. How can you measure the force needed to use an inclined plane?

Exploration

1. Lay an end of the smaller board on one book as shown.
2. Place a roller skate on the board. Hook a bent paper clip around the tied shoelace. Attach a rubber band.
3. Pull the skate slowly up the board. Measure with a ruler how much the rubber band stretches (or measure the pull with a spring scale).

4. Now make the inclined plane or "hill" three books high. Do steps 2 and 3 again.

Concept Invention

1. What was the difference in rubber band stretch in the two trials?
2. How much stretch will there be with "hills" of different heights? Measure also a height of two books, then five and six books. (Do not measure four books now.) Record what you find on a graph such as this:

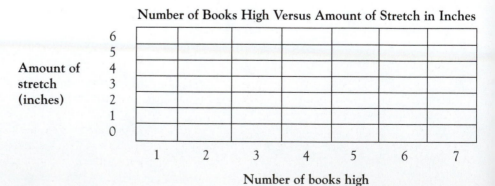

Number of Books High Versus Amount of Stretch in Inches

Amount of stretch (inches)

Number of books high

3. Examine your graph data for heights of one, two, three, five, and six books. Can you predict the stretch for four books? Write this down and then test your prediction.
4. Examine your data again. Can you predict the stretch for seven books?
5. What pictures of different inclined planes can you bring to school?

Concept Application

The force needed to go up an inclined plane increases with height and decreases with distance. Switch this board for one twice as long. Suppose you used one through seven books again. What do you think your results would be? Write down your ideas and then test them.

 Teaching Tips

One long board, rather than two different-sized boards, can be used to demonstrate how differing board lengths affect the force needed to go up a given height. The books may first be placed under the midpoint of the board, and the board tilted. The tilted part beyond the books may be ignored; this may confuse some students, however, especially the younger ones. Pairs of boards of almost any lengths may be used, but the larger one should be twice as long as the smaller one.

A spring scale is likely to yield more accurate measurements than a rubber band. A rubber band may not stretch uniformly and, of course, does not indicate force in standard units. Try several rubber bands; select one that stretches easily for heights of one to seven books. If needed, snip and use a single strand.

Two kinds of predicting occur in this inquiry. The child predicts within the data (interpolating) and beyond the data (extrapolating).

Adapting for Students with Exceptionalities

When working with exceptional students, use predetermined and explicit teaching procedures before, during, and after instruction. Take the time to review directions and accurately record data. (See Mercer & Mercer, 2005, for a discussion on accommodations involving instruction.)

SCREWS AND INCLINED PLANES CONCEPTS

For any machine to do work, force must overcome gravity, inertia, molecular cohesion (the binding force that holds materials together), and friction. Machines may be used to reduce the force needed to do work, speed up work, or change the direction of a force.

Inclined Planes ─────────

Although they may not have thought about it, even small children have had experiences with inclined planes, such as climbing stairs, walking up a hill, or coasting down a slanted driveway on roller skates. They know from these experiences that it is harder to climb a steep hill than a gradual hill. Children may even unknowingly use the idea that distance may be increased to decrease force, as when a bicycle rider rides diagonally back and forth up a hill. This background of common experiences lets us focus on force–distance relationships fairly quickly when working with inclined planes.

INQ **Figure 6–1**   An inclined plane.

Does an inclined plane or other simple machine make work "easier"? No, if we mean that some part of the total effort is saved. In terms of work, or force moving a resistance over a distance, it is impossible to get out of a machine any more than is put into a machine. Another way of saying this is:

Effort times distance equals resistance times distance, or ED = RD

Let's apply this idea to the inclined plane in INQ Figure 6–1. Suppose we want to push a 50-pound barrel to a height of 5 feet and the inclined plane is 10 feet long. If we were to push the barrel up the incline, it would take less force (25 pounds of force) than if we were to pick it straight up (50 pounds of force). The total amount of force to move the barrel up the incline would be the distance of the incline, which is 10 feet, times the effort required, which is 25 pounds. This is a total of 250 foot-pounds. Notice that this equals the 250 foot-pounds of work that would be required to lift the barrel straight up a distance of 5 feet times an effort of 50 pounds.

In both cases, we assume that we are physically able to do the work. Yet, it is easier for us to apply less force for a longer distance and time. Muscles get tired quickly from concentrated, heavy work. In that sense, then, a simple machine makes work "easier."

The reduction of force provided by a simple machine is called its mechanical advantage. This is a number found by dividing the force of the resistance by the force of the effort. In the foregoing example, the *mechanical advantage* is

R (50 pounds)/E (25 pounds) = 2

In other words, it is twice as easy to lift the barrel with the inclined plane as without it. Or, we can say it takes half as much effort.

Children can make crude measurements to grasp the force–distance relationship. For instance, a string can be used to compare the length of an inclined plane with the height to which it rises. A rubber band attached to an object may have a ruler held beside it to measure different degrees of applied force in terms of "stretch." A spring scale, if available, is even more effective than a rubber band.

Wedges

A *wedge* can be thought of as a combination of two inclined planes. Although the classic use of this machine has waned, along with professional rail-splitters and woodchoppers, the wedge principle is utilized in many other ways. For example, streamlining is a way of better enabling objects to pierce air and water. More speed can be achieved with the same amount of applied force. Paper cutters, knives, pencil sharpeners, nails, and needles are all wedges we use every day for cutting or piercing functions.

INQ Figure 6–2   The pitch of a screw is the distance between its threads.

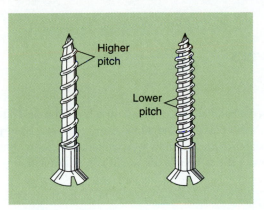

Screws

"The screw is just an inclined plane wrapped around a nail." This is what one child said, and it is a fairly accurate description. We usually think of the screw as a nail-like object with a spiral thread that holds together pieces of wood or metal. But other applications of this machine are all around us: spiral staircases, roads that wind around steep hills or mountains, vises for workbenches, clamps to hold things together, adjustable piano stools, and the adjustable parts of wrenches, to name just a few. Sometimes a screw is not so obvious, like propellers for ships and airplanes.

When a screw is used to lift objects, its mechanical advantage is the greatest of any simple machine. It is relatively easy for a small person to lift the front of an automobile with a screw-type jack, and jackscrews employed by house movers actually lift entire houses off their foundations. As with an inclined plane, though, the price paid for such a gain in force is increased distance.

Each time a screw is given a complete turn, it advances into a piece of wood or lifts an object only as far as the distance between its threads. This distance is called pitch and is illustrated in INQ Figure 6–2. The paired drawings show that two screws of similar size but different pitches would vary in the number of times turned if screwed into some wood or used to lift an object. We expect a steep spiral staircase to take more effort to climb than a longer, gradual one when walking up to the same height. Likewise, the steeper (or higher) the pitch of a screw, the more force needed to make it rotate. However, it advances farther and faster than one with a narrower (or lower), more gradual pitch.

The mathematical relationships here are identical to those of other simple machines. Mechanical advantage is again found by dividing resistance by effort.

LEVER Inquiry

Common Levers

MATERIALS

- Real or picture examples of levers in everyday things (canoe paddle, crowbar, paper cutter, baseball bat, seesaw, post puller, house broom, can opener, wheelbarrow, tennis racket, golf club, boat oar).

Invitation

Have you ever used a baseball bat, a seesaw, or a house broom? These and many other objects we use are examples of levers. How levers work can be surprising. Some that are similar in appearance may actually work differently. Some that are different in appearance may work the same way. How can you tell in which ways levers are alike and different?

Exploration

1. The illustration shows a fishing pole in action. Notice how this lever is used. The tip carries the load, or resistance (R). The opposite end, which is held, moves very little. This is the fulcrum (F). To pull up the resistance takes effort (E). This happens between the fulcrum and the resistance.
2. Study the three smaller drawings in the illustration. Levers can be grouped into three classes, depending on how they are used. Each group has a place for the fulcrum, resistance, and effort. But notice that, in each group, the placement of these points is different. This is a good way to tell them apart.

Concept Invention

1. In which group does the fishing pole belong?
2. Examine real or picture examples of many levers. Use them, or think of how they are used. In which group does each belong? Following is a way to record what you find.

Lever	1. RFE	2. FRE	3. FER
Fishing pole			
Paper cutter			
Others			

3. Which of these levers are really alike?
4. Examine your forearm. It is a lever, too. In which group does it belong?
5. Play a game with some friends. Think of a common lever. Can they find out what it is by asking questions? You can answer only yes or no. If they get stuck, act out the way it is used. A good way for them to begin is to find out the resistance (load)–fulcrum–effort order.

Teaching Tips

It is the internal order of resistance–fulcrum–effort that counts in classifying levers. So, there is no difference between R–F–E and E–F–R, for example. (This may be a difficult concept for a few students.) It is not important for children to memorize the internal order of each class, but it is worthwhile for them to develop skill in observing and classifying likenesses and differences in objects.

In step 4 of Concept Invention, the part played by the upper arm muscle (bicep) in moving the forearm may be confusing. The actual pull on the forearm is just below and opposite the elbow on the inside.

Adapting for Students with Exceptionalities

Some students may experience difficulty with the vocabulary of this activity. Provide a glossary of the key terms with illustrations of the sample lever classes and the associated resistance, effort, and fulcrum points. (See Mercer & Mercer, 2005, for a discussion on accommodations involving instructional materials.)

Concept Application

Levers may be grouped by where places on each are used for the resistance, fulcrum, and effort. What other real or picture examples can you find? In which group does each belong? Illustrate and label some levers of your choice.

Common Double Levers

Invitation

Scissors are an example of a double lever that has cutting parts. We use many tools that are double levers. How many can you name or describe? Some that are similar in appearance may work differently. Some that are different in appearance may work about the same way. How can you tell in which ways double levers are alike and different?

MATERIALS

- Scissors
- Pliers
- Tweezers
- Lemon squeezer
- Nutcracker
- Sugar tongs
- Tin snips

In classifying double levers, it is the internal order of the resistance–fulcrum–effort that counts, just as it did with single levers. There is no difference between R–F–E and E–F–R, for example.

Exploration

1. In the pair of scissors, notice how the parts are used, especially the cutting parts. When you cut something, it resists being cut. So, each part that does this work is called the *resistance* (R).
2. Notice where the two parts of the scissors join and pivot. This is the *fulcrum* (F).
3. Observe the handles in action. To cut something requires force, or effort, so each of these parts is called the *effort* (E).

Concept Invention

1. All tools that are double levers have parts for the resistance (R), fulcrum (F), and effort (E). But they are not always in that order. Examine some real or picture examples of double-lever tools. Which tools are arranged differently? How many different arrangements do you find?
2. You can classify these and other double levers by how the three parts are arranged. In which group will each fit?

   Following is a way to record what you find.

Double Lever	1. RFE	2. FRE	3. FER
Scissors			
Pliers			
Others			

3. Can you name parts of your body that work like a double lever?

Concept Application

Double levers may be grouped by how places on each are used for the resistance, fulcrum, and effort. What other real or picture examples of double levers can you find? In which group does each belong? Illustrate and label some double levers of your choice.

The Making of a Mobile

Invitation

Notice the balanced group of objects shown. This is a *mobile*. The word means "something that moves." Even a tiny breeze can move the objects. They may almost seem to be alive! What kinds of mobile objects would you like to make? Fish, birds, butterflies, balloons, and airplanes are all fun to do. You can even use cutout letters of your name. How can you make a mobile?

Ruler taped to chair

Straw

> **MATERIALS**
>
> - Plastic soda straws
> - Tagboard
> - Thin knitting yarn
> - Sticky tape
> - Paper clips
> - Ruler
> - Scissors
> - Crayons or paints and brushes

Exploration

1. Cut some strings of yarn 20 to 30 centimeters (8 to 12 inches) long.
2. Tie one end of each string to a paper clip.
3. Decide what shapes of objects to hang. Then cut three or four object shapes from tagboard.
4. Set up a place to hang your mobile. Tape a ruler to a chair. Put the chair on a table.
5. Hang the shapes from a straw with yarn. Loop the yarn once around the straw. Make half a knot. Then, pull the yarn tight. Clip the paper clip to each shape in the usual way.
6. Try to balance the shapes. Slide the yarn on the straw. Change where each shape is clipped if necessary.

Scaffolding for English Learners

As students are learning the concepts related to levers, they could use shapes of objects labeled with the English word on them to reinforce English vocabulary. (See Ovando, Collier, & Combs, 2003, for a discussion of the use of integrated content and language development with English learners.)

Concept Invention

1. How can you make a mobile with more straws and shapes? It will help to draw your mobile on paper first. Start with a few materials and then add more as you are building your mobile.

2. What can you do to balance your shapes?
3. How can you keep the shapes from touching?
4. How big should each shape be?
5. Where should each shape be placed?
6. How long should each string be?
7. Where is it best to clip the string on each shape?

8. How can you color your shapes with crayons or paints?

Concept Application

For mobile shapes to balance, we consider such variables as size and shape, weight, string length, best positions for the shapes, and where to fasten them. Design a mobile below. Use a combination of shapes from heavy and light materials.

LEVER CONCEPTS

No one knows who actually first contrived the lever, but it has been known and used for a very long time. The ancient Greek scientist Archimedes is purported to have said to King Hiero that he could move the world if given a long enough lever, a fulcrum, and a place to stand. It is widely assumed that primitive people also had knowledge of levers in a practical way.

The principles of this simple machine are used in so many ways that a moment's reflection produces surprising examples: The ancient Japanese sport of judo is based on knowledge that the human skeleton is comprised of lever systems. Also, a golfer with long arms may swing the club head faster than a golfer with shorter arms.

Three Parts

The seesaw is a lever familiar to most children. It has three parts: (a) *fulcrum*, the point on which it pivots; (b) *effort arm*, the part on which the force is exerted; and (c) *resistance*, or load, *arm*, the part that bears the load to be raised. When the seesaw is perfectly balanced on the fulcrum, the resistance and effort arms will alternate if two equally heavy riders alternately push against the ground to make the seesaw go up and down.

As in other machines, effort multiplied by the distance (from the fulcrum) equals resistance times distance (from the fulcrum). This is shown in INQ Figure 6–3. The me-

INQ Figure 6–3   To find the mechanical advantage of a lever, divide the effort-arm length by the resistance-arm length.

Resistance × distance = Effort × distance
10 lb × 1 ft = 2 ft × 5 lb

chanical advantage in this example is 2. Another way to calculate the mechanical advantage is simply to divide the effort-arm length by the resistance-arm length. Friction is usually so minor in the lever that it does not need to be taken into account.

Primary students can arrive at an intuitive understanding of the "law of levers" if they are given experience with balancing objects.

Three Classes

Levers are found with parts arranged in three different combinations called classes. Children do not need to memorize these combinations or even their examples; but analyzing how everyday levers work can sharpen their observation and classification skills. Notice the three arrangements in INQ Figure 6–4.

Seesaws, crowbars, and can openers are first-class levers. Two levers of this kind are placed together in tools such as scissors and pliers. By varying the effort-arm length, you change the amount of required force or gain in speed and distance. This type also changes direction of movement. You exert force in a direction opposite to which the load moves. With both effort and resistance arms equal in length, however, a first-class lever will only be able to change the direction of a force. Neither reduced force nor gain in speed and distance takes place.

The wheelbarrow and post puller illustrate second-class levers. A nutcracker illustrates joined, double levers of this type. Speed or distances are not as likely to be considerations when using a second-class lever as in the first-class lever.

A very basic and tangible example of a third-class lever is your arm. Your elbow is the fulcrum, your bicep provides the effort at a point just below and opposite the elbow, and your fist represents the load or resistance. Other common applications are found in the broom, baseball bat, fly swatter, and fishing pole, to name just a few. Sugar tongs or ice cube tongs represent double levers of the class. Analysis of this lever reveals that force is traded to get added speed or distance. With a fishing pole, for example, you want to increase the speed of your hands to hook a nibbling fish securely before it can react and get away.

INQ Figure 6–4   Three classes of levers; R is resistance, E is effort.

INQ Figure 6–5   **A tagboard and paper clip mobile.**

Mobiles

A mobile is a combination of several suspended levers with attached figures. In some mobiles, even the figures may function as levers (INQ Figure 6–5).

When children work on mobiles, they may have problems balancing the figures and keeping them from touching. For solutions, they need to think about variables such as figure size and shape, string length, best position for figures, and where to fasten them. This task sharpens their thinking skills. Mobiles are also an interesting way to combine artwork with science.

Archimedes and the Application of Levers

We began the lever concepts section with the bold statement to King Hiero that Archimedes could move the earth if he had a big enough lever. Even today, it would be an impossible engineering feat considering you would need a lever that was 88,000,000,000,000,000,000,000 miles long (Berquist, 1995).

Archimedes did show, however, that the principles behind the lever could be applied in useful ways even back in 215 B.C.E. In addition to designing a block-and-tackle system to move a huge ship and the Archimedean screw that is used to pump water even today, Archimedes was called upon to develop war machines to protect Syracuse from the battle between Rome and Carthage. Responding to King Hiero's challenge, Archimedes designed a massive catapult that could hurl enormous masses of stone against an enemy. The historian Plutarch (as cited in Downs, 1982) noted that just the noise and violence that Archimedes' catapults produced sent soliders running away. Archimedes also developed immense cranes that could lift enemy ships right out of the water if they came too close to Syracuse.

Archimedes' practical applications of his geometric ideas are found everywhere. Even the mobiles discussed in the previous section relate back to Archimedes. His experiments with equilibrium and the center of gravity showed that the balancing point of an object is not always at its center. He experimented with finding the centers of gravity of triangles, parallelograms, and other plane figures. Could you design an "Archimedean" mobile to find the centers of gravity for geometric shapes?

WHEEL AND AXLE Inquiry

Easier Work

Invitation

How does a screwdriver handle make work easier?

Exploration

1. Use a hammer to tap in the screw so that it sticks into the wood.
2. Hold the screwdriver below the handle at the steel shank. Try to turn the screw.
3. Now hold the handle. Again, try to turn the screw.

Concept Invention

1. Which was easier?
2. Maybe your hand slipped on the smooth steel shank. Probably it did not slip on the handle. What will happen if you wrap masking tape around both parts and try again?
3. Which is easier this time?

Concept Application

Look at the screwdriver on end from the steel tip toward the handle. Notice the difference in width between the steel shank and the handle. Why do you think it is easier to turn a screw by using the handle rather than by using the shank?

MATERIALS

- Screwdriver with round handle
- Masking tape
- Piece of soft wood
- Screw
- Hammer

Wheel–Belt Systems

Invitation

Have you ever noticed how bicycle gears turn? A chain connects the two gears. As one gear rotates, the other gear moves, too. A *gear* is just a wheel with teeth. There are many ways to connect wheels. Often, they are connected with belts. Several connected wheels are called a *wheel–belt system*. You can make your own wheel–belt system with spools and rubber bands. How can you make a wheel–belt system?

Exploration

1. Pound four nails into the board as shown.

MATERIALS

- Four empty sewing spools
- Board (about the size of this page)
- Four finishing nails
- Four rubber bands
- Crayon
- Hammer

2. Make one crayon dot on the rim of each spool.
3. Put a spool on each of two nails.
4. Place a rubber band around the two spools.
5. Turn one spool. Watch the other spool turn too.

Part of an end piece from a discarded vegetable crate is ideal for the wheel–belt system base. Be sure that only finishing nails are pounded into the wood. These nails have small heads, allowing the spools to slip easily over them.

This investigation deals only with the direction the spools turn. By using different-sized spools, children can also study how size governs the speed of turning. Because much slipping will happen with the rubber bands, the size–speed relationship cannot be determined accurately. Children can get the idea better by inverting a bicycle and studying the relative turnings of the large gear and the small gear.

Concept Invention

1. How will the spools turn when connected in different ways? Notice the eight drawings in the first illustration. Each set of spools starts with the left spool. An arrow shows how each is turning. Another spool in the set has a question mark. It is next to a dot on the spool rim. See how the spools are connected.

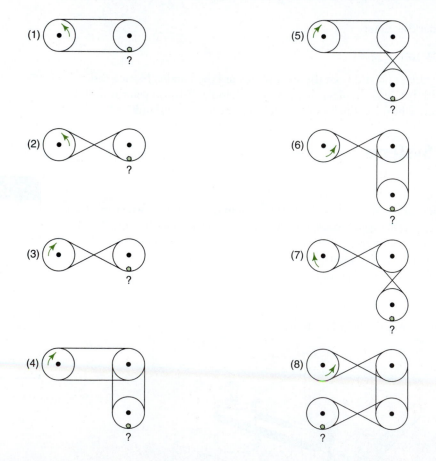

2. Will the dot on the rim turn left or right? Make a record of what you think. Then use your wheel–belt board to find out.

3. Notice the four drawings in the second illustration. How should the spools be connected to turn in these ways? How many different connections can you think of? Make drawings of what you think. Then, use your wheel–belt board to find out if they work.

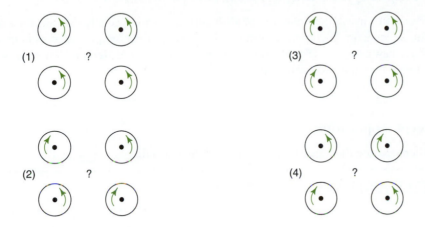

Concept Application

A wheel–belt system can be used to change the direction of a force. What wheel–belt systems can you invent? Record them below. Make up and trade some problems with friends. Fix your board so that you can use more spools.

Gearing Up for Speed ———————

Invitation

How do bicycle gears affect speed?

MATERIALS

• Ten-speed bicycle

• Chalk

Exploration

1. Observe the different-sized gears or sprockets on the rear wheel of the bicycle. Notice that all are smaller than the large pedal sprocket. See how a chain connects the large sprocket with a smaller one.
2. Adjust the chain so that it is on the largest of the small gears.
3. Turn the bicycle upside down. Face the chain side.
4. Move the near pedal around. Notice how the rear wheel turns.
5. How many times will the wheel turn, in comparison to the pedal?
6. Chalk a spot on the rear tire. Crank the pedal around one full turn. Count the turns made by the chalked wheel.
7. Adjust the chain so that it is on the smallest rear gear. (You may have to set the bicycle upright to do so.)
8. Crank the pedal one full turn. How many times does the rear wheel turn now?

 Teaching Tips | Ten-speed bicycles have two different-sized front sprockets. When the smaller one is used, it causes the pedals to revolve faster. This decreases the forward speed but allows less force to be used. For simplicity, use only one front sprocket in this activity.

Concept Invention

1. How does changing the rear gear size affect how fast you can go?
2. Try several gear combinations to see if your theory is correct.

Adapting for Students with Exceptionalities

Activities involving force and motion concepts are especially difficult for exceptional students. Incorporate examples from the students' experiences to help reinforce new concepts. (See Mastropieri & Scruggs, 2004, chapter on science and social studies for a discussion on activities related to force and motion.)

Concept Application

Where else are there gears that may help change speed?

WHEEL AND AXLE CONCEPTS

The *windlass,* or wheel and axle, is a commonly misunderstood simple machine. Although a windlass looks like a wagon wheel and axle, it is different. We put wheels on a wagon to reduce friction by lessening the surface area that comes in contact with the road. The axles are stationary. Greater "leverage" is indeed present in a large wheel, compared with a small wheel. This is why a large wheel can roll over uneven ground more easily than a small wheel. Still, a wagon wheel and axle combination is not regarded as a simple machine.

In a windlass, the axle and wheel are firmly fixed together. Spinning the axle causes the wheel to rotate; force at the axle is traded off to gain an advantage in speed and distance on the outside of the wheel. By turning the wheel, though, an advantage in force can be gained; speed and distance are then reduced or sacrificed at the axle.

A windlass is really a continuous lever on a continuous fulcrum. Therefore, when a handle is placed anywhere on the wheel, it becomes the end of the force arm. The axle's radius is the load arm. INQ Figure 6–6 illustrates this idea. The theoretical mechanical ad-

INQ Figure 6–6   **A windlass is a lever.**

INQ Figure 6–7 A pencil sharpener can be used as a wheel and axle.

vantage in a windlass is calculated like that of a lever. If the effort-arm length is 45 centimeters (18 inches) and the resistance-arm length is 5 centimeters (2 inches), the mechanical advantage equals 9. Because friction is so great with a windlass, however, actual mechanical advantage is found only through dividing resistance by effort.

Placing the windlass handle (effort) ever farther away from the axle (fulcrum) decreases needed effort, just as it did with the lever. At the same time, it increases the distance through which the effort is applied.

Understanding the force–distance relationship makes it easy for children to see why a pencil sharpener with a normal size handle (INQ Figure 6–7) works better than one with a short, broken handle. Children may also realize that a large steering wheel is easier to turn than a smaller one.

Gears, Chains, and Belts

Wheel-and-axle combinations may be modified to interact with one another by using belts, chains, and wheels with toothlike projections (gears). The bicycle is a common example of two modified wheels and axles joined by a chain. Because the front gear, or sprocket, is larger than the rear sprocket, one turn of the larger sprocket forces several or more turns of the smaller rear one. Older students can find the theoretical mechanical advantage of the larger sprocket by counting and comparing the number of teeth on each sprocket.

PULLEY Inquiry

How Pulleys Work —————

MATERIALS

- Two single-wheel pulleys
- Sticky tape
- Rubber band or spring scale
- Book
- Strong cord
- Ruler
- Broom handle or stick
- Scissors
- Paper clip
- Two chairs

Invitation

Many people use pulleys to help them work. Have you used a pulley to raise and lower a flag on a flagpole? Painters and roofers use pulleys to haul supplies up and down. Sometimes people work with only a single pulley, but often two or more are used together. How can you set up one or more pulleys to lift a load?

Exploration

1. Make a place to hang the pulley. Lay a stick over the backs of two separated chairs. Use tape to keep it from sliding. Loop and tie cord around the stick. Hang a single-wheel pulley from the loop. Hook a rubber band at the free end to act as a handle.
2. Set up a single pulley as illustrated in part A. This is a fixed pulley. Use a book for the load. Pull the cord down to lift the load. Practice a few times.
3. Now set up the pulley differently, as shown in part B. This is a movable pulley. Pull the cord up to lift the load. Practice a few times.

A   B   C

Concept Invention

1. What differences do you notice in using both pulleys?
2. Which takes less force to lift the load—the fixed pulley or the movable pulley? How much less? To measure, hook a rubber band to the pull cord with a paper clip. Measure the stretch with a ruler, or use a spring scale.
3. How far must you pull the cord to lift the load 1 meter (3 feet) with each pulley? Measure length of pull from where the cord leaves the pulley.
4. Refer to part C in the illustration. It shows a fixed and a movable pulley working together. This is a *block and tackle*. Which do you think takes less force to lift a load—a single fixed pulley or a block and tackle? How far must you pull the cord with each to lift the book 1 meter (3 feet)? Predict and then measure to answer each question.
5. Compare the block and tackle with the single movable pulley. Which do you think takes less force to lift a load? How far must you pull the cord with each to lift the book 1 meter (3 feet)? Predict and then measure to answer each question.
6. What examples of pulleys can you find in the classroom? What examples of pulleys can you find in the school? How do they work?

Teaching Tips

If a spring scale is used, be sure the load does not exceed its capacity. If you plan to do this investigation in a whole-group setting, consider placing the broomstick holder and supporting chairs on a table. This will allow students a clearer view.

Concept Application

A fixed pulley changes the direction of a force. A movable pulley reduces the force needed to lift a load. What other pulleys can you collect and try? How do they compare with the three pulleys of this investigation?

PULLEY CONCEPTS

Pulleys for teaching can be bought through science supply houses. Yet, in elementary school activities, two clothesline pulleys or two smaller single pulleys, found in most hardware stores, should work just as well. A single pulley has one grooved wheel or sheave. Some pulleys have two or more sheaves for combined use with other pulleys in heavy lifting.

Fixed and Movable Pulleys

As its name implies, a fixed pulley is securely fastened to some object. A movable pulley moves vertically—or laterally, as the case may be—with the load (INQ Figure 6–8). The pulley's similarity to a lever and windlass is diagrammed in INQ Figure 6–8. As with a windlass, the wheel-like arrangement is really a continuous lever.

Observe why a fixed pulley can do no more than change the direction of a force. Like a seesaw whose fulcrum is centered, the effort arm and the resistance arm are of equal length. There is no useful mechanical advantage. If 30 centimeters (1 foot) of rope is pulled downward, the resistance moves upward 1 foot. This happens, for example, when a flag is raised on a flagpole.

Note that a movable pulley offers a theoretical mechanical advantage of 2. The resistance arm is only half the effort-arm length. Like a wheelbarrow, this is a variation of a second-class lever. Distance is traded for decreased effort. We must pull the rope 2 feet for each 1 foot the load is lifted.

INQ Figure 6–8   A fixed pulley offers no mechanical advantage because its effort and resistance arms are equally long. A movable pulley, however, does make work easier because its resistance arm is only half the length of its effort arm.

INQ Figure 6–9   Block and tackle.

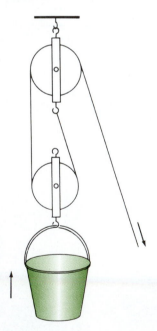

Block and Tackle

By placing a fixed and a movable pulley in combination, we are able not only to change the direction of a force but also to decrease the force necessary to lift a load. Such an arrangement is called a *block and tackle* (INQ Figure 6–9). By adding more movable pulleys (or pulleys with two or more sheaves), effort can be reduced even further.

Friction limits how far we can go in adding pulleys to reduce effort. It can be partly overcome by greasing or oiling the axle. Because each rope in a block-and-tackle setup supports an equal fraction of a load, it is easy to know the theoretical mechanical advantage. Two supporting ropes have a mechanical advantage of 2, three ropes 3, and so on. Because of friction, though, actual mechanical advantage must be calculated by dividing resistance by effort, as with all simple machines.

Children may use a rubber band (or spring scale) in the activities to measure differences in the force needed to lift objects by using pulleys. To attach a rubber band, first fashion a paper clip hook. Simply pierce or loop the pulley cord at the place where you wish to measure needed force, insert the hook, and then attach a rubber band to it. As before, a ruler can measure the amount of stretch.

Power Pulleys

The use of a pulley is not limited to lifting an object. Pulleys can be used in a system to deliver power. A smaller pulley can turn a larger pulley that goes slower, but provides more torque. One example of the use of a pulley system is in an automobile. A fan belt, powered by a pulley connected to the engine, is used to rotate the water pump (to circulate water to the radiator), the fan (to blow cooler air across the radiator), and the alternator (used to recharge the battery). In the home, pulleys are used to rotate the drum of the clothes dryer or to move the wheels attached to a computer hard disk or VCR head, to mention just a few examples.

Power pulley systems were used extensively in early factories. A water wheel, and later a steam engine, was used to supply energy to the layshaft, a long, cylindrical bar with small pulley wheels that rotated and transmitted power down the center of the workspace. Various machines such as power looms (used in weaving fabrics), lathes (machines for shaping a piece of material), or magnets (in generators to produce electricity) were connected to the layshaft by large belts and pulleys.

MOTION AND FRICTION Inquiry

Moving Parts ————

Invitation

How do machines and their parts move?

Exploration

1. Some machines move mostly in a straight line when they work, such as a locomotive and roller skates. Some machines or their parts go back and forth, such as a swing and the pendulum in a grandfather clock. Some machines or their parts go around, such as a merry-go-round and a bicycle wheel. Find pictures of machines and machine parts in magazines.
2. Cut out and group the pictures by how the machines or their parts seem to move.
3. Which machines or parts move mostly in a straight line?
4. Which machines or parts go back and forth?
5. Which machines or parts spin or go around as they work?
6. Which machines or parts do all of these things?
7. Which machines or parts do some of these things?
8. How do some toy machines and their parts move?

Concept Invention

1. Look for real examples of machines working.
2. Watch how they and their parts move.
3. Make a record of what you find out.

Scaffolding for English Learners

Look for opportunities to apply science concepts into the community. What machines are representative of your student's cultures? How do the parts on these specific machines move? Using community resources will assist in concept development of your English learners. (See Ovando, Collier, & Combs, 2003, for a discussion of the importance of community resources in science education for English learners.)

Concept Application

What machine can you make up and draw below? How will your machine or its parts move? What work will it do?

Pendulums

Invitation

Have you ever seen an old-fashioned grandfather clock? One kind has a long, weighted rod underneath that swings back and forth. The swinging part is called a *pendulum*. You can keep time with your own pendulum made with a string. How can you make a string pendulum?

Exploration

1. Tape a pencil to a table edge so that it sticks out.
2. Bend a paper clip into a hook shape. Tie one string end to the hook.
3. Loop the free end of the string once around the pencil. Tape the string end to the tabletop.
4. Put two washers on the hook, as shown.
5. Move the washers to one side and then let go. Each time the washers swing back to that side, count one swing. Be sure the string does not rub against the table edge.

MATERIALS

- Thin string (about 1 meter, or 1 yard, long)
- Meterstick or yardstick
- Pencil
- Three heavy washers
- Paper clip
- Clock or watch with second hand
- Sticky tape
- Graph paper
- Table

Concept Invention

1. How many swings does the pendulum make in 1 minute? Have someone help by observing the second hand on a clock. Then you can count the swings.
2. Do wide swings take more time than narrow swings? Suppose you let go of your pendulum far to one side. What difference might that make in the number of swings it takes in 1 minute?

The timing of events is possible with a pendulum because its to-and-fro motion recurs with near-perfect regularity. Through manipulating variables, children can discover that the length of the weighted string affects the swing rate, or *period*, of a pendulum. Be sure children realize that one complete swing consists of the swing out and return movement.

An easy way for younger children to see the effect of manipulating a variable is to set up two identical pendulums. When both are set to swinging, they should perform in the same way. Thereafter, change only one variable at a time with one pendulum—weight or width of swing or length—so that its performance may be contrasted with the unchanged pendulum.

3. Does the amount of weight used change the swing time? What might happen if you use a one-washer weight? What might happen if you use a three-washer weight?
4. Does the length of string used make a difference in swing time? (Measure length from the pencil to the end of the washers.) What might happen if you use a shorter string? What might happen if you use a longer string?
5. How can you get your pendulum to swing 60 times in 1 minute?
6. How well can you predict with your pendulum? Make a graph such as the one shown. Try several string lengths for your pendulum. Count the swings for each length. Let's say you find that a 20-centimeter (8-inch) string swings 65 times in 1 minute. Make a mark on your graph where lines running from these two numbers meet, as shown in the graph. Make marks for three or four other string lengths and their swings. Then draw a straight line between the marks. Suppose you know the length of a pendulum but you have not yet tried it. How can you use your graph to predict its number of swings? Suppose you know the number of swings of a pendulum but you have not yet measured its length. How can you use your graph to predict the pendulum's length? How can you make your predictions more accurate?

Concept Application

A pendulum is any object that swings regularly back and forth; its length affects its swing rate. Suppose you had a grandfather clock that was running slow. What could you do to its pendulum to correct it? What if it was running fast?

Friction

Invitation

Suppose someone asks you to slide a wooden box across the floor. On what kind of floor surface would it be easiest to start the box sliding? What kind would be the hardest? When an object catches or drags on a surface, we say much friction is present. If it slides or moves easily, little friction is present. How can you find out about the friction of different surfaces?

Exploration

1. Place a wooden block on a wooden table. Fasten a rubber band to it with a thumbtack.
2. Hook a thin rubber band with an opened paper clip. Hold the rubber band end over the end of a ruler as illustrated here.
3. Pull the rubber band very slowly. Observe where the rubber band end is over the ruler. How far does the band stretch before the block moves? Read the ruler to the nearest whole number. Always make the reading before the block starts to slide.

MATERIALS

- Two same-sized wooden blocks
- Paper clip
- Ruler
- Two round pencils
- Thumbtack
- Sheets of sandpaper
- Sticky tape
- Waxed paper
- Thin rubber band
- Three wide rubber bands
- Kitchen foil
- Construction paper
- Table

Concept Invention

1. How much will the rubber band stretch if you pull the block a second time?
2. How much will the rubber band stretch if you pull the block a third time? Record the results and the average for the three trials as shown below:

Surface Tested	Predicted Stretch	Stretch for Each Trial (cm)	Average Stretch (cm)
Wood	10	11, 15, 13	13
Others			

3. How much will the band stretch if the block is placed on other surfaces? Tape a small piece of kitchen foil to the table, and place the block on it. Test this and other surfaces such as sandpaper, waxed paper, or construction paper. (To prepare

Two identical wooden play blocks can be used for this investigation, or cut two 4-inch squares from a 2-inch by 4-inch piece of wood. A thin rubber band works best to pull with. To make it even "stretchier," cut and use it as a single strand. If available, a spring scale may be used to compare results. There should be little relative difference, although the spring scale may be calibrated in grams or ounces.

Caution: Make sure the tack that holds the rubber band to the block is secure before the band is pulled.

Younger children may not be ready to use a ruler for measurements. Instead, they may mark a piece of paper, in place of a ruler, to show the rubber band's relative amounts of stretch. Before this is done, allow time for them to play with and become familiar with the different materials.

a rubber surface, wrap three wide rubber bands around the block.) Try to predict first how far the band will stretch each time. Record the results.

4. How much will the band stretch if the block is placed on its side? How much will the band stretch if a second block is put on top?
5. How much will the band stretch if two round pencils are placed under the block?

Concept Application

Friction between two surfaces depends on the force that presses the surfaces together and the materials that make up the surfaces. Some surfaces have more friction than others. How can you make the most friction between the block and surface? How can you make the least friction between the block and surface? (Use more materials if necessary.)

MOTION AND FRICTION CONCEPTS

Most machines we use are complex; that is, they are combinations of simple machines. It is interesting to see how these machines and their parts move and interact.

Three Basic Motions

Some machines have mainly a *straight-line motion*. A few examples are toy or real trains, a bicycle (turning requires some leaning), roller skates, and steamrollers. Some machines or their parts make a repeated forward and backward movement called *periodic motion*. The pendulum in a grandfather clock is one example. Others are a swing, a mechanical walking doll, a metronome, and some lawn sprinklers.

Some machines or their parts make a continuous spinning motion in one direction as they work. This is *rotary motion*. A few examples are the merry-go-round, the turntable on a record player, a rotary lawn sprinkler, and clock hands. It can be fascinating to examine mechanical toys and other machines; their parts are designed to produce a particular motion and, in some cases, to change it.

Any moving machine or part continues to produce its designed motion unless another force is applied to alter, reverse, or stop it. When we rotate a telephone dial, for instance, a metal stop prevents us from going beyond one rotation. A spring then returns the dial to its original position. Also, the front wheel of a moving bicycle may be turned by applying a force to the handlebars. But what happens if the force is applied too strongly? Perhaps painful experience has taught you that bicycle and rider will continue in a straight line until road friction finally stops both.

Friction

Accompanying all motion is *friction*, the resistance produced when two surfaces rub together. No surface is perfectly smooth. The tiny ridges in a "smooth" surface, or the larger bumps and hollows in a rough one, catch and resist when surfaces rub together. The mutual attraction of molecules on the opposing surfaces also adds to the resistance we call friction. Surface pressure is another condition that affects friction. A heavy object has more friction than a lighter one.

Lubricating a surface is effective because the oil or grease fills in the spaces between the ridges and bumps. Opposing surfaces mostly slide against the lubricant, rather than rub against each other.

In many machines, ball bearings or roller bearings are used to change sliding friction to rolling friction. Rolling friction is less than sliding friction because a load-bearing rolling object rolls over tiny surface ridges or bumps, rather than catches against them.

Friction reduces a machine's efficiency by robbing some of its power (and so its energy). It also creates heat as surfaces rub and wears out parts. But not all its effects are bad. Friction also allows us to brake a car or bicycle, walk or run, or write on paper. A frictionless world would create far more problems than it would solve.

References

American Association for the Advancement of Science (AAAS). (1993). *Benchmarks for science literacy*. New York: Oxford University Press.

Berquist, L. (1995). *Archimedes and the door of science*. Warsaw, ND: Bethlehem Books.

Downs, R. (1982). *Landmarks in science: Hippocrates to Carson*. Littleton, CO: Libraries Unlimited.

Mastropieri, M., & Scruggs, T. E. (2004). *The inclusive classroom: Strategies for effective instruction* (4th ed.). Upper Saddle River, NJ: Merrill/Prentice Hall.

Mercer, C. D., & Mercer, A. R. (2005). *Teaching students with learning problems* (7th ed.). Upper Saddle River, NJ: Merrill/Prentice Hall.

National Research Council (NRC). (1996). *National science education standards*. Washington, DC: National Academy Press.

Ovando, C. J., Collier, V. P., & Combs, M. C. (2003). *Bilingual and ESL classrooms: Teaching in multicultural contexts*. Boston, MA: McGraw-Hill.

Selected Trade Books: Simple Machines

For Younger Children

Barton, B. (1987). *Machines at work*. New York: Harper & Row.

Gibbons, G. (1982). *Tool book*. New York: Holiday House.

Hodge, D. (1998). *Simple machines* (Starting with science series). Toronto, Ontario: Kids Can Press.

Kiley, D. (1980). *Biggest machines*. Austin, TX: Raintree.

Lampton, C. (1991). *Marbles, roller skates, doorknobs: Simple machines that are really wheels*. Brookfield, CT: Millbrook Press.

Lampton, C. (1991). *Sailboats, flag poles, cranes: Using pulleys as simple machines*. Brookfield, CT: Millbrook Press.

Lampton, C. (1991). *Seesaws, nutcrackers, brooms: Simple machines that are really levers*. Brookfield, CT: Millbrook Press.

Lauber, P. (1987). *Get ready for robots*. New York: Scholastic.

Pipe, J. (2002). *What does a wheel do?* Brookfield, CT: Copper Beech Books/Millbrook.

Robbins, K. (1983). *Tools*. New York: Macmillan.

Rockwell, A., & Rockwell, H. (1985). *Machines*. New York: Harper & Row.

Tompert, A. (1993). *Just a little bit*. Boston: Houghton Mifflin.

Wade, H. (1979). *Gears*. Austin, TX: Raintree.

Wade, H. (1979). *The lever*. Austin, TX: Raintree.

Weiss, H. (1983). *The world of machines*. Austin, TX: Raintree.

Wells, R. (1996). *How do you lift a lion?* Morton Grove, IL: Albert Whitman.

Wilkin, F. (1986). *Machines*. Danbury, CT: Childrens Press.

Wyler, R. (1988). *Science fun with toy cars and trucks*. Parsippany, NJ: Julian Messner.

For Older Children

Adkins, J. (1980). *Moving heavy things*. Boston: Houghton Mifflin.

Baines, R. (1985). *Simple machines*. New York: Troll Associates.

Barrett, N. S. (1985). *Robots*. Danbury, CT: Watts.

Brown, W. F., & Brown, M. G. (1984). *Experiments with common wood and tools*. New York: Macmillan.

Busby, P. (2003). *First to fly: How Wilbur and Orville Wright invented the airplane*. New York: Crown Books for Young Readers.

Catlin, D. (n.d.) *The inventa book of mechanisms*. London, UK: Valiant Technology.

DeWeese, B. (1994). *Playground physics: Simple machines*. Monterey, CA: Evan-Moor.

Fleisher, P., & Keeler, P. (1991). *Looking inside: Machines and constructions*. New York: Macmillan.

Friedhoffer, B. (1997). *Physics lab in a hardware store*. Danbury, CT: Watts.

Gardner, R. (1980). *This is the way it works*. New York: Doubleday.

Glass, A. (2003). *The wondrous whirligig: The Wright Brothers first flying machine*. New York: Holiday House.

Hellman, H. (1971). *The lever and the pulley*. Philadelphia: J. B. Lippincott.

Hewitt, P. G. (1998). *Conceptual physics for parents and teachers—Mechanics*. Newburyport, MA: Focus.

Hulls, J. (2003). *Rider in the sky: How an American cowboy built England's first airplane*. New York: Crown Books for Young Readers.

James, E., & Barkin, C. (1975). *The simple facts of simple machines*. New York: Lothrop, Lee & Shepard Books.

Jupo, F. (1972). *The story of things (tools)*. Upper Saddle River, NJ: Prentice Hall.

Lasky, K. (2003). *The man who made time travel*. New York: Farrar, Straus, and Giroux.

Rockwell, A. (1985). *Planes*. New York: Dutton's Children's Books.

Sauvain, P. A. (1992). *Motion*. New York: Macmillan.

Taylor, B. (1990). *Force and movement*. Danbury, CT: Watts.

VanCleave, J. P. (1993). *Janice VanCleave's machines*. Hoboken, NJ: John Wiley.

Weiss, H. (1983). *Machines and how they work*. New York: Harper & Row.

Resource Books

Butzow, C. M., & Butzow, J. W. (1989). *Science through children's literature: An integrated approach*. Englewood, CO: Teacher Ideas Press. (force and movement topics, pp. 197–199)

Cordel, B., Erickson, S., Hillen, J., & Winkelman, G. (Eds.). (1993). *Machine shop*. Fresno, CA: AIMS Education Foundation. (lever, pulley, inclined plane, wheel, and friction activities)

Goldfluss, K., & Sima, P. (1993). *Thematic unit: Inventions*. Huntington Beach, CA: Teacher Created Materials. (thematic invention activities)

Merrell, J. (1994). *Thematic unit: Simple machines*. Huntington Beach, CA: Teacher Created Materials. (thematic simple machine activities)

Shaw, D. G., & Dybdahl, C. S. (1996). *Integrating science and language arts. A sourcebook for K–6 teachers*. Boston: Allyn & Bacon. (wheel and gear topics, pp. 96–100)

Tolman, M., & Morton, J. (1986). *Physical science activities for grades 2–8*. West Nyack, NY: Parker. (simple machine activities, pp. 137–187)

PLANT LIFE

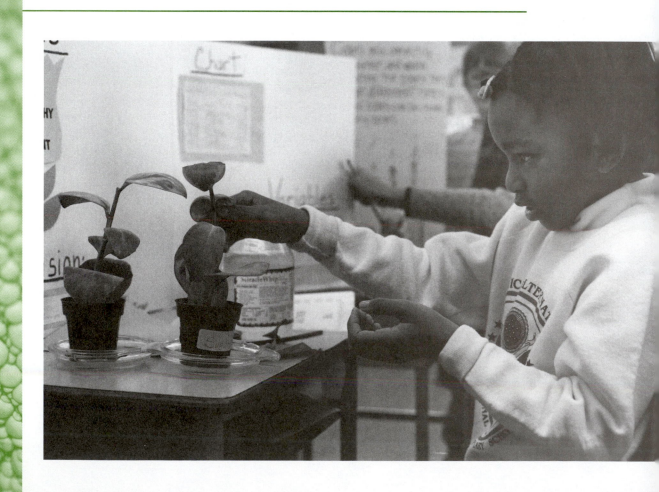

"Chances for open-ended experiments are greater with plants than with any other area of elementary school science." That is what one longtime teacher said, and we agree. At the same time, there is more need for planning ahead and keeping track of activities so that they may be interrelated. Living things take time to grow, and growth rates can seldom be predicted exactly. The most complex and familiar plants we see are those that produce seeds, of which there are two basic groups. One group is the *gymnosperms*. These plants are flowerless; they develop seeds attached to open scales or cones. Evergreens such as pine, hemlock, spruce, juniper, fir, and redwood are examples of gymnosperms. There are about 600 species.

The second and far larger group (about 250,000 species) is the *angiosperms*, or flowering plants. These form their seeds in closed compartments or cases within the flowers.

In this section, we consider seeds and how they grow, how new plants can be started from plant parts, how environmental conditions affect plants, how plant parts work, and how plants respond to their environment. A brief, final section takes up the tiny plantlike organisms called *molds*.

Benchmarks and Standards

Throughout the elementary years, it is important that children build an understanding of biological concepts through direct experiences with living things. Plants are excellent sources for observational activities, classification tasks, and experimentation. A sampling of benchmarks and standards related to the study of plants in the elementary classroom follows:

Sample Benchmarks (AAAS, 1993)
- Plants and animals have features that help them live in different environments. (By Grades K–2, p. 102)
- Plants and animals both need to take in water, and animals need to take in food. In addition, plants need light. (By Grades K–2, p. 119)

Sample Standards (NRC, 1996)
- Each plant or animal has different structures that serve different functions in growth, survival, and reproduction. (By Grades K–4, p. 129)
- Plants and some microorganisms are producers; they make their own food. (By Grades 5–8, pp. 157–158)

SEED-RELATED Inquiry

Seed Parts

Invitation

What is inside a bean seed? Can you draw a picture of how it might look inside? How can you find out about the parts of seeds?

Exploration

1. Soak some bean and corn seeds in water overnight.
2. Use your thumbnail to open a soaked bean seed.

 Teaching Tips Seeds from flowering plants have three things in common: a protective seed cover, a baby plant (embryo), and a food supply. The food nourishes the sprouted embryo as it pushes up through the soil and grows into a young plant. When its food supply is gone, a green plant can make (photosynthesize) its own food from substances in air, water, and soil if light shines on it. In the seeds of some plants, such as the bean and sweet pea, the food supply is located in two seed halves, or *cotyledons*. In the seeds of other plants, such as corn and rice, there is only a single cotyledon; the food supply is located there.

If possible, let older children gather and examine some seeds from evergreen plants such as the pine, hemlock, spruce, fir, juniper, and redwood. They may observe how the seeds are attached to open scales or cones. Have them look up information about the reproductive process of such plants.

Baby plant

Food for the baby plant   Seed cover

Concept Invention

1. What do you notice about your seed?
2. How many different parts do you find?
3. How does the seed feel to you without its cover?
4. What does the seed smell like?
5. Open the corn seed. How is it like the bean seed? How is it different?

Concept Application

Most seeds have a baby plant, a food supply, and a cover. Soak and open other kinds of seeds. In what ways are they alike and different? How well can you describe a seed? Put a seed among three different kinds of seeds. Describe it. Will someone be able to pick it out?

The Growth of Seeds ——————

Invitation

Where do green plants originate? Have you planted seeds? What did you do? How can you plant seeds so they may grow?

Exploration

1. Use a pencil or large nail to poke holes into the carton or cup bottom.
2. Put the carton on a pie pan.
3. Fill the carton almost full with soil.
4. Water the soil slowly until water leaks into the pie pan.
5. Poke a hole in the soil. Make it about as deep as the seed you plant is long.

MATERIALS
• Soil
• Bean seeds soaked overnight in water
• Water
• Paper towel
• Pencil or large nail
• Topless milk carton or paper cup
• Pie pan
• Glass or watering container
• Paper strips
• Paste
• Large sheet of paper
• Sand, sawdust, or different soils for planting seeds
• Salt
• Freezer
• Boiling water
• Seeds (bean, pea, and flower)

6. Put the bean seed into the hole. Cover it with wet soil. Tap the soil down lightly.
7. Water the soil when it feels dry to your touch, but not more than once a day.
8. Measure your growing plant three times a week. Put a strip of paper alongside. Tear off some to match the plant's height. Date the strips and paste them on a large sheet of paper. What can you tell from this plant record?

Concept Invention

1. Experiment with more materials. In what kind of soil will a seed grow best? Try sand, sawdust, or soil from different places; or mix your own soil from some of these.
2. Will a seed live and grow if you water it with saltwater? How much salt can you use? What else might you use to "water" a growing seed?

3. Will a broken or damaged seed grow? Will a seed that was frozen or boiled grow? Will a seed grow if the seed cover is taken off?
4. Does the position of a seed make a difference? For example, what will happen if you plant a seed upside down?

Adapting for Students with Exceptionalities

Avoid excessive watering when growing plants. Set up a detailed schedule with students' names, amounts of water, and how the water is to be measured (predetermined mark on a measuring cup). (See Mastropieri & Scruggs, 2004, for a discussion on activities related to plants in the chapter on science and social studies.)

Concept Application

Some plants grow from seeds; proper conditions are needed for seeds to sprout and grow. Design an activity to see if the same conditions work well for different types of seeds. For example, do pea seeds and bean seeds like the same conditions? How about flower seeds? Do not forget to use a control group with this experiment.

Deep Down Seeds

MATERIALS

- Six sprouted bean seeds
- Soil
- Sticky tape
- Tall, clear jar with straight sides
- Black paper
- Radish seeds

Invitation

How deep can you plant a seed and still have it grow?

Exploration

1. Plant two seeds in soil at the bottom of the jar. Place the seeds next to the sides of the jar so that they can be seen.
2. Add more soil. Plant two seeds in the middle of the jar the same way.
3. Add more soil. Plant two seeds near the top of the jar.
4. Tape black paper around the jar. Remove the paper for a short time each day to observe the seeds. Water the seeds as needed.

Concept Invention

1. Which seeds will have enough food energy to grow to the surface?
2. What happens to the seeds that do not reach the surface?

Adapting for Students with Exceptionalities

Slow-growing plants may lose students' interest. Try substituting Fast Plants® (*http://www.fastplants.org/*) for the bean seeds. (See Mastropieri & Scruggs, 2004, for a discussion on activities related to plants in the chapter on science and social studies.)

Concept Application

What would happen if you planted smaller seeds, like radish seeds? Why are some seeds larger than others?

Where Are the Seeds? ———————

Invitation

In what places are seeds in the soil?

Exploration

1. Line some shoe boxes with plastic bags.
2. Half-fill each shoe box with bare soil from a different place. Try garden soil, soil where weeds grow, and other bare soils.
3. Use a marker to label where each place is on the box.
4. Water the soils so that they are damp.
5. Cover each box with clear kitchen wrap.
6. Leave each box in a warm, well-lighted place for several weeks or more.

Concept Invention

1. In which box do you expect seeds to grow?
2. In which box, if any, did seeds grow?

Concept Application

Would wild plants grow in the exact places from which you took soil? Observe these places from time to time and record your observations.

> **MATERIALS**
> - Shoe boxes
> - Bare soil from outdoor places
> - Clear kitchen wrap
> - Small shovel
> - Plastic bags
> - Marker
> - Water
> - Glass or watering container

SEED-RELATED CONCEPTS

"Where do seeds come from?" is a question curious children may ask when they study flowering plants. Seeds are produced in the *ovary*, in the central part of the flower. As the ovary ripens, its seeds become enveloped either by a fruity pulp, a pod, or a shell, depending on the kind of plant.

Pears and peaches are fruits whose pulp we eat. Beans, peas, and peanuts are examples of seeds enclosed in pods. When we "shell" string beans, lima beans, peas, or peanuts, we are removing these seeds from their pods. Walnuts, pecans, and coconuts have hard outer shells.

Seed Parts ———————

Seeds come in many shapes, colors, and sizes. Still, they have three things in common: a protective seed cover, a baby plant (embryo), and a food supply that nourishes the seed as it pushes up through the soil and grows into a young plant. In the seeds of some plants, such as the bean and sweet pea, the baby plant's food supply is in two seed "leaves," or *cotyledons* (INQ Figure 7–1). In the seeds of other plants, such as corn and rice, there is a single cotyledon; the baby plant's food supply is in there.

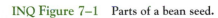

INQ Figure 7–1   Parts of a bean seed.

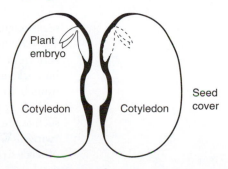

Growth Stages ———————

What happens when a seed grows into a young plant, or *seedling*? INQ Figure 7–2 is an illustration of the growth stages. In A, the seed swells from absorbing

INQ Figure 7–2   Growth stages: from seed to seedling.

moisture from the soil. The coat softens and splits. A tiny root and stem emerge. In B, the upper part of the stem penetrates the soil surface and lifts the folded cotyledons out of the seed cover. In C, the cotyledons and tiny plant leaves unfold. Roots deepen and spread. In D, roots become more extensive. The cotyledons are smaller and shriveled. Nearly all the food supply has been consumed. The plant begins to make its own food through photosynthesis within its maturing leaves. In a short while, the shriveled cotyledons, now useless, will drop off the growing plant. This growth process, from seed to seedling, is called *germination*.

Survival Conditions

Some flowering plants produce thousands of seeds a year. If they all grew into plants, before long there would scarcely be room on the earth for anything else. Fortunately, a variety of factors enable only a small percentage of wild seeds to grow. Birds, insects, bacteria, and other organisms destroy seeds, and unless proper conditions of moisture, temperature, and oxygen are present, seeds remain dormant. After several years in a dormant state, all but a few kinds of seeds lose their potential ability to germinate. These few, however, may not lose this ability for hundreds or even thousands of years.

Weeds are everywhere about us. What makes them so prolific? Perhaps you have noticed that weeds appear at different times during a growing season. They grow in different seasons because the growth requirements of moisture, temperature, and oxygen vary greatly among different kinds of seeds. Of course, this diversity has great survival value.

How Seeds Travel

We know that people plant seeds in gardens. But they do not plant weeds in fields and vacant lots. Nor do they plant seeds in many other places where plants grow. Where do these seeds originate?

Children can learn that seeds travel in several ways. Some are scattered through the actions of animals and people. For example, the sharp hooks or barbs on the cocklebur, burdock, and beggar tick cling to clothing or animal fur (INQ Figure 7–3). Birds eat fleshy fruits but may not digest the hard seeds; the seeds pass out of their bodies some distance away. People throw away fruit pits or watermelon seeds. The wind blows many seeds. Some, such as the goldenrod, milkweed, and dandelion, have "parachutes"; maple tree seeds have "wings." Water can carry seeds from place to place because many seeds float. The capacity of seeds to disperse widely and in different ways is another survival feature.

INQ Figure 7–3 **Some common seeds.**

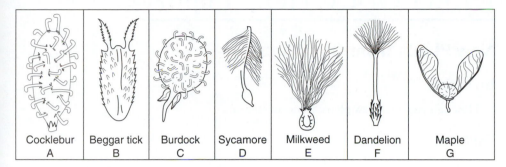

| Cocklebur A | Beggar tick B | Burdock C | Sycamore D | Milkweed E | Dandelion F | Maple G |

Sprouting Seeds ———

It is much less expensive to buy seeds (the kind you eat) at a grocery store than at a seed store even though a smaller percentage will grow. Some easy-to-grow seeds are kidney beans, lima beans, pinto beans, whole green peas, and yellow peas. To ensure that only live, healthy seeds are planted, treat them as follows:

- Soak the seeds in water for several hours to soften them.
- Remove the seeds from the water and drop them into a mixture of one part liquid bleach to eight parts water.
- Take out the seeds immediately after immersing them.

To sprout the treated seeds, first soak several paper towels in water. Fold and place them in an aluminum pie pan or dish. Place the treated seeds on top of the wet towels. Then cover the pan with clear plastic wrap to prevent the water from evaporating.

Inspect the seeds every day. Within several days to a week, many bean or pea seeds will have parts sticking out of their seed covers. These sprouted seeds are alive. They are likely to grow into plants, if planted while moist and cared for properly.

Soil ———

All containers may be filled with garden soil, sand, sawdust, or vermiculite, an inexpensive insulating material of fluffy bits of mica. Only the garden soil will have minerals needed for healthy growth of plants beyond the seedling stage.

Other "soil" materials allow air to circulate around the seed cover and plant roots. They are also more porous in order to protect the plant from excess water. Plants rooted in these materials may be more easily removed, examined, and replanted without serious root damage.

Small holes punched in containers will aid good drainage. Any water runoff can be caught in a saucer placed below. If holes cannot easily be made, as with a glass jar, include 2.5 centimeters (1 inch) of gravel in the jar bottom before adding soil. Water only when the soil surface feels slightly dry.

Instruct students to plant seeds only slightly deeper than the seed length; but always follow instructions on the seed package for seed store varieties. Because it takes energy to push through the soil, a small seed planted too deeply runs out of food before it reaches the surface. Also, keep the soil somewhat loose so that air can get to the roots.

VEGETATIVE REPRODUCTION Inquiry

New Plants from Old Plants

MATERIALS

- Three clear plastic drinking glasses
- Soil
- Sand
- Water
- Knife
- Healthy geranium plant
- Ruler

Invitation

How can you grow new plants from cut stems?

Exploration

1. Cut a strong stem about 13 centimeters (5 inches) long from the plant. Cut just below where leaves join the stem. Trim away all but two or three leaves from the top of the plant.
2. Stick the cutting into a glass half-filled with water. Watch every day for roots to appear.

Concept Invention

1. Some cuttings grow roots faster when placed in sand or soil. Make two more cuttings. Plant one at a slant in a glass containing sand. Plant the other the same way in soil. The stem end should be against the glass. In this way, you will be able to see roots start.
2. Keep the soil or sand damp.
3. In which container does the cutting grow roots fastest?

Caution: Handle the knife yourself or closely supervise its use.

Teaching Tips

Concept Application

Does the thickness of a cutting affect root growth? Does the length of a cutting affect root growth? Record your findings from what is observed.

Sweet Potatoes

Invitation

How can you grow sweet potato vines?

MATERIALS

- Sweet potato
- Wide-mouthed plastic drinking glass
- Three toothpicks
- Water

Exploration

1. Sweet potatoes are the swollen root ends of the sweet potato plant. You can grow beautiful, trailing vines from them indoors.
2. Place the sweet potato into a glass of water, stem end up. (This end has a small scar where it was attached to the plant.) Stick toothpicks in the sides to support it, if needed. Only about one third of the sweet potato should be in the water. Keep the water level the same during this activity.
3. Leave the glass in a warm, dark place until buds and roots grow. Then put it in a sunny or well-lighted place.

Concept Invention

1. How long does it take before you see the first growth?
2. What changes do you notice as the buds and roots grow?
3. What happens to the sweet potato as vines grow?

Concept Application

What are similar plants that will grow vines? Experiment with different types of plants and write your conclusions.

Tapping into New Growth ————————

Invitation

How can you get new growth from taproots?

Exploration

1. Cut off the top 5 centimeters (2 inches) of each carrot. (You may eat the rest.) Trim away any stems and leaves growing from the top.
2. Put gravel into each tumbler. Stick each carrot top about halfway into the gravel.
3. Fill each jar with just enough water to cover the bottom. Leave each tumbler in a warm, well-lighted place. Observe each day.

Concept Invention

1. How long does it take for stems and leaves to grow?
2. What happens to the taproot part as stems and leaves grow?
3. Which, if either, carrot top shows more growth?
4. What will happen if you plant the carrot tops in soil?

Concept Application

Can you get new growth from other taproots? Try a beet, turnip, and parsnip and describe the results.

Teaching Tips | **Caution:** For safety, you may wish to cut the carrots for the children.

VEGETATIVE REPRODUCTION CONCEPTS

Many people think that only seeds produce new flowering plants. Yet, some of the most useful and interesting ways to grow new plants are through the propagation of roots, stems, and even leaves. This technique is called *vegetative reproduction*.

Roots ————————

Consider the orange taproot of the carrot plant (the part we eat). A carrot plant is usually grown from seed in the spring and harvested some months later. If left in the ground, however, all parts above the soil surface die as the weather becomes cold. No growth occurs during this time. As warmer weather approaches, tender shoots grow from the taproot and emerge into the sunlight. These grow into stems and leaves. Some time thereafter, flowers and seeds are produced. Like a seed, a taproot provides the food energy needed for shoots to emerge and grow. Parsnips and beets are other examples of taproots that grow in this way (INQ Figure 7–4).

New plants may be grown from taproots in the classroom by embedding them in moist sand or garden soil. A favorite method of many teachers is to cut off all but the top quarter of a taproot and embed it in a small bowl containing a layer of pebbles and some water. At least half of the root cutting is above water to ensure a sufficient oxygen supply. When sufficient foliage and roots have emerged, cuttings are planted in garden soil for full growth.

Stems

Most ground-cover plants, such as grass, strawberry, and ivy, spread quickly after planting. These plants send out stems or runners that take root, push up shoots, and develop into new plants. These lateral stems may spread above ground, as the strawberry plant and Bermuda grass do, or below ground, as quack grass does. The most persistent weed grasses are of the underground-stem variety, as frustrated lawn growers will testify.

New geranium and begonia plants may be propagated from stem cuttings. Other common plants whose stems grow independently are the coleus, oleander, philodendron, and English ivy. Dipping the ends of stem cuttings in a commercial hormone preparation may start root growth in half the usual time.

Sometimes, on opening a bag of white potatoes, we find some of them beginning to sprout. Usually, this happens when the potatoes have been left undisturbed for a time in a dark, warm place. White potatoes are swollen parts of underground stems, called *tubers*. The dark spots, or "eyes," are buds from which shoots may grow.

Farmers today seldom, if ever, use potato seeds in growing potato crops. Instead, they cut potatoes into several bud-bearing parts and plant these. Each bud grows into a new plant that produces more potatoes.

Occasionally, we see shoots growing from onion bulbs stored in the home pantry. Bulbs, too, are modified stems. All contain thick, fleshy leaves wrapped tightly around a

INQ Figure 7–4   Carrots, parsnips, and beets have taproots.

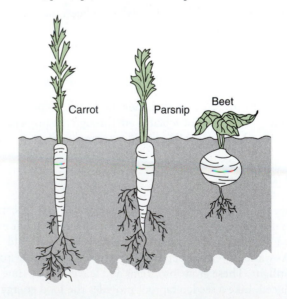

small, immature stem. Tulips and gladioli are typical flowers that may be grown from both bulbs and seeds.

Leaves

Even some leaves may develop into whole plants. Suggestions follow for using an African violet, echeveria, and bryophyllum plant.

Use a fresh African violet leaf with attached *petiole* (leaf stalk). Put the stalk into 2.5 centimeters (1 inch) of water in a drinking glass. For better support of the leaf, use an index card with a hole punched in it placed across the glass rim. Insert the leaf petiole through the hole and into the water. After roots begin to grow, plant the leaf in rich soil. The bryophyllum leaf is sometimes sold in variety stores under the name "magic leaf." To propagate, pin it down flat on damp sand with several toothpicks or straight pins. Tiny plants should grow from several of the notches around the leaf rim.

Why Vegetative Reproduction?

Sometimes children ask, "If plants can grow from seeds, why are the other ways used?" There are several reasons: All of these methods result in whole plants in far less time. Also, some plants cannot be grown from seed (e.g., seedless oranges). In this case, branches of seedless oranges are grafted onto an orange tree grown from seed. But the most important reason for growing plants in other ways besides seeds is quality control. We can never be sure of the results when we plant seeds of some plants. Vegetative reproduction ensures that the new plants will be very much like the parent plant. If large, healthy potatoes are cut up and planted, for instance, we probably can harvest near-identical specimens.

Today, as the demand for plants to feed us and provide energy is on the rise and farmable land is becoming scarcer, vegetative propagation techniques are being used in conjunction with genetic engineering to provide new plants. These *transgenic* plants carry new genes from other species of plants or animals in order to grow better fruit, vegetables, and grains; change flavors; resist disease and insects; or better tolerate herbicides used to kill weeds growing around new plants. For example, an antifreeze protein from a cold-water fish is being used to develop strawberries that can be grown in cold climates (Jefferis, 1999). This growing body of research will provide many new plants to help us meet our energy needs, become healthier, and enjoy tastier foods.

All the foregoing methods of vegetative reproduction are *asexual*. In other words, reproduction does not require involvement of plant sex organs. Certain lower animal-like forms also can reproduce themselves asexually. In another section, we discuss sexual reproduction in flowering plants—that is, how fertile seeds are produced.

ENVIRONMENTAL CONDITIONS Inquiry

How Colored Light Affects Plant Growth

Invitation

Plants need light to grow. But must it be white sunlight? Perhaps plants will grow just as well or better in colored light. What can you do to find out how plants grow in colored light?

Exploration

1. Cut out the bottoms of four shoe boxes. Leave a 2.5-centimeter (1-inch) border on all sides.
2. Cover each cutout bottom with a different color of cellophane. Fasten the sheets with sticky tape.
3. Place the shoe boxes close together, with cellophane sheets facing up, on a healthy patch of lawn, as illustrated. Lift the boxes once each day for 2 weeks to observe the grass. Water the grass as needed but do not mow it.

Teaching Tips

As illustrated, other kinds of plants may be tested with shoe boxes as well. Punch holes in the sides of the boxes for adequate air circulation. The boxes may be slipped off quickly for observing, measuring, and watering the plants.

Cellophane taped over opening

Cardboard end removed

Concept Invention

1. What differences, if any, do you notice each day in the grass under the boxes?
2. How do the grass samples compare in height and color?
3. What kind of a record can you make to keep track of what happens?
4. What color seems best for grass growth?
5. What color seems worst for grass growth?
6. What other colors can you test?
7. How will the grass be affected?

Teaching Tips Some children may also like to try growing plants under artificial light. A gooseneck lamp with a 50-watt bulb works well as a light source. If the bulb is left on 24 hours a day, the children may discover that plant growth slows down.

Adapting for Students with Exceptionalities

Use instructional conversations with rich dialogue as opposed to question-and-answer formats when working with students who have hearing impairments, especially on activities that may involve difficult concepts. Be sure to focus on the concepts and content (e.g., why light is needed for plant growth, why colored light may make a difference in plant growth, the "colors" that white light contains). (See Turnbull, Turnbull, Shank, & Smith, 2004, for a discussion on augmenting instruction of students who have hearing impairments through instructional conversations.)

Concept Application

Plants grow better in natural light than in colored light. How can you test other plants? How will they be affected? Try out your ideas and record the results.

How Saltwater and Other Liquids Affect Plants

Invitation

Many places have too little freshwater to grow plants. So, some people want to use ocean water, which is salty. How do you think saltwater would affect land plants? How can you find out what saltwater does to plants?

Exploration

1. Mix 1 teaspoonful of salt into 0.5 liter (1 pint, or 2 cups) of water.
2. Water one container of plants with only this saltwater.
3. Water a matched container of plants with only freshwater.
4. Observe both sets of plants each day.

MATERIALS

- Two matched containers of healthy young radish plants
- Matched containers of other land plants
- Two measuring cups
- Water
- Iodine-free salt
- Other liquids
- Teaspoon

Teaching Tips

If ocean water is available, it may be used in place of the saltwater mixture. If needed, ocean water may be diluted with freshwater. Steps in the Exploration require two containers with three radish plants each. Steps in the Concept Application require similar containers of different kinds of plants.

Younger children will be able to do the activities if given help in matching plants and otherwise controlling variables.

Concept Invention

1. What changes do you notice from day to day?
2. Keep a record of what you observe.
3. Will the plants live if any salt is in the water?
4. How much can you use?

Concept Application

When watered with saltwater, land plants die or grow poorly. How will other plants be affected by saltwater? What other liquids can be used to water plants? How do you think the plants will be affected?

ENVIRONMENTAL CONDITIONS CONCEPTS

Plants grow and flourish only when the environment provides proper amounts of minerals, water, light, temperature, and—more indirectly—space. Because the classroom is an artificial habitat, or home, for plants, children will need to furnish the conditions the plants need for survival.

Growth Conditions

Children will find that soil-watering requirements for plants are like those for germinating seeds. Excess watering causes plants to die of oxygen deprivation or disease. Not enough watering usually results in droopy, malnourished plants. The absence of vital soil minerals and extremes in temperature also has a weakening, or even fatal, effect on plants.

Crowding of plants is harmful to growth largely because competition deprives individual plants of enough of what they need for good growth. Even the hardiest plants develop to less-than-normal size under crowded conditions.

Green plants need light energy, but not necessarily sunshine, to manufacture their own food. Electric lights may be substituted. Many commercial flower growers take advantage of this fact to regulate the growth rates or blooming times of their flowers to coincide with different holidays. Plants generally grow faster when exposed to light for increased time periods, but overexposure retards growth and delays normal blooming times.

Three Habitats

Even the casual observer can notice that different kinds of plants live in different habitats. Cacti are unlikely to be found in woodlands, and ferns do not ordinarily live in deserts. It may be difficult for us to take children directly to different habitats. It is possible, though, to bring several habitats to the classroom in miniature form.

The terrarium is a managed habitat for small land plants and, if desired, small animals likely to be found with the plants. Three basic kinds are the woodland, marsh, and desert terrariums. Almost any clear, large, glass or plastic container will do for the basic structure. An old aquarium tank is usually best, but a large jar turned on its side will also do. The container should be thoroughly cleaned before use. To make a woodland terrarium, cover the bottom of the container with a 2.5-centimeter (1-inch) layer of pebbles, sand, and bits of charcoal mixed together. This layer will allow drainage, and the charcoal will absorb gases and keep the soil from turning sour. Add to the bottom layer a second layer, about twice as thick, consisting of equal parts of rich garden soil and sand mixed together with a bit of charcoal. Sprinkle water on the ground until moist, but do not leave it wet, as molds may develop.

Dwarf ivy, ferns, liverworts, and lichens are ideal plants. Partridgeberry and mosses provide a nice ground cover, if desired.

After a week or so, the plants should take hold, and a few small animals may be introduced. A land snail, earthworms, a small land turtle, a salamander, or a small frog are suitable for a miniature woodland habitat. A little lettuce will feed the snail or turtle; earthworms get nutrition from the soil. Appropriate foods for frogs and salamanders include small live insects, such as mealworms, flies, sow bugs, and ants. A small, shallow dish pressed into the soil can serve as a water source.

Keep the terrarium covered and out of the sunlight to avoid the buildup of heat. A glass sheet loosely fitted to permit air circulation will help keep high humidity inside, reducing the need to water the soil. Here, too, water will evaporate from the soil, condense on the underside of the glass cover, and fall as "rain" in a miniature water cycle.

To make a marsh terrarium, the soil must be more acidic and damper than in the previous terrarium. Cover the container bottom with pebbles. Add to that a 6-centimeter (2.5-inch) layer of acid soil and peat moss mixed in about equal parts. These materials can be bought at a plant nursery. Suitable plants are the Venus flytrap, sundew, pitcher plant, mosses, and sedges. Appropriate animals include frogs, toads, small turtles, and salamanders. Again, press a small, shallow dish of water flush with the soil surface for the animals. Keep this terrarium covered and in a cool part of the room.

To make a desert terrarium, cover the container bottom with about 3 centimeters (1 inch) of coarse sand. Sprinkle this lightly with water and an equally thick layer of fine sand on top. Get a few small potted cacti or other desert succulents. Bury these so that the pot tops are flush with the sand surface. Sprinkle the plants lightly with water about once a week. Suitable animals are lizards, including the horned toad. Push a partly buried dish of water into the sand for their water source. Mealworms and live insects will do for their food. Place a stick and a few stones in the sand on which the animals may climb or rest. This terrarium may be left uncovered and in the sun.

Terrarium Investigations ————————

A woodland terrarium can be a good source of further investigation for your students. Many terrarium-related activities are suggested in the GEMS *Terrarium Habitats* book (Hosoume & Barber, 1994). For example, investigating and then later adding earthworms to the terrarium will help to introduce the concept of a *decomposer*. A decomposer feeds on and, in turn, breaks down dead plant and animal matter. This action is essential to the terrarium because it recycles the organic nutrients, making them available for the remaining plants to grow in the terrarium or any other ecosystem. You will want to have a hand lens available for the students to look at the earthworms, both inside and outside of the terrarium. It will be surprising to see how students will respond to the chance to investigate earthworms up close.

Another animal that you may introduce to a moist woodland terrarium is the pillbug, a small terrestrial crustacean in the isopod subgroup. Pillbugs breathe through gill-like structures and acquired their name because they roll up in the shape of a pill when agitated or in danger of dehydrating. Students can investigate the anatomy of pillbugs, where they hide out, where they walk, how they move, and other characteristics. A good source of activities for these investigations is *The Pillbug Project* (Burnett, 1992).

A desert terrarium provides a good environment to observe how plants and animals adapt to harsh conditions. Students can investigate where the animals go during the heat of the day or how they eat and drink in the desert environment. In addition to investigations of the cacti, lizards, and other plants and animals that you have in your desert terrarium, you may want to use the AIMS book *Exploring Environments* (Mercier & Hoover, 1999) to study other species of plants and animals that have adapted to desert conditions.

PLANT PART AND FUNCTION Inquiry

Plant Roots

Invitation

What do plant roots look like? What are some of the characteristics?

Exploration

1. Dig up some small weeds from both dry and wet places if possible. Try not to damage the roots. Dig deeply and loosen the soil around each weed. Then slip the shovel under it.
2. Soak the roots in water to remove the soil.
3. Carefully place each plant inside a folded sheet of newspaper. Observe the plant roots in class.

Concept Invention

1. Which plants have a single, large taproot with smaller branching roots?
2. Which plants have branching roots?
3. Can you see tiny root hairs with a hand lens?
4. On what parts of the roots do most appear?

> **Scaffolding for English Learners**
>
> Cultures vary on their use of plants for medicinal purposes. Some parents are very knowledgeable on the effects of various roots, stems, leaves, and flowers of plants. Invite select parents into the classroom to discuss plant parts and functions.

Concept Application

What other differences among the roots do you notice? What similarities have you observed? Where would you most likely find a lot of plants in the environment?

How Water Rises in Plant Stems

Invitation

We usually water the roots of a plant. How, then, does water in the roots get to the leaves? How can you use a celery stalk to study how water travels in plant stems?

Exploration

1. Put a few drops of red coloring into a glass of water. This will help you see how the water moves through the stalk.
2. Use a knife to cut off the lower end of the stalk at a slant.

MATERIALS

- Places where weeds grow
- Newspaper
- Small shovel
- Hand lens
- Pail of water

MATERIALS

- White celery stalk (fresh, with many leaves)
- Other celery stalks
- Red food coloring or water-soluble ink
- Other food colorings
- Two glasses of water
- Liquids other than water
- Knife
- Ruler
- White flower with long stem (such as a carnation)

3. Put the stalk into the colored water right away.
4. Leave the stalk where it will get bright light.

Concept Invention

1. Check the stalk every hour. How far does water rise in 1 hour? How far does water rise in more than 1 hour? Make a record of what you see each time.
2. After a few hours, or the next day, remove the stalk. Cut the stalk across near the bottom. What do you notice about this cutoff part?
3. Cut the stalk the long way. What do you notice? Can you find any long colored tubes?
4. Use other celery stalks for experiments. What can you do to change how fast the water rises? For example: Does the number of leaves on the stalk make a difference? Does the amount of light make a difference? Does wind make a difference? Will using liquids other than water make a difference? Have a race with someone to see whose celery stalk wins.
5. How can you prevent water from rising in the stalk if it stands in water?

Teaching Tips

Sometimes the water-conducting tubes in a celery stalk or flower stem become clogged. To open the tubes, make a fresh diagonal cut across the stalk or stem base. Immerse it quickly to keep air bubbles from forming in the tubes.

Concept Application

Stems conduct liquids from one part of a plant to another. Light, wind, and the condition and number of attached leaves affect the conduction rate. Get a white carnation with a long stem, or some other white flower. How can you make it a colored flower? Suppose you split the flower stem partway up and stand each half in a different color of water. What do you think will happen to the flower?

The Properties of Leaves ───────

Invitation

Have you ever collected different kinds of leaves? There are more than 300,000 different kinds! How can you tell one leaf from another? What do you look for? How can you describe the properties of leaves?

Exploration

1. Size: How large is the leaf? Compare their sizes with the sizes of other things in the classroom.
2. Shape: What is the shape of the leaf? Some are oval; some are almost round. Others are shaped like a heart, a star, or another figure.
3. Color: What is the color of the leaf? Most fresh leaves are green, but some are darker or lighter than others. Some leaves have other colors.
4. Veins: Veins are the small tubes that carry liquids throughout the leaf. How do the veins look? In some leaves, they are side by side. In others, the veins look like many Vs in a row with a main center vein. Some leaves have several long veins with Vs. In a few leaves, veins cannot be seen.
5. Edges: What do the leaf edges look like? Some are smooth. Some edges look like saw teeth. Others are wavy. An example of each is shown in the drawings.
6. Feel: How does the leaf feel to you? Is it rough? Is it smooth? Is it waxy? Is it hairy? Is it slippery? Is it sticky?
7. Smell: What does the leaf smell like? Some leaves may not have a noticeable smell.

MATERIALS

- Six or more different kinds of leaves
- Partner
- Pencil and paper

Important: To further the processes of careful observation and communication, use only leaves that are roughly similar in this investigation. You want different kinds of leaves, but leaves that are grossly and obviously different from others will defeat the purpose of the investigation. It is best to do this investigation with fresh, unblemished leaves, such as weed leaves. Copy leaves on a copy machine and have children cut them out to use in class if needed.

Concept Invention

1. Play a game with a partner. Sort your leaves into two groups according to one property (shape, veins, etc.). Let your partner study your groups. Can your partner tell which property you used to sort your leaves? Try other properties. Take turns with your partner in this sorting game.
2. How well can you describe your leaves? Can you make a chart that someone else can use to identify them? Make a chart of all the properties you observe about your leaves. Label your leaves in A, B, C order. Try to remember which is which.

Leaf	Size	Shape	Color	Veins	Edges	Feel	Smell
A							
B							
C							
D							

3. Give your completed chart and your leaves to your partner. They should be out of order, so your partner must study your chart to tell which leaf is A, B, C, and so on. Which chart descriptions were helpful? Which confused your partner? How could you make these descriptions clearer?

Concept Application

Leaves vary in size, shape, color, texture, vein pattern, and other properties; no two leaves are identical. Describe how you think scientists may classify leaves.

How Leaves Lose Water

Invitation

A plant usually takes in more water than it can use. What do you think happens to the extra water? How can you find out if water is lost from leaves?

Exploration

1. Fill one glass almost full with water.
2. Use scissors to make a small hole in the center of a piece of cardboard.
3. Cover the glass with the cardboard.
4. Take a fresh leaf. Use a knife to cut off at a slant the tip of its stalk.
5. Quickly put the stalk into the hole in the cardboard.
6. Seal around the hole with petroleum jelly.
7. Put another glass upside down on top of the cardboard.
8. Leave the glass in sunlight for several hours.

Seal hole w
petroleum je

Water

MATERIALS

- Fresh leaf with stalk
- Water
- Four matched plastic water glasses
- Petroleum jelly
- Knife
- Paper towel
- Two cardboard squares
- Scissors

Concept Invention

1. Do water drops form inside the top glass? Where do you think they originate?
2. Maybe water drops would appear in the glass without the leaf. How could you find out?
3. What affects how many water drops appear—leaf size? the kind of leaf? the freshness of the leaf? Does the amount of light affect how many drops appear? How can you find out?

Concept Application

Plants lose water through tiny openings in their leaves; the amount of water lost depends on several conditions. From which side does the leaf give off water—the top? the bottom? both sides? Describe how you could use petroleum jelly to find out. Try out your idea and keep a record of your results. Compare your record with the records of others.

Teaching Tips

Many tiny openings, called *stomata* (singular, *stoma*), are found in a green leaf, where gases enter and exit during the leaf's food-making process. Water, in the form of water vapor, also releases through the stomata. In this activity, the released water vapor is trapped by the plastic cover. It then condenses into visible water drops on the plastic. In land plants, stomata are usually found in the bottom leaf surface. Water loss varies with weather conditions and the size and kind of leaf.

Leaf Rubbings

Invitation

How can you make leaf rubbings?

Exploration

1. Place tissue paper over a fresh leaf.
2. Rub a crayon back and forth on it. A beautiful vein pattern will appear.
3. Try different colors and leaves.

Concept Invention

1. Play a matching game with someone.
2. Can your partner match each of your patterns with the right leaf? Can you match your partner's patterns and leaves?

Concept Application

What does your leaf rubbing tell you about your leaf? How can you use your patterns to make holiday or greeting cards?

MATERIALS

- Different leaves with thick veins
- Tissue paper
- Crayons
- Construction paper
- Partner

A Budding Activity

Invitation

How can you learn about plant buds?

Exploration

1. Find a low tree or bush with fallen leaves.
2. Look for small branches or twigs that have buds.
3. Observe just above where each leaf was attached to the twig or stem.
4. Cut off a few twigs that have buds. (Ask permission first.)

MATERIALS

- Small branches and twigs from plants
- Thin nail
- Pruning shears or knife
- Jar of water

The beginning of spring is a good time to collect twigs for budding.

Concept Invention

1. How are the buds arranged on the twigs?
2. What patterns, if any, do you notice?

Concept Application

Pick apart one or two buds with a thin nail. How can you describe the buds? Which of the remaining buds will grow leaves? To see, stick the twig into a jar of water. Change the water every 2 or 3 days and record your findings.

Inside a Flower ———————

MATERIALS

- Several flowers
- Straight pin
- Newspaper
- Hand lens

Invitation

What is inside flowers?

Exploration

1. Bend back a few petals to see inside the flower, as shown.
2. Remove one of the stamens. Pick apart the anther, the part on the end. Can you see any dustlike pollen?
3. What color is it?
4. How does the pollen look under a hand lens?
5. Examine the pistil end.
6. What does it look like? Is it sticky when touched?
7. Carefully use a pin to slit open the pistil's thicker end.
8. Can you see any baby seeds inside? What do they look like?

 Florists are usually willing to donate to schools flowers that are unable to be sold.

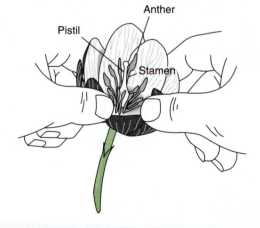

Concept Invention

1. Examine other flowers in the same way.
2. How are other flowers alike?
3. How are other flowers different?

Concept Application

Draw a diagram of the inside of one of the flowers you explored. How does it compare to the flower illustrated?

PLANT PART AND FUNCTION CONCEPTS

Children are usually surprised to learn that, besides fruits and vegetables, all the meat they eat has originally been derived from green plants. Flesh-eating animals depend on plant-eating animals. This is true in the ocean as well as on land. Everything alive basically depends on food synthesized from raw materials in the leaves of green plants.

A plant itself depends on the proper working of its several parts to produce this food. In this section, we examine how these parts work. Let's begin with plant roots.

Roots

The experience of weeding a garden makes us very conscious of one function of roots: They anchor plants. We also know that food storage in roots enables plants to survive when food making cannot occur. Another function of roots is the absorption of soil water.

Plants that are transplanted sometimes grow poorly for a while, or even die. This is usually the result of damage done to the tiny, very delicate root hairs that grow from the older root tissue (INQ Figure 7–5). It is the root hairs, not the older fibrous material, that absorbs all of the water for the plant.

A single plant may have billions of root hairs, enough to stretch hundreds of kilometers if laid end to end. If laid side by side in rows, they would take up the floor area of an average-size home. Root hairs are so small that they are able to grow in the tiny spaces between soil particles and make direct contact with water and air trapped within the soil. Root growth takes place largely at the tip of a root. A tough root cap protects the sensitive growing portion as it punches through the soil. Because soil is abrasive, the root cap tissue is continually worn off and replaced by new tissue.

Stems

Water absorbed by the roots goes into the stems, through which it is transported by narrow tubes to all parts of the plant. Dissolved minerals in the water are deposited within the cells of these parts. When water reaches the leaves, some of it evaporates into the air.

Exactly how does this continual movement of water happen in the plant? This process was a mystery until recent times. Modern molecular theory gives an answer. As you know, molecules that are alike have an attractive force that binds them together (cohesion). These molecules may also be attracted to unlike molecules (adhesion). The thin tubes that transport water in a plant run from root to stem to leaf. Adhesion of water molecules to the tube walls helps support the narrow water column. Cohesion causes the water molecules to stick together. As water molecules evaporate into the air, they "tug" slightly at the molecules below because of cohesive attraction. Because of cohesion, all the other molecules rise in a kind of chain reaction unless an air bubble separates some molecules to a distance beyond their effective cohesive attraction.

INQ Figure 7–5   A seedling has many root hairs.

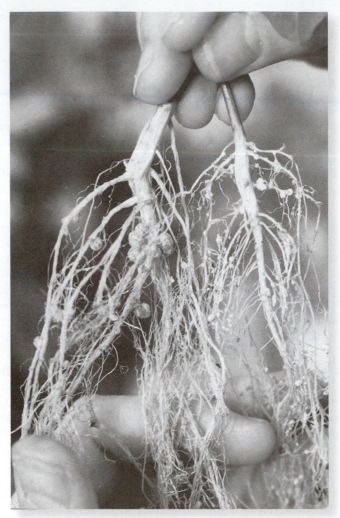

Leaves

A leaf seems thin and simple in structure from the outside. Yet, the intricate mechanisms within it, which produce the world's food supply, have never been fully duplicated by scientists.

Inside the leaf cells is a green-pigmented chemical, chlorophyll. Chlorophyll enables a leaf to chemically combine carbon dioxide from air with water to form a simple sugar. The energy needed to power this chemical synthesis in the leaf comes from sunlight, which is absorbed by the chlorophyll. *Photosynthesis*, as the process is called, literally means "to put together with light."

From the sugar that the leaves manufacture, the plant's cells make starch, which may be stored in all parts of the plant. With additional compounds received from the soil and through soil bacteria, plant cells can manufacture proteins and vitamins.

Carbon dioxide is taken up in photosynthesis, and oxygen is released as a waste product. But when a plant consumes the food stored in its cells, it takes up oxygen and gives off

INQ Figure 7–6   Guard cells regulate the stomata in a leaf.

carbon dioxide as a waste product. Fortunately for us, much more oxygen is released to the air through photosynthesis than is used by plants in oxidizing their stored food. In fact, green plants are the chief source of the world's current oxygen supply.

How do these gases enter and leave the leaf? Thousands of microscopic openings, called *stomata*, may be found in a green leaf. In land plants, these are largely, but not exclusively, located in the leaf's underside. Each stoma is surrounded by two special cells that regulate the size of the opening (INQ Figure 7–6). As water moves into and out of the guard cells, their shape changes slightly, opening and closing the opening (stoma) between them. Water in the leaf evaporates into the air through the stomata, a process called *transpiration*. Regulation of these openings has great survival value. In dry spells and at night, the stomata stay closed, thereby preventing any appreciable loss of water.

Interestingly, most photosynthesis on the earth happens in the ocean within uncountable numbers of microscopic algae that float on and near the water's surface. We have not yet learned how to use the tremendous food supply this source potentially affords to a hungry world.

Flowers

Many people value flowers because of their beauty. But for flowering plants, flowers have a more vital function. They are the only means by which species can naturally survive. The flower is the reproductive system of a flowering plant. Its two principal organs are the *pistil*, which contains unfertilized egg cells, and *stamens*, which produce dustlike pollen cells (see INQ Figure 7–7).

When a pollen grain lands on the sticky end of a pistil, a tube begins to grow that "eats" its way down to the pistil base, or ovary. There, it joins onto an egg cell, or *ovule*. A sperm cell released from the pollen grain travels down the tube and unites with the ovule. Other ovules in the ovary may be fertilized by additional pollen in the same way.

The ovules, now fertilized, begin growing into seeds. The entire ovary begins to swell as a fleshy fruit begins to grow around the seeds. As the ovary becomes larger, parts of the flower drop off. Finally, a whole fruit forms. In the apple, for example, the ovary is enveloped by a stem part that swells up around it. The next time you eat an apple, look at the core end opposite the fruit stem. Quite likely, the tiny dried-up remains of the pistil and stamens will be visible.

It is best to examine single flowers, such as tulips and sweet peas, with children rather than composite flowers, such as daisies and sunflowers. The centers of composite types con-

INQ Figure 7–7   Parts of a flower.

sist of many tiny flowers, each complete with pistil and stamens that are very minute. With these parts not readily observable, a description of the parts of a flower may be confusing to younger children.

Pollination ———————

Self-pollination happens when pollen from a flower's own stamens fertilizes its ovules. *Cross-pollination* occurs when pollen from another flower performs this function. Pollen must be from the same type of flower, however, for fertilization to take place.

Much pollination depends on gravity, as when pollen simply falls from tall stamens onto a shorter pistil; or pollen may fall from a flower high up on a stem to one lower down. Insects are also primary distributors of pollen. As they sip nectar from flowers, pollen grains rub off onto their bodies. When the insects visit other flowers, these grains may become dislodged. It is interesting to note that brightly colored and fragrant flowers are visited by the most insects. Wind is also an important distributor of pollen. In spring, the air contains billions of pollen grains, bringing pollination to plants and hay fever to many people.

Life Cycles ———————

Many garden flowers and vegetables grow from seeds, then blossom, produce seeds, and die in one growing season. These are known as *annuals*. Examples are petunias, zinnias, beans, and tomatoes. Those that live two seasons are *biennials*. Examples are hollyhocks, forget-me-nots, carrots, and turnips. Plants that live more than two growing seasons are *perennials*. Trees and most shrubs fit into this classification.

ADAPTATION AND SURVIVAL **Inquiry**

Plants and Gravity

Invitation

How does gravity affect a growing plant?

Exploration

1. Line the inside of a glass with a wet, folded paper towel.
2. Crumple and stuff some towels inside the lined glass. These will hold the first towel in place.
3. Put a soaked radish seed between the glass and the first towel. The seed should be in the middle of the glass.
4. Pour about 2.5 centimeters (1 inch) of water into the glass.
5. Observe the seed in the glass every day.
6. Wait until the seed sprouts, grows leaves, and roots. Then pour out what water is left. Cover the glass with plastic wrap to keep the towel lining moist.
7. Tip over the glass onto one side.

Concept Invention

1. What happens to the upper stem of the plant over the next few days?
2. What happens to the roots?
3. What will happen if you tip over the glass onto the opposite side?

> ### MATERIALS
> - Paper towels
> - Water
> - Soaked radish seed
> - Plastic drinking glass
> - Plastic kitchen wrap

Scaffolding for English Learners

The English as a Second Language (ESL) Standards of the Teachers of English to Speakers of Other Languages (TESOL) organization recognize that upon entry to school, English learners must acquire an additional language and culture and learn the English language competencies that are characteristic of native English speakers. As you complete the geotropic and phototropic activities, think about how you are addressing these standards. We know that language acquisition takes place "during activities that are of a cognitive or intellectual nature where learners have opportunities to become skilled in using language for reasoning and mastery of challenging new information" (ESL Standards Introduction, TESOL, 1997). Are you providing students opportunities to use English as they interact with these activities? Do you provide feedback on their language use? (See the *http://www.tesol.org* weblink for the text of the standards.)

Concept Application

Predict what would happen if you again turned the glass after a few more days. Record your prediction. Try tipping the glass to check your prediction. Was your prediction correct?

Growing to the Light ———

MATERIALS

- Small and large paper cups
- Bean seeds
- Soil
- Water
- Pencil

Invitation

How can you make a plant grow toward the light?

Exploration

1. Plant one or two bean seeds in a small paper cup of soil. Water the plant as needed.
2. Wait until leaves appear.
3. Use a pencil to punch a hole into the side of the large paper cup.
4. Cover the small cup with the large cup. Uncover it briefly when you need to water the plant.
5. Leave the cups in a well-lighted place. Be sure the cup hole faces the light.

Concept Invention

1. What do you notice after a few days?
2. What do you think would happen if you turned the plant around? Try it. (Be sure the cup hole faces the light.)

Concept Application

Can you grow a plant in total darkness? Record your prediction. Try to grow a plant in a dark closet. Describe what happens.

ADAPTATION AND SURVIVAL CONCEPTS

Adaptation ———

If you were asked to invent a plant, what adaptive features would you want it to have for survival value? Whatever your design, it would be wise to have your plant regulate itself to some extent according to its needs.

Assume that it has the same needs as other plants. Because it requires water, and because water soaks down into the soil, you would want your plant's roots to grow downward. But what if the soil below the roots contained no water? You would want your plant to have roots that could overcome the pull of gravity and grow toward a water source, even if the source were to one side or above the roots.

Because your plant would need light, you would want the stem to have the ability to grow toward a light source. At the same time, it would be desirable to design the leaf stalk to give the leaf maximum exposure to sunlight. An efficient stalk should be able to grow longer if another leaf blocks its light. The stalk might also turn its leaf perpendicular to the sun's rays as the sun appears at different positions in the sky. Most green plants respond to gravity, water, light, and touch. These responses to environmental stimuli are called plant *tropisms*. Let's see why they happen.

Tropisms ———

INQ Figure 7–8 shows a radish seedling growing on wet blotting paper inside a glass. The glass has been placed on its side for 24 hours. Notice that the seedling shoot, or stem, is beginning to curve upward although the root is starting to grow downward. Both reactions are responses to gravity.

INQ Figure 7–8 Seedling shoots curve upward and roots grown downward almost as soon as sprouting occurs.

Why the opposite directions? Check the magnified sections of the seedling. Gravity concentrates plant hormones (auxins) all along the bottom cells from the beginning of the stem to the root tip. The cells along the bottom of the stem are stimulated by the hormones to grow faster than cells above. Growth of these cells is fastest by the stem tip (see INQ figure 7-8, left inset). As these bottom cells elongate, the stem begins to curve upward. Root cells, however, are much more sensitive than stem cells. So, the concentration of hormones along the bottom root cells has the opposite effect; it inhibits cell growth. Top cells are least affected and elongate faster, so the root tip begins to curve downward. Cell growth is fastest by the tip.

Geotropism, or the plant's response to gravity, is only one of many reactions of a plant to its environment. Hydrotropism is the plant's response to water. Generally it is the increased growth of roots in soil as a response to increased moisture. Scientists have observed that roots that happen to grow into an area of moist soil will grow more and branch more than roots that happen to grow into a dry area. Chemotropism, or a plant's ability to grow roots toward needed nutrients in the environment, is a subject of controversy in the scientific community.

Phototropism can be defined as a plant's movement to (positive tropism) or away from (negative tropism) a light source. When the light source is sunlight, the plant's response is called heliotropism. Plants that require sunlight will turn leaves around to grow toward the light. As with the case of geotropism, this response is driven by the hormone auxin. On the side of a plant facing the light, the auxin is inactivated and only the side away from the light elongates and continues to grow. The result is the plant tends to bend toward the light. Alternatively, shade plants will use this mechanism to turn their leaves away from bright light.

Charles Darwin (1989) is credited with demonstrating that the growing tips of plants bend toward a light source. Related to phototropism, scientists have also observed that vine tips will move slowly along the ground toward vertical objects by responding to the stimulus of the darkest sector of the nearby horizon. This response is called skototropism, or growing toward darkness. This response is widely used in vines of the tropical rain forests. Vines must grow away from the dim light and into darkness until they reach a tree trunk where they can grow upward to reach full sunlight.

Thigmotropism is another tropism in which contact with a solid or a rigid surface is the orienting factor for the plant. Haptotropism is a response of an organism to stimulation by touch or contact. Since vines depend on other plants or surfaces for support, there is a tendency of the vine to respond to touch or contact with such supports. In this case, vines such as the sweet pea or Boston ivy will attach specialized tips of leaves known as *tendrils* to continue their growth. Another example of the response to touch is found in the sticky hairs of a sundew plant, which bend around an insect when it comes into contact with them.

Tropistic responses seem to be the result of plant hormones that concentrate in various parts of the plant. As we have seen, this difference causes some cells to grow faster than others. Such responses can happen only in growing tissue.

Survival and Environment

The survival of plant (and animal) species is more than a matter of properties the organism inherits by chance. The environment also plays a part because it is continually changing.

For example, a long dry spell will favor plants with small, bad-tasting leaves and deep roots. Why? Large-leafed plants will lose too much water to survive. Shallow-rooted plants will not be able to tap moisture deep down. Plants with tasty leaves will be eaten first by hungry, thirsty animals.

MOLDS AND FUNGI Inquiry

How Molds Grow

Invitation

On what things have you seen molds? How did the molds look? How can you make a mold garden?

Exploration

1. Fill a large glass jar about one-third full with sand.
2. Put the jar down on its side. Shake the jar so that the sand settles evenly.
3. Place a flattened piece of clay under the jar to keep it from rolling.
4. Use a spoon to sprinkle some water on the sand to make it damp.
5. Put different objects that might mold on the sand.
6. Screw the lid on the jar. Do not remove it.
7. Leave the jar where you can observe it each day.

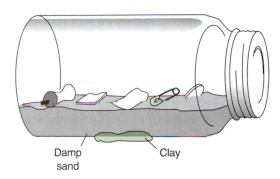

Damp sand   Clay

MATERIALS

- Aluminum foil
- Large pickle jar with lid
- Sand
- Baby food jars with lids
- Water
- Bread slice
- Hand lens
- Small pieces of different foods
- Tissue paper
- Clay
- Spoon
- Medicine dropper

Concept Invention

1. On which objects do you think molds will grow?
2. Which objects will not mold?
3. Which do you think will be covered by molds first?
4. Which do you think will be covered by molds last? Keep a record of your results.

Concept Application

Some molds grow well under dark, moist, and warm conditions. Try some experiments. How can you get a fresh piece of bread to mold? Keep the bread inside a baby food jar (or plastic bag). Keep the lid on each jar after starting each experiment. Is water needed for molds to grow on bread? If so, how much water is needed? Fresh bread may contain some moisture. How can you start with dry bread? Will bread molds grow better in the dark or the light? How about dim light? How can you prevent mold from growing on a piece of bread? What other experiments would you like to try?

 Teaching Tips

For bread experiments, try to get the white home-baked kind or store bread without preservatives. Commercial bread often contains a mold-inhibiting chemical called sodium propionate.

Caution: The molds or other organisms in this investigation are typically harmless. Play it safe, however, by having children (a) keep all moldy materials covered, (b) wash their hands if they touch a mold, (c) avoid sniffing molds, (d) avoid growing molds in soil samples, and (e) dispose of all used, still-closed containers in a tightly sealed bag.

MOLDS AND FUNGI CONCEPTS

In recent years, growing molds has become popular in elementary science programs. It offers students many chances to experiment with variables at several levels.

Molds are a subgroup of a broader group of organisms called *fungi*. Some common examples of other fungi are mushrooms, mildews, puffballs, and yeasts. Molds will grow on a wide variety of animal and plant materials and some synthetic materials.

Tiny, seedlike spores from molds are found in the air almost anywhere. When the spores settle on a substance, they may grow. Molds get the nutrients they need to live from the materials on which they grow. Unlike the green plants, molds and other fungi cannot manufacture their own food.

Molds grow under a wide variety of conditions. But those found commonly in classrooms are most likely to thrive when their environment is dark, moist, and warm.

References

American Association for the Advancement of Science (AAAS). (1993). *Benchmarks for science literacy*. New York: Oxford University Press.

Burnett, R. (1992). *The pillbug project: A guide to investigation*. Arlington, VA: National Science Teachers Association.

Darwin, C. (1989). *The power of movement in plants* (Reprint ed.). New York: New York University Press.

Hosoume, K., & Barber, J. (1994). *Terrarium habitats*. Berkeley, CA: Great Explorations in Math and Science.

Jefferis, D. (1999). *Cloning: Frontiers of genetic engineering*. New York: Crabtree.

Mastropieri, M., & Scruggs, T. E. (2004). *The inclusive classroom: Strategies for effective instruction* (4th ed.). Upper Saddle River, NJ: Merrill/Prentice Hall.

Mercier, S., & Hoover, E. (1999). *Exploring environments*. Fresno, CA: AIMS Educational Foundation.

National Research Council (NRC). (1996). *National science education standards*. Washington, DC: National Academy Press.

Turnbull, R., Turnbull, A., Shank, M., & Smith, S. J. (2004). *Exceptional lives: Special education in today's schools* (4th ed.). Upper Saddle River, NJ: Merrill/Prentice Hall.

Selected Trade Books: Plant Life

For Younger Children

Brown, R. (2001). *Ten seeds*. New York: Knopf/Random House Children's Books.

Busch, P. (1979). *Cactus in the desert*. New York: Thomas Y. Crowell.

Challand, H. (1986). *Plants without seeds*. Danbury, CT: Childrens Press.

Cole, J. (1995). *The magic school bus meets the rot squad: A book about decomposition*. New York: Scholastic.

Cole, J. (1995). *The magic school bus plants seeds: A book about how living things grow*. New York: Scholastic.

Cole, J. (1996). *The magic school bus gets eaten: A book about food chains*. New York: Scholastic.

Gibbins, G. (1991). *From seed to plant*. New York: Holiday House.

Gibbins, G. (1998). *Marshes and swamps*. New York: Holiday House.

Goodman, S. E. (2001). *Seeds, stems, and stamens: The ways plants fit into their world*. Brookfield, CT: Millbrook Press.

Heller, R. (1999). *The reasons for a flower*. Ossining, NY: Paper Star.

Kirkpatrick, R. K. (1985). *Look at seeds and weeds*. Austin, TX: Raintree.

Kuchalla, S. (1982). *All about seeds*. New York: Troll Associates.

Lauber, P. (1981). *Seeds: Pop, stick, glide*. New York: Crown.

Miner, O. I. (1981). *Plants we know*. Danbury, CT: Childrens Press.

Moncure, J. B. (1990). *What plants need*. Plymouth, MN: Child's World.

Moss, M. (2000). *This is the tree*. Lajolla, CA: Kane/Miller Book Publishers.

Orr, R. (1995). *Nature cross-sections*. New York: Dorling Kindersley.

Penn, L. (1986). *Wild plants and animals*. Torrance, CA: Good Apple.

Pfeffer, W. (1997). *A log's life*. New York: Simon & Schuster.

Posada, M. (2000). *Dandelions: Stars in the grass*. Minneapolis, MN: Carolrhoda Books/Lerner.

Schories, P. (1996). *Over under in the garden: An alphabet book*. New York: Farrar, Straus & Giroux.

Selsam, M. E., & Hunt, J. (1977). *A first look at flowers*. New York: Walker.

Silverstein, S. (1964). *The giving tree*. New York: Harper & Row.

Taylor, B. (1991). *Growing plants*. Danbury, CT: Watts.

Tresselt, A. (1992). *The gift of a tree*. New York: Lothrop, Lee & Shepard Books.

Webster, V. (1982). *Plant experiments*. Danbury, CT: Childrens Press.

For Older Children

Bates, J. (1991). *Seeds to plants: Projects with botany*. Danbury, CT: Watts.

Cochrane, J. (1987). *Plant ecology*. Danbury, CT: Watts.

Coldrey, J. (1987). *Discovering flowering plants*. Danbury, CT: Watts.

Conway, L. (1980). *Plants*. Torrance, CA: Good Apple.

Conway, L. (1986). *Plants and animals in nature*. Torrance, CA: Good Apple.

Gallant, R. A. (1991). *Earth's vanishing forests*. New York: Macmillan.

Hogner, D. C. (1977). *Endangered plants*. New York: Thomas Y. Crowell.

Holley, B. (1986). *Plants and flowers*. Cincinnati: Penworthy.

Lambert, M. (1983). *Plant life*. Danbury, CT: Watts.

Leutscher, A. (1984). *Flowering plants*. Danbury, CT: Watts.

Marcus, E. (1984). *Amazing world of plants*. New York: Troll Associates.

Patent, D. H. (2003). *Plants on the trail with Lewis and Clark*. New York: Clarion Books.

Penn, L. (1987). *Plant ecology*. Danbury, CT: Watts.

Pratt, K. (1992). *A walk in the rainforest*. Nevada City, CA: Dawn.

Ryden, H. (2001). *Wildflowers around the year*. New York: Clarion Books.

Sabin, L. (1985). *Plants, seeds, and flowers*. New York: Troll Associates.

Taylor, K., & Burton, J. (1993). *Forest life*. New York: Dorling Kindersley.

Resource Books

American Forest Foundation, & Western Regional Environmental Education Council. (1995). *Project learning tree*. Washington, DC: Author.

Butzow, C. M., & Butzow, J. W. (1989). *Science through children's literature: An integrated approach*. Englewood, CO: Teacher Ideas Press. (tree topics on pp. 49–54; seed topics on pp. 55–60)

Butzow, C., & Butzow, J. (1999). *Exploring the environment through children's literature: An integrated approach (through children's literature)*. Englewood, CO: Teacher Ideas Press. (hands-on environment activities)

Echols, J. C., & Kopp, J. (1993). *Tree homes*. Berkeley, CA: Great Explorations in Math and Science. (appreciation for trees)

Fredericks, A. D., Meinbach, A. M., & Rothlein, L. (1993). *Thematic units: An integrated approach to teaching science and social studies*. New York: HarperCollins. (plant topics on pp. 123–131)

Hillen, J., & Hoover, E. (Eds.). (1990). *Primarily plants*. Fresno, CA: AIMS Education Foundation.

LeCroy, B., & Holder, B. (1994). *Bookwebs: A brainstorm of ideas for the primary classroom*. Englewood, CO: Teacher Ideas Press. (seed activity on p. 69)

Malnor, B., & Malnor, C. (1998). *A teacher's guide to a walk in the rainforest*. Nevada City, CA: Dawn.

Mercier, S., Richmond, B., Mitchell, D., Hoover, E., & Wagner, B. V. (1999). *Exploring environments*. Fresno, CA: AIMS Education Foundation. (plant interactions with the environment)

Shaw, D. G., & Dybdahl, C. S. (1996). *Integrating science and language arts. A sourcebook for K–6 teachers*. Boston: Allyn & Bacon. (plant topics on pp. 60–62)

Wilson, J., Cordel, B., & Hillen, J. (Eds.). (1995). *Magnificent microworld adventures*. Fresno, CA: AIMS Education Foundation.

Winkleman, G., & Hillen, J. (Eds.). (1995). *The budding botanist*. Fresno, CA: AIMS Education Foundation.

Animal Life

Can a gnat have anything in common with an elephant? Despite their enormous diversity, all animals share certain common needs and physical properties. By carefully observing how animals are formed, we can place them into groups with common properties. These groups enable us to learn many of the interesting adaptations of animals without having to study each group member.

This section discusses animals with backbones, animals without backbones, and interactions of living things with each other and their environment, or ecology. But right now, let's briefly consider some ways to classify animals.

Benchmarks and Standards

Elementary students place animals high on their list of topics they are most curious about and want to explore further. Animals provide basic understandings of interrelationships, habitats, cycles, structures, and functions. Many concepts are related to animals, the following of which are provided as examples of basic benchmarks and standards:

Sample Benchmarks (AAAS, 1993)

- A lot can be learned about plants and animals by observing them closely, but care must be taken to know the needs of living things and how to provide for them in the classroom. (By Grades K–2, p. 15)
- All living things are composed of cells, from just one to many millions, whose details usually are visible only through a microscope. Different body tissues and organs are made up of different kinds of cells. (By Grades 6–8, p. 112)

Sample Standards (NRC, 1996)

- Organisms have basic needs. For example, animals need air, water, and food. (By Grades K–4, p. 129)
- Millions of species of animals, plants, and microorganisms are alive today. (By Grades 5–8, p. 158)

CLASSIFICATION OF ANIMALS Inquiry

Animal Classification

MATERIALS

- Computer with Internet access and a printer
- Scissors
- Tape
- Newsprint end rolls (available from newspaper publishers)

Invitation

How can you classify animals?

Exploration

1. Search the Internet for pictures of animals. Print out pictures of various animals.
2. Cut out the pictures and arrange them on the newsprint according to your own classification system.
3. Compare your classification system with those of other students.

Adapting for Students with Exceptionalities

Using the Internet may be difficult for students with visual impairments. Allow classmates to print large pictures for students with visual impairments to use with this activity. (See Turnbull, Turnbull, Shank, & Smith, 2004, for a discussion on adapting instruction for students who have visual difficulties.)

Teaching Tips

Older children can look up scientific classifications of the animals and compare systems after they have developed their own classification system. Pictures from magazines may also be substituted for Internet pictures. As an extension activity, children can search the Internet for sites that show live animals, such as viewable Ant Farms®.

Concept Invention

1. How are your systems the same?
2. How are your systems different?

Concept Application

How do you think your system would compare with the scientific system?

CLASSIFICATION OF ANIMALS CONCEPTS

Of some 1,250,000 different forms of living things, animals make up almost 1,000,000. They run, walk, crawl, fly, slither, and swim. They range in size from microscopic organisms to the blue whale, which may be up to about 30 meters (100 feet) long. Their colors embrace all shades of the spectrum. The diversity of animals is truly amazing.

How do scientists keep track of them? A system developed by the Swedish naturalist Carolus Linnaeus (1707–1778) provided the foundation for modern classification. Its basis is the physical structure of the living thing. His six main categories range from the general to the particular description of group properties. For example, a dog is classified in INQ Table 8–1.

Most children think of living things as either animals or plants. Scientists, however, classify living things into five kingdoms:

- **Animalia:** multicellular animals that are heterotrophic (cannot make their own food), are eukaryotic (have a membrane-bound nucleus), and reproduce sexually.
- **Plantae:** multicellular plants that are generally autotrophic (make their own food through photosynthesis), are eukaryotic, and reproduce sexually.

Table 8-1

Classification of the Common Dog

Category	Name	General Meaning of Each Category
Kingdom	Animalia	The subject belongs to the animal, not any other, kingdom.
Phylum	Chordata	It has a backbone or a notochord.
Class	Mammalia	It is a mammal.
Order	Carnivora	It eats meat.
Family	Canidae	It belongs to a group with doglike characteristics.
Genus	Canis	It is a coyote, wolf, or dog.
Species	familiaris	It is a common dog.

- *Protista:* single-celled or multicelled plantlike and animal-like organisms that are autotrophic or heterotrophic, are eukaryotic, and reproduce either sexually or asexually (no male and female).
- *Monera:* single-celled bacteria that are autotrophic or heterotrophic, are prokaryotic (no membrane-bound nucleus), and reproduce asexually (some also reproduce sexually).
- *Fungi:* single-celled or multicelled organisms that are eukaryotic, are heterotrophic, and generally reproduce asexually (some also reproduce sexually through conjugation).

Such a classification system has important advantages to biologists. It is possible to pinpoint most living things and to note relationships that otherwise might be easy to miss. Scientists throughout the world use this system.

For elementary school science, however, you will want to work with a simpler classification scheme. The following one should be useful and will fit into the more formal structure a child will develop later in high school and college. Although we do not study all of the subgroups described, the overall classification scheme should be helpful to you.

We can divide the entire animal kingdom into two huge groups, each with a manageably small number of subgroups.

Animals with Backbones (Vertebrates)

Mammals (e.g., human, dog)

Birds (e.g., sparrow, penguin)

Reptiles (e.g., turtle, lizard)

Amphibians (e.g., frog, toad)

Fishes (e.g., carp, bass)

Animals without Backbones (Invertebrates)

Echinoderms Animals with spiny skins (e.g., sand dollar, starfish)

Arthropods Animals with jointed legs: insects (e.g., fly, moth); arachnids (e.g., spider, scorpion); crustaceans (e.g., crab, lobster); myriapods (e.g., millipede, centipede)

Mollusks Animals with soft bodies (e.g., clam, snail)

Worms (e.g., flatworm, segmented worm, ribbon worm, round worm)

Corals and relatives (e.g., sea anemone, coral)

Sponges (The natural sponges we use are the fibrous skeletons of these animals.)

When young children use the term *animal,* they are inclined to mean mammal or, at best, another animal with a backbone. Yet, the five classes of vertebrates—mammals, birds, reptiles, amphibians, and fishes—make up a scant 5% of the known animal species. Animals without backbones make up the rest. Insects, which make up 70% of all animals, represent by far the largest class of invertebrates—more than 800,000 species. (A *species* is a group in which the members can only reproduce among themselves.)

Animal Classification Extensions ──────────

One way to extend classification activities is to challenge your students to see how male, female, juvenile, or animal groups are classified. For example, when classifying a gerbil, the baby is a pup, the male is a buck, the female is a doe, and the family is called a horde. Peafowl include peacocks, peahens, and peachicks with the family name of muster, ostentation, or pride. Crocodiles are bulls, cows, and crocklets and the families are basks or congregations. Sharks are bulls, females, pups, or cubs and the families are schools or shivers (University of Alberta, 2001).

Classifying male, female, juveniles, or groups of animals can be a fun way to lead into other activities such as a "Find It" activity (Carratello & Carratello, 1994). This activity involves finding animals in the schoolyard and then completing a chart with the name and type of animal, a hand-drawn picture of the animal, and descriptive words related to the animal. Once charts are complete, topics such as *diversity* and *animal traits* can be discussed. Later, as students discuss what an animal is, they will better understand how diverse the animal kingdom is.

ANIMALS WITH BACKBONES Inquiry

Bones

Invitation

What bones make up a chicken skeleton?

Exploration

1. See the drawing of a chicken skeleton. Notice the different kinds of bones for each of its parts.
2. Examine the chicken bones brought from home.
3. Can you find the leg bones?
4. Which are the large back and breast bones?
5. Which are the rib bones?
6. Which are the wing bones?
7. What other bones can you find? Can you tell what they are?

> **MATERIALS**
> - Chicken bones (boiled and stripped clean)
> - Tray or newspaper

> **Teaching Tips** The head bones and feet are usually not provided with store-bought chickens.

Concept Invention

1. Why do the bones differ in structure?
2. Do you think turkey bones are similar?

Concept Application

Without referring to the drawing, sketch how the bones you have may be put together. Which bones seem to be missing?

Tadpoles

Invitation

How can you raise and observe tadpoles?

> **MATERIALS**
> - Pond water containing water plants and algae
> - Aquarium tank or plastic shoe box
> - Sloping rock for tank
> - Hand lens
> - Frog or toad eggs
> - Fish food
> - Small net

Teaching Tips It is likely that the school semester will end before the tadpoles grow into adult frogs or toads. If this is the case, you may release them where the eggs were found or with the parents' permission, allow children to take them home.

Exploration

1. Put the frog or toad eggs and pond water into the tank. The water should have a few plants and algae for the tadpoles to eat.
2. Place a large, sloping rock into the tank. It should rise out of the water at one end. When the tadpoles grow legs, they can crawl onto the rock.
3. When the tadpoles grow legs, sprinkle some dry fish food into the tank twice a week.
4. Every 2 weeks, replace the old pond water with fresh pond water. Use a small dip net to transfer the tadpoles.
5. Use a hand lens to observe the tadpoles.

Concept Invention

When can you see the following things happening?

- Tiny tadpoles with gills hatching from the eggs
- Tiny tadpoles sticking closely to the water plants
- Bodies and tails getting longer
- Hind legs starting to grow
- Gills disappearing
- Front legs developing
- Tails shrinking

Concept Application

What else can you notice about tadpoles?

How to Train Goldfish

MATERIALS

- Two goldfish in tank
- Fish food
- Flashlight
- Guppies

Invitation

Have you trained a dog or other pet to do something? Many animals can learn to respond to some signal. You can even train goldfish. How can you get goldfish to respond to the light from a flashlight?

Exploration

1. Shine the flashlight into a corner of the tank. The goldfish should not swim toward the light.
2. Each day, sprinkle a little food near the same corner of the tank. At the same time, shine the flashlight on the food, as illustrated. Watch the fish swim toward the lighted food.
3. Do this for at least 4 days in a row.
4. At the next feeding time, just shine the light.

Concept Invention

1. How do the fish act now when only the light, but no food, is used?
2. How many times will the fish respond if only the light is used? (Do not skip more than 2 feeding days.)
3. How can you train the goldfish to respond to an unlit flashlight?
4. How can you train the goldfish to respond to a sound?
5. What differences, if any, do you notice in the behavior of the two goldfish?
6. How will other fish, such as guppies, respond to training?

Teaching Tips

If the fish do not respond, try extending the training period. Also, make sure the fish are fed only sparingly. Should more fish and containers be available (plastic containers can be used), small groups can pursue different discovery problems.

Children enjoy telling others about training animals. Reporting their attempts and successes allows many chances for verbal and written language development (science journals).

Adapting for Students with Exceptionalities

Make sure to avoid overfeeding. Set up a detailed schedule with students' names, amounts of food, and how the water is to be placed for the animal to eat. When using animals in the classroom, be sure to follow school rules and restrictions. (See Mastropieri & Scruggs, 2004, for a discussion on adapting activities related to animals in the chapter on science and social studies.)

Concept Application

Animals can be conditioned to respond to signals. Are some fish "smarter" (more quickly trained) than others? How could you find out?

Changing Temperatures

MATERIALS

- Goldfish in small bowl of water
- Pitcher of ice water
- Watch with second hand
- Thermometer

Invitation

How do temperature changes affect a fish?

Exploration

1. Notice how the fish's gills open and close. This is called a *gill beat*.
2. How many gill beats does it make in 1 minute? Take the water temperature and record it.
3. Slowly pour ice water into the bowl. Do not lower the temperature more than about 10°C (15°F) below the starting temperature. Observe the gill beats again.
4. How many beats does the fish make in 1 minute now?
5. Wait long enough for the water temperature to rise again to the first reading.

Concept Invention

About how many gill beats per minute do you think the fish will make? Watch and find out.

Concept Application

What do you think happens if fish go from cool winter waters to hot waters that are discharged from industrial sources?

Making Casts of Animal Tracks

MATERIALS

- Place with damp dirt
- Paper towel
- Thin cardboard
- Scissors
- Old plastic bowl
- Sticky tape
- Plaster of paris
- Newspaper
- Stick for mixing
- Water
- Petroleum jelly
- Flat-bladed, dull knife

Invitation

When animals walk in mud or on damp ground, they leave tracks. By examining these tracks closely, we may be able to tell many things about an animal. A large, heavy animal may leave deep, large tracks. A track of a running animal may be pushed up a little at one end. Each kind of animal leaves a different track. Animal tracks are interesting to study and keep, but rain can wash them away. There is a way you can save them. You can make a cast of an animal track. How can you make a cast of an animal track?

Exploration

1. Have someone in your class make a shoe print in the damp ground. (It will be more fun if you don't know who that person is.)
2. Make a low wall around the shoe track with cardboard. Tape it closed.
3. Spread petroleum jelly thinly on the inside surface of the wall. This will keep the plaster from sticking to it.
4. Mix plaster of paris and water in a bowl. Go easy on the water. Make the mixture like a thick milkshake. Pour about 2.5 centimeters (1 inch) of the mixture into the wall, as illustrated.
5. Wait about 1 hour for it to harden. Remove the cast from the shoe print and take off the cardboard. Notice that the cast is an opposite, or raised model, of the shoe print. To make a model that looks like the real shoe print, you must make a second cast, or mold.

Petroleum
jelly
inside

Teaching Tips

Check the local school policy about the use of plaster of paris. Some districts or schools discourage or ban its use.

If plaster is in short supply, you might have students begin with a small animal track rather than a human footprint. Caution children not to spill plaster on their clothing. Small spills, however, may be brushed off after drying. Almost any large discardable container will serve to mix the plaster and water. A flexible plastic container can be bent to pour the mixture more neatly into a narrow form.

6. Spread petroleum jelly thinly over the top of the first cast. Place it on newspaper. Put a cardboard wall, also coated thinly on the inside with petroleum jelly, around the cast. Tape it closed.
7. Pour about 2.5 centimeters (1 inch) of plaster mix into the wall. Wait again 1 hour for it to set.
8. Remove the wall. Carefully slip a knife between the two casts to separate them. Clean off the petroleum jelly with a paper towel. The second cast should now look like the original shoe print.

Concept Invention

1. What can you tell from the cast of the shoe print?
2. Do you think a girl or a boy made the print?
3. How large or heavy might the person be?
4. What kind of shoe was worn?
5. Does anyone's shoe fit the mold?

Concept Application

We can infer some things about an animal from its tracks. Make a cast of a track from an animal that does not wear shoes. What bird or other animal do you think it might be? How large or heavy might it be? Was it walking or running? Where can you find the most animal tracks around your school? Where can you find the most animal tracks around your home? What kind of collection of animal track casts can you make?

ANIMALS WITH BACKBONES CONCEPTS

Despite their fewer numbers, the five classes of vertebrates represent the highest forms of life on this planet. We begin here with the most advanced form, mammals.

Mammals ———

Look around long enough, and you will find animals everywhere: below the ground (e.g., mole, gopher, woodchuck); on the ground (e.g., human, giraffe, elephant); in trees (e.g., monkey, sloth, tree squirrel); in the air (e.g., bat); and in the water (e.g., whale, seal, dolphin). What can such a diverse collection of creatures have in common? All of them are *mammals*; that is, all have some fur or hair, and all have milk glands. To be sure, you will not find much hair on a whale, only a few bristles on the snout; and sometimes fur or hair is greatly modified, as with the porcupine's quills. But look closely enough, and if it is a mammal, it has hair.

Both male and female mammals have *mammary*, or milk, *glands*. (You can see how the term *mammals* originated.) Ordinarily, of course, only the female produces the milk used in suckling the young.

Another distinction of mammals is their intelligence, the highest of all animal groups. But other unique properties are few and subtle.

Internal Development

Mammals are born wholly formed, and then continue to grow to the adult stage of the life cycle. The embryo develops within the mother from a tiny egg fertilized by a sperm cell from a male of the same species.

During its development, the embryo is attached to the mother by a placenta, or membranous tissue. Water, oxygen, and food pass from mother to embryo through this tissue. In turn, liquefied waste materials flow the other way. These are absorbed into the mother's bloodstream, sent to the kidneys, and eliminated. The navel pit in the abdomen of humans, or "belly button," is a reminder of this early state of our development. The two known exceptions to this developmental pattern are the spiny anteater and duck-billed platypus, both of Australia. Each lays eggs. The hatched young, though, are cared for and suckled by the mother just like other mammals.

Warm-Blooded

Mammals are warm-blooded and have efficient hearts with four definite chambers. Their blood temperatures stay at relatively the same level, whether the air warms or cools. Animals of lesser complexity are cold-blooded; that is, their blood temperature changes as their environmental temperature changes.

It is both an advantage and a disadvantage to be warm-blooded. Vigorous activity is possible within most air temperature ranges. But the body heat of mammals must be conserved or else death occurs.

In cold climates, thick blubber or fur performs this function, as do hibernation and, in some cases, migration. In warm climates, humans perspire. Some animals *estivate*, or become relatively inactive for a period in whatever suitably cool refuge can be found.

Some cold-blooded animals can withstand great cold or heat, but most depend on a narrow temperature range for normal activity or survival. We go into more detail later with several specific animals.

Although the terms are still relative, it is more accurate to say "constant-temperatured" and "variable-temperatured" rather than "warm-blooded" and "cold-blooded" when we refer to animals. In hot weather, for example, a cold-blooded animal might have a higher body temperature than a warm-blooded one.

Teeth

The teeth of mammals are particularly interesting to observe because they seem adapted to specific uses. We can see the four main kinds of teeth by examining our own in a mirror. In front are the chisel-like *incisors*. On both sides of these teeth are the conelike *canines*. Farther back are the *front molars*, and last, the *back molars*. Now note how these teeth are used by several kinds of mammals.

Prominent, sharp incisors are characteristic of gnawing mammals such as rats, mice, gerbils, guinea pigs, hamsters, muskrats, beavers, and rabbits. The incisors of these rodents grow continuously at the root and are worn down at the opposite end by gnawing. When such an animal is prevented from gnawing, its incisors may grow so long that the animal cannot close its mouth, and so starves to death.

The flesh eaters have small incisors and prominent canines, sometimes called "fangs." Their molars have curved, sharp edges. The canines are useful for tearing meat. The molars are suited for chopping it into parts small enough to swallow.

Plant eaters have wide, closely spaced incisors and large, flat-surfaced molars. Canines do not appear. The incisors work well in clipping off grasses and plant stems. The molars grind this material before it is swallowed.

You and I are omnivores; in other words, we are capable of eating both plants and animals. Human teeth include all four types.

Classroom Mammals

The classroom is likely to be a restrictive place for mammals, so it is wise to select those that can be reasonably taken care of and live well in that type of environment. It is also important to get an animal that can be used to fulfill some lasting educational purposes. (Most school districts have policies on what animals, if any, are permitted in classrooms.)

Experienced teachers often recommend use of white rats and gerbils (INQ Figure 8–1) over common classroom animals such as white mice, hamsters, and guinea pigs. Although

INQ Figure 8–1   A gerbil.

INQ Figure 8–2   **A commercially produced cage such as this is well suited for housing white rats.**

simple cages for rodents can be homemade from strong screening material, a commercial cage is usually more secure and better suited to the animals' needs. A commercial cage, like that shown in INQ Figure 8–2, should serve well and last indefinitely.

Following are some suggestions for housing and caring for a female and male white rat or gerbil.

Cage

Use a commercially produced cage with exercise wheel and inverted water bottle as recommended. Cover the floor with a four-page thickness of newspaper. Scatter a generous covering of sawdust, wood shavings, peat moss, or shredded newspaper over the paper. Remove the floor covering and replace with fresh materials twice a week or more often if odor develops.

The cage should be in a draft-free location, as rodents are quite susceptible to colds. Ideally, the temperature should not fall below 15°C (60°F). A deep floor covering, however, usually provides some insulation against the loss of heat energy, because the animals will burrow into it.

Food

Dry food pellets for small laboratory animals, including rats, are sold at most pet and feed stores. In addition, provide bits of carrot, lettuce, cheese, and bread for the animal to eat. A constant supply of pellets and other nonperishable food may be left in a small, flat container in the cage. However, remove any perishable food within an hour after it has been offered. A fresh bottle of water and tray of pellets should last over weekends, but provisions for feeding will need to be made for longer periods.

Handling

White rats are typically very gentle, likable creatures. They should be handled daily for a short period. This tames them and accustoms them to being around children. Although there is little chance that a white rat will bite if treated gently, remind children to keep their fingers away from the animal's mouth when handling it. Notify the school nurse immediately if any classroom animal bites a child. Although the bite itself is usually minor, germs the animal may harbor in its mouth may cause infection unless the wound is promptly treated.

Breeding

Rats will usually breed within a few days. Provide some loose cotton or shredded newspaper for the female to use in preparing a nest. Remove the male from the cage after it appears obvious that the female is pregnant. Return the male to the pet store, or give it to the Humane Society.

About 3 to 4 weeks after mating, the female will give birth to eight or more young in the nest. Do not disturb the female for 10 days after this event. The newborn young will be blind and hairless. They may be weaned gradually to a regular diet after they are about 2 weeks old. Feed them milk that contains soft bread crumbs for a week and adult food thereafter.

All rats should be given to a responsible party after completion of this activity. Abandoned rodents become wild and add quickly to the local pest population.

During the 8 weeks or so of working with these animals, try to have time for frequent, short class discussions about the behavior and habits of the caged rats. Emphasize the birth, appearance, care, feeding, and physical development of the young. You may note rapid day-to-day improvement in children's verbal reporting skills as they tell the latest news about their rats. It is also an excellent journal-writing activity.

Use a chart with rotating names for assigning such tasks as replacement of water, paper, and food. Most children are delighted to serve. This may be an excellent opportunity to motivate children and help them achieve a greater sense of responsibility.

Birds

"A bird is an animal with feathers." This is a primary child's definition, but it really cannot be much improved. Almost all other properties we see in birds may be found here and there among other animal groups, although not in the same combinations. The coloring and construction of birds' feathers vary tremendously, from the luxuriant plumage of a peacock to the scruffy covering of a New Zealand kiwi.

Although we ordinarily think of birds as fliers, chickens and roadrunners seldom fly, and some birds, like the ostrich, penguin, and kiwi, cannot fly at all.

Food and Heat Loss

"He eats like a bird." How often we have heard a person who eats sparingly described this way. It is hardly fitting. Few other animals possess such voracious appetites for their size. Many birds must eat their weight in food each day just to stay alive.

To see why this is so, examine a small, flying bird closely. Notice that its body volume is relatively small when compared to the large surface area of its skin. As body volume decreases, the relative size of skin surface increases. If this seems unclear, inspect a pint and a quart milk carton. The small carton holds only half as much but clearly has more than half the surface area of the larger carton.

A large skin surface area causes heat energy to radiate rapidly away from the body. This is bad when the body volume is small, because the heat-generating capacity is also small. To generate enough heat energy for normal functioning when heat energy is being radiated away quickly, a high *metabolic rate* (the rate at which food is oxidized and assimilated) must be maintained. The rapid burning of fuel causes body temperatures in birds of 39° to 43°C (102° to 110°F), the highest of any animal group.

The same principle of volume relative to surface area applies to mammals. Smaller mammals usually eat more for their size than larger ones. As we travel toward the earth's polar regions, we can observe a general increase in mammals' body size. As body volume increases, the relative size of skin surface decreases. Comparatively less heat energy is radiated away. This has great survival value.

Flight Adaptations

The bodies of most birds are well suited for flight. Inside are several air sacs connected to the lungs. Many bones are hollow, or nearly so, and further reduce body weight. Even a chicken has relatively little marrow in its longer bones. It is said that the evolutionist Charles Darwin had a pipe stem made from a wing bone of an albatross.

The body of a bird is streamlined and closely fitted with three kinds of feathers. Next to the skin are fluffy, soft *down feathers*. These contain numerous "dead air" pockets that help conserve body heat. *Contour feathers* hug the body closely, and large *flight feathers* help propel and steer the bird as it flies.

Most birds continually preen their feathers. This is done by using the bill to press a drop of oil from a gland located just above the tail and then spreading the oil over the feathers. A shiny, waterproof coating results. It is so effective that a duck can float for many hours without becoming waterlogged. If the oil were suddenly removed, a swimming duck would disappear into the water like a slowly submerging submarine.

If you can locate a large, recently molted feather, dip it in water before and after washing it in soap or detergent. Notice how water soaks in after the washing.

The thick white meat or breast section on poultry is partly the result of selective breeding by humans. However, nearly all birds have their largest and strongest muscles in this section because these muscles control the major wing movements.

Senses

The remarkably keen eyesight of birds has been well known. Less acknowledged is the fact that they have three eyelids. Two shut the eye, and the third, which is transparent, sweeps back and forth, cleaning away dust or other foreign matter without the need for blinking. The eyes of most birds are located on the sides of the head. So, birds must continually cock the head to one side to see directly forward. Their hearing is also acute despite the lack of outer ears. Two small ear holes suffice. Birds do not appear to discriminate well, however, among various odors or tastes.

Beaks and Feet

Most birds have horny beaks; their various shapes show great diversity of function. Although all known modern birds are toothless, fossil records indicate that a variety of toothed birds lived in ancient times. The feet of birds are equally diverse in form. On the legs we find scales, which reveal their evolutionary connection to the reptiles.

INQ Figure 8–3 shows some common structures and functions of birds' bills and feet. The duck's bill is useful for scooping up small fish and plants in water because it is shaped like a shovel. The scooped-up water spills out through the uneven sides of the bill, but the food remains inside. The duck's webbed feet are useful for paddling in water.

The woodpecker's bill is like a large, pointed nail, useful for digging insects out of tough tree bark. (The bills of most other insect catchers are more slender.) Its feet can dig securely into a vertical tree trunk.

The sparrow's bill is small but strong enough to crack open seeds and some nuts, similar to a pet canary. Its feet are useful for perching because they automatically close around a tree limb. It requires no effort, and the bird may sleep in this position without danger of falling.

The hawk's bill is like a sharp hook, useful for tearing the flesh from bones of field mice and other small animals of preys. Its feet are useful for grasping and holding prey.

INQ Figure 8–3 (A) Duck, (B) woodpecker, (C) sparrow, (D) hawk.

Reproduction

As in mammals, sexual reproduction begins with an egg cell fertilized within the female by a sperm cell. However, fertilization is not necessary for an egg to be laid. Many chickens lay an egg every day. We eat these unfertilized eggs. An egg acquires its hard shell in the lower part of the hen's *oviduct*, or egg-conducting tube. Glands produce a limy secretion that gradually hardens over a period of hours before the egg is laid. The shell is porous and permits oxygen to enter and carbon dioxide to leave. In a fertilized egg, this gas exchange is essential for life in the developing chick embryo.

Chick Hatching

It is fairly easy to hatch chicks in the classroom. To do so, you will need fertilized eggs and an incubator. Get the eggs from a hatchery or farmer. Buy a small incubator from a pet shop or scientific supply house. It is essential to success that a near-constant temperature of 38° to 39°C (101° to 103°F) be maintained for the 21-day incubation period. Fertilized eggs should be turned over twice a day. This change in position keeps the growing embryo from sticking to the shell. A mark placed on the egg will allow you to keep track of egg positions.

In 21 days, or sooner if the eggs have not been freshly laid, the hatching will take place. This process may take several or more hours. Because some hatching may happen at night, it is good to have several eggs. This will increase the chance that a few chicks will hatch during school hours.

Children can observe how a chick breaks out of its shell by using a tiny "egg tooth" on top of its beak. This projection drops off shortly after the chick emerges (see INQ Figure 8–4). The chick will look wet and scraggly until its downy feathers dry. No food is necessary for at least 24 hours, as it will have digested the egg yolk and some egg white before breaking out

INQ Figure 8–4   **A chick starts to peck itself out of the egg. Notice the egg tooth.**

of the shell. (It is a common misconception that an egg yolk is the undeveloped embryo, rather than the chick's principal food.)

Caring for Chicks

Chicks need constant warmth furnished by a brooder or warm box. An incubator can be used temporarily if the lid is raised, but it may be too confining after a few days. If the chicks are to be kept for more than several days, use a cardboard box with a shielded, gooseneck lamp shining into it.

Chick feed may be bought at a pet store. Leave some feed and clean water in dishes within the brooder at all times. A fresh newspaper floor cover each day will keep the brooder clean.

Reptiles

Many children know that snakes are reptiles but are unaware that the group also includes turtles, lizards, alligators, and crocodiles. What do these animals have in common? Typically, they have dry, scaly skin. Those with feet have five clawed toes on each foot. They all have lungs in order to breathe, or are lung breathers, which means that even an aquatic turtle will drown if placed underwater for an extended time period.

Cold-Blooded

Reptiles have well-developed hearts with three chambers (some have almost four). Unlike mammals and birds, reptiles are cold-blooded. In winter, reptiles in relatively cold climates hibernate below ground; they become unable to move when the temperature drops very low. It is no accident that reptiles are rare in regions beyond the temperate zones and proliferate in the tropics.

Reproduction

In reptiles, reproduction begins with the internal fertilization of an egg, similar to mammals and birds. But the process thereafter is different enough to warrant our attention. All turtles and most lizards and snakes lay eggs in secluded areas on land. The eggs have tough, leathery covers and for the most part depend on the sun's warmth for incubation.

Some snakes and lizards retain the fertilized eggs internally until the incubation period is complete. The young are then born alive. However, the process differs from the development of mammalian young.

INQ Figure 8–5   A typical small lizard, the Eastern fence swift.

In mammals, as was noted, the embryo is attached to the female and nourished directly through a placental membrane. In reptiles, there is no internal attachment. The egg incubates until the growing embryo inside is sufficiently developed to hatch and so leave the female.

Eyes

Turtles and most lizards have three eyelids on each eye, as do birds. Snakes have no eyelids. A transparent, horny cover over the eye protects it from injury as the animal moves among sticks and vegetation. Just before a snake sheds its skin, up to several times a year, the transparent eye cover becomes milky in color. Interestingly, the only easy way to tell the several species of legless lizards from snakes is to note whether the eyes blink.

Common Lizards

Children may bring lizards, often swifts, to class (see INQ Figure 8–5). In the southwestern United States, it is common for children to bring in the gentle and easily tamed horned toad. Nearly all lizards may be housed satisfactorily in a terrarium containing some sand and placed where it is sunny. The anole (American chameleon), the kind often bought at fairs and pet shops, is more suited to a woodland terrarium.

Chameleons (anoles) are interesting for children to observe. Like many lizards, they change body color under different conditions of light, temperature, and excitation. However, the color change is greater in chameleons than in most other lizards. It is brought about by dilation and contraction of blood vessels in the skin.

Many lizards have fragile tails that break off easily when seized. In some species, the broken-off tail wriggles about animatedly, thereby often distracting the attention of a would-be captor until the lizard escapes. Lizards can *regenerate*, or grow back, new tails.

Classroom Snake

If possible, try to get a small, tame snake for the children to examine. Let the children touch it and learn that it has dry, cool skin, rather than a slimy coating. Children can learn that nearly all snakes in this country are highly beneficial to humans and that snakes consume many thousands of destructive rodent and insect pests each year.

At the same time, children should learn an intelligent respect for snakes. If poisonous snakes are found locally, show pictures of them. Instruct children never to hunt for snakes unless accompanied by a responsible and informed older person. In the continental United States, the rattlesnake, copperhead, water moccasin, and coral snake are dangerous to humans.

Amphibians

Amphibians are animals that typically spend part of their lives in water and part on land. The main kinds are frogs, toads, and salamanders. Amphibians represent an interesting evolutionary link between fishes and reptiles and have many properties of both groups. If animal life originally began and evolved in the sea, as is generally hypothesized, it is probable that early amphibians were the first vertebrates to emerge from the water and live successfully on land.

Cold-Blooded

Amphibians are cold-blooded and have hearts with three chambers. Like other cold-blooded animals, they hibernate in cold weather, usually by burrowing in the ground or mud. The adults breathe through lungs but are also able to absorb some oxygen through the skin. The latter method of breathing is especially useful in hibernation. Still, skin breathing is inadequate for sustained activity, and even a frog will drown eventually if forced to remain underwater.

Frogs and salamanders usually have moist, smooth skins that must remain moist if they are to survive. For this reason, a bowl of water is needed in a terrarium that houses these creatures.

Frogs and Toads

One day, a child may show you a small amphibian and ask, "Is this a toad or a frog?" Although it is difficult to distinguish between them all the time, a toad usually has dry, rough skin and a broad, fat body. In addition, its eyelids are more prominent than those of frogs. Another indicator is where it was caught. Frogs are more likely to live by water, whereas toads are mostly land dwellers (INQ Figure 8–6).

INQ Figure 8–6   Toad (left) and frog (right). Notice the external eardrum, just behind and below the eye.

Can toads cause warts? Many children think they can. The toad's warty-looking tu-bercles are glands that secrete a fluid that can sicken attacking animals, but the substance cannot cause warts. It may irritate the eyes, though, if they are rubbed after the person has handled a toad. Advise children to wash their hands after playing with a toad.

Salamanders

Less common than frogs and toads are salamanders; chances are that few children will have these as pets. Typically, a salamander has four legs of the same size and a long, tu-bular body with a tail. Superficially, they resemble lizards and are often mistaken for them. They differ from lizards in several ways: Each foreleg of a salamander has four toes instead of five and no claws; typically, the skin is smooth rather than rough. A salaman-der's skin may secrete a mild poison, so hands should be thoroughly washed after han-dling it.

Reproduction

Perhaps the most striking difference between amphibians and the other groups we have ex-amined is in their means of reproduction. Female amphibians lay their eggs in water or in very moist places on land. Immediately after the eggs are laid, the males fertilize them by shedding sperm over them. Therefore, fertilization is external, unlike that in higher order animals. A single female frog or toad may lay several thousand eggs at one time. The eggs are coated with a thick, jellylike substance that quickly absorbs water and swells in size. This substance protects the developing embryos and serves as a first source of food. Eggs may often be found in ponds in spring. Look for gelatinous clumps (frog) or strings (toad) near grassy edges or where cattails grow.

After 1 to 2 weeks, the embryos hatch as tadpoles, or "polliwogs," which look com-pletely unlike the adults. Only after several months to several years, depending on the species, do tadpoles acquire the adult body form (see INQ Figure 8–7). This process of

INQ Figure 8–7   Metamorphosis of the frog.

changing forms, called *metamorphosis*, is another distinct departure from the growth and development pattern of higher animals.

In their initial growth stages, tadpoles breathe like fishes; that is, they obtain oxygen from water through gills. Thus, be sure to "age" tap water for at least 24 hours to rid it of chlorine before adding it to the container in which the tadpoles are kept. Use tap water only if pond water is not available.

Fishes ───────

Next to mammals, fishes are the vertebrates that present the greatest diversity in appearance, adaptations, and habits. Certainly, fishes are most numerous, both as individuals and in numbers of species. (When only one species is referred to, *fish* is both singular and plural. *Fishes* means those of several species.) Fossil records show that these creatures were the first animals with true backbones.

Breathing

Fishes are cold-blooded and have hearts with only two chambers. They breathe through gills instead of lungs. Their gills are composed of thousands of blood vessels contained in hairlike filaments located in back of the head on both sides. We cannot easily see these filaments on a live fish, as gill covers conceal them.

A fish breathes by opening and closing its mouth. In the process, water is taken into the mouth and then is forced out the gill openings. As water passes over the gills, oxygen dissolved in the water enters the filaments and blood vessels and then circulates throughout the body. At the same time, carbon dioxide leaves the filaments and is swept away. One advantage of carefully classifying living things by structure is that it enables us to see relationships we might otherwise miss. In fishes, for example, an organ called the *air bladder* appears to be a forerunner of the lung. The air bladder is an air-filled sac usually located in the middle of a fish between its kidney and stomach. By compressing and expanding its air bladder, a fish can rise and descend in the water.

In the lungfish, this organ has been modified into a crude lung, enabling it to breathe air directly in addition to breathing through the gills. A lungfish typically lives in a muddy pond or marsh, which may dry up in summer. It survives by burrowing into the mud and breathing air supplied through a hole in the mud cover. When its pond fills again with seasonal rainfall, the lungfish resumes the normal gill-breathing behavior of fishes. The lungfish appears to be a clear link between fishes and amphibians in the long evolutionary march of vertebrates from the sea.

Body

The body of a fish is well suited for its environment. Its streamlined contours offer a minimum of resistance to the water. A slimy, mucouslike secretion that exudes between the overlapping body scales further reduces friction and insulates the skin from attack by microorganisms. A large tail fin, wagged from side to side, propels it through the water. Vertical fins on top and bottom keep the fish on an even keel while it is moving. Two pairs of side fins, one pair near the gills (pectoral fins) and the other pair farther back (pelvic fins), balance the fish when it is stationary. These fins are also used to assist turning, in the manner of oars, and for swimming backward. When held out laterally, they brake the swimming fish to a stop. Pectoral fins correspond to forelegs, and pelvic fins correlate to hind legs, in other animals.

Senses

The eyes of a fish are always open because it has no eyelids. Focusing is done by shifting the pupil forward and back, rather than by changing the lens shape, as in humans. So-called flatfish, such as the flounder and halibut, lie on one side. Both eyes are arranged on one side of the head. Because these fish are typically bottom dwellers, this eye arrangement permits greater vision.

Although fishes have no external ears, they hear with *auditory capsules* deep within the head. In many fishes, a *lateral line* of sensory scales extends along both sides of the body from head to tail. These scales are particularly sensitive to sounds of low pitch. Some expert anglers claim that a fish can hear heavy footsteps (always of other, inexpert anglers, of course) on a nearby bank.

The taste sense appears to be mostly lacking, but a fish is sensitive to smells. Nostril pits on the snout lead to organs of smell just below. The whole body, and especially the lips, seems to be sensitive to touch. In species like the catfish, extra touch organs are found in the form of "whiskers."

Reproduction

In fishes, reproduction is accomplished by either external or internal fertilization of the egg, depending on the species. The female goldfish, for example, lays eggs on aquatic plants. The male fertilizes the eggs by shedding sperm cells over them. Goldfish usually reproduce only in large tanks or ponds. Guppies and many other tropical varieties use internal fertilization. The male has a modified anal fin that carries sperm. The fin is inserted into a small opening below the female's abdomen, and sperm cells are released. Fertilized eggs remain in the female's body until the embryos hatch and are "born." Many of the young guppies are eaten by the adult fish unless sufficient plant growth makes it difficult to detect them.

To raise as many guppies as possible, place the pregnant female (its underside will look swollen) and some plants in a separate container. After the young are born, remove the mother. The young may join the adult guppies safely in about 1 month. Try not to be too efficient at breeding guppies, however. Someone good at arithmetic has calculated that a single pair will become 3 million guppies in a year, assuming that all generations and off-spring stay alive. A female guppy may produce several dozen young every 4 to 6 weeks at a water temperature of 21° to 27°C (70° to 80°F).

Male guppies differ from the females in several ways. They are about half the size (exclusive of the tails), much narrower in body, and more brilliantly colored (INQ Figure 8–8).

Setting Up an Aquarium

An aquarium is an excellent source to observe ecological principles firsthand. In this watery habitat, plants and animals interact with each other and their environment, and reproduction takes place in several ways. It is possible to see a near balance of nature through the interactions, and the consequences when there is an imbalance.

It is easy for children to set up small aquariums for short-range observations of a week or two. For the containers, they may use large, wide-mouthed jars or plastic shoe boxes. One or two goldfish and a few sprigs of water plants per container should do nicely. Tap water can be put into the containers and aged for at least 24 hours before the fish are introduced. A tiny amount of fish food, no more than the fish can eat in a few minutes, should be sprinkled on the water once a day. A more elaborate, long-range habitat for aquatic animals and plants is described next.

INQ Figure 8–8   Female (left) and male (right) guppy.

Tank

The materials needed are a tank, some clean sand (not the seashore variety), a few aquatic snails and plants, and several small fish. A rectangular tank of 19- to 23-liter (5- to 6-gallon) capacity serves best for a classroom aquarium. The rectangular shape has less viewing distortion than a bowl. It also permits more oxygen from the air to dissolve in the water because of the relatively greater surface area exposed at the top.

The tank must be clean. Dirt, grease, or caked lime can be removed by scrubbing thoroughly with salt and water. The salt is abrasive enough to have a scouring effect. Should detergent or soaps be needed, repeated rinsing of the tank is essential. Any residue may be harmful to future inhabitants. About 5 centimeters (2 inches) of clean sand may then be placed and spread evenly on the bottom of the tank.

Plants

A pet store can supply several varieties of inexpensive plants, any of which will serve well. Sagittaria and vallisneria will produce more oxygen than others and are rooted plants. Anchor the plants firmly in the sand. If necessary, also anchor them with several clean stones. Placing the plants toward the back of the tank will permit easier viewing of the fish.

Water

Put a large piece of paper or cardboard over the plants before pouring or siphoning water into the tank. This prevents the plants from becoming dislodged and helps keep the sand in place. The paper should be removed immediately thereafter. Should tap water be used, it must stand for at least 24 hours to permit the chlorine to escape and the water to reach room temperature. The water level should be about 2.5 centimeters (1 inch) lower than the tank top.

Moving the tank after it is filled may warp the tank seams and start a leak. (If a leak does occur, apply epoxy glue to the inside joints and seams after thoroughly drying out the tank.)

Animals

Goldfish and guppies are among the best fishes to use, as they can withstand a broad temperature change. But do not mix the two, because goldfish prey on guppies.

Freshwater angelfish are also a popular aquarium fish. Angelfish have many variations such as silver, gold, black, and marble. The juveniles and adults are colored differently in many species. Most species of angelfish are a few centimeters long, but some may reach lengths of 60 centimeters (2 feet). Angelfish will breed on broadleaf plants and will care for their young if not frightened. If angelfish do become threatened, they might eat their young. Angelfish are sometimes aggressive and will fight with each other or eat small fish of other species.

The neon tetra is another freshwater fish that is often kept in aquariums. Tetras have blue and red markings and, like the angelfish, originate in the Amazon waters of South America. Tetras are a good community fish and often move throughout the aquarium in groups. They should not be kept with larger fish since they are easy prey.

The black molly is a hybrid tropical fish that does not have a native counterpart living in the wild. Black molly fish are very hardy so it is easy to breed them in an aquarium. The females are livebearers and produce a large number of fry.

"Chinese" algae eaters that come from Northern India and Thailand are useful to remove unwanted algae. As juveniles, they are peaceful and stay to themselves. As adults, however, they tend to be very aggressive and territorial. An alternative to the Chinese algae eater is the plecostomus catfish that is notoriously good at keeping an aquarium free of algae. The fish has an elongated, brown body and a large head. It cleans the tank by sucking at the aquarium glass or tank decorations with its strong mouth. Small catfish, sunfish, minnows, zebras, and bullheads are also easy to keep and are interesting to observe.

If several water snails are bought at the pet store along with the plants and fish, they will add interest and value. Snails keep the aquarium clean by scavenging excess fish food and eating the green slime (algae) that may form on the glass. Only a few are needed, as they multiply rapidly and can become a problem. Children delight in examining snails' eggs, laid on the glass sides, and seeing the snails scrape off and eat the algae. A few hand lenses placed around the aquarium make the viewing easier.

A properly set-up aquarium needs little attention. Plants give off some of the oxygen needed by the animals and absorb some of their waste materials. The animals also provide carbon dioxide needed by the plants for photosynthesis. What if the aquarium is not properly set up? Here, we can look for clues that may indicate improper light, temperature, oxygen, and feeding.

Light

If algae grow rapidly on the sides, the tank is getting too much light. A northeast corner location or other place of good but indirect light will work best. Adding more snails and wrapping black paper around the tank for a while can retard growth of algae, but it may also be necessary to clean the tank. Algae will not hurt the fish unless they are so abundant that some decay; however, visibility into the tank may be obscured.

Temperature

If the temperature is too low, reproduction will slow noticeably or stop. Some fish may die. The best temperature range for fish recommended here is 10° to 21°C (50° to 70°F). An exception is the guppy, which requires 21° to 29.5°C (70° to 85°F) water to reproduce.

When most kinds of tropical fishes are used, a heater is a necessity. This can be in the form of a light mounted in the cover of the tank, although an immersible heater works better.

Oxygen Supply

Insufficient oxygen is indicated when fish stay very close to the surface. This is where the greatest amount of oxygen dissolved directly from the air is located. Occasionally, some fish might be seen to break the surface and gulp air directly. Insufficient surface area or over-crowding can cause this condition.

One small, approximately inch-long, goldfish (not including the tail) per gallon of water is proper. If guppies are used, about six fish per gallon are satisfactory. Having too many snails will also add to an oxygen-poor condition. Increase the number of sagittaria and vallisneria for more oxygen.

Cloudy Water

A cloudy water condition occurs from excess feeding or from not removing dead plants and animals. Bacterial action on uneaten food and other organic matter poisons the water and promotes the growth of other microorganisms. The most practical solution is to discard everything but the fish, filter, and gravel, carefully clean the tank, and begin again.

Feeding

Only a small sprinkling of packaged fish food every other day (enough to be completely eaten in 5 minutes) is required for feeding. Tiny bits of chopped beef and earthworm may also be used. Feeding is not needed over weekends, but some means for feeding during vacations is necessary.

Cover

A glass top or piece of kitchen plastic wrap may be used to cover the aquarium. For better air circulation, leave some space open or punch a few holes in the plastic-wrap cover.

A top helps keep the water clean and cuts down on loss of water through evaporation or loss of an overly athletic fish. It also shows condensation and precipitation in a small water cycle, because water droplets form on the bottom surface and fall back into the tank.

ANIMALS WITHOUT BACKBONES Inquiry

Mealworms and What They Do

Invitation

Have you ever seen a mealworm? You can buy mealworms at a pet store to feed to lizards and fish. It's fun to observe mealworms and what they do. How can you find out about mealworms and what they do?

Exploration

1. Take a mealworm out of the jar of bran. Put one in an upturned shoe box lid.
2. Use a spoon and card to move it to where you want.
3. Use a hand lens to see it more clearly.

Concept Invention

1. What do you notice about the mealworm? How many legs does it have? How many feelers on its head? What is on its tail end? How many body segments, or parts, does it have?
2. Put the mealworm on a rough paper towel, and then on a smooth surface. On which does it seem to travel more easily?
3. Put a few more mealworms in the shoe box lid. Observe how they look and act. In what ways can you tell different mealworms apart?
4. In what ways can you get a mealworm to back up? Which way is best?
5. Suppose you place the mealworms on a slant. Will they go up or down? Does the amount of slant make a difference?
6. How far can a mealworm go in half a minute?
7. Which food do mealworms seem to like best? Try cornflakes, flour, bread, crackers, and other foods.
8. Suppose you put two mealworms into a narrow straw, one at each end. What do you think will happen when they meet?
9. Do mealworms like moisture? How could a cotton swab be used to find out? How else might you find out?
10. Will a mealworm move toward or away from a cold place? How could an ice cube be used to find out?
11. Will a mealworm move to a dark or light place? How can black paper be used to find out?

MATERIALS

- Mealworms
- Spoon
- Three rulers
- Small card
- Shoe box lid
- Small jar of bran
- Hand lens
- Cotton swab
- Rough paper towel
- Water
- Clock with second hand
- Samples of foods (cornflakes, flour, bread, crackers, and others)
- Ice cube
- Drinking straw
- Sheet of black paper

Teaching Tips

Mealworms are the larval stage of the grain beetle, an insect often found in rotting grain or flour supplies. They may be bought inexpensively at pet stores and are fed to a variety of small animals, including some fishes. Mealworms can be kept in closed glass jars containing bran or other cereal flakes. Punch small holes in the jar lids for air. A potato or apple slice can be added to provide extra moisture. When the old bran looks powdery, dump out everything and then wash and dry the jar. Put fresh bran and the live, healthy-looking mealworms back into the jar.

12. In each of the four illustrations, which way will a mealworm go?
13. How can you get a mealworm to go in a straight line for at least 10 centimeters (4 inches)? No fair touching it!

(1)   (2)

(3)   (4)

Concept Application

Some behaviors of an animal are inborn, and some are influenced by its environment. What are some other questions about the mealworm's behavior that you would like to investigate? Watch the mealworm go through its life cycle. What do you notice at the different stages of life?

Crickets

Invitation

How can you raise crickets?

Exploration

1. Put about 5 centimeters (2 inches) of dry soil into the container.
2. Fill the custard cup with soil. Sprinkle water on it until it is all damp. Bury it in the dry soil so that the damp soil is even with the dry soil. (This is where the female can lay eggs.)
3. Scatter some pieces of torn paper towel around the container. (The crickets can hide underneath when needed.)
4. Scatter some dry oatmeal and a few raisins at one end.
5. Put no more than three or four crickets inside the container. Cover it with a screen large enough to bend down at the sides.

Concept Invention

1. How do the crickets act?
2. How do they use the pieces of toweling?
3. How do the females lay eggs?
4. How do the crickets eat?
5. How do the crickets move about?
6. What happens when cricket eggs hatch?
7. What do the young (nymphs) look like?
8. What do they look like as they get older? (Use a hand lens to help you see.)

Concept Application

What else can you observe about the crickets?

MATERIALS

- Several male and female crickets
- Plastic shoe box
- Custard cup or small dish
- Screen top for shoe box
- Paper towel
- Ruler
- Water
- Dry soil
- Dry oatmeal or bran
- Raisins
- Hand lens

Teaching Tips

If children are unable to catch crickets in fields, they may often be bought at fish-bait stores. The female may be recognized by a long slender "tail," or ovipositor, through which it deposits eggs in damp soil. Development from egg to adult takes about 6 months, and adults live about 3 months.

MATERIALS

- Vial of brine shrimp eggs
- Tap water
- Noniodized salt
- Hand lens
- Plastic teaspoon
- Small baby food jars with lids
- Measuring cup
- Crayon or marker
- Baking soda
- Small package of brewer's yeast

Brine Shrimp

Invitation

Have you ever visited a salt lake? If so, maybe you have seen brine shrimp. These small animals lay tiny eggs. You can find out many interesting things about brine shrimp, but first you will need to hatch the eggs. How can you hatch brine shrimp eggs?

Exploration

1. Let a cup of tap water stand overnight. Then mix 4 teaspoons of salt into it.
2. Pour the water into several baby food jars.
3. Use one jar now. Cap and save the other jars for later use.
4. Take just a tiny pinch of eggs from the vial. Sprinkle them on top of the water.
5. Observe the eggs closely a few times each day. Use a hand magnifier to see the eggs more clearly.

Brine shrimp are sold at pet stores for fish food. The eggs may be hatched in saltwater. You can use about 4 teaspoons of salt per cup of water for both hatching and growth; but the shrimp may hatch within a wide range of salt concentrations. Be sure to use either noniodized or marine salt.

About 6 weeks are needed for the shrimp to reach maturity under the best conditions. A water temperature of about 27°C (80°F) is ideal. Children will be able to distinguish female from male adults most easily by the females' egg pouches. It is harder to keep brine shrimp alive for a lengthy period than it is to hatch them. Some precautions will help. Have children use a crayon to mark the beginning water level on each jar. Be sure that any evaporated water is replaced by aged tap water containing the proper salt concentration.

The water should stand for at least 24 hours to allow the chlorine to escape. Put a tiny pinch of baking soda into each shrimp container once a week to neutralize the acid that builds up. Above all, do not overfeed the shrimp. A tiny pinch of brewer's yeast once a week is adequate to grow the bacteria on which the shrimp feed. As with other long-range observational activities, this one is ideal for motivating artwork and language experiences.

Concept Invention

1. When do you first notice changes in the eggs? What changes do you see?
2. When do you first notice tiny brine shrimp? How do they look to you? Can you describe what they are doing?
3. What changes do you notice as the brine shrimp grow? Observe them each day.
4. Do brine shrimp ever seem to rest or sleep? How can you find out?
5. How long does it take for a shrimp to start growing?
6. How long can you keep a brine shrimp alive?
7. Do newly hatched shrimp go where it is light or dark? How about month-old shrimp? How can you find out?
8. How can you tell which brine shrimp are female?
9. Will brine shrimp eggs hatch in freshwater?
10. Will brine shrimp eggs hatch in water with twice as much or more salt than you first used?

Concept Application

Brine shrimp will hatch and grow from eggs, stay alive, and reproduce when conditions are like those of their natural habitat. Suppose you hatch many shrimp eggs in one jar and only a few in another. What do you think will happen as the shrimp grow? What else would you like to investigate about brine shrimp?

Snails and What They Do ———

Invitation

Have you ever seen a snail? If so, where? Many water snails live in and around the edges of ponds. Land snails can be found in gardens, lawns, and around damp soil. They are easiest to find early in the morning or at night. Land snails are usually larger than water snails, so they are easier to observe. What they do is surprising. How can you find out about land snails and what they do?

Exploration

1. Put a snail on a pie plate.
2. Use a spoon and card to move it where you want.
3. Use a hand lens to see it more clearly.

Concept Invention

1. What do you notice about the snail? How does it move? How can you describe its head? How can you describe its shell? How can you describe its other parts?
2. How many stalks (feelers) do you observe on its head? Which seem to have eyes? Which seem to be used for feeling?

MATERIALS

- Live land snail
- Small stiff card
- Wide-mouthed glass jar, with lid, containing some damp soil
- Hand lens
- Spoon
- Aluminum pie plate
- Ruler
- Sheet of black paper
- Piece of lettuce
- Paper towel
- Small paper cup of water
- Clock with second hand
- Paper and pencil
- Samples of different foods

Teaching Tips

Land snails can be found where there is plenty of vegetation and moisture. They seem to prefer cool, shady places, especially under leaves, logs, and rocks. Early morning is probably the easiest time to collect snails, when leaves are heavy with dew. If you collect them in a dry "resting" condition, place them on a water-soaked paper towel to reactivate them. Several collected snails may be kept in one glass jar covered with a lid that has holes punched into it for air. Place 2.5 to 5 centimeters (1 to 2 inches) of soil inside and keep it damp. For extra moisture, sink a bottle cap flush with the soil surface and fill it with water. Leave a small piece of lettuce inside for food. Keep the jar in a shady place. After several days, the jar will need to be cleaned. Try to have several snails available for observation and experiments; even when treated gently, this animal needs a rest period between activities.

3. What happens when you gently touch the two longer stalks? What happens when you gently touch the two shorter stalks? How close can you get before the stalks move?
4. How can you get the two longer stalks to move in different directions?
5. What happens when you tap the snail's shell gently?
6. Try to put the snail upside down on its shell. Can the snail right itself? If so, how?
7. Put the snail on black paper. Observe the silver trail it makes. How far does the snail go in 1 minute?
8. How well can you draw an animal? Make a drawing of your snail. Show it to someone who does not know you are studying snails. Can that person tell it is a snail?
9. How well can you describe an animal? Write a description of your snail without saying what it is. Show the description to someone who does not know you are studying snails. Can that person tell that you described a snail?
10. Give the snail some lettuce to eat. Use a hand lens to observe its mouthparts. How does it eat?
11. What foods does your snail seem to like best? Circle your snail with bits of different foods. Which does the snail go to first? What happens when you try this several times? How long should you wait between each trial? Why?
12. Will a snail go to the dark or the light? Put your snail into the pie pan. How can you use a sheet of black paper to find out?
13. Will a snail go where it is dry or wet? How can you use a paper towel to find out?

Adapting for Students with Exceptionalities

To assist students with exceptionalities, when doing this activity, try using a concept diagram that includes the "concept name" (snail behavior), "overall concept" (animal behavior), "key words" (snail, head, stalks, shell, trail, and mouthparts), "characteristics" (responds to touch and light, eats, leaves a trail, body parts), "exploration of examples" (likes lettuce, likes cucumbers, does not like carrots), "practice with a new example" (similarities with an earthworm), and "definition" (snails are soft-bodied mollusks that have a single shell and secrete mucus). (See Mastropieri & Scruggs, 2004, chapter on science and social studies for a discussion on concept diagrams.)

Concept Application

Some behaviors of an animal are inborn, and some are influenced by its environment. What other experiments would you like to try with snails? What other kinds of snails can you find to try?

ANIMALS WITHOUT BACKBONES CONCEPTS

The invertebrates make up most of the animals on earth. Of these, insects are by far the largest group. We begin this section with insects and why they have done so well and then consider four more animals you might have for many classroom activities: crayfish, brine shrimp, snails, and earthworms.

Insects and Life Cycles

If we were to eliminate all insects, some very undesirable consequences would result. Here are only a few: Probably half of all the flowering plants on the earth would disappear, because bees, flies, moths, and butterflies help pollinate them. Most land birds would vanish because their main source of food is insects. Biological research would be hampered because the short life cycles of insects are ideal for quick results in medical and hereditary studies.

As mentioned, insects make up an astounding 70% of all animal species. Hundreds of new species are discovered each year. They are found almost everywhere on the earth. What makes them so successful?

Legs and Skeleton

The first things we might note about insects is that they have jointed legs and segmented bodies. Instead of an internal skeleton, such as we find in vertebrates, they have an external skeleton made of a crusty substance called *chitin*. Muscles and other body parts are attached inside to this semirigid exterior. To continue growing, an immature insect must *molt*, or shed its outside covering from time to time. We can see that the need for molting greatly limits insect size. A heavy body would collapse before the soft, new covering hardened. Jointed legs and an external skeleton are also typical of the several other classes that make up the phylum of arthropods.

The Adult Insect

The easiest way to recognize an adult insect is to look for three pairs of legs and three body parts: head, thorax (chest), and abdomen (INQ Figure 8–9). Notice that these two characteristics leave out spiders, which have four pairs of legs, and many other arthropods, such as sow bugs, centipedes, or scorpions.

The *head* contains a primitive "brain" and mouthparts that vary considerably among insect orders. Most insects have one pair of compound eyes, which are aggregates of many lenses, and several simple eyes as well, each of which has only one lens. The eyes are always open because they lack eyelids. Two hairlike feelers, or *antennae*, sensitive to touch and sometimes smell, are also found on most insect heads.

The middle section, or thorax, is where the legs and wings are attached. Some insects have one pair of wings, and others have two pairs; a few have none.

The *abdomen* contains the organs of digestion, excretion, and reproduction. Tiny holes (*spiracles*) in the thorax and abdomen furnish air for breathing. The air is piped into the internal organs by a network of connected tubes.

INQ Figure 8–9 Insects have three distinct body parts and three pairs of legs.

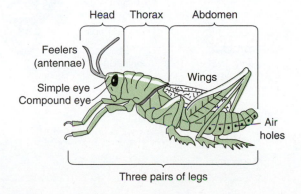

Crickets and katydids hear through a tiny eardrum located on each foreleg just below the "knee" joint. Look for an oval spot of slightly different color. Grasshoppers also have visible eardrums. These are located on each side of the abdomen's first section. Lift up the insect's wings and look for a disklike membrane just above where the rear legs are attached.

Survival Features

Insects have survived so successfully for several reasons. Most can fly; this provides a great range for potential food. Insects typically have very sensitive nervous systems; they are particularly sensitive to odors related to their food. The thorax may be packed with striated muscles that can contract immediately on signal; this makes many insects difficult to catch. The compound eyes increase this advantage because they cover a wide-angle view.

Although insects are cold-blooded, as are all known invertebrates, their small size often permits them to secure adequate shelter when the weather becomes cold. Many pass through the winter months in a resting or inactive stage. Perhaps most important for their survival as a group is how quickly they produce new generations.

Life Cycles

The life cycles of insects are most interesting. Eggs are fertilized internally and hatched externally. In most species, the insect goes through a complete metamorphosis of four stages as it matures: egg, larva, pupa, and adult. The fertilized *egg* hatches a *larva* (caterpillar), which eats continually and sheds its skin several times as it grows. Then it either spins a cocoon (e.g., moth larva) or encases itself in a chrysalis (e.g., butterfly larva) and enters the *pupa* stage. The body tissues change during this "resting" period. Sometime later an *adult* insect emerges.

Some insects, such as the grasshopper, cricket, termite, and aphid, go through an incomplete metamorphosis of three stages: egg, nymph, and adult. The fertilized *egg* hatches a young, or *nymph,* which resembles the *adult* except that it appears out of proportion and lacks wings. As it grows, molting takes place several times. There is no pupa stage (see INQ Figure 8–10).

Students will enjoy observing some insects go through several stages of their life cycles, and they will learn from this procedure. Suggestions for doing so with crickets and mealworms are included in upcoming activities.

INQ Figure 8–10   **Grasshopper and butterfly metamorphoses.**

Butterflies and Moths

Insects are distributed throughout the world, from the polar regions to the tropics. They range in size from microscopic to more than 60 centimeters (2 feet). With 800,000 species already found, scientists believe more than 800,000 insect species could be on the earth. Common insects are the butterfly, moth, and mealworm.

Some teachers like to show stages in the life cycles of butterflies and moths. Children will not be able to locate eggs, as these are usually too small to see. Even so, they should be able to find and bring in caterpillars, cocoons, and chrysalises. Remind them to take several leaves from the plant on which the caterpillar was feeding when captured. A fresh supply may be needed every few days.

Use a glass jar or similar container to house each of these specimens (INQ Figure 8–11). Place inside some soil and an upright twig from which the larva might suspend its chrysalis. Either a cheesecloth lid secured with an elastic band or a perforated jar top should provide enough air. Moisten the soil occasionally for cocoons and chrysalises, as they may dry up without sufficient humidity.

For a larger, more elaborate insect terrarium, see INQ Figure 8–12. You will need two cake pans, a section of wire screen, paper fasteners, an upturned jar lid (for water), several twigs and leaves, and some soil. Roll the screen into a cylinder to fit inside the cake pans. Secure the screen seam with several paper fasteners. Put soil in the base. To make the base heavier and firmly implant a small branch, you may want to pour some mixed plaster of paris into the bottom cake pan before adding the soil.

To show the entire life cycle of an insect from egg to adult, raise some silkworm moths in class. Within about 8 weeks, children will see larvae hatch from the eggs, feed busily for a time, spin cocoons and pupate, emerge from the cocoons as adult moths, mate, lay eggs, and die. Eggs and specific instructions can be purchased inexpensively from a biological supply house. The mulberry leaves on which the larvae feed are found in most parts of the continental United States.

Another insect with a short (6–8 weeks) life cycle is the greater wax moth. It also may be bought from several biological supply companies.

INQ Figure 8–11   A transparent jar may permit children to observe the life cycles of some insects.

INQ Figure 8–12   A homemade terrarium for butterflies and moths.

Cake pan

Paper
fastener

Mealworms

The grain beetle (*Tenebrio molitor*) is one of the easiest insects to keep and observe. It, too, undergoes a complete four-stage metamorphosis. This insect has a particularly interesting larval stage, during which time it is called a *mealworm*. Mealworms shed their skin from 10 to 20 times during the 4 to 5 months they remain in the larval stage. The entire metamorphosis takes 6 to 9 months. Cultures of this insect can be bought inexpensively at pet stores.

Crayfish and Brine Shrimp

Crayfish, shrimp, lobsters, crabs, water fleas, barnacles, and sow bugs are in a class of animals called *crustaceans*. Like insects and other animals with jointed legs, most crustaceans have external skeletons made of chitin. Muscles and other body parts are attached inside to this semirigid exterior. Like insects, crustaceans need to shed their outside covering, or molt, several times in order to grow.

Unlike insects, which have three body parts, crustaceans have only two: a fused-together head and thorax, and an abdomen. All crustaceans but the sow bug and its relatives live in water. All breathe through gills and have two main pairs of feelers, or antennae.

Crayfish

With its hard shell and five pairs of legs, the crayfish looks much like a lobster (INQ Figure 8–13). Crayfish are widely found in the United States, living in and along the banks of muddy freshwater streams, marshes, and ponds.

Crayfish are caught with minnow traps, scooped up with small nets, or simply pulled up when they grasp a chunk of fish dangling at the end of a string. Biological supply houses (see Appendix C) also furnish them.

Crayfish are found more easily at night, when they emerge from burrows or from between stones to prey on small fish and insects. During the day or night, they may also be caught by flipping over flat stones and quickly grasping them by hand from the rear. They

INQ Figure 8–13   A crayfish.

INQ Figure 8–14   Brine shrimp.

can be safely brought back to the classroom in a plastic bucket loosely filled with wet grass and pond weeds and just enough water to cover the bucket bottom.

Crayfish need a roomy, shallow water habitat. A child's plastic wading pool is suitable for keeping them in a classroom. Their behaviors there give many chances for observing, reporting, and other language activities. Their interactions are particularly interesting to observe, as a recognizable "pecking order" soon emerges.

Brine Shrimp

Adult brine shrimp are no more than 12 millimeters (0.5 inch) long (INQ Figure 8–14). However, these animals are crustaceans, just like their distant cousins, the shrimp, which we eat. Their tiny eggs are found around the shores of salt lakes and salt flats.

Brine shrimp eggs may be hatched in saltwater within a wide range of salt concentrations. The eggs are produced in a curious way. The first group of eggs produced by the female hatch inside her body. What emerges are tiny, almost transparent brine shrimp. Any further eggs produced by the same female are released directly into the water. These eggs will hatch only if they are first dried. They may survive for years in a dry condition before being hatched.

Snails ——————

Snails belong to one of the largest animal phyla, the soft-bodied *mollusks*. Most live in the ocean; they include the squid, octopus, oyster, clam, and many other less familiar animals. Mollusks are divided into three subgroups according to how the foot is attached.

Snails are among the belly-footed mollusks (*gastropods*). A snail has a single shell and travels on what seems to be its abdomen, but what is really a soft, muscular *foot*. The foot secretes a *mucus*, or slime, that reduces friction and protects it from being irritated as the snail moves over different surfaces. The mucus is so effective that a snail may travel over a row of upturned razor blades without injury (although children should not try this).

Water, or pond, snails have one pair of stalks, or tentacles, each with a tiny eye at the base. Most are smaller than the land snails, and many breathe through gills. Land, or garden, snails are lung breathers and have two pairs of tentacles. The upper pair has primitive eyes at the tips. The lower pair carries organs of smell. When threatened, land snails retract their tentacles; water snails do not.

Like the water snail, each land snail has both male and female sex organs. It lays tiny, single eggs, up to about 100 at a time. These may be found in small depressions in the soil, often by the base of a plant. The tiny snails that hatch from the eggs eat leaves, as do the adults. The adults live for about 5 years.

Land snails need a humid environment to be active. When its habitat begins to dry out, a land snail usually attaches itself to some object. A mucous secretion forms and dries over its shell opening. This seal greatly reduces water loss. The snail may remain in this inactive state for months, until its habitat becomes humid again.

Snails have filelike tongues that shred vegetation into bits small enough to be swallowed. In an aquarium, the tongue of a snail may be observed with a hand lens as it scrapes green algae off the sides of the tank.

Earthworms ——————

The earthworm is a *segmented worm*, the most developed of three broad groups of worms. Its body may have more than 100 segments. The earthworm's peculiar way of eating makes it valuable to farmers and gardeners: It literally eats its way through the soil. The decaying plant and animal matter in the soil is digested as it passes through the earthworm's body. The soil that the earthworm eliminates from its body is improved in fertility, but the side effects are even more important: The soil is loosened and aerated. Also, mineral-rich soil below the surface is brought up and mixed with mineral-depleted surface soil. The earthworm moves through and on the soil by alternately stretching and contracting its body.

Earthworms are skin breathers; that is, they take in oxygen and release carbon dioxide directly through the skin. For this to happen, the skin must be moist. It is important to have wet hands or use a wet file card and spoon when handling them since this dries out their skin.

ECOLOGICAL Inquiry

Food Chains

Invitation

What is a food chain? Plants need the sun to grow. Many insects eat plants, many toads eat insects, many snakes eat toads, and many hawks eat snakes. This is one example of a food chain. What do you think happens when a food chain is broken?

Exploration

1. Each person should pin a card to his or her clothes.
2. Stand in line and hold hands in this order: sun, plant, insect, toad, snake, and hawk.
3. What animals would die if they had no snakes to eat? (The snake person should drop hands now.)
4. What animals would die if they had no toads to eat? (The toad person drops hands.)
5. What animals would die if they had no insects to eat? (Insect person drops hands.)
6. What animals would die if they had no plants to eat? (Plant person drops hands.)
7. What would happen if there were no sun to help plants grow? (Sun person drops hands.)

Concept Invention

1. What would happen if there were no hawks?
2. Do hawks belong to other food chains?
3. Do we belong to any food chains?

> **MATERIALS**
>
> - Six cards with one of these words or pictures on each (*sun, plant, insect, toad, snake, hawk*)
> - Six persons
> - Six pins

Teaching Tips

Be sure to point out that these animals might eat a wider variety of food than is shown in this simple chain, but the basic idea of interdependence is valid. This idea can be clarified further by making more food chains. Older children can connect two or more food chains to make a more complicated *food web.* Run strings between and among individuals in the web to show the intricate interrelationships involved.

Scaffolding for English Learners

One way to make this activity easier and more meaningful for English learners is to use computer drawing or animation software in the development of a sample food chain. (See Buxton, 1999, for a discussion of the value of using software with English learners.)

Concept Application

Can you think of other animals and plants that might comprise a food chain? List them, and draw lines and arrows showing who eats what in your food chain.

How Color Protects Animals ———

MATERIALS

- Brown and green construction paper
- Lawn area
- Scissors
- Bare dirt area
- 1/2 cup of birdseed
- Set of food colorings
- Jar
- Stopwatch or nonelectric clock with second hand

Invitation

If you were an insect that lived in the grass, what enemies might you have? How might having the right color protect you from being eaten by birds and other animals? How can you test whether color affects the chances to survive?

Exploration

1. Cut out 100 same-sized pieces of green paper and 100 of brown paper. Make each piece about the size of your thumbnail.
2. Have someone scatter 50 pieces of each color on a lawn area.
3. Pretend the paper pieces are insects and you are a bird. Try to find as many pieces as you can in 1 minute. As shown, let some partners help you.

 Teaching Tips Try to have the colors of the construction paper match as closely as possible the lawn and bare dirt areas. For the birdseed activity, allow several hours between scattering the seeds and locating the surviving seeds. Make sure students realize that they may not be able to locate all the surviving seeds. How can they increase their chances of locating survivors? They may decide to enclose groups of seeds with string or to try other methods.

Concept Invention

1. How many pieces of each color of paper did you find? Which color would be better if you were a lawn insect?
2. Suppose you were an insect that lived in a bare dirt area. Which color would be better? What could you do to find out?
3. How could colored seeds be tested with real birds? Mix a few drops of food coloring with water in a jar. Drop in the seeds to color them.
4. Observe closely the insects on different plants. How are their colors like those of the plant? How are their colors different from those of the plant?

Concept Application

Survival chances increase when an animal's color matches its surroundings. How are other animals protected by their skin colors? Look in books and magazines for colored pictures of animals in their natural habitats. Describe what you find.

Ant Responses to Sweeteners ——————

Invitation

Some people do not use regular sugar because it has a high energy value. Instead, they may use an artificial sweetener, which has a low energy value. Many people cannot tell the difference between the tastes of the two. You probably know that ants and some other insects are attracted to sugar. But what attracts them? Is it the taste or something else? How can you test ant responses to real and artificial sugar?

Exploration

1. Mix about one bottle cap each of sugar and water in a cup. Use a spoon to stir. Pour the mixture into one cap until it is full.
2. Do the same with sweetener and water. Use a second cap and cup. Remember to rinse the spoon clean before you stir again.
3. Place both caps close together where there are ants. Mark which cap contains the sugar. Watch what happens.

MATERIALS

- One or more artificial sweeteners
- Sugar
- Two small matched bottle caps
- Water
- Two paper cups
- Teaspoon
- Outdoor area with ants

Teaching Tips You may want to check where children put the caps. They should be equally accessible to the ants.

Concept Invention

1. What do you notice? Which mixture attracts more ants?
2. What will happen if you test the sweetener by itself?
3. What will happen if you test it with different kinds of ants?
4. What will happen if you test different sweeteners?

Concept Application

The ability to respond to a high-energy food can help an animal survive. How can you find out how other insects will act toward artificial sweeteners? Keep a record of your findings. Look it over. How do the responses of these animals help them stay alive?

MATERIALS

- Wild birds
- Different kinds of bird food (bread crumbs, seeds, bacon bits)
- Handkerchief
- Meterstick or yardstick

The Fright Distances of Wild Animals ——————

Invitation

One difference between wild and tame animals is how easily they are frightened. How close have you come to a wild bird before it flew off? How about other wild animals? What are the fright distances of some wild birds?

Teaching Tips

Children can usually notice differences in bird species, but they often have trouble communicating what they see. A simple bird identification book can help. If possible, let children repeat this activity over several days. They will discover that birds and other wild animals typically decrease their fright distances if the same harmless stimulus is presented each time. Remember that children should never touch wild animals that approach humans and never feed them by hand. Such animals are abnormal and may be ill.

Exploration

1. Go where there are some wild birds.
2. Sprinkle some breadcrumbs on the ground at different distances from you.
3. Watch where the birds pick up the crumbs each time. Measure the closest distance the birds dare to come near you.

Concept Invention

1. What is the fright distance of these birds? Is every bird in this group frightened at the same distance? Are other kinds of birds frightened at another distance?
2. What would be the fright distance if you tried other foods?
3. Suppose you go to the same place and drop crumbs each day for a week. What do you think the fright distance of the same birds would be then?
4. How close can you get to different birds without food? Slowly walk toward each perched bird until it flies away. Measure the distance between you and the perch place each time.
5. How do different sounds and noises affect fright distance? different movements?

Concept Application

Fright behavior is an inborn property of wild animals that helps them survive. Fright distance may decrease when animals become familiar with objects or events. What are the fright distances of other wild animals? Find squirrels, chipmunks, and other animals. Make a record of what happens with other animals.

Bird Nests —————

Invitation

Have you ever seen a bird nest close up? Birds do not have to learn how to make nests. This is an inborn behavior. Birds use the nest to lay and hatch eggs. The hatched chicks stay there until they grow up enough to go out on their own. The materials used for the nest may come from many different things. Sometimes the materials birds use are quite surprising. How can you find out more about how some birds make nests? Given choices, what materials will some birds pick to make nests?

Exploration

1. Look for abandoned bird nests in trees and large bushes. Collect several nests. Ask a responsible adult to help you. Bring the nests to class.
2. Punch many holes in the cardboard with a large nail. Wiggle the nail in each hole to make it larger. Cut narrow pieces of cloth, paper, and foil. Cut small pieces of string and yarn. Thread these materials partway through the cardboard's holes. Label under each hole what is there. Tack the cardboard to a tree where other trees and bushes grow. Check the board each day to see what is missing.

MATERIALS

- Several abandoned bird nests
- Pencil
- Tweezers
- 60-centimeter (2-foot) cardboard square
- Aluminum foil
- Large nail
- Different kinds of string
- Scissors
- Different kinds of cloth
- Different colors of yarn
- Different kinds of paper
- Tack or nail
- Hammer

Concept Invention

1. What is the size and shape of each nest that was collected? How is each made? How are the nests alike? How are the nests different? What materials were used to make these nests? Use tweezers and a pencil to help you pick apart the nests.

2. Make a list of the materials. Which seem to come from where the birds live? Which, if any, seem to come from far away? What kind of bird probably made each kind of nest? Get some bird books from the library. See if they can help you find out.

3. Which of your materials were taken first when birds were making new nests? Replace these materials right away. Will they be taken again before other materials? Check again to see.

4. How can you change the picked materials to make them less attractive? You might cut longer pieces of yarn, for example, or cut wider cloth strips. How can you make the unpicked materials more attractive?

5. What will happen if you move the board to another place? How will your findings compare with those before?

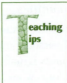

Teaching Tips — Bird nests are usually abandoned by winter and are rarely used again. So, winter is a good time to collect nests. In the unlikely event that eggs are found, the nest should be left undisturbed. The materials-selection board is best placed off the ground on a tree trunk or low limb away from traffic, but visible and accessible to the children.

Concept Application

Birds use materials from the environment to build their nests; the ability to build nests has survival value. Make a list of the materials selected by the birds to make new nests. How does it compare with the list of nest materials in the nests that you found?

ECOLOGICAL CONCEPTS

In previous sections, you have seen some ways that animal bodies are adapted to the requirements of their physical environments. In this section, we take up some factors that influence the numbers and quality of animal populations. To do so, we first need to examine some concepts from *ecology*, or the study of interactions of living things with each other and their physical environment.

Habitats and Their Dwellers

A *habitat* is the specific environment or place where an animal or plant lives. There are many different kinds of habitats. On land, we see desert, woodland, frozen tundra, farm, vacant lot, and garden habitats, to name just a few. Each contains animals and plants equipped to live in these locations. The many freshwater and saltwater habitats contain diverse living things, too. Some habitats fluctuate between a semidry and a watery condition, like seashores. Here, too, we see creatures equipped to live and continue their kind.

Populations

Within a habitat, we usually can find any number of organisms of the same kind that live and reproduce there. This is a *population*. A habitat is likely to have more than one population. For example, a "vacant" lot may contain a half-dozen different animal populations: worms, snails, mice, spiders, or various insects. It most likely will contain different plant populations as well: dandelions, alfalfa, clover, or various grasses or weeds.

Communities

A human community is made up of people with different skills and needs. When groups of these persons interact properly, the community sustains itself. Likewise, a natural *community* is made up of interacting plant and animal populations. Plants grow when their needs for raw materials are met. Plant eaters eat some of the plants, and animal eaters eat some of the plant eaters.

Food Chains and Webs

The connection between plants, plant eaters, and animal eaters is called a *food chain*. For example, in a freshwater habitat, tiny fish called minnows eat water plants, and the minnows in turn are eaten by frogs. We can diagram the relationship like this:

Water plants → minnows → frogs

The arrows show the direction of food transfer.

Real-life food chains and food webs are seldom so simple. Usually, more animals are involved, and they eat more than one kind of plant or other animal. For example, we may see something like INQ Figure 8–15.

We can classify the organisms in this food web into three groups: *producers* (plants), *consumers* (animals), and *decomposers* (bacteria and molds). All three types are usually present in a food web. Consumers are further grouped as *predators* (animal eaters) and *prey* (animals eaten by the animal eaters). Most preyed-upon animals are plant eaters.

A large percentage of plants and animals do not complete their life cycles because they are consumed. Those that do complete their cycles finally become food for the decomposers. These organisms are essential to new life because, through decay, they break down animal and plant matter into minerals, water, and gases. The minerals become part of the soil. The water and gases go back into the air. These elements are used again by growing plants.

An Ecosystem and Its Energy

To survive, animal and plant communities depend on interactions with the physical environment and with each other. Air, water, soil, temperature, and light all play a part in sustaining life. This web of relationships between a community and its physical environment is called an *ecosystem*. There is no strict agreement about its size. Some scientists regard the whole earth as one ecosystem. Others regard the term as referring to the interactions within a small habitat.

All life in any ecosystem depends on the transfer of energy. You saw how this happens with food webs. But some source must start the energy transfer. That source is the sun. The process that makes the energy usable, of course, is photosynthesis. Even our fossil fuels hold the sun's energy, locked up millions of years ago in buried plant and animal forms.

INQ Figure 8–15   Food web.

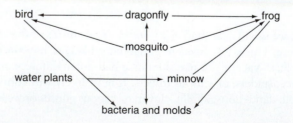

Biotic Potential ———————

Earlier, we jokingly suggested that you not be too efficient at breeding guppies. A single pair might result in 3 million guppies in a year. A huge reproductive capacity is found in many other living things as well. The greatest increase possible in a population without deaths is called its *biotic potential*. For many reasons, no population achieves this potential. Let's look at some of these reasons.

Limiting Factors

Every known organism needs certain environmental conditions to survive. Without certain supplies of air, chemicals, water, light, or proper temperature, for example, living things typically die. If only a certain amount of these factors is present, organisms may barely survive but not reproduce. Every organism seems to have an optimum range of conditions in which it flourishes. Knowing these conditions is the key to success at cultivating plants and raising animals.

Physical barriers, disease, and predators also limit populations. Sea plant growth stops at the shores, animals suffer from diseases just as humans do, and predators must eat to stay alive.

Adaptations

Both animals and plants have some adaptations that allow many to survive when limiting factors come into play. When winter comes, some birds migrate and some mammals hibernate or grow thicker coats of fur. At other times, many insects go undetected by predators because their body colors blend into their surroundings. Grasshoppers may literally fly on to greener pastures when they run low on food. In a huge population, the sheer number allows some members to survive even with a combination of bad conditions.

With less prolific animals, such as birds and mammals, fewer offspring would seem to pose a greater risk to population survival. But these animals compensate for the lack of numbers by an increased capacity to care for their young.

For example, a bird may build a nest for its eggs and feed its young until they are ready to fly. It has the capacity to pick the proper materials from its environment and assemble them in a way that suits the function. The bird does not have to learn this task from older birds; it does the intricate job properly the first time.

So-called instinctive behavior is a common property of animals. A spider does not have to learn how to make its complex web. Nor does an ant have to learn to choose between a solution of high-energy sugar water and an artificial sweetener of little caloric value. Nature abounds with many such examples.

Such adaptations bring about a dynamic balance in population sizes. Limiting factors reduce populations, but adaptive behaviors counter these factors enough so that population sizes stabilize.

The significant exception to the rule, of course, is the human animal. By eradicating most diseases and predators, the human population has grown at a fantastic pace. In the long run, however, limiting factors will exact their toll unless we, too, live in ways that make ecological sense.

Pollution

The problem of environmental pollution is that it introduces another limiting factor into ecosystems. Pollution usually happens faster than organisms can adapt to the changes introduced. The result is a decline in at least some of the populations subjected to the pollution. The populations most likely to decline are the more complex forms of plant and animal life, incluidng humans. Those less likely to decline are the primitive plants and animals, the decomposers, and their kin.

INQ Figure 8–16   Carbon dioxide–oxygen cycle.

INQ Figure 8–17   Nitrogen cycle.

Material Cycles

Scientists refer to the earth as a *closed ecosystem;* that is, almost no new raw materials enter or leave the system. Because an ecosystem ultimately depends on its raw materials, it is essential to life that these materials are never used up. Fortunately, they never are. The materials basic to life are used over and over in a kind of cycle. Next, we consider three important cycles.

Carbon Dioxide–Oxygen Cycle

Living things need oxygen to convert stored food into energy. As a by-product, they give off carbon dioxide. This is true of plants as well as animals. Decomposers also release carbon dioxide as they work. Fortunately, plants need carbon dioxide to carry on photosynthesis. During this process, plants take in carbon dioxide and give off much oxygen.

Decomposers and animals give plants carbon dioxide, and plants give all living things oxygen. The process is continual and may be diagrammed like INQ Figure 8–16.

Another side to this gas exchange is important to realize. An essential part of living cells is the element carbon. Plants get the carbon they need from the food they make during photosynthesis. Animals get carbon from the plants they eat or from animals that eat plants.

Nitrogen Cycle

Another cycle occurs with the element nitrogen. It, too, is an essential part of living cells. The air contains plenty of nitrogen, but neither plants nor animals can use it in a gaseous form. How can it be converted into a form living things can use? The basic way this is done in nature is through bacteria attached to the roots of such plants as clover, beans, alfalfa, and peas. The bacteria combine nitrogen with other elements to make chemical compounds called *nitrates*. Plants absorb the nitrates as they grow. Animals eat the plants and therefore get the nitrogen they need. When the animals die, decomposers convert the nitrogen into a gaseous form again as part of the decay process. This process is continual and may be diagrammed as illustrated in INQ Figure 8–17.

Water Cycle

As you may know, water on the earth's surface continually evaporates, condenses at some altitude in the sky, and falls again as rain, hail, or snow. Living things need water to transport chemicals to cells and remove waste materials from cells. Plants release water through *transpiration*, a process whereby water vapor passes out mainly through holes in the leaves into the air. Animals release water through exhalation, through perspiration, and in waste products. The released water goes into the air and becomes part of the water cycle.

Seen in this way, it is possible that a trace of the water that sustains you today may once have fallen on a dinosaur or on Julius Caesar's Rome.

References

American Association for the Advancement of Science (AAAS). (1993). *Benchmarks for science literacy*. New York: Oxford University Press.

Buxton, C. (1999). Designing a model-based methodology for science instruction: Lessons from a bilingual classroom. *Bilingual Research Journal, 32*(2, 3). Retrieved November 13, 2004, from http://brj.asu.edu/v2323/articles/art4.html

Carratello, P., & Carratello, J. (1994). *Animals (hands-on minds-on science series)*. Huntington Beach, CA: Teacher Created Materials.

Mastropieri, M., & Scruggs, T. E. (2004). *The inclusive classroom: Strategies for effective instruction* (4th ed.). Upper Saddle River, NJ: Merrill/Prentice Hall.

National Research Council (NRC). (1996). *National science education standards*. Washington, DC: National Academy Press.

Teachers of English to Speakers of Other Languages (TESOL). (2001). *Position statement on language and literacy development for young English language learners*. Alexandria, VA: Author. Retrieved November 13, 2004, from www.tesol.org/s$$$tesol/bin.asp?CID532&DID5371&DOC5FILE.PDF

Turnbull, R., Turnbull, A., Shank, M., & Smith, S. J. (2004). *Exceptional lives: Special education in today's schools* (4th ed.). Upper Saddle River, NJ: Merrill/Prentice Hall.

University of Alberta. (2001). *Animal terms or what do you call a . . . ?* Retrieved April 1, 2001, from www.biology.ualberta.ca/uamz.hp/name.html

Selected Trade Books: Animal Life

For Younger Children

Aaseng, N. (1987). *Meat-eating animals*. Minneapolis: Lerner.

Aaseng, N. (1987). *Prey animals*. Minneapolis: Lerner.

Berger, M. (2003). *Let's-read-and-find-out science books—Spinning spiders*. New York: HarperTrophy.

Breeden, R. (Ed.). (1974). *Creepy crawly things*. Washington, DC: National Geographic Society.

Bruchac, J. (1992). *Native American animal stories*. Golden, CO: Fulcrum.

Carle, E. (1987). *The very hungry caterpillar*. New York: Philomel.

Carle, E. (1995). *The very lonely firefly*. New York: Philomel.

Cousins, L. (1991). *Country animals*. New York: Morrow.

Crump, D. (1983). *Creatures small and furry*. Washington, DC: National Geographic Society.

Day, J. (1986). *What is a mammal?* New York: Golden Books.

Dewey, J. O. (2002). *Once I knew a spider*. New York: Walker and Company.

Dreyer, E. (1991). *Wild animals*. New York: Troll Associates.

Fleming, D. (1993). *In the small, small pond*. New York: Henry Holt.

Fowler, A. (1992). *It's best to leave a snake alone*. Danbury, CT: Childrens Press.

Freedman, R. (1980). *Tooth and claw: A look at animal weapons*. New York: Holiday House.

George, T. C. (2001). *Jellies: The life of jellyfish*. Brookfield, CT: Millbrook Press.

Glaser, L. (2003). *Brilliant bees*. Brookfield, CT: Millbrook Press.

Greenway, S. (1992). *Can you see me?* Nashville, TN: Ideals Children's Books.

Heiligman, D. (1996). *From caterpillar to butterfly*. New York: HarperCollins.

Lauber, P. (1965). *Who eats what? Food chains and food webs*. New York: HarperCollins.

Llewellyn. C. (2003). *Starting life butterfly*. Chanhassen, MN: Northword Press.

Markle, S. (2002). *Growing up wild: Penguins*. New York: Antheneum.

Mastro, J., & Wu, N. (2003). *Antarctic ice*. New York: Henry Holt & Co.

Miller, D. S. (2000). *River of Life*. New York: Clarion Books.

Oppenheim, J. (1986). *Have you seen birds?* New York: Scholastic.

Palotta, J. (1992). *The icky bug counting book*. Watertown, MA: Charlesbridge.

Pandell, K. (1996). *Animal action ABC*. New York: Dutton Children's Books.

Patent, D. H. (2003). *Fabulous fluttering tropical butterflies*. New York: Walker and Company.

Patent, D. H. (2003). *Slinky scaly slithery snakes*. New York: Walker and Company.

Penn, L. (1983). *Young scientists explore animal friends*. Torrance, CA: Good Apple.

Penny, M. (2000). *Giant panda: Habitats, life cycles, food chains, threats (natural world)*. Austin, TX: Raintree Steck-Vaughn Publishers.

Pfloog, J. (1987). *Wild animals and their babies*. Cambridge, Ontario: Western.

Posada, M. (2002). *Ladybugs: Red, fiery, and bright*. Minneapolis: Carolrhoda Books/Lerner.

Priestly, A. (1987). *Big animals*. New York: Random House.

Rockwell, A. (2001). *Let's-read-and-find-out science 1—Bugs are insects*. New York: HarperCollins.

Savage, S. (1992). *Making tracks*. New York: Lodestar Books.

Sayer, A. P. (2002). *Army ant parade*. New York: Henry Holt.

Sill, C., & Sill J. (2003). *About arachnids: A guide for children*. Atlanta: Peachtree Publishers.

Stone, L. M. (1983). *Marshes and swamps*. Danbury, CT: Childrens Press.

Sutton, F. (1983). *The big book of wild animals*. New York: G. P. Putman.

Tagholm, S. (2000). *Animal lives: The rabbit*. New York: Kingfisher.

Tatham, B. (2001). *Let's-read-and-find-out science series—Penguin chick*. New York: HarperCollins.

Urquhart, J. C. (1982). *Animals that travel*. Washington, DC: National Geographic Society.

Walker, S. M. (1998). *Sea horses (early bird nature)*. Minneapolis: Carolrhoda Books/Lerner.

Walker, S. M. (2001). *Fireflies*. Minneapolis: Lerner Publications.

Wildsmith, B. (1991). *Animal homes*. Norway, ME: Oxford Group.

Winer, Y. (2002). *Birds build nests*. Watertown, MA: Charlesbridge Publishing.

Wozmek, F. (1982). *The ABC of ecology*. Los Altos Hills, CA: May Davenport.

Zemlicka, S. (2002). *From egg to butterfly*. Minneapolis: Lerner Publications.

Zuchora-Walske, C. (2000). *Leaping grasshoppers*. New York: Kingfisher.

For Older Children

Branzei, S. (1996). *Animal grossology*. Reading, MA: Planet Dexter/Addison-Wesley.

Bright, M. (1987). *Pollution and wildlife*. Danbury, CT: Watts.

Crenson, V. (2003). *Horseshoe crabs and shorebirds: The story of a food web*. New York: Marshall Cavendish Corporation.

Crump, M. (2002). *Amphibians, reptiles, and their conservation*. North Haven, CT: Linnet Books.

Dean, A. (1977). *How animals communicate*. Parsippany, NJ: Julian Messner.

Dean, A. (1978). *Animal defenses*. Parsippany, NJ: Julian Messner.

Earle, S. A. (2000). *Sea critters*. Washington, DC: National Geographic Society.

Earthbooks Staff. (1991). *National Wildlife Federation's book of endangered species*. Winchester, VA: Author.

Fichter, G. S. (1991). *Poisonous animals*. Danbury, CT: Watts.

Galan, M. (1997). *There's still time: The success of the Endangered Species Act*. Washington, DC: National Geographic Society.

Gallant, R. A. (1986). *The rise of mammals*. Danbury, CT: Watts.

Hansard, P., & Silver, B. (1991). *What bird did that? A driver's guide to some common birds of North America*. Berkeley, CA: Ten Speed Press.

Heinz, B. J. (2000). *Butternut hollow pond*. Brookfield, CT: Milbrook Press.

Hickman, P. (1998). *Animal senses: How animals see, hear, taste, smell, and feel*. Toronto, Ontario: Kids Can Press.

Horowitz, R. (2000). *Crab moon*. Cambridge, MA: Candlewick Press.

Hostetler, M. (1996). *That gunk on your car: A unique guide to insects of North America*. Berkeley, CA: Ten Speed Press.

Imes, R. (1992). *The practical entomologist: An introductory guide to observing and understanding the world of insects*. New York: Simon & Schuster/Fireside.

Jenkins, S. (1997). *What do you do when something wants to eat you?* Boston: Houghton Mifflin.

Johnson, J. (2000). *National Geographic animal encyclopedia*. Washington, DC: National Geographic Society.

Kaufman, K. (2000). *Focus guide to the birds of North America*. Boston: Houghton Mifflin.

Leon, D. (1982). *The secret world of underground creatures*. Parsippany, NJ: Julian Messner.

Lerner, C. (1998). *Butterflies in the garden*. New York: HarperCollins.

Mason, C. (1998). *Everybody's somebody's lunch*. Gardiner, ME: Tilbury House.

Maynard, T. (1991). *Animal inventors*. Danbury, CT: Watts.

Patent, D. H. (2002). *Animals on the trail with Lewis and Clark*. New York: Clarion Books.

Penny, M. (1987). *Animal evolution*. Danbury, CT: Watts.

Pringle, L. (1987). *Home: How animals find comfort and safety*. New York: Macmillan.

Reed-Jones, C. (2001). *Salmon stream*. Sierra Nevadas, CA: Dawn Publications.

Ross, M. E. (2000). *Pond watching with Ann Morgan*. Minneapolis: Carolrhoda Books/Lerner.

Sabin, F. (1985). *Ecosystems and food chains*. New York: Troll Associates.

Sanders, J. (1984). *All about animal migrations*. New York: Troll Associates.

Swinburne, S. R. (2002). *The woods scientist*. Boston: Houghton Mifflin.

Thomas, P. (2000). *Marine mammal preservation*. Brookfield, CT: Twenty-First Century Books/Millbrook Press.

Witmer, L. (1995). *The search for the origin of birds*. Danbury, CT: Watts.

Yamashita, K. (1993). *Paws, wings, and hooves*. Minneapolis: Lerner.

Resource Books

Barrett, K. (1986). *Animals in action*. Berkeley, CA: Great Explorations in Math and Science.

Beals, K., Parizeau, N., & MacPherson, R. (2003). *Life through time*. Berkeley, CA: Great Explorations in Math and Science. (evolution activities)

Berg, C. (1994). *Chameleon condos: Critters and critical thinking*. Arlington, VA: National Science Teachers Association.

Burnett, R. (1992). *The pillbug project: A guide to investigation*. Arlington, VA: National Science Teachers Association.

Butzow, C. M., & Butzow, J. W. (1989). *Science through children's literature: An integrated approach*. Englewood, CO: Teacher Ideas Press. (animal reproduction and development topics on pp. 61–65; ducks, ants, spiders, ladybugs, and fish topics on pp. 66–94; animal adaptation topics on pp. 102–106)

Cordel, B. (Ed.). (1998). *Cycles of knowing and growing*. Fresno, CA: AIMS Education Foundation.

Cordel, B. (Ed.). (1998). *Field detectives*. Fresno, CA: AIMS Education Foundation.

Council for Environmental Education. (1992). *Project WILD*. Bethesda, MD: Author.

Echols, J. C. (1987). *Animal defenses*. Berkeley, CA: Great Explorations in Math and Science. (predator–prey relationships)

Echols, J. C. (1999). *Buzzing a hive*. Berkeley, CA: Great Explorations in Math and Science. (bee social behavior and habitat)

Echols, J. C. (1999). *Ladybugs*. Berkeley, CA: Great Explorations in Math and Science. (ladybugs and animal adaptation)

Echols, J. C. (2000). *Penguins and their young*. Berkeley, CA: Great Explorations in Math and Science. (penguin characteristics and social behavior)

Echols, J. C., Blinderman, E., & Kopp, J. (2001). *Elephants and their young*. Berkeley, CA: Great Explorations in Math and Science. (elephant characteristics and social behavior)

Echols, J. C., Hosoume, K., & Kopp, J. (1996). *Ant homes under the ground*. Berkeley, CA: Great Explorations in Math and Science.

Echols, J. C., Kopp, J., Blinderman, E., & Hosoume, K. (1999). *Mother opossum and her babies*. Berkeley, CA: Great Explorations in Math and Science. (opossum adaptations)

Fredericks, A. D., Meinbach, A. M., & Rothlein, L. (1993). *Thematic units: An integrated approach to teaching science and social studies*.

New York: HarperCollins. (animals and how they grow topics on pp. 111–122)

Hillen, J., Wiebe, A., & Youngs, D. (Eds.). (1992). *Critters*. Fresno, CA: AIMS Education Foundation.

Hoover, E., & Cordel, B. (Eds.). (1999). *Exploring environments*. Fresno, CA: AIMS Education Foundation.

Hosoume, K., & Barber, J. (1994). *Terrarium habitats*. Berkeley, CA: Great Explorations in Math and Science.

LeCroy, B., & Holder, B. (1994). *Bookwebs: A brainstorm of ideas for the primary classroom*. Englewood, CO: Teacher Ideas Press. (animal activities on pp. 30–31)

Mason, C., & Markowsky, J. (1998). *Everybody's somebody's lunch teachers' guide: The roles of predators in nature*. Gardiner, ME: Tilbury House.

Shaw, D. G., & Dybdahl, C. S. (1996). *Integrating science and language arts: A sourcebook for K–6 teachers*. Boston: Allyn & Bacon. (animal life topics on pp. 57–59)

THE HUMAN BODY AND NUTRITION

By any measure, the human body is a masterpiece of organization. It is composed of millions of tiny cells, many of them differing in shape, size, and internal makeup according to the work they do. Groups of cells that work together are called *tissues*. Examples are the connective tissue that holds the body together, muscle tissue, nerve tissue, blood tissue, and epithelial (skin) tissue. Tissues that work together are called *organs*. Examples are the lungs, heart, stomach, and eyes. Organs that work together are *systems*.

We now consider several body systems, including the skeletal and muscle systems, which support and move the body; the nervous system, which controls the body; the circulatory and respiratory systems, which move the blood and permit breathing; and the digestive system, which fuels the body by breaking down foods into simpler forms. A final section examines nutrition: the makeup of foods and how they affect the body.

Benchmarks and Standards

As students progress through the elementary years, they gain a more comprehensive understanding of the complexity of the human body and the need to care for it through proper nutrition and exercise. Examples of specific standards related to the human organism are as follows:

Sample Benchmarks (AAAS, 1993)

- People need water, food, air, and waste removal, and a particular range of temperatures in their environment. (By Grades K–2, p. 128)
- Food provides energy and materials for growth and repair of body parts. Vitamins and minerals, present in small amounts in foods, are essential to keep everything working well. (By Grades 3–5, p. 144)

Sample Standards (NRC, 1996)

- Humans have distinct body structures for walking, holding, seeing, and talking. (By Grades K–4, p. 129)
- The human organism has systems for digestion, respiration, reproduction, circulation, excretion, movement, control, and coordination, and for protection from disease. These systems interact with one another. (By Grades 5–8, pp. 156–175)

SKELETAL AND MUSCLE SYSTEMS Inquiry

Soft Bones

MATERIALS

- Narrow jar and cap
- Vinegar
- Safety goggles
- Two clean matched chicken bones
- Water

Invitation

What happens when minerals are removed from a bone?

Exploration

1. Put one bone in the jar. Leave the other one outside.
2. Put on safety goggles. Fill the jar with enough vinegar to cover the bone.
3. Cap the jar and remove your safety goggles. Wait 5 days.
4. Remove the bone from the jar and rinse it with water.

Concept Invention

1. Compare the bones. In what ways are the two bones different?
2. How easily does each bone bend?
3. How are the bones still alike?

Concept Application

What difference would it make if your bones had no hard minerals? What foods are rich in minerals?

All Thumbs

MATERIALS

- Paper clip
- Pencil and paper
- Tape

Invitation

How useful are your thumbs?

Exploration

1. Make a list of some things you can do now with one or two hands. Which do you think you cannot do without thumbs? Which might you do less well? Which might you do as well?
2. You might record what you think on a chart. You can make a check mark first for what you think, and then an X for what you find out.

Can Do With Thumbs	Can't Do Without Thumbs	Do Less Well	Do as Well
Pick up paper clip	✓		
Tie shoelace	✓		
Write my name		X	
Shake hands			
Button a shirt			
(Other)			

3. Ask someone to tape your thumbs to your hands.
4. Try doing the things on the list without using your thumbs.

Concept Invention

1. What surprises, if any, did you find?
2. How do your thumbs help you?

Concept Application

What would it be like if other mammals had thumbs like ours? How would this change their ways of doing things or survival?

Tired Muscles

Invitation

What happens when you overwork your muscles?

Exploration

1. Open one hand all the way and then quickly close it to make a tight fist.
2. Open and close it just like that for 1 minute without stopping. Do it as fast as you can.
3. Count and record what you are able to do during the first and last 30 seconds.

Concept Invention

1. How do the first half and the last half figures compare?
2. What difference might it make if you change hands?

> **Scaffolding for English Learners**
>
> When identifying the muscles or bones of the body, try to use no more than 12 new vocabulary words in a lesson. (See Fathman, Quinn, & Kessler, 1992, for more information on language principles for English learners.)

Concept Application

If you went more slowly, would you be able to make more fists in 1 minute? Can you make as many fists in a second trial? If not, how long must you rest in between to do so?

MATERIALS
• Pencil and paper
• Watch with second hand

SKELETAL AND MUSCLE SYSTEMS CONCEPTS

It is difficult to imagine how the human body would look without bones. It has more than 200 bones joined into a skeletal framework that gives the body its overall shape and support. The bones are not all individual, unique pieces that fit together. Rather, the bones are in groups, all well fitted for their specialized work.

Groups of Bones

The main part of the skull consists of eight relatively flat bones joined into the characteristic helmetlike shape. In children, the joints between the bones are movable. This allows the bones to grow as children get older. In adults, the skull bones will have grown together into a solid, curved surface with immovable joints. The only head bone we can ever move voluntarily is the jawbone. Chewing and normal conversation depend on this movement.

The skull is joined to a stack of oval and irregular small bones called the *vertebrae*, or spine. The vertebrae permit bending and twisting motions. Between each small bone is a pad of tough, elastic tissue called *cartilage*. The cartilage pads keep the spinal bones from grinding or hitting together during movement. As we age during adulthood, the pads continue to compress, making us shorter. Between ages 40 and 70, for example, we may lose 2.5 centimeters (1 inch) or more in height.

Each spinal bone also has a hole in its middle. The holes in the bones are lined up, making the vertebrae into a kind of hollow tube. The bundle of nerves that make up the spinal cord runs through the length of this protective tube of vertebrae. Side holes in the vertebrae permit nerve branches from the spinal cord to go out to other parts of the body.

Many children think that "standing up straight" means having a straight backbone. This is not so. Although the vertebrae are stacked in a column, the column is curved in a shallow S form. This shape permits better balance than a vertical backbone.

Attached to the backbone are 12 pairs of *ribs*. The top 10 pairs curve around and join the *breastbone* in front. But if you feel your two pairs of bottom ribs, you may notice that they are not joined in front. For this reason, they are called "floating ribs."

The ribs form a flexible cage that protects the heart, lungs, and other organs in the chest area. The cartilage that fastens the ribs is somewhat elastic, and the ribs are bendable. This is why the chest can expand and contract during breathing. The hipbones are fastened at the other end of the backbone. With the bottom of the backbone, they form a large and open shallow bowl in front, called the *pelvis*. The bowl helps support the body and protects some of the organs below the waist. The lowest parts of the hipbones are used for sitting.

The long bones of the arms and legs are the levers that allow us to walk, run, and throw. These bones are strong but also light for their size, because they are mostly hollow inside. If they were solid, the increased weight would slow us down considerably. Long bones are thicker at the ends than in the center section and fit the ends of adjoining bones.

Composition of Bones

A soft material called *marrow* is found inside many bones, particularly the long bones. There are two kinds of marrow. Red marrow is found at the ends of the bones, where red blood cells are manufactured. Yellow marrow is stored inside the middle of the bones and is mainly composed of fat.

A newborn baby's skeleton is composed mostly of soft cartilage. As the baby grows, its body continually replaces the cartilage with calcium and other minerals from digested food, so the skeleton continually hardens. Children's bones typically are softer than those of adults because they contain more cartilage. This makes their bones less likely to break under stress. Some cartilage never changes to bone, like the ears and the tip of the nose.

Movable Joints ———————

A rigid skeletal framework would be of little use to us. We can move because many bones are held together by movable joints. Tough, thick cords of elastic tissue, called *ligaments*, join bone to bone. We have several kinds of movable joints, and each allows different movements. *Hinged joints* allow us to bend the elbow, knee, and fingers. Notice that the movement is in only one direction.

The thumb is particularly interesting. It has only two hinged joints, yet we can move the thumb so that it opposes any finger. A third joint up near the wrist makes this movement possible.

A *ball-and-socket joint* at the shoulder allows rotary motion of the arm. A similar socket connects the upper leg bone at the hip, but movement in this case is more restricted. Other kinds of joints allow wrist, head, foot, and other motions. In all, we have six kinds of movable joints.

Muscles ———————

Under the skin and inside the body are about 600 muscles, two thirds of which are *voluntary muscles*. These muscles are connected to bones, and we can move them on command. Some muscles, such as those that move food through the intestines and those that make the heart beat, cannot ordinarily be controlled. These are *involuntary muscles*.

Muscles can only pull, not push. In other words, they work in opposite pairs. This is easiest to see with the jointed leg bones. If you swing a leg forward, muscles in the front part of the thigh and hip contract and pull the leg forward. If you swing the leg back, muscles in the back part of the thigh and hip contract and pull the leg back.

Tendons ———————

Muscles are attached to bone and cartilage by *tendons*. These are tough, white, twisted fibers of different lengths. Some are cordlike; others are wider and flat. Tendons are enclosed in sleeves of thin tissue that contain a slippery liquid. This lubricating liquid permits them to slide back and forth without rubbing.

Tendons are strong and unstretchable. Some that are easy to observe are found inside the elbow and at the back of the knee. One of the strongest and thickest tendons in the body is the Achilles tendon, located just above the heel of the foot. Also easy to observe are the tendons that pull the finger bones as you wiggle your fingers. If you try this and touch the forearm with the opposite hand, you will notice that muscles in the forearm, not muscles in the hand, mainly move the fingers. Children are usually surprised by this.

Makeup of Muscles ———————

How do muscles work? Why do they get tired? Why does exercise make us warm? A microscope reveals that voluntary muscles are made up of bundles of fibers, each about the size of a human hair but far stronger. Like the entire muscle, each fiber shortens as it pulls and lengthens as it relaxes. The number of fibers that work depends on how heavily the muscle is strained. Also, not all the fibers work simultaneously. Each is rapidly and continually switched on and off by the nervous system as the muscle works. This allows each fiber some rest and greater overall endurance for the muscle.

The energy to move a muscle comes from a form of sugar called *glycogen*. It is found inside the muscles' cells. About one fourth of the energy released by this sugar goes into moving the muscle; the rest is released as heat. The faster a muscle is used, the more heat is produced. This is why heavy exercise makes us warm.

Sooner or later, heavy exercise fatigues the muscle. Not only is the supply of glycogen consumed, but waste products also build up in the cell faster than they can be removed. As the waste products build up, the muscle fibers work more and more slowly.

NERVOUS SYSTEM Inquiry

Eye Blinking

Invitation

When do your eyes blink? Do they blink when something suddenly comes near them? Eye blinking can protect your eyes. Have you also found that your eyes blink at other times? Regular eye blinking wipes your eyes clean and keeps your eyes soft and moist. How much can you control your protective eye blinking?

Exploration

1. You will need to make an eye shield. Cut out the center of a large file card. Leave at least a 2-centimeter (1-inch) border.
2. Stick a double layer of clear kitchen plastic wrap to the border with tape.
3. Hold up the shield to your eyes. Look at your partner through the clear wrap, as illustrated. Let him gently toss a tiny wad of tissue toward it.

Teaching Tips

Closely monitor this activity. Blinking is an automatic reflex that children like to investigate. Many children find it hard to prevent the protective blinking reaction when the wad is tossed at the shield. This is good because the reaction has survival value. Regular blinking, of course, is easily controllable when we are conscious of the act. The rate varies widely among persons and is influenced by a variety of factors.

Concept Invention

1. Do your eyes blink each time the wad hits the shield? Can you stop your eyes from blinking?
2. Are you able to control your eye blinking with practice? If so, how much practice? Keep a record.
3. Trade places with some other people. How does their protective eye blinking compare with yours?
4. How often do a person's eyes blink the regular way? Secretly observe the number of times someone blinks for 1 minute. Compare the blinking rates of different people. Do their blinking rates change when they know you are observing them?

Adapting for Students with Exceptionalities

It may be hard for some students with physical handicaps to complete this activity. Allow them to work in groups of three so that they can have an extra partner for assistance or observation.

Concept Application

Eye blinking is a protective reflex action that is partly controllable. The rate of blinking varies among different people. How often do some animals blink their eyes? Which animals can you observe?

Your Reaction Time

Invitation

Have you ever had to stop fast when riding your bike? The time between when we sense something and when we act is called our *reaction time*. What people would you expect to have fast reaction times? What people would you expect to have slowed reaction times? How can you find out about your reaction time?

Exploration

1. Have your partner hold up a ruler just above your open thumb and forefinger. The ruler's lowest marked number should be facing down. Keep your eye on this ruler end.
2. Have your partner drop the ruler without warning. When you see it drop, close your fingers quickly and catch the ruler.
3. At what number did you catch the ruler? Read the closest whole number just above your two closed fingers. This is your reaction time number.

MATERIALS

- Ruler
- Paper
- Partner
- Pencil

Teaching Tips

For meaningful comparisons, it is important that students do the test in the same way. It is also important that the ruler be turned before it is dropped. You want the flat part of the ruler, not the ruler edges, to be pinched by the two fingers.

Concept Invention

1. What persons in your class may have faster reaction times than yours? What persons in your class may have slower reaction times? Test these persons and your partner. Keep a record.
2. Will you react to a sound you hear faster than to what you see? Have your partner make a sound just as she drops the ruler. Your eyes should be closed. Catch the

ruler when you hear the sound. Compare this reaction time number with the one made when you saw the ruler drop.

3. Will you react to a touch faster than to sound or sight? Your eyes should be closed. Your partner can touch your head lightly when she drops the ruler. Catch the ruler when you feel her touch. Compare this reaction time with the other times.

Concept Application

People have different reaction times. The sense signal people react to also makes a difference in their reaction times. Does the time of day affect your reaction time? Does practice make a difference? Does which hand you use make a difference? How can you find out? What other ideas would you like to try?

How Practice Improves Learning

Invitation

Suppose you learn to do something one way, and then someone says you must learn to do it another way. Why might this be hard to do? How might learning to draw or write backward be a problem? How might practice help? How can you learn to do mirror drawing or writing?

Exploration

1. Draw a triangle on paper, no larger than the one pictured here.

Start

2. Arrange the paper, a mirror, and a book as shown. Use two pieces of clay to hold up the mirror.

3. Sit so that you must look into the mirror to see the triangle.
4. Place your pencil point on the triangle corner at "start."
5. Observe a watch and notice the time.
6. Draw a line inside and around the whole triangle. Look at the mirror to see what you are doing. Keep the line between the inside and outside border of the triangle. If you go beyond the borders, stop drawing. Start again from the place where you left the border.
7. When you complete the drawing, check the time again. Record in seconds how long it took for this first trial.

Teaching Tips

You may have to help some children with the line graphs if they lack experience. Also, expect some children to have trouble deciding how many seconds it takes to draw completely around each figure.

Number of Trials	Time to Finish (Seconds)
1	160
2	140
3	100
4	70

Concept Invention

1. How will practice affect the time needed to draw around the triangle? How much faster will your second trial be? How much faster will your third trial be? How much faster will your fourth trial be? Make a record like this of what you find out.
2. Make a graph of your findings. Notice how to do this on the graph shown here. Suppose it took 160 seconds to finish the first trial.
3. Put your finger on 1 at the bottom. Follow the line up to and opposite 160. Place a dot where the two lines cross. Check to see how the other figures are recorded. See how a line has been drawn from one dot to the next. This line is called a *curve*. The graph tells about learning, so the line may be called a *learning curve*.
4. Study your own learning curve. How fast do you think you can draw the triangle after 6 trials? after 7 trials? after 8 trials? after 9 trials? after 10 trials? Record your findings on your graph and complete your learning curve.
5. How does your learning curve compare with those of others? Do some people learn mirror drawing faster than others?

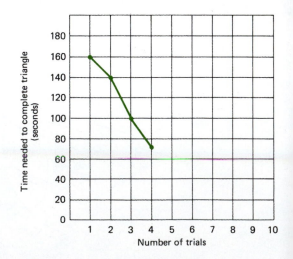

Concept Application

An earlier learning may interfere with a later learning. Proper practice can improve one's performance. Try a mirror drawing of another figure, such as a large 8 like the one shown here. What shape will your learning curve be for this figure? Will people who learned fast before learn fast again? What other problems about learning mirror drawing can you investigate?

Start

Your Sense of Touch ──────────

Invitation

What can you tell about an object by touch? What are some small objects you might know just by touching them? What objects can you match just by touch?

Exploration

1. Blindfold your partner or ask him to close his eyes. He should not see what you are doing.
2. Put two small, unlike objects inside the box, which should be upside down.
3. Place another small object outside the box. It should match one of the objects inside. Let your blindfolded partner feel it.
4. Next, have your partner feel the objects inside the box. Can he tell which one matches the outside object?
5. Take turns with your partner in playing this game. Use different objects each time. Later, use as many objects each time as you can.

Concept Invention

1. Which objects are hard to tell apart? Which are easy? What makes them easy or hard to tell apart?
2. Can you use touch to put objects in order by size? Can you use touch to put objects in order by roughness? Which objects?
3. Is it easier to tell what an inside object is if you can see the outside objects? How can you find out?
4. Is it easier to tell what an inside object is with two hands than with one? How can you find out?

MATERIALS

- Cloth blindfold
- Open cardboard box (with a hand–sized hole cut in each side)
- Matched pairs of small objects
- Partner

Teaching Tips

Many small objects around the classroom and home may be used in this activity. Among objects easily paired are chalk, pencils, leaves, erasers, crayons, nails, coins, washers, rubber bands, cloth of various sizes and textures, paper, foil, and toy figures. Size, texture, shape, hardness, and, to a minor extent, weight will be the properties used by children to identify objects by touch.

Concept Application

Several properties of an object can be discovered by touch. Try a challenging variation that stresses communication skills. One child holds an object behind her and describes its properties to a partner. The partner touches several objects inside the box and selects one that matches the description. The described and selected objects are then compared to see if they are identical. To make the task harder, make the differences among the objects less obvious. Also, put more objects inside the box. Describe your experiences.

The Sensitivity of Your Skin ————

MATERIALS

- Ruler
- Paper and pencil
- Partner
- Paper clip

Teaching Tips

Many of our nerve ends are found near the skin surface and are distributed unevenly. Typically, our fingertips are more sensitive to touch than other body parts, because a high concentration of nerve endings is located there. It is important that children who are being tested keep their eyes closed. Otherwise, their perception of touch may be altered by what they see. Supervise this activity closely to ensure that the paper clip points are touched lightly to the skin.

Invitation

Suppose you could not tell if something was touching your skin. How might this change your life? How can you find out how sensitive your skin is to touch?

Exploration

1. Open up and then bend a paper clip into a U shape.
2. Push the two points together so that they meet.
3. Touch the points lightly to the palm of your partner's hand. His eyes should be closed.
4. Ask your partner if he feels two points or one.
5. Separate the two points a short distance, as shown. Ask again if he feels two points or one.
6. Keep repeating this action. Each time, move the two points farther apart until your partner feels two points. Then measure the distance between the two points with a ruler.
7. Switch with your partner so that you can have your skin tested.

Concept Invention

1. Where on your skin can you feel the two points soonest? Let your partner measure and make a record like the one shown.

Body Part	Distance Between the Points
Fingertip	
Palm of hand	
Back of hand	
Back of neck	
Lips	

2. Look carefully at your completed record. Which seems to be the most sensitive place measured?
3. In what order should the places go if arranged from least to most sensitive?

Concept Application

Some places on the skin are more sensitive to touch than other places; also, some people are more sensitive to touch than others. How does your record compare with those of other people? Are some people more sensitive than others? If so, which people? Are certain places on people's skin more sensitive than others? If so, which places?

Your Sensitivity to Temperature

Invitation

Suppose you have two containers of water. One is slightly warmer than another. Could you tell by touch a temperature difference in the water? Does it depend on how much the difference is? How can you find out the smallest temperature difference you can feel?

Exploration

1. Dip a finger into each cup, as illustrated. It is probably easy now for you to tell which cup of water is cooler and which is warmer.

2. Let your partner pour a little of the cooler water into the warmer water. You can probably still easily feel the temperature difference.
3. Have your partner continue to reduce the temperature difference between the two cups. She can do this by pouring a little water back and forth between the cups. Keep feeling the water in both cups each time.
4. Stop when you can just barely tell there is a temperature difference. Make sure you are not just imagining this. Close your eyes and let your partner switch around the cups a few times. Tell your partner which cup is cooler or warmer each time. Always keep your eyes closed when the cups are switched.
5. Put the thermometer into each cup for at least half a minute. What is the difference between the two readings?

MATERIALS

- Two cups half-filled with water (one water sample should be warm)
- Paper and pencil
- Partner
- Thermometer (waterproof type)
- Clock with second hand

Teaching Tips

The beginning temperature difference between the two water samples should be obvious, but it need not be a wide one. If you do not have access to a hot-water tap, warm some water on a hot plate. Or, draw two half-cups of tap water and slip an ice cube into one for several minutes. Children will need the ability to read thermometers to do this investigation. The average child can detect a temperature difference as little as 1.5°C (3°F). Some children will detect an even smaller difference. The tester's eyes should be closed for each test.

Concept Invention

1. What is the smallest temperature difference your partner can feel?
2. Get some more warm and cool water and find out.

Concept Application

People differ in their sensitivity to temperature. Are some people more sensitive than others? Are people with thin fingers more sensitive than those with thicker fingers? Are toes more sensitive than fingers?

NERVOUS SYSTEM CONCEPTS

The Nerves ———————

What happens inside the nervous system when we sense an object and react to it? The central part of the nervous system is composed of the brain and spinal cord. Nerves connected to the brain and spinal cord branch out in ever smaller tendrils to all parts of the body.

When nerve endings are stimulated in some sense organs, ordinarily an electrical message is zipped through *sensory nerves* from the receptors to the spinal cord and then to the brain. In turn, the brain flashes back a message along *motor nerves*, which control muscles. The time between when the brain receives a signal and when it returns a command to the muscles is called one's *reaction time*.

Quick Reflexes ———————

A curious thing happens, however, when a quick reflexive action is required. The brain is bypassed until the *reflex* action happens. For example, if you should touch a finger to a hot stove, the electrical impulses travel from the finger to the spinal cord. But instead of the signal going on to the brain, the spinal cord itself flashes a signal along the motor nerves, which immediately activate muscles to jerk the hand away. Meanwhile, the spinal cord also sends impulses to the brain that cause you to feel pain. The sensation, though, is felt after you have already reacted to the danger. This process, of course, has survival value.

The Brain ———————

The brain is the control center of the body. Instead of a single mass, it consists of three parts: the cerebrum, the cerebellum, and the medulla. Each has a different job.

The *cerebrum* is the brain's largest part. It consists of two halves that occupy the top portion of the skull. This is the part that governs the conscious, rational processes and that receives signals from the senses. The cerebrum also controls the body's voluntary muscles.

The *cerebellum* is a far smaller part and is located below and behind the cerebrum. It governs perception of balance and coordinates the voluntary muscles.

The *medulla* adjoins the top of the spinal column at the base of the skull. It governs the involuntary muscles used for digesting food, coughing or sneezing, breathing, pumping blood, and the like.

Learning

How successfully we adapt to the environment often depends on our ability to learn. We learn in several ways. At the lowest level is trial-and-error learning. This is how we learn to do handwriting or hit a golf ball. The brain works in combination with the senses and muscles to provide corrective feedback.

Learning increases when we organize our data. Recognizing patterns, outlining, and drawing diagrams are some ways we improve learning. Learning also increases when we associate something we do not know with something we do know. Using memory devices to learn names or to remember spelling words are examples. Reasoning and problem solving are at the highest levels of learning.

The Senses

We receive most of the sensations that our brains turn into perceptions through five organs: the eye, ear, nose, tongue, and skin. How do they work? Let's look at each in turn.

The Eye

In the eye, as in the other sense organs, are the tiny nerve endings of neurons, or nerve cells. The *retina,* or back section of the eyeball, contains two kinds of light-sensitive neurons: rods and cones. The *cones* are clustered in and around the center of the retina and are sensitive to color. The *rods* are distributed outside the cones and are sensitive to light but not to color. The nerve endings of both rods and cones join into a bundle called the *optic nerve,* which leads to the brain. Electrical impulses from our eyes travel along this nerve to the brain. At that point, we see.

The Ear

The ear has three parts: outer, middle, and inner. The first two parts pass on sound vibrations to the inner ear, located deep inside the skull. The inner ear contains the *cochlea,* a spiral passage shaped like a snail's shell. Inside are sound-sensitive nerve endings and a liquid. When vibrations move into the inner ear, the cochlea's liquid vibrates and stimulates the nerve endings. This movement instantly transmits electrical impulses to the *auditory nerve,* which then zips them to the brain. At that point, we hear.

If you have ever been seasick, you can probably blame your inner ear. It has an intricate part that controls our sense of balance. The part consists of three tubes, formed in half circles, called the *semicircular canals.* The tubes contain a thin liquid and are arranged in three different positions relative to each other. These positions correspond to the three ways we move our head: up and down, sideways tilt, and the turning motion. Each motion of the head sloshes the liquid in one of the canals, stimulating nerve endings inside. The impulses are flashed along a branch of the auditory nerve that leads to the cerebellum rather than to the large cerebrum.

One seasickness theory states that the several motions felt in the inner ear conflict with what we see. This is especially so below deck. The sensory conflict triggers the body reaction we know as seasickness.

The Nose

The nose has nerve endings in the nasal cavity that are sensitive to chemicals. When breathed into the nose, the chemicals dissolve in the moist film of mucus that covers a membrane in the nasal cavity. There, nerve endings are stimulated to send signals to the sensory nerves and brain. Continual exposure to one odor causes the nerve cells to become insensitive to that odor. Yet, other odors may be detected very well at the same time.

Nerve cells of the nose seem to sense only four primary odors: burnt, rancid, acid, and fragrant odors. Some scientists think that every other odor may simply be some combination of two or more of the four primary odors.

The Tongue

Exactly what we taste is an individual matter, even though our tongues are similarly constructed. The tongue contains clusters of nerve cells in the tiny bumps we call *taste buds*. Taste buds are sensitive to four flavors: sweet, sour, salty, and bitter. Most buds are clustered in the tip, on the edges, and in the back of the tongue. The tip tends to be sensitive to sweet and salty flavors, the sides to sour flavors, and the back to bitter flavors. However, the exact places vary with people. The taste buds clump into small mounds called *papillae*. These are connected to a sensory nerve that leads to the brain.

Do you remember how tasteless food is when a head cold causes a stuffy nose? It is easy to confuse the sense of taste with that of smell. As we eat, the odors given off by the food stimulate the sense of smell. So, the organs of taste and smell work together.

Sometimes the sense of smell dominates. For example, if you chew a tiny piece of radish while you hold a small fresh piece of apple or onion under your nose, you will believe that you are eating the apple or onion.

The Skin

Our skin contains no fewer than five kinds of nerve endings, which are sensitive to pressure, touch, pain, heat, and cold. These nerve endings are positioned at various depths in the skin. Pressure, for example, is felt much deeper in the skin than touch.

Our nerve endings are also scattered unevenly. The lips and fingertips have many more endings clustered together than other places such as the back of the neck or arm. This is why they are so sensitive.

CIRCULATORY AND RESPIRATORY SYSTEMS Inquiry

People's Pulse Beats

Invitation

Your heart pumps blood through long tubes in your body called *arteries*. Your arteries are very elastic. They stretch and then shrink slightly each time the heart pumps more blood through them. These tiny movements are called *pulse beats*. You can tell how fast your heart pumps by feeling your pulse beats. How can you feel and measure how fast your pulse beats are?

MATERIALS

• Watch or clock with second hand

• Paper and pencil

Exploration

1. Press on the inside part of your wrist with four fingers as shown.

2. Find where you can best feel your pulse.
3. Count how often your pulse beats in 1 minute while sitting. The number of pulse beats in 1 minute is your "resting" pulse rate (this would differ when exercising).
4. Record your pulse rate on paper.

Concept Invention

1. How does what you do change your pulse rate? For example, how does standing affect your pulse rate? How does lying down affect your pulse rate? How does exercise affect your pulse rate?
2. How do your pulse rates compare before and after eating?
3. Where else on your body can you feel your pulse? Is the pulse rate there the same as at the wrist?

Teaching Tips

The pulse may also be felt quite easily on each side of the throat just under the chin. The pulse rate usually slows with age and size. Also, boys have slightly slower rates than girls. Seven-year-olds average around 90 beats per minute, which is almost twice the rate for the very aged. Athletic training also reduces the rate because it helps to develop a stronger heart. These factors similarly influence animal pulse rates, particularly size. An elephant, for example, has a very slow pulse rate. This investigation provides several opportunities to make useful graphs. For example, how long does it take for the pulse to return to a resting rate after exercise? What is the effect of eating on the rate? Also, watch for chances to control variables and make operational definitions: What is a tall, young, old, heavy, or tired person? If we are testing for age, how can we control height and weight?

Scaffolding for English Learners

When working on activities involving the human body, ensure that activities are culturally acceptable for all students. (See Laplante, 1997, for a discussion of approaches to teaching that are sensitive to culture.)

Adapting for Students with Exceptionalities

For students with a hearing impairment, use a stethoscope when listening to the heart. (See Mastropieri & Scruggs, 2004, for a discussion on activities involving anatomy in the chapter on science and social studies.)

Concept Application

One's pulse rate is a measure of how fast the heart beats in 1 minute. A variety of conditions may affect it. How do the pulse rates of different people compare? For example, how do the pulse rates of boys and girls compare? How do adults and children compare? How do young and old adults compare? Does tallness make a difference in a person's pulse rate? Does weight make a difference in a person's pulse rate? What else do you notice about people or what they do that might affect pulse rates? How do you think the pulse rates of dogs, cats, and other animals compare with those of humans? How can you find out?

The Volume of Air You Breathe

MATERIALS

- Large bowl or pail, placed in a sink
- Masking tape
- Plastic or glass bottle with cap (1 gallon, or 4 liter)
- String
- Rubber tube
- Ruler
- Paper strips
- Partner
- Pencil
- Water
- Graph paper

Invitation

How much air do you breathe in a single breath? How big a container do you think you would need to hold it? How can you find out how much air you breathe?

Exploration

1. Stick a strip of tape down the side of the bottle.
2. Mark the strip into 10 equal parts.
3. Partly fill a large bowl or pail with water.
4. Fill the bottle with water and cap it.
5. Put the bottle, upside down, into the bowl.
6. Remove the cap while the bottleneck is underwater.
7. Put one end of the tube into the bottle. (You may have to tip the bottle a little. Have someone hold the bottle so it does not go far over.)
8. Wrap a paper strip around the other end of the tube.
9. Take a regular breath. Then blow out the air through the tube. Quickly pinch the tube shut when you finish blowing. Observe how much water was forced out of the bottle. This tells you how much air you blew out.

10. Refill the bottle each time you try a breath test.

Concept Invention

1. By what tape mark is the water level for a regular breath? Make a record, so that you can compare it with other marks.
2. How much more air can you hold when you breathe deeply? Take a deep breath. Blow out all the air you can. Compare the new and old marks.
3. How much air can other persons blow out in one breath? (Wrap a fresh piece of paper around the tube end each time a new person blows through it.)
4. Make a graph of your findings. Use each person's chest size, or height, or weight for one part of your graph. Use each person's water level mark for the other part, as shown.

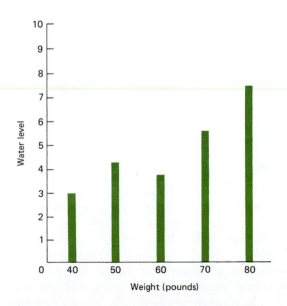

Concept Application

The volume of water displaced by "lung" air is a rough measure of lung capacity. People's lungs vary greatly in air capacity. Can you use your graph to predict more findings? For example, will two persons who weigh the same get the same results? Will two persons with the same height or chest size get the same results? What else do you notice about people that might affect how much air they can hold? For example, do athletes have more lung space than others? What is an "athlete"?

How Fast People Breathe ——————

Invitation

MATERIALS

- Watch or clock with second hand
- Pencil and paper

How many breaths do you take each minute? Does everyone breathe equally fast? What conditions may affect how fast people breathe? How can you find out how many breaths you take each minute?

Exploration

1. Count one breath each time you breathe out while sitting.
2. Observe the time on a clock. Count the number of times you breathe out in 1 minute.
3. Record the number on a piece of paper.

Teaching Tips

The main purpose of this investigation is to help children record and think about data. Children will discover a variety of breathing rates, but reasons for these differences will be inconclusive at their level of understanding. You might mention that there is no single proper breathing rate for everyone. What is natural for one person may not be for another.

Concept Invention

1. How fast do you breathe after exercise? Bend and touch your toes or do some other easy exercise for 1 minute. Then count your breaths for 1 minute.
2. How fast do other people breathe while sitting? Compare people who are different in weight, height, and sex. Tell them how to count their breaths. Keep time for 1 minute. Record each person's name and how fast each breathes.
3. How fast do other people breathe after exercise? Record your findings.
4. Can you predict how fast some people will breathe? Study your records and observe the people. What are the people like who are slow breathers? What are

the people like who are faster breathers? Perhaps other people who are like them will also be fast or slow. Pick a few people you have not tested before and find out.

Concept Application

People have different breathing rates. Exercise affects one's breathing rate. What else about people or about what they do might affect how fast they breathe?

CIRCULATORY AND RESPIRATORY SYSTEMS CONCEPTS

Circulatory System

It would be difficult to design a better system than the human blood system for the same function. *Blood* is the vehicle that transports food, chemicals, and oxygen to all parts of the body. It picks up wastes from the cells and moves them through organs whose job is to remove them. Blood also protects the body.

The liquid part of blood is a clear, yellowish substance called *plasma*. In the plasma are three kinds of solid materials: red blood cells, white blood cells, and platelets. The *red blood cells* are most numerous and give the blood its characteristic color. They carry oxygen from the lungs to the body's cells and carbon dioxide from the cells back to the lungs. *White blood cells* are larger and move about freely among the body's cells, attacking and consuming disease germs. *Platelets* also have an important function; they help make the blood clot wherever the body is injured and bleeding.

Blood moves throughout the body because the *heart*, a powerful muscle about the size of one's fist, pumps it by alternately contracting and relaxing. Oxygen-poor blood flows into one side of the heart. Squeezing motions pump this blood to the lungs, where it picks up oxygen and gets rid of carbon dioxide. The oxygen-rich blood then flows back into the opposite side of the heart, from where it is pumped to the rest of the body.

In a sense, the circulatory system is really a combination of two interconnected networks of tubes of various sizes. One network sends the blood from the heart to the lungs and back again to the heart. The other sends the blood from the heart to the rest of the body and returns it to the heart.

Oxygen-rich blood flows from the heart to the body through thick tubes called *arteries*. Arteries branch out all over the body, getting progressively narrower until they become extremely fine *capillaries*. Capillaries may be as narrow as one fiftieth the diameter of a human hair and are threaded throughout the cells. Digested food and oxygen pass out of the blood in the capillaries and into the adjacent cells. Blood in the capillaries also takes up carbon dioxide and other waste products from the cells. The waste-carrying capillaries join into progressively larger tubes called *veins*, which carry blood back to the heart. The entire trip takes about 15 seconds. Note that the veins do not carry "blue" blood, as most children's science text illustrations would indicate. Those of us who have donated blood realize that it is a dark red, as opposed to the bright red of oxygenated blood found in arteries.

Respiratory System

The body's cells use oxygen to *oxidize*, or "burn," food. This process releases energy. Carbon dioxide and water vapor are by-products of this process, just as they are when a candle burns inside an inverted jar. A candle goes out when the oxygen supply is diminished. Likewise, oxidation of food requires a steady supply of enough oxygen. The job of the respiratory system is to replace the carbon dioxide and water vapor in the blood with oxygen. Let's see how this is done.

As we breathe in air through the nose, it passes through hollow nasal passages above the mouth where it is warmed and filtered. Hairlike, moving cilia inside the passages catch dust and airborne particles. These particles are swept to the mouth and coughed up or swallowed. The membrane lining the passages is coated with mucus, which also traps airborne materials.

The air then moves through the voice box, or *larynx*, and down into the throat. Two tubes are found there. One tube channels food into the stomach and is called the gullet, or *esophagus*. A second tube, the windpipe, or *trachea*, is located in front of the esophagus. It goes to the lungs. A flap of tissue, the *epiglottis*, covers the windpipe automatically when we eat or drink. This action usually prevents food or liquids from entering the windpipe.

The windpipe shortly divides into two tubes called *bronchi*. One bronchus is attached to each *lung*. In the lungs, the bronchi split into progressively smaller branches of tubes. Each of the tiniest tubes ends in a tiny air sac. Because of the many thousands of these sacs, the lungs have a soft, spongy appearance.

Each sac swells like a tiny balloon when we breathe air into our lungs. Surrounding each sac are many capillaries. Oxygen from breathed-in air in the sac passes through the sac's thin wall into the blood in the capillaries. Carbon dioxide and water vapor in the capillaries pass the opposite way into the air sacs; these gases then move up through the branched tubes and are exhaled.

Your students may read that body cells use oxygen to "burn" digested food and that carbon dioxide is one by-product of the process. But don't be surprised if most still assume that the air they breathe out is the same as the air they breathe in (Mintzes, 1984).

To show them the difference, you might get some limewater (calcium oxide in water; an indicator for carbon dioxide) from a drugstore, two identical balloons and small glass jars, and a bicycle tire pump. Pour the clear limewater into each of the two jars until half full. Have a child fill one balloon with the pump and the other using lung power. Release the air from one balloon under the limewater surface of one jar, and then do this with the second balloon and jar. The limewater exposed to the lung air should turn milky, an indication that carbon dioxide is present; the other should stay about the same.

Breathing

Children typically believe that the act of breathing in forces the lungs to draw in air and expand. This is not what happens. Breathing in occurs because of unequal air pressure. Examine the process yourself.

Notice what happens when you take a deep breath: The chest cavity enlarges. It enlarges because rib muscles contract and pull the ribs up and outward. At the same time, the *diaphragm*, a thin sheet of muscle between the chest and the abdomen, pulls downward. This further enlarges the chest cavity. Enlarging the chest cavity lowers the air pressure inside the lungs. So, the higher outside air pressure forces air into the air passages and lungs.

When we breathe out, the diaphragm relaxes and moves upward. At the same time, the rib muscles relax, and the ribs move down and inward. This reduces the size of the chest cavity, which forces air out of the lungs.

The Cardiopulmonary System and Vital Signs

Your temperature, pulse rate, respiratory rate, and blood pressure are indications of your health, called *vital signs*. Temperature is measured with a glass or electronic thermometer orally, axillary, rectally, or aurally. The normal oral temperature is 37°C (98.6°F) and is slightly less when taken axillary, within the armpit, and slightly more when measured rectally or aurally.

The rhythmical throbbing in the arteries that is produced by the heart's regular contractions causes your pulse. A pulse rate is generally found by compressing your radial artery with an index and middle finger and then feeling the throb for 1 minute. Pulse rates vary from 150 beats per minute in an embryo to about 60 in the elderly. The respiration rate is taken immediately after a pulse, so that you do not know the measurement is being taken. In an adult, the normal resting respiratory rate is between 14 to 20 breaths per minute.

Blood pressure is the force exerted by circulating blood against the walls of the blood vessels. It is greatest when the heart contracts (systole) and lowest when it relaxes (diastole). The pressure is measured with a sphygmomanometer, or blood pressure cuff. To take a blood pressure reading, wrap the cuff around the upper arm and inflate the bladder by pumping a rubber bulb. The health professional listens to a stethoscope that is placed against an artery lower on the arm. As the cuff expands, it compresses the artery and stops the blood circulation. Systolic pressure is measured when no pulsations can be heard. As the cuff is slowly deflated, a spurting, or Korotkoff, sound occurs as the heart contraction forces blood through the compressed artery. Diastolic pressure is measured when the blood is flowing smoothly again and the spurting sound is no longer heard. The blood pressure measurements are given as a ratio of maximum over minimum; normal blood pressure is in the range of 110/60 to 140/90 millimeters of mercury. Blood pressure varies with factors such as a person's age, level of physical fitness, weight, general heath, strength of the heartbeat, and elasticity of the arterial walls.

DIGESTIVE SYSTEM Inquiry

Sweet Crackers

Invitation

How does changing starch into sugar help the body?

Exploration

1. Bite off a piece of sugarless cracker and chew it for at least 1 minute.
2. How does the taste of the cracker change as you chew it?
3. A soda cracker is made up mostly of starch. The saliva in your mouth starts changing the starch into a sugar. It is changed the rest of the way in your small intestine. Before food can be used by your body cells, it must be in a dissolved form.

Concept Invention

1. Does changing a starch into a sugar help it dissolve? Find out for yourself.
2. Half-fill two small jars with water.
3. Put 1 teaspoon of sugar in one jar. Use a second teaspoon to put 1 teaspoon of starch in the other. Mix each for 1 minute with its correct spoon.
4. Which food dissolves? Will stirring help to dissolve the food even more?

Concept Application

What other starches can you turn into sugars by chewing? Try out some starchy foods and record your results.

MATERIALS

- Two small jars or glasses
- Two teaspoons
- Starch
- Sugarless soda cracker
- Sugar
- Water

 Teaching Tips In the Concept Invention, children will need to know that when a material dissolves it is no longer visible. The solution looks clear.

DIGESTIVE SYSTEM CONCEPTS

We can eat food, but when is it inside the body? The answer to this seemingly simple question depends on whose point of view we take.

Most people would say that food is inside the body once it is swallowed. To biochemists, however, any food still within the 9-meter (30-foot) digestive tube they call the *alimentary canal* is considered outside the body. This definition underlines the uselessness of foods we eat until they are *digested,* or chemically broken down and dissolved into a form that can be used in the cells. The digestive system (INQ Figure 9–1) is marvelously suited to this function. Let's see how it works.

The Mouth

The digestive process begins when we start chewing food. Our front teeth (*incisors* and *canines*) cut and tear the food. Back teeth (*molars*) crush it into small particles. At the same time, saliva pours into the food from six salivary glands in and near the mouth. *Saliva* softens the food and begins the chemical breakdown of starches. A gradual, sweetening flavor is experienced when we chew starchy foods such as cooked potato, soda cracker, or bread. The saliva contains an enzyme called *ptyalin* that reduces large starch molecules into simple sugar molecules. (An enzyme is a *catalyst*, or chemical that brings about or speeds up chemical reactions without itself becoming altered.) Besides ptyalin, several other enzymes in the body's digestive system help break down food into usable form.

The Food Tube

Swallowed food passes into the *esophagus*, or food tube. It is squeezed down into the stomach by regular, wavelike contractions of smooth muscles that surround the esophagus. Similar muscles are located all along the alimentary canal. Because muscle action (*peristalsis*), not gravity, moves the food inside the canal, it is possible to eat and swallow while standing on our heads.

The Stomach

Peristaltic motions continue in the *stomach*. The food is churned slowly in gastric juices secreted from the stomach lining. Several enzymes and diluted hydrochloric acid break down most of the proteins. Digestion of starch stops because acid prevents ptyalin from working. Some fats are broken down, but for the most part, fats go through the stomach undigested.

If the stomach's hydrochloric acid is so powerful, why doesn't this corrosive liquid digest the stomach itself? Only in recent years have researchers pinpointed the reason. A small amount of ammonia (this is an alkali or base) is secreted in the lining of the stomach. It effectively neutralizes acid next to the lining without interfering with the acid's digestive action elsewhere in the stomach. We use the same principle of neutralizing an acid when we drink seltzer or soda water to settle a "sour" stomach.

The Intestines

After about 2 to 6 hours in the stomach, depending on what and how much has been eaten, the partially digested food materials are pushed into the *small intestine*. Here, glands within intestinal walls produce digestive juices with enzymes that begin working on the food. Additional digestive juices are secreted into the small intestine from small tubes connected to the liver and pancreas.

Throughout the small intestine, peristaltic motion continues as digestive juices complete the breakdown of carbohydrates into simple sugars, proteins into amino acids, and fats into fatty acids and glycerin. At various portions of the small intestine, the sugars and amino acids are absorbed into blood vessels within its lining. Digested fats are first absorbed into the lymph system and then later are transported into the bloodstream.

Nondigestible material, or waste, composed chiefly of cellulose, passes into the large intestine. Much of the water contained in waste material is absorbed into the intestinal walls. The remaining substance is eliminated from the body.

Food products dissolved in the blood are distributed to the body cells after the liver processes them. In the cells, these products are oxidized, changed into protoplasm, or stored as fat.

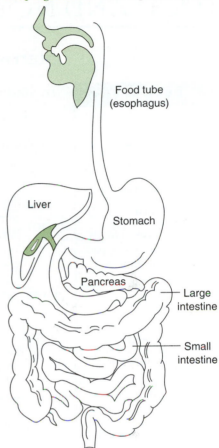

INQ Figure 9–1 The digestive system.

Food tube (esophagus)

Liver

Stomach

Pancreas

Large intestine

Small intestine

FOOD AND NUTRITION Inquiry

Starchy Foods

Invitation

Which foods have starch?

Exploration

1. Place a bit of cornstarch on waxed paper. Crush a small piece of white chalk next to it with a spoon.
2. Put on safety goggles. Place a drop of iodine on each goggle. Notice how the cornstarch turns purple-black. The chalk should look red-brown. When a food turns purple-black, it has starch.
3. Test your food samples with the iodine. Crush each sample first with the spoon. Wash the spoon off each time.

Concept Invention

1. Which samples seem to have starch? Which do not?
2. Taste a little piece of unripe banana and a little piece of very ripe banana. Now try the starch test on part of an unripe banana. Now try the starch test on part of an unripe banana. Then test part of a very ripe banana.
3. What difference do you notice? When does a banana seem to have more starch? When does it seem to have more sugar?

Concept Application

Make a list of predictions of starchy foods to test with the iodine. Test the foods and make a chart of your correct and incorrect predictions.

MATERIALS

- Iodine
- Safety goggles
- Piece of white chalk
- Medicine dropper
- Cornstarch
- Tiny pieces of foods (such as white bread, rice, macaroni, cheese, potato, cereals)
- Teaspoon
- Waxed paper
- Piece of very ripe banana
- Piece of unripe banana

Fatty Foods

Invitation

Which foods have fats?

Exploration

1. Spread a drop of oil on the brown paper. Fat is mostly oil.
2. Spread a drop of water alongside it. Allow it to dry.

Concept Invention

1. Hold up the paper to the light.
2. Notice the difference in the two spots. Fat shows as a shiny, oily spot.

Concept Application

Which foods do you think have fat? Make a list and then test the foods you can. Rub each small piece into the brown paper. Record which made an oily stain. How do your findings compare with what you thought?

MATERIALS

- Brown paper bag
- Drop of oil
- Small pieces of different foods (such as bacon, olive, margarine, bread, apple, cheese)
- Drop of water

Some Properties of Powdered Foods ———

MATERIALS

- White powders (such as baking powder, baking soda, white flour, powdered sugar, cornstarch, powdered milk)

- Small jar of water

- Three medicine droppers

- Two teaspoons

- Small jar of iodine solution

- Safety goggles

- Paper towel

- Small jar of white vinegar

- Hand lens

Invitation

You eat many different white powders. Cake is made with baking powder. White bread is made with white flour. Cornstarch helps make gravy. You can even make milk by mixing powdered milk with water. If you take a quick look at any white powder, they seem alike. But each is really different in several ways. How can you tell one white powder from another? (Do not use the sense of taste for this investigation.)

Exploration

1. Put less than a quarter-teaspoon of one powder on a paper towel. Only a little is needed, as shown.
2. Observe it carefully through a hand lens. How does it look?
3. Feel the powder with your fingers. How does it feel?
4. Put a drop of water on the powder. What happens?
5. Put on safety goggles. Put a drop of iodine solution on the powder. What happens?
6. Put a drop of vinegar on the powder. What happens?

Concept Invention

1. How does this powder compare with other powders? Test a few more powders (make sure to wear safety goggles). Record what you observe on a chart such as this:

Powder Tested	How It Looks Magnified	How It Feels	Reaction to Water	Reaction to Iodine	Reaction to Vinegar
Cornstarch					
Flour					
Baking Soda					
(Others)					

2. Which test(s) seem most useful to tell the powders apart? Which test(s) seem least useful to tell the powders apart?

Any material has certain physical properties that may be used to identify it. By performing certain tests, children may learn some different properties of similar-looking powdered foods, as well as other powders. Small baby-food jars make excellent containers for the powders and test liquids. For the iodine solution, mix two full medicine droppers of iodine in a half-full baby-food jar of water. Children may try additional tests, such as heating the powders and mixing them with water. A small cup can be formed from kitchen foil and held over a candle flame with a spring clothespin.

Caution: Supervise closely for safety. Only a tiny amount of powder needs to be heated. A powder may also be mixed in water in a clear glass jar and then compared with other water–powder mixtures. Students should not taste powders. Explain that some powders they should not eat may get mixed with some powdered foods in this investigation. For example, some nonfoods they may want to test are powdered detergent, white tempera paint powder, crushed white chalk, talcum powder, alum, scouring powder, tooth powder, and plaster of paris.

3. Can you identify an unknown powder? Ask someone to put a quarter-teaspoon of powder on a fresh paper towel. You should not know what powder it is, but it should be one recorded on your chart. Make some tests and use your chart to identify it.
4. Can you identify two unknown powders mixed together? Have someone choose two chart powders and mix them. Then you test the mixture.

Adapting for Students with Exceptionalities

For students who have difficulty reading the directions or following the steps of these activities, record the directions on tape. (See Mercer & Mercer, 2005, for a discussion on accommodations involving instructional materials.)

Concept Application

A material may be identified by tests to reveal its physical properties. What other ways can you test white powders? What other powders can you test?

FOOD AND NUTRITION CONCEPTS

We may eat hundreds of foods combined in thousands of ways. But nutritionally speaking, there are four kinds of foods: sugars, starches, fats, and proteins. Some persons would add three more: vitamins, minerals, and water. These seven nutrients may be combined into three groups:

1. Foods for energy: sugars, starches, and fats
2. Foods for growth and repair of cells: proteins
3. Foods for regulation of body processes: vitamins, minerals, and water

Carbohydrates

If we heat table sugar in a test tube, the sugar will gradually turn black, and water vapor will be given off. The black material is carbon. The water is formed as hydrogen and oxygen atoms given off by individual sugar molecules combine. Heat some starch, and again carbon and water appear. Both sugar and starch are *carbohydrates*, a name that means "carbon and water."

Although sugars and starches are composed of the same elements, these elements may appear in various combinations and form relatively small or large molecules. *Simple sugar* molecules, for example, are the smallest carbohydrate molecules. They may be found in grapes and many other fruits. When two simple sugar molecules become attached, a *complex sugar*, such as table sugar, is formed. A starch molecule is nothing more than a long chain of sugar molecules tightly attached to one another.

In digestion, carbohydrates are broken down into simple sugars. Only in this form are these molecules small enough to pass through cell membranes into the cells, where they "burn" and release energy. The burning is a result of *oxidation*, a process in which oxygen chemically combines with fuel—in this case, sugar—and releases heat energy. (Rusting is a form of slow oxidation; fire is very fast oxidation.) The oxygen comes from the air we breathe.

Fats

Analysis shows that fats are also composed of carbon, hydrogen, and oxygen. However, fat molecules have relatively fewer oxygen atoms than carbohydrates. Because they are oxygen "poor," fat molecules can combine with more oxygen atoms and yield about twice as much energy as carbohydrates.

Foods rich in carbohydrates and fats provide our principal source of energy. But when we eat more than we need of these materials, the cells store any excess in the form of fat. Fat storage does not occur uniformly throughout all body cells, as every figure-conscious person knows.

Proteins

Proteins are extremely complex, large molecules. A single protein molecule may contain thousands of atoms. Like the preceding nutrients, proteins are made up of carbon, hydrogen, and oxygen; but proteins also contain nitrogen and, typically, sulfur. Proteins are the main source of materials (amino acids) needed for growth and repair of body cells. Excess proteins can be oxidized in cells and so provide energy.

Although all animal and some plant foods (mainly beans, peas, and nuts) are rich in proteins, no single plant source contains sufficient amino acids for complete growth and repair of body cells. A combination of legumes and grains (beans and rich), however, can furnish all the needed amino acids.

Vitamins

Vitamins are essential to health because they regulate cell activities. These substances permit biochemical processes to take place. Without proper vitamins, the body may suffer from several deficiency diseases, such as scurvy, rickets, and anemia. A balanced diet is usually all that is needed to prevent the disease. Particularly in the last decade, however, scientists have found clues that vitamins may play a larger role than previously thought in achieving optimal health and in preventing some chronic diseases such as cancer, decline of the immune system in the aged, heart disease, and eye degeneration. This is why some nutritionists recommend a daily multivitamin as "insurance." Most researchers, however, see the need for more evidence before they can recommend large doses of vitamins aimed at specific diseases or conditions.

Minerals

Several minerals are essential because they help regulate cell activities. In addition, some minerals are incorporated into body tissue. Calcium and phosphorus form the hard portions of our bones and teeth. Milk is especially rich in these two minerals. Iron and copper help form red blood cells. A proper amount of iodine is needed in the thyroid gland for normal oxidation to take place in cells. Salt is often iodized to prevent goiter, an iodine deficiency. Some minerals cannot be used by cells unless specific vitamins are present. Most fruits and vegetables are rich in vitamins and minerals.

Water

For many reasons, water is essential to life and good nutrition. It changes chemically to form part of protoplasm. Water is the chief part of blood. It cools the body and carries away accumulated poisons. It is important to digestion and excretion. About two thirds of the body itself is composed of water.

Besides drinking water directly, we take in much water in the food we eat. For example, celery is about 95% water, and fresh bread is about 35% water.

Choosing a Healthful Diet

Years ago, many Americans suffered from malnutrition. Today, the problem is often the opposite. Most of us eat too much, particularly of foods rich in fat, such as meat and dairy products. This food consumption increases the risk of heart disease, stroke, and diabetes and may also increase the incidence of certain types of cancer. Nutritionists today recommend that we eat far more grains, fruits, and vegetables than has been customary in the American diet.

Most children and adults realize that they must eat a variety of foods to have a proper, or "balanced," diet but are unsure of what to eat or what are proper serving sizes. To help us select healthful combinations of nutrients, the U.S. Department of Agriculture publishes "MyPyramid." This food pyramid helps children and adults choose foods and serving sizes that are right for them by taking into account individual differences in activity levels, age, and gender.

To determine your appropriate number of calories, including serving sizes of grains, vegetables, fruits, discretionary calories, milk, meat and beans, log on to the http://www.mypyramid.gov/mypyramid/index.aspx website. The intent of MyPyramid is to promote variety in the foods we eat as well as stressing proportionality and moderation by eating more foods that are healthy and less foods that are high in trans fats, sugar, salt, and cholesterol.

INQ Figure 9–2   Food guide pyramid.

Source: U.S. Department of Agriculture, Washington, DC, 2005.

References

American Association for the Advancement of Science (AAAS). (1993). *Benchmarks for science literacy*. New York: Oxford University Press.

Fathman, A. K., Quinn, M. E., & Kessler, C. (1992). *Teaching science to English learners, grades 4–8*. Washington, DC: National Clearinghouse of Bilingual Education. Retrieved November 13, 2004, from *www.ncela.gwu.edu/pubs/pigs/pig11.htm*

Laplante, B. (1997). Teaching science to language minority students in elementary classrooms. *Journal of the New York State Association for Bilingual Education, 12*, 62–83. Retrieved November 13, 2004, from *www.ncela.gwu.edu/pubs/nysabe/vol12/nysabe124.pdf*

Mastropieri, M., & Scruggs, T. E. (2004). *The inclusive classroom: Strategies for effective instruction* (4th ed.). Upper Saddle River, NJ: Merrill/Prentice Hall.

Mercer, C. D., & Mercer, A. R. (2005). *Teaching students with learning problems* (7th ed.). Upper Saddle River, NJ: Merrill/Prentice Hall.

Mintzes, J. J. (1984). Naive theories in biology: Children's concepts of the human body. *School Science and Mathematics, 84*(7), 548–555.

National Research Council (NRC). (1996). *National science education standards*. Washington, DC: National Academy Press.

Selected Trade Books: The Human Body and Nutrition

For Younger Children

Adler, D. A. (1991). *You breathe in, you breathe out*. Danbury, CT: Watts.

Berger, M. (1983). *Why I cough, sneeze, shiver, hiccup, and yawn*. New York: Harper & Row.

Bishop, P. R. (1991). *Exploring your skeleton*. Danbury, CT: Watts.

Carle, E. (1997). *From head to toe*. New York: HarperCollins.

Cole, J. (1989). *The magic school bus inside the human body*. New York: Scholastic.

Cole, J. (1999). *The magic school bus explores the senses*. New York: Scholastic.

Hawcock, D. (1997). *Amazing pull-out pop-up body in a book*. Hillsdale, NJ: DK Publishing.

Hoover, R., & Murphy, B. (1981). *Learning about our five senses*. Torrance, CA: Good Apple.

Hvass, U. (1986). *How my body moves*. New York: Viking.

Janulewicz, M. (1997). *Yikes! Your body up close*. New York: Simon & Schuster.

Kindersley, D. (1991). *What's inside my body?* Hillsdale, NJ: DK Publishing.

Mayer, G. (1998). *This is my body (Little Critter)*. New York: Golden Books.

Parker, S. (1991). *Eating a meal: How you eat, drink, and digest*. Danbury, CT: Watts.

Penn, L. (1986). *The human body*. Torrance, CA: Good Apple.

Sattler, H. R. (1982). *Noses are special*. Nashville, TN: Abingdon Press.

Showers, P. (1982). *You can't make a move without your muscles*. New York: Thomas Y. Crowell.

Simon, S. (1999). *The Heart*. New York: HarperTrophy.

Simon, S. (2000). *Muscles*. New York: HarperTrophy.

Simon, S. (2003). *Eyes and ears*. New York: HarperCollins.

Sproule, A. (1987). *Body watch: Know your insides*. New York: Facts on File.

For Older Children

Allison, L. (1976). *Blood and guts: A working guide to your own little insides*. Boston: Little, Brown.

Arnold, N. (1998). *Horrible science: Blood, bones, and body bits*. New York: Scholastic.

Behm, B. (1987). *Ask about my body*. Austin, TX: Raintree.

Berger, M., & Berger, G. (1998). *Why don't haircuts hurt? Questions and answers about the human body*. New York: Scholastic.

Brynie, F. H. (2003). *101 Questions about sex and sexuality: With answers for the curios, and cautious, and confused*. Minneapolis: Lerner Publishing Group.

Davidson, S., & Morgan, B. (2002). *Human body revealed*. New York: Dorling Kindersley Publishing.

De Bruin, J. (1983). *Young scientists explore the five senses*. Torrance, CA: Good Apple.

Gabb, M. (1991). *The human body*. Danbury, CT: Watts.

Galperin, A. (1991). *Nutrition*. Broomall, PA: Chelsea House.

Harlow, R., & Morgan, G. (1991). *Energy and growth*. Danbury, CT: Watts.

Hausherr, R. (1989). *Children and the AIDS virus: A book for children, parents, and teachers*. New York: Clarion Books.

Klein, A. E. (1977). *You and your body*. New York: Doubleday.

Knutson, R. (1999). *Fearsome fauna: A field guide to the creatures that live in you*. New York: Freeman.

Mayle, P. (1997). *What's happening to me?* Secaucus, NJ: Carol.

Parker, S. (1991). *Nerves to senses: Projects with biology*. Danbury, CT: Watts.

Patent, D. (1992). *Nutrition: What's in the food we eat*. New York: Holiday House.

Rayner, C. (1980). *The body book*. Hauppauge, NY: Barron's.

Rutland, J. (1977). *Human body*. Danbury, CT: Watts.

Simon, S. (1979). *About the foods you eat*. New York: McGraw-Hill.

Suzuki, D. (1991). *Looking at the body*. New York: John Wiley.

Taylor, R. (1982). *How the body works*. St. Paul, MN: EMC.

Walker, R. (2004). *Guide to the human body*. Buffalo, NY: Firefly Publishing

Walpole, B. (1987). *The human body*. Parsippany, NJ: Julian Messner.

Ward, B. R. (1991). *Diet and health*. Danbury, CT: Watts.

Wilson, R. (1979). *How the body works*. New York: Larousse.

Wolf, D., & Wolf, M. L. (Eds.). (1982). *The human body*. New York: G. P. Putnam.

Wong, O. (1986). *Your body and how it works*. Danbury, CT: Childrens Press.

Wyatt, V. (1999). *Earthlings inside and out: A space alien studies the human body*. Toronto, Ontario: Kids Can Press.

Zim, H. S. (1979). *Your skin*. New York: Morrow.

Resource Books

Butzow, C. M., & Butzow, J. W. (1989). *Science through children's literature: An integrated approach.* Englewood, CO: Teacher Ideas Press. (nutrition topics on pp. 107–111)

Cordel, B., & Hillen, J. (1994). *Sense-able science.* Fresno, CA: AIMS Education Foundation.

Fredricks, A. D., Meinbach, A. M., & Rothlein, L. (1993). *Thematic units: An integrated approach to teaching science and social studies.* New York: HarperCollins. (health topics on pp. 140–145; body system topics on pp. 189–194)

Harris, R. (1994). *It's perfectly normal.* Cambridge, MA: Candlewick Press.

Jasmine, G. (1995). *Thematic unit: My body.* Huntington Beach, CA: Teacher Created Materials.

Jefferies, D. (1993). *Thematic unit: The human body.* Huntington Beach, CA: Teacher Created Materials.

Shaw, D. G., & Dybdahl, C. S. (1996). *Integrating science and language arts: A sourcebook for K–6 teachers.* Boston: Allyn & Bacon. (circulatory system topic on pp. 65–67)

VanCleave, J. (1995). *The human body for every kid.* New York: John Wiley.

Wiebe, A. (Ed.). (1986). *Jaw breakers and heart thumpers.* Fresno, CA: AIMS Education Foundation.

Wiebe, A., Ecklund, L., & Mercier, S. (Eds.). (1986). *From head to toe.* Fresno, CA: AIMS Education Foundation.

THE EARTH'S CHANGING SURFACE

Shifting sand dunes, eroding hillsides, weeds growing on an asphalt playground, and muddy water running in gutters are all evidence that the earth's surface is changing. This section of the book examines forces that wear down and build up the earth and their rock and soil products. The four parts are weathering and erosion, soil and its makeup, the building up of the land, and the formation of rocks.

Benchmarks and Standards

Most children have explored with soil, rocks, and play sand or seen pictures or movies that include volcanoes and earthquakes. Activities in elementary school should further refine these explorations and allow children to discover additional properties about the earth. Sample benchmarks and standards include the following:

Sample Benchmarks (AAAS, 1993)

- Chunks of rocks come in many sizes and shapes, from boulders to grains of sand and even smaller. (By Grades K–2, p. 72)
- Waves, wind, water, and ice shape and reshape the earth's land surface by eroding rock and soil in some areas and depositing them in other areas, sometimes in seasonal layers. (By Grades 3–5, p. 72)

Sample Standards (NRC, 1996)

- Soils have properties of color and texture, capacity to retain water, and ability to support the growth of many kinds of plants, including those in our food supply. (By Grades K–4, p. 134)
- Some changes in the solid earth can be described as the "rock cycle." (By Grades 5–8, p. 160)

WEATHERING AND EROSION Inquiry

Breaking Rocks

MATERIALS

- Two small topless milk or juice cartons
- Moist soil
- Plaster of paris
- Stick
- Bean seeds
- Jar of water
- Ruler

Invitation

How can seeds break up rocks?

Exploration

1. Soak some bean seeds in a jar of water overnight.
2. Plant them in a small carton half-filled with moist soil.
3. Use a stick to mix some plaster of paris and water in a second carton. Make the mixture like a thick milkshake.
4. Pour the plaster mixture lightly over the soil. Make the cover about 0.5 centimeter (0.25 inch) thick.

Concept Invention

1. Will the growing seeds be strong enough to break through the hard cover? If so, how long do you think it will take?
2. If the seeds do break through, how thick a plaster cover will beans go through?

Concept Application

What examples can you find of plants breaking up rocks and other hard materials? Look for plants growing in cracks in rocks, sidewalks, asphalt, and other paved surfaces. Record what you find.

How Weathering Breaks Down Minerals

MATERIALS

- Plain iron nails
- Container of dry soil
- Container of wet soil
- Container of water
- Steel wool

Invitation

Over time, gases in the air can cause a chemical change in many different minerals in rocks. The process is called *chemical weathering*. A rock that is chemically weathered becomes loose and easily crumbled. Something like this happens when iron or steel breaks down as it rusts. You can learn more about chemical weathering by making things rust. How can you make an iron nail rust?

Exploration

1. Rub a nail with steel wool for a few seconds. This will take off any chemical that may have been put on to prevent rusting.
2. Get a container of wet soil. Bury the nail just under the surface. Dig up the nail each day to see if, or how much, it is rusting. Put the nail back in the same way each time. Keep the soil damp.

Concept Invention

1. When does rust first appear?
2. How quickly is the whole nail covered with rust?
3. Will a nail rust more quickly on the wet soil's surface than below it? What do you think?
4. What would happen if you put a nail in water?
5. What would happen if you buried a nail in dry soil?
6. Will a piece of steel wool rust faster than a nail?

Concept Application

Gases in the air may cause chemical weathering in rocks. Rust is an example of chemical weathering. What are some other materials that might rust? In what other ways can you get them to rust? How can you prevent materials from rusting? Record your ideas.

Teaching Tips

Make sure that any steel wool used is the variety without soap. Plastic margarine or cottage cheese containers are handy to hold soil for this activity. Soil may be dried, if needed, by spreading it on a newspaper and exposing it to sunlight.

Oxygen chemically combines directly with many minerals, as in the rusting process. Carbon dioxide also produces chemical weathering, but indirectly. It dissolves in rainwater to form a weak acid called *carbonic acid*. This acid attacks limestone and cementing materials that hold minerals together in some rocks.

Cave Deposits

Invitation

How do mineral deposits form in caves?

Exploration

1. Fill a large paper cup three-fourths full with water. Dissolve as much Epsom salt in it as you can.
2. Pour the solution into the two small paper cups.
3. Tie a small stone to each end of the string to weigh them down. Put one string end into each small paper cup. Have the string sag between cups.
4. Place the cups on top of the washcloth. Leave at least 4 centimeters (1 3/4 inches) between the cloth and the string. Allow a few days for mineral deposits to form on the string and cloth, as illustrated.

MATERIALS

- Epsom salt
- Two small paper cups
- Thick, soft string
- Large paper cup
- Spoon
- Two small stones
- Thick washcloth or piece of towel
- Water
- Ruler

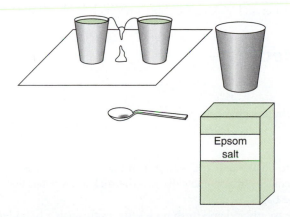

Concept Invention

1. In a real cave, water with dissolved minerals in it drips from the cave ceiling to the floor. The water leaves minerals behind as it evaporates at both places. Little by little, the mineral deposits build up to look like "icicles" of stone. Those that hang down are called *stalactites*. Those that point up are called *stalagmites*. (To remember them, think of C for "ceiling" and G for "ground.") In your model, where is the stalactite?
2. Where is the stalagmite in your model?

Concept Application

Describe how your model compares with real stalactite and stalagmite formations. Research related terms such as *speleothems*, *speleologist*, *spelunking*, *columns*, *helictites*, and *flowstone*.

Freezing Water and Rocks ————

Invitation

How does freezing water break up rocks?

Exploration

1. Leave some rocks in a container of water for several hours. Use cracked rocks and those that soak up water. Sandstone and limestone are good to use.
2. Put the rocks into a bag. Place the bag in a freezer overnight. Examine the rocks the next day.

MATERIALS

- Several porous or cracked rocks
- Freezer bag
- Container of water
- Freezer

Concept Invention

1. What, if anything, happened to the rocks?
2. How can you explain your results?

Concept Application

If some rocks broke, maybe the cold in the freezer alone did it. How can you experiment to make sure it was the freezing water that actually broke the rocks in this case? Try placing similar soaked and unsoaked rocks in the freezer. What happens? Could you use porous and nonporous rocks (porous rocks may be detected by placing some rocks in water and looking for those on which bubbles form) to test your theory?

Changing Rocks ————

Invitation

How does weathering change a rock?

Exploration

1. For safety, to break open a rock, put it into a thick paper bag. Hold the bag against a cement curb or sidewalk. Hit the rock a few times with a hammer through the bag.
2. Look at the weathered and fresh rock surfaces through a hand lens.

MATERIALS

- Several different weathered rocks
- Thick paper bag
- Soft paper towel or facial tissue
- Hand lens
- Empty egg carton
- Hammer

Concept Invention

1. How are they different?
2. How are they alike?

Concept Application

Make a weathered rock display. Take two of the larger pieces of a rock. Wrap one piece in tissue or a soft towel so that only the weathered part shows. Wrap the other so that only the fresh surface shows. Place them in opposite spaces in an egg carton. Do this with other broken rocks, too, until you fill the carton. What will happen if you shift the rocks around so that the samples are not opposite one another? How many of the rocks will your friends be able to match? If someone shifts them for you, how many will you be able to match?

Soil Erosion

Invitation

After a rain, have you noticed how water has carried away, or eroded, soil? Splashing raindrops and running water are responsible for much soil erosion. But not all places with soil erode, and some places erode much more than others. How can you test to see what affects soil erosion?

Exploration

1. Use a hammer and small nail to punch 10 holes in the bottom of one juice can. Use the hammer and a medium-sized nail to punch 10 holes in the second can. Both cans should be open at the top.
2. Fill a saucer level and to the brim with soil. Put the dish into a pie pan to catch any spilled material.
3. Place a meterstick or yardstick upright behind the dish. Hold the small-holed can 60 centimeters (2 feet) above the dish.
4. Have someone pour a half-cup of water into the juice can. When the can stops "raining," observe the soil and pie pan.

MATERIALS

- Two throwaway pie pans
- Soil
- Two matched plastic saucers
- Two small matched juice cans
- Measuring cups
- Meterstick or yardstick
- A small- and a medium-sized nail
- Hammer
- Water
- Several leaves

Teaching **T**ips
Finding actual samples of erosion is important to achieving full understanding.

Concept Invention

1. What, if any, signs of erosion can you observe?
2. How will a heavier "rain" affect erosion? Fill a second saucer with soil. Use the medium-hole can for rain and compare the results with the first trial.
3. How does loose soil erode, compared with tightly packed soil? Prepare two saucers and find out.
4. How will tilted soil erode, compared with level soil?
5. How will covered soil erode, compared with bare soil? Cover the soil in one dish with several leaves.

Scaffolding for English Learners

The soil erosion activity provides a good opportunity to learn. Teachers of English learners see opportunity to learn as a key to English language acquisition. (See TESOL, 1992, for a discussion of the opportunity to learn for English learners.)

Concept Application

What conditions seem to reduce soil erosion? What conditions seem to increase soil erosion? If rainfall, soil cover, degree of incline, and compactness of the soil affect soil erosion, what examples can you find outdoors that show some or all of these conditions?

Wind Erosion

MATERIALS

- Two rulers
- Sticky tape
- Crayon
- Scissors
- Small empty milk carton
- Open, unpaved area outdoors
- Sand or soil
- Large sprinkling can
- Directional compass

Invitation

What happens to loose soil on a windy day? The moving of soil or rocks from one place to another is called *erosion*. Soil erosion by wind is a big problem in some places. How can you find out about wind erosion in your area?

Exploration

1. Make a wind erosion recorder. Cut two narrow slots on top of a small milk carton.
2. Stick two rulers through the slots.
3. Fill the carton with sand or soil to make it heavy.
4. Cut two 45-centimeter (18-inch) strips of sticky tape.
5. Put one strip evenly over the top of each ruler, sticky side out. Use tape to fasten the strip ends to each ruler.
6. With crayon, draw an arrow on the carton top.
7. Place your recorder where the wind is blowing loose soil. Point the arrow north. Leave the recorder for 30 minutes. Notice how bits of windblown soil collect on the sticky tape.

Teaching **T**ips
Some children may not realize at first that some variables need to be controlled in this investigation. If two areas are to be tested, two identical recorders must be exposed to wind within equal areas at the same time. When possible, let the children discover this for themselves.

Tape, sticky side out

MILK

Concept Invention

1. Examine the sticky tape on all four sides. Which side has the most soil? From which direction did the wind blow most?
2. Where do you think is the most wind erosion around the school? Where do you think is the least wind erosion? Make more recorders. Put one in each place and find out. What reasons can you give for what you find?
3. What difference in wind erosion is there between grass-covered and bare soil? How can you find out?
4. What difference in wind erosion is there between dry and damp soil? How can you find out?
5. Collect windblown soil bits each day for a week with your recorder. Change the sticky tape each day. Can you arrange the strips in order from most to fewest soil bits? On what day did the most wind erosion occur? On what day did the least wind erosion occur? Can you tell from which main direction the wind blew each day?

Concept Application

Soil erosion by wind depends on how hard the wind blows and how the soil is protected from the wind. When during the day does the most wind erosion occur where you live? How can you find out? What else can you discover with your recorder? Record your ideas.

Glaciers

Invitation

How do glaciers change the land?

MATERIALS

- Aluminum pie pan
- Freezer
- Rocks and pebbles
- Place with bare soil
- Water
- Meterstick or yardstick

Exploration

1. Put some rocks and pebbles into a pie pan. Spread them about halfway around the inside edge of the pan as shown.
2. Put some water into the pan, but let the tops of the rocks stick out of the water.
3. Leave the pan in a freezer overnight.
4. Remove your frozen glacier model from the pan. Turn it over so that the rocks sticking out are underneath.
5. Place the model flat on some bare dirt. Push it so that the stones are forward. Press down at the same time. Push it in a straight line for about 60 centimeters (2 feet).

6. Let your model stay and melt at the end of that distance. Come back to this place several hours later after the model has melted. Observe carefully everything that has been left behind.

Concept Invention

1. How can you tell the direction in which the "glacier" moved?
2. How can you tell how wide it was?
3. How can you tell where the forward part of the glacier stopped and melted?

Concept Application

What geological features show that glaciers were once in the United States? Describe these features and their locations.

WEATHERING AND EROSION CONCEPTS

Perhaps the only permanent feature of the earth's surface is the continuous process of change it reveals. The forces that weather and erode the land are powerful and ceaseless.

Weathering refers to the breaking down of rocks into smaller parts through the action of such agents as plants, chemicals, frost, and changes of temperature. *Erosion* includes weathering plus the process of transporting weathered material from one location to another, as in the action of running water, wind, and glaciers.

Plant Actions ———————

It is difficult for some children to realize at first that plants break down rocks. After all, rocks are "hard" and plants are "soft," they reason. But plants weather rocks in several ways.

Growing roots may wedge deeply into a cracked rock and force it apart. As dry plant seeds absorb water, they swell with surprising force and may perform a similar wedging

INQ Figure 10–1 Lichens play a part in weathering rock.

function. Tiny flat plants called *lichens* grow on bare rock (INQ Figure 10–1). Acids released by these plants decompose and soften the rock. Larger plants may then follow in a long succession, each contributing to the rock's destruction.

Chemical Weathering

Oxygen and water in the air combine with rock surfaces to produce "rust." Reddish soils, for example, usually contain oxidized iron compounds.

Falling rain picks up a small amount of carbon dioxide in the air and forms carbonic acid. Although it is well diluted, this substance slowly wears down limestone. Older limestone buildings and statuary have a soft, worn look from the dissolving effect of acidic rainwater. This is especially noticeable in England and in several areas in the northeastern United States, where coal burning has been prevalent. Abnormal quantities of sulfur dioxide released into the air increase the acidic content of rain and hasten weathering.

Rainwater that percolates into the ground may encounter a limestone formation and dissolve some of it, thus forming a cave. This is how Carlsbad Caverns of New Mexico, Luray Caverns of Virginia, and Mammoth Caves of Kentucky were formed. Because the surface appearance of a rock is somewhat altered by chemical weathering, we must often chip or break it to note its natural color.

Expansion and Contraction

Frozen water also contributes to weathering. Many rocks are relatively porous. Water, you may remember, is one of the few substances that expands as it freezes. As absorbed water in a rock expands, bits of rock are broken off. In addition, ice may wedge apart cracked rocks.

Stones placed around campfires are sometimes cracked because rocks conduct heat poorly. The difference between a hot surface and the cooler interior may produce strains that cause parts to flake off. But some of this *exfoliation*, as it is called, may be from expansion that results from release of pressure. Rocks formed underground are subjected to great pressures. When they finally appear on the surface because of erosion or other means, these rocks may have a tendency to "unsqueeze" slightly, thus starting some cracks.

Running Water

Moving water is no doubt the most erosive force on the earth. Abrasive, waterborne rocks and particles have gradually formed the Grand Canyon over millions of years. Millions of tons of soil daily wash from banks and hills over the world into streams and are eventually carried into the ocean. Ocean waves ceaselessly pound huge cliffs and boulders into sand.

Water running down hills usually forms gullies. As the slope angle increases, water moves more swiftly, so hastening erosion. Rain splashing on near-level fields has a different erosive effect. Broad sheets of soil wash off into lower places without obvious gullying.

Wind Erosion

The effect of wind erosion became dramatically apparent to millions of Americans in the Dust Bowl years of 1934–1935. Prairie lands originally covered by a grassy sod had been broken up for agriculture. A combination of dry weather and marginal farming practices resulted in the most destructive dust storms ever seen in the United States.

Glacial Erosion

Glaciers also contribute to land erosion. Huge snow deposits build up when snowfall exceeds the melting rate. Gradually, some of the underlying snow compacts into ice and the glacier flows slowly downhill, as in the case of mountain valley glaciers.

Continental glaciers are much larger, ranging to thousands of square kilometers in size. At one time, a large part of North America was buried under snow and ice. Today, such glaciers cover much of Greenland and Antarctica. Gravity forces these glaciers to spread out as more and more snow piles on top. When glaciers move, they scour the land under their tremendous weight, scooping out basins and leveling hills. As they melt, huge deposits of soil and rocks are left at the sides and leading edge. Effects of glaciation may be seen in many parts of our country, particularly in New England and the north central states (INQ Figure 10–2).

Interplanetary Weathering

How does the interplanetary space environment change the rocky and icy surfaces of planetary bodies? How can this information help us better understand the weathering processes here on earth or the formation of the solar system? Finding answers to these questions is an ongoing research emphasis of planetary geologists.

An important step in understanding interplanetary weathering involves the study of the samples of soils and rocks that the *Apollo* astronauts retrieved from the surface of the moon. Along with other observations, scientists have been able to begin to understand the effect of impacts and solar wind on the moon. *Galileo* spacecraft images of asteroids

INQ Figure 10–2 About 11,000 years ago, glaciers advanced deeply into what is now the northern United States.

Sea ice

Sea ice

951 Gaspra and 243 Ida revealed to planetary geologists that the surfaces of these asteroids undergo space weathering. NASA's Near-Earth Asteroid Rendezvous mission that touched down on the asteroid 433 Eros on February 12, 2001, also confirmed this information. Similarly, the *Galileo* and *Cassini* spacecraft may provide results for space weathering questions about surfaces such as the icy moons of Jupiter and Saturn. The Spitzer Space Telescope was launched in August of 2003 to study infrared radiation and the effect of heat. In 2005, the Deep Impact spacecraft was launched to study comets and their weatering patterns.

SOIL AND ITS MAKEUP Inquiry

The Makeup of Soils

MATERIALS

- Bags of two different types of fresh soil
- Spoon
- Three glass jars with caps
- Newspaper
- Water
- Four sheets of white paper
- Hand lens
- Paper cup
- Partner

Invitation

What are some things you eat that grow in soil? How is soil important in your life? What do you think makes up soil? How can you find out what makes up soil?

Exploration

1. Spread newspaper on a table or desk. Put a sheet of white paper on top.
2. Pour some soil from one bag onto the white paper, as shown. What is the color of the soil?
3. Spread out the soil with a spoon. Use a hand lens to better observe the soil. What animals or animal parts do you see? (Put live animals into a paper cup.) What plant or plant parts do you see? Animal and plant materials in soil are called *humus*.
4. Feel the soil between your fingers. Rough soil has more large rock bits or particles than smooth soil. Use a hand lens. Can you find three sizes of rock particles? Which size makes up most rock particles in your sample?
5. Sort the different humus and rock materials into layers, as follows: Fill a glass jar half full with the soil you are observing. Fill the rest of the jar with water. Cap the jar and shake it. Then let it settle for an hour. Where does the humus settle? How much is there? In what order do the different-sized rock particles settle? How much is there of each size?

Concept Invention

1. How good a soil detective are you? Can you tell which two soil samples are from the same place? Have a partner pour some soil onto three white sheets. Two soil samples should come from one bag and one soil sample from the other bag. (Do not look while this is done.)
2. Try to identify the two soil samples from the same bag. Observe color, humus, and rock particles. Try the shake test.

Teaching Tips

The two bags of soil in the Exploration should come from two very different locations. Make sure the materials in each bag of soil are fairly evenly distributed. Otherwise, it will be difficult to match soil samples that come from the same bag.

Concept Application

Soil consists of humus and rock particles. The kinds and amounts of these materials may identify different soils. What is the makeup of soil from different places? Get samples of different soils around school and home. How are the soil samples alike and different? How does deeper soil compare with surface soil from the same place? How many soil samples can you match?

How Water Sinks into Different Soils

Invitation

Some rain that falls on soil runs off it into streams. Some rain also soaks into the ground. This water can help crops grow. If water sinks deep below the surface, it may be pumped to the surface for many uses. How fast water soaks into soil depends on several conditions. You can find out some for yourself. What can you do to test how fast water sinks into soils?

Exploration

1. Get a can that is open at both ends. Scratch a mark sideways on the can's side 2.5 centimeters (1 inch) from one end.
2. Go to a place with soil outdoors. Use your foot to press the can into the soil up to the mark.
3. Fill the second can with water. Pour the water into the first can without spilling any, as illustrated. With a watch, check how long it takes for all the water to sink in.

> **MATERIALS**
> - Two matched cans (one with both ends removed)
> - Watch with second hand
> - Water
> - Different outdoor places with soil

 Teaching Tips A steel can is likely to hold up better than an aluminum can for this activity. Some hard soils may require an adult's weight to push the can down to the mark.

Mark

Concept Invention

1. How much time is needed for the water to sink into the soil?
2. Compare the sink times of different soils. How will soil with grass compare with the same kind of soil without grass?

3. How will sandy soil compare with sticky soil?
4. How will hard-packed soil compare with loose soil?
5. How will soil that is usually in the sun compare with soil that is usually in the shade?
6. How will soil on a hill compare with soil that is on a flat surface?

Concept Application

Permeable soils tend to be loosely packed and consist of coarse mineral particles with little or no humus. What are some things about soil that seem to make water sink in quickly or slowly?

SOIL AND ITS MAKEUP CONCEPTS

Many children understand that weathering and erosion can wear underlying rock into small particles; but they often do not realize that productive soil is more than just rock particles. Not until decomposed plant and animal matter is added (or manufactured chemicals applied) does the soil become productive enough to support agriculture (INQ Figure 10–3).

Humus, as this organic matter is called, supplies plants with essential elements such as nitrogen, phosphorus, and potassium. The decomposition of organic material is done by soil bacteria. Acids released in decomposition also dissolve other minerals in the soil particles. Humus retains water well and so keeps soil from drying out rapidly. The darkish color of humus-laden soil absorbs sunlight efficiently, and so it is warmer than light-colored soil. This warmth speeds up plant growth and reduces seed failure.

Earthworms, you may recall, are important to soil for several reasons. They help break up the soil and so allow air, as well as water, to reach the plant roots. (Root cells die unless they absorb sufficient oxygen.) As earthworms eat through soil, they mix it and leave castings that contain rich fertilizing ingredients.

Soil Makeup

The composition of soil is easily studied if you mix some earth in a water-filled jar and allow the jar to stand several hours. Gravity causes the various materials to settle in order. Heavier, coarser particles like pebbles settle first, followed by sand, silt, and clay. Any humus present floats on the water's surface.

The best soil for most plants is *loam*, composed of sand (30% to 50%), silt (30% to 50%), clay (up to 20%), and abundant humus. Silt and clay have small particles that retain water well. Having been eroded from rocks rich in certain minerals, they contain elements that plants need for healthy growth. Coarser sand particles make soil porous, enabling air and water to reach plant roots. A soil composed of sand or clay alone lacks the moderate degree of porosity that seems best for watering plant roots.

Soils differ greatly in their degree of acidity and alkalinity. Strawberry plants thrive in acidic soil. Many grasses grow well in alkaline or basic soils. Clover does best in soil that is neither basic nor acidic, but neutral.

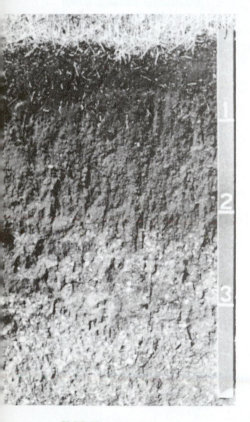

INQ Figure 10–3 A soil profile, or cross section, 3 feet (0.9 meter) deep. Subsoil becomes coarser and contains less humus with depth.

Soil Conservation

One reason why erosion is a fearsome enemy of the farmer is the time required for good soil to form. It may take up to 500 years for a single inch of good topsoil to be produced by natural means. With a rapidly multiplying world population, topsoil conservation is a serious concern.

Methods that farmers can use to preserve topsoil are shown in INQ Figure 10–4. Each is directed toward a specific problem. *Contour plowing*, for example, is used when plowing hilly land. Plowing straight up or down a hill will cause gullies to form during rain or irrigation; plowing around the hill reduces gully erosion. *Strip cropping* alternates a row crop that has much bare soil exposed, such as corn, with a ground cover crop, such as clover. This method reduces wind erosion. A *tree windbreak* will also help if the field is located where a strong wind usually blows from one direction. *Terracing* may be used to prepare relatively flat areas for growing crops on steep slopes. *Check dams* of stones or logs may be used to slow water in a stream or to prevent a gully from widening.

Another good farming practice for conserving farm topsoil is called *residue management*. This method does away with the plow, because even the best plowing practices bare soil to water and wind erosion. Now, many farmers leave the residue or stubble from harvested crops in place to hold soil and moisture. Tractor-pulled machines gouge places for seeds, which then sprout and grow through the decomposing residue. Besides minimizing erosion, the method actually rebuilds the precious topsoil.

INQ Figure 10–4 **Ways of preventing erosion: (A) contour plowing, (B) strip crops, (C) terraces, (D) check dams, and (E) tree windbreak.**

BUILDING UP OF THE LAND Inquiry

The Earth's Changing Crust ─────────

Invitation

What are some forces acting on the earth's crust? When rocks melt underground, they form a thick, fiery-hot liquid called *magma*. Hot gases and steam that are released when the rocks melt mix with the magma and build up great pressure. This pressure forces the magma to squeeze into cracks or weak places under the earth's crust. Magma may push up and bend rock layers above without coming to the surface. This can make a dome mountain. Can you make a model of one? Earthquakes may also change the earth's surface. In the three types of earthquakes, the crust moves horizontally, diagonally, or vertically. How can you demonstrate the three types of earthquakes?

MATERIALS

- Box lid or tray
- Round balloon (large, deflated)
- Sand or dry soil
- Three chocolate sheet cakes (unfrosted)
- Ruler
- Relief globe

Exploration

1. Spread a thin layer of sand or soil in a box lid or tray.
2. Lay a balloon on the sand. Let its neck stick out over the lid's side. Cover the balloon with about 5 centimeters (2 inches) of sand or soil. Make the "land" surface level.
3. Slowly blow air into the balloon so that it is partly filled.
4. Now, holding the first of the three cakes with one hand on each side, push the cake together until a crack develops in the cake. This is a *fault*.
5. Hold the second cake on its side with both hands and gently pull the cake apart until a "fault" forms a *trench*.
6. Hold the final cake as above, but with your left hand pull toward your body and with your right hand pull away from your body, producing a *strike slip fault*.

Teaching Tips

A large, round balloon is recommended. Small balloons are hard to inflate, and the weight of the soil will make this even harder to do. A small plastic bag may also be easily inflated if its opening is tightly wrapped around the end of a drinking straw and fastened with sticky tape.

Thin layers of alternating chocolate and vanilla cake simulate rock layers when performing the earthquake activity.

Concept Invention

1. What happened to the land surface when you blew up the balloon? What in the model is like the magma? What is like the layers of rock above the magma?
2. Compare and contrast each of the three faults made with the cakes.

Scaffolding for English Learners

Be sure to include your students' countries of origin when discussing the earth's changing surface. Have them chart the patterns of volcanic and earthquake activity from their native region onto a classroom world map. Many online data sources provide information on volcanic and seismic activity.

Concept Application

Look on a raised surface (relief) globe for examples of volcanoes and faults similar to those you made here. Where do you find volcanoes occurring? Where are examples of each type of fault found?

BUILDING UP OF THE LAND CONCEPTS

Careful geological studies show that the powerful forces of weathering and erosion should have long ago worn down the earth's surface to a low-lying plain. Then why does the earth have mountains? Part of the answer is seen in volcanic activity.

Magma

Fiery molten rock from deep underground, called *magma*, thrusts up through weak spots and cracks in the earth's crust. When this material reaches the surface, it is called *lava*.

Sometimes the accumulation of magma and high-pressure gases is so great that the molten rock shoots up to the surface in a spectacular eruption. This can happen under the ocean, as well as on land. The Hawaiian Islands are the eroded tops of volcanoes, as are the Azores in the Atlantic Ocean.

Sometimes magma may quietly ooze up through great cracks in the crust and spread out over the ground. Large parts of the Pacific Northwest are covered with hardened lava beds to depths of thousands of meters. Similar lava flows have occurred in Iceland.

Several types of magmatic activity are not directly visible until erosion has worn away parts of the crust. Magma may stop flowing and cool before it reaches the surface, or it may push up part of the crust, forming a dome, or *laccolith*. Erosion of the surrounding crust uncovers the dome and makes the dome more prominent (INQ Figure 10–5).

Where does heat energy for volcanoes originate? Several theories have been developed. Some scientists think that radioactive rocks are responsible in some places. One radioactive element is uranium, which continually shoots off helium atoms and changes to

INQ Figure 10–5   A volcano and a laccolith.

Magma

lead, and in the process, generates a tiny amount of heat energy. If many rocks of this type become concentrated, it is conceivable that they could bring about enough heat energy to melt rocks, thus forming magma.

Earthquakes and Faults ──────────

There has been a lot of attention given to earthquakes and earthquake monitoring since the December 26, 2004 earthquake off the coast of Northern Sumatra, but what causes earthquakes? Earthquakes happen when the earth's crust breaks under the strain of its deforming forces. Parts of the crust may move horizontally, diagonally, or vertically along a huge crack, or *fault*. Over a long time, *block mountains* may develop through tilted or vertical movements along a fault line. This seems to be how the Sierra Nevada range was formed.

Other mountains seem to be made through *folding*. Immense forces push parts of the crust into giant wrinkles. The Appalachians are an example.

Plate Theory ──────────

How do scientists explain such major changes in the earth's crust? When we look at a world map, certain land masses of the earth, though far apart, seem to fit together like pieces of a jigsaw puzzle. The east coast of South America and the west coast of Africa are examples. Could it be that these and other continents were once joined?

Many earth scientists infer this. They think the earth's thin crust was once solid, but now is fragmented into six to eight immense "plates" and several smaller ones that fit in between. The plates drift on the earth's fiery mantle of molten rock some 100 kilometers (60 miles) or so below. The continents float on the plates like passengers on rafts. Plate edges do not necessarily coincide with the edges of continents. According to *plate tectonics* theory, the plates continually pull apart, collide, grind edges, or partially slide under each other.

Ocean floors, for example, form when two plates drift apart. Magma pushes up from the mantle and fills the ever-widening gap between the plates. When one plate pushes into or under another, folded mountains and block mountains may be formed. A plate edge that thrusts downward under another melts into the fiery mantle below. Some of the magma resulting from this thrusts up through weak spots in the solid crust to form volcanoes. Earthquakes may happen as plates slide past each other in opposite directions. The great friction between the two massive plates may cause the movements to stop temporarily. However, stresses build up until the crust suddenly fractures and the plates grind onward.

Plate movements are surprisingly fast, up to 20 centimeters (8 inches) a year in some locations, given the approximate age of the earth at 5 billion years. Apparently, the force needed to move the rigid plates comes from convection currents in the molten mantle below.

Note the correlation between regions of earthquake and volcanic activity in INQ Figure 10–6. Many scientists infer that these active regions reveal some boundaries of the huge, drifting plates. The "Cakequake" (Hardy & Tolman, 1991) is a fun way to introduce plate tectonics through types of plate movements.

INQ Figure 10–6 Earthquake (A) and volcanic (B) regions of the world.

A

B

HOW ROCKS ARE FORMED Inquiry

The Properties of Rocks

MATERIALS

- Penny
- Six different rocks
- Large iron nail
- Partner
- Glass baby-food jar
- Pencil and paper
- Vinegar
- Safety goggles
- Piece of white tile
- Paper cup
- Hand lens

Invitation

Have you ever heard the saying, "It's as hard as a rock"? Does this mean all rocks are equally hard? What do you think? How can you find out the hardness of different rocks? What other properties of rocks can you observe and describe?

Exploration

1. Study the following hardness scale for help in grouping your rocks.

Hardness Scale	Rock Test
Very soft	Can be scratched with your fingernail.
Soft	A new penny will scratch it. A fingernail will not.
Medium	A nail will scratch it. A penny will not.
Hard	It will scratch glass. A nail will not scratch it.

2. Test each rock according to this scale. Record the hardness of each rock. One way is to label each rock with a different letter. Write the letter on a slip of paper. Then put the rock on the slip, as illustrated. Record each rock's letter and hardness on a sheet of paper.

Color streak — Tile

3. What is the color of each rock? Note that some rocks have several mixed colors.
4. What is the color of the streak left by rubbing the rock on a tile? Rub the rock on the rough side of some tile, as shown. What color is the streak?

5. How does the rock feel to you? Is the rock's texture rough? Is it smooth? Is it soapy?
6. Does the rock seem to be made up of flat layers pressed together? Use a hand lens to get a closer look.
7. Does the rock have many small holes in it?
8. Put on safety goggles. Place the rock into a small cup of vinegar. Do many tiny bubbles appear?
9. Can you see tiny parts of seashells or other such materials? Use a hand lens to get a closer look.
10. How heavy or light does the rock seem for its size?
11. What other properties of your rocks can you observe?

 Teaching Tips Only about 30 minerals make up most common rocks. So, you will observe some of the same minerals many times in different rocks.

Concept Invention

1. Will someone else who tests your rocks' hardness agree with you? Let your partner test your rocks. They should be on the lettered paper slips. Have her record each rock's letter and hardness. How much is this record like yours? Are there differences? Why? How can you put your six rocks in order from softest to hardest? (*Hint:* How can scratching one rock with another help?) What other rocks can you test for hardness? How much will someone else agree with you if they test the same rocks?
2. Try comparing color, streak, texture, or other properties of your rocks. How can these properties be used to classify rocks?

Concept Application

Rocks vary in hardness, color, texture, and other properties. To understand these properties better, play a game with a partner. Sort some of your rocks into two groups according to one property (use hardness, color, feel, or other properties). Can your partner tell which property you used to sort them? Also play the "I'm-Thinking-of-a-Rock" game with a partner. Place four or more rocks in a row. Think of just one rock and some of its properties. Can your partner find out which rock you have in mind? He must ask you only questions that can be answered by *yes* or *no*. Example: "Is it a rough rock?" (Yes) "Does it have holes?" (No) How well can you describe your rocks? Can you make a chart that your partner can use to identify them (see following example)? Make a chart of all the properties you observe about your rocks. Label your rocks and try to remember which rock is which. Show your completed chart and rocks to your partner. The rocks should be out of order, so he must study your chart to tell which rock is A, B, C, and so on. Which chart descriptions were helpful? Which confused your partner? How could these be made clearer?

Rock	Hardness	Color	Feel	Layers	Holes
A	Medium	Gray	Smooth	No	Yes
B					
C					

Growing Crystals ————

Invitation

It is interesting to see the crystals that make up some rocks. Most crystals are formed underground when melted minerals collect and grow in size as they cool. You can learn more about crystals and how they "grow" by making some yourself. How can you grow crystals?

Exploration

1. Wear safety goggles for steps 1 and 2. Stir as much salt into a half-cup of hot water as will dissolve.
2. Pour the salt solution into a saucer. Put a short string in the solution. Leave part of it out of the liquid so that you can pick up the string later. Put the saucer where it will not be disturbed.
3. Wait several days until most of the salt solution has evaporated. Carefully pour off what is left. Then give the crystals forming on the saucer bottom and string a day to dry.
4. Examine the dry crystals with a hand lens.

MATERIALS

- Glass or ceramic saucers
- String
- Scissors
- Hand lens
- Hot water
- Table salt
- Cup
- Alum (potash)
- Spoon
- Borax
- Safety goggles
- Refrigerator

 Teaching Tips
Alum (potash) is sold in drugstores, rather than in grocery stores. Sugar is another substance from which a solution may be prepared for crystal growing. All solutions should be very heavy or saturated for good crystals to form. A solution that cools quickly forms small crystals; this is like molten rock that cools relatively quickly at or near the earth's surface. A solution that cools more slowly has time to form larger, coarser crystals; this is like molten rock that cools slowly deep underground.

Concept Invention

1. How do the salt crystals look? Study their shape, size, and cohesiveness.
2. What do alum and borax crystals look like? Prepare crystals from these materials as you did from salt. Remember to wear safety goggles. Study the crystals carefully with a hand lens.
3. Have someone show you strings of crystals prepared from salt, alum, and borax. Can you tell which is which without being told?
4. How, if at all, does quickness of cooling affect crystal size?

Adapting for Students with Exceptionalities

Some students may become impatient with this activity because of the time involved. Set up a classroom observation schedule (wall chart) with names, dates, and observation times. Have students fill in what they see each day to help maintain interest.

Concept Application

Crystals may form from molten rock or may be grown from mineral solutions. The size of crystals depends on how fast the molten rock and solutions cool. Prepare two solutions of alum in separate saucers. Refrigerate one so that it will cool fast. Put the other where it will cool slowly. Examine each solution the next day. Record your results.

HOW ROCKS ARE FORMED CONCEPTS

"What are rocks made of?" children often ask. Rocks are made of minerals, natural inorganic materials that constitute most of the earth's crust. Some minerals are a single element, such as copper or carbon. A beautiful diamond is an example of almost pure carbon formed under enormous pressure underground. Other minerals are compounds of two or more minerals, such as mica or quartz. The chemical makeup of a mineral is the same anywhere it is found on the earth. A pure copper or quartz sample is as recognizable in Asia as in North America.

Geologists have developed many ways of identifying a mineral. These include observing its color, hardness, luster, crystal structure, and density, and how it splits along a plane, breaks, and reacts to chemicals.

Just as a word may be made up of one or more letters of the alphabet, rocks may be composed of one or more minerals. But there are far more known minerals than letters of the alphabet (about 2000). Most are seldom seen. Fewer than 100 minerals make up the bulk of the earth's crust.

Usually, rocks are given the same name when they contain essentially the same minerals, like granite. Some samples, though, may contain a greater proportion of one or more of the minerals than other samples. So, not all granite samples look alike, nor do many other rock samples that are given a certain name. Although there are many minerals, rocks are formed in just three ways.

Sedimentary Rocks ————————

Sediments from eroded rocks are the raw materials for new *sedimentary rocks*. The sediments are usually moved and deposited by rivers into coastal trenches and basins. Some rivers deposit sediments into large lakes. Sand, clay, silt, pebbles, and stones are common sedimentary materials. Sediments gradually collect layer upon layer where they are deposited, which makes the layers press harder and harder on the lower sediments. The enormous pressure, plus chemicals dissolved in the water, act to cement the sediments together. Sand particles become sandstone, mud or clay becomes shale, and pebbles and rocks and sand combine to form conglomerate.

Not all sediments come from eroded materials. Limestone and chalk are examples of rock formed on the ocean floor from the compressed skeletons and shells of billions of ocean animals, including clams, mussels, and corals. Some sedimentary rock may also form from previously dissolved chemicals that deposit out of solution when the water can no longer hold them.

Igneous Rocks ──────────

A second way rocks are formed is through the cooling of magma or lava, creating *igneous rocks* (the word *igneous* means "formed from fire"). A common example of igneous formation happens in volcanic domes, or *laccoliths*. Magma squeezes under a surface rock layer, slowly cools, and becomes solid. When the surface rocks erode away, the underlying hardened magma rock is exposed. Granite is the most frequently found rock of this kind. Its large crystals reveal that it cooled slowly.

Lava that is blown from a volcano or that flows out of cracks in the crust cools quickly. So, it has small crystals or no visible crystals. The light, spongy rock called *pumice* and the black, glassy rock called *obsidian* are examples.

Metamorphic Rocks ──────────

Sedimentary and igneous rocks may be subject to severe pressure and heat as parts of the crust move, fold, thrust deeper under the ground, or are buried under lava flows. This may cause physical and chemical changes in the rocks, making them *metamorphic rocks* (the word *metamorphic* means "changed in form"). Sedimentary rock such as limestone becomes the metamorphic rock marble, sandstone may become quartzite, and shale becomes slate. Igneous rock, such as granite, changes to gneiss (pronounced "nice"), or soft coal changes to hard coal.

Metamorphic rocks are harder than the original rock material. They often have compression bands of different colors. Usually, crystals are small. Still, it is easy to confuse metamorphic rocks with igneous rocks.

INQ Table 10–1 shows 12 kinds of rocks that children can use to become acquainted with the three basic rock types. They are fairly distinctive and easy to obtain. Some, and perhaps all, of these rocks may be included in specimens children bring to school. If not, they may be acquired from local rock collectors, museums, and science supply companies.

Fossils ──────────

The remains or signs of animals or plants in rock are called *fossils*. The most likely rocks in which fossils are found are sedimentary. Occasionally, fossils are found in partly metamorphosed sedimentary rocks, but pressure and heat usually destroy fossils.

Fossils are formed in different ways. When some animals died, sediments covered them. The soft body parts decomposed, but teeth and skeletons remained, preserved by hardened layers of sediment. In other cases, even the skeletons disintegrated, but before they did, mineral-laden water infiltrated into the bones and replaced bone with minerals. This process left a perfect cast replica of the skeleton in many cases. Some trees have left casts in a similar way. This is how specimens of the Petrified Forest in Arizona were formed. Additional fossils have been discovered frozen in ice, found in tar pits, and other places.

The so-called fossil fuels—coal, oil, and natural gas—were formed from the remains of plants and animals that died millions of years ago. Mud, silt, and other sediments covered

Igneous, Sedimentary, and Metamorphic Rocks

Igneous Rocks	Description	How Formed
Pumice	Grayish, fine pores, glassy, frothy, light, floats on water.	From rapid cooling of frothy, surface lava containing gases.
Volcanic Breccia	Consolidated fragments of volcanic ash, such as glass, pumice, quartz.	From being exploded high into the air from a volcano and settling.
Obsidian	Black, glassy, no crystals.	From very rapid surface cooling of lava.
Basalt	Dark, greenish-gray, very small crystals, may have some holes.	From very rapid cooling of lava close to the surface. Escaping gases form holes.

(continued)

Igneous, Sedimentary, and Metamorphic Rocks—Continued

Igneous Rocks	Description	How Formed
 Granite	Coarse crystals, white to gray, sometimes pinkish.	From slow, below-surface cooling of molten rock (magma), as when domes are formed.

Sedimentary Rocks	Description	How Formed
 Conglomerate	Rounded pebbles, stones, and sand cemented together.	From loose materials compacted by pressure of overlying sediments and bound by natural cement.
 Sandstone	Sand grains clearly visible, gray, yellow, red.	From sand compacted by pressure of sediment, bound by natural cement.
 Shale	Soft, smells like clay, fine particles, green, black, yellow, red, gray.	From compacted mud bound by natural cement.

Sedimentary Rocks	Description	How Formed
Limestone	Fairly soft, white, gray, red, forms carbon dioxide gas bubbles when touched with acids.	From dead organisms that used calcium carbonate in seawater in making body parts; from evaporation of seawater containing calcium carbonate.

Metamorphic Rocks	Description	How Formed
Marble	Different, mixed colors, may have colored bands, medium to coarse crystals, fizzes if touched with acids.	Formed when pure limestone is subjected to intense heat and pressure.
Slate	Greenish-gray, black, red, splits in thin layers, harder than shale.	Formed when shale is subjected to intense heat and pressure.
Quartzite	Very hard, white, gray, pink, indistinct grains, somewhat glassy.	Formed when sandstone is subjected to intense heat and pressure.

huge masses of organic matter in swampy forests. Gradually, the sediments formed into stony layers. Pressure and heat from immense crustal movements caused physical and chemical changes in the buried organic matter. Some formed into seams of coal trapped between shale and slate. Some deposits changed into thick, black oil and natural gas, often trapped between layers of folded rock.

Rock Cycle ————————

The same processes that formed rocks in the past continue today. Over many thousands of years, rocks change their forms. Even so, much evidence indicates that the same mineral materials are used over and over in a kind of rock cycle. INQ Figure 10–7 shows what seems to happen.

All three kinds of rocks erode when exposed on the earth's surface. The resulting sediments, under pressure, form into rock cemented with water-borne chemicals. When these rocks undergo further pressure, torsion, and heat, they metamorphose. The metamorphic rocks turn into magma when heated further. When the magma cools and hardens, it becomes igneous rock. Some of the magma may metamorphose if folded, twisted, or heated again. Some of the magma may also erode, and the cycle continues.

INQ Figure 10–7   The rock cycle.

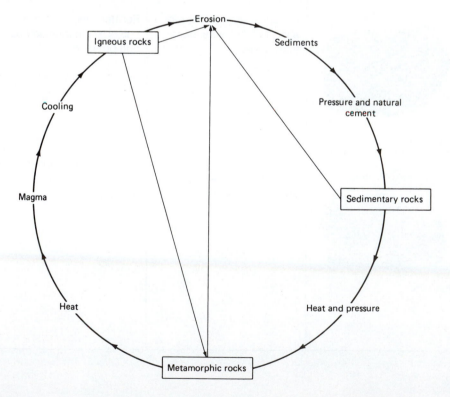

References

American Association for the Advancement of Science (AAAS). (1993). *Benchmarks for science literacy.* New York: Oxford University Press.

Hardy, G. R., & Tolman, M. N. (1991). Cakequake! An earthshaking experience. *Science and Children, 29*(1), 18–21.

Mastropieri, M., & Scruggs, T. E. (2004). *The inclusive classroom: Strategies for effective instruction* (4th ed.). Upper Saddle River, NJ: Merrill/Prentice Hall.

National Research Council (NRC). (1996). *National science education standards.* Washington, DC: National Academy Press.

TESOL (Teachers of English to Speakers of Other Languages). (1992). *TESOL Statement on the education of K-12 language-minority students in the United States.* Alexandria, VA: Author.

Selected Trade Books: The Earth's Changing Surface

For Younger Children

Baylor, B. (1974). *Everybody needs a rock.* New York: Aladdin Paperbacks.

Booth, E. (1985). *Under the ground.* Austin, TX: Raintree.

Branley, F. (1986). *Volcanoes.* New York: HarperTrophy.

Branley, F. M. (1994). *Earthquakes.* New York: HarperTrophy.

Butler, D. (1991). *First look under the ground.* Milwaukee, WI: Gareth Stevens.

Cole, J. (1988). *The magic school bus inside the earth.* New York: Scholastic.

Cole, J. (1996). *The magic school bus blows its top: A book about volcanoes.* New York: Scholastic.

Dorros, A. (1990). *Feel the wind.* New York: HarperTrophy.

Harris, S. (1979). *Volcanoes.* Danbury, CT: Watts.

Hiscock, B. (1988). *The big rock.* New York: Aladdin Paperbacks.

Ingoglia, G. (1991). *Look inside the earth.* New York: G. P. Putnam.

Leutscher, A. (1983). *Earth.* New York: Dial.

Lewis, T. (1971). *Hill of fire.* New York: HarperTrophy.

Lindop, L. (2003). *Probing volcanoes (science on the edge).* Brookfield, CT: Twenty-First Century Books/Millbrook.

McNulty, F. (1979). *How to dig a hole to the other side of the world.* New York: HarperCollins.

Merrians, D. (1996). *I can read about earthquakes and volcanoes.* New York: Troll Associates.

Pellant, C. (2000). *The best book of fossils, rocks, and minerals.* New York: Larousse Kingfisher Chambers.

Podendorf, I. (1982). *Rocks and minerals.* Danbury, CT: Childrens Press.

Roberts, A. (1983). *Fossils.* Danbury, CT: Childrens Press.

Rosenblum, R. (1994). *Earthquakes: Let's read and find out about science.* New York: HarperTrophy.

Ross, M. E., & Smith, W. (2000). *Exploring the earth with John Wesley Powell (Naturalist's Apprentice).* Minneapolis, MN: Carolrhoda Books/Lerner.

Schwartz, L. (1991). *My earth book.* Santa Barbara, CA: Learning Works.

Simon, S. (1999). *Mountains.* Topeka, KS: Econo-Clad Books.

Sipier, P. (1986). *I can be a geologist.* Danbury, CT: Childrens Press.

Williams, L. (1986). *The changing earth.* Bothell, WA: Wright Group.

Wyler, R. (1987). *Science fun with dirt and mud.* Parsippany, NJ: Julian Messner.

Zoehfeld, K. (1995). *How mountains are made.* New York: HarperTrophy.

For Older Children

Aulenbach, N. H., & Barton, H. A. (2001). *Exploring caves: Journeys into the earth.* Washington, DC: National Geographic Society.

Blobaum, C. (1999). *Geology rocks: 50 hands-on activities to explore the earth.* Charlotte, VT: Williamson.

Bramwell, M. (1987). *Planet earth.* Danbury, CT: Watts.

Challand, H. (1983). *Volcanoes.* Danbury, CT: Childrens Press.

Downs, S. F. (2000). *Earth's fiery fury.* Brookfield, CT: Twenty-First Century Books/Millbrook Press.

Fordor, R. V. (1978). *Earth in motion: The concept of plate tectonics.* New York: Morrow.

Fordor, R. V. (1983). *Chiseling the earth: How erosion shapes the land.* Springfield, NJ: Enslow.

Gallant, R. A. (1986). *Our restless earth.* Danbury, CT: Watts.

Hooper, M. (1996). *The pebble in my pocket: A history of our earth.* New York: Viking.

Lampton, C. (1994). *Earthquake (a disaster book).* Brookfield, CT: Millbrook Press.

Lauber, P. (1991). *Volcanoes and earthquakes.* New York: Scholastic.

Levine, E. (1992). *If you lived at the time of the great San Francisco earthquake.* New York: Scholastic.

Levine, S., & Grafton, A. (1992). *Projects for a healthy planet.* New York: John Wiley.

Levy, M. (1997). *Earthquake games: Earthquakes and volcanoes explained by games and experiments.* New York: Margaret McElderry.

Lye, K. (1991). *The earth.* Brookfield, CT: Millbrook Press.

Marcus, E. (1984). *All about mountains and volcanoes.* New York: Troll Associates.

Nixon, H. H., & Nixon, J. L. (1980). *Glaciers: Nature's frozen rivers.* New York: Dodd.

Rickard, G. (1991). *Geothermal energy.* Milwaukee, WI: Gareth Stevens.

Ruthland, J. (1987). *The violent earth.* New York: Random House.

Rydell, W. (1984). *Discovering fossils.* New York: Troll Associates.

Selden, P. (1982). *Face of the earth.* Danbury, CT: Childrens Press.

Sussman, A. (2000). *Dr. Art's guide to planet earth: For earthlings ages 12 to 120.* Chelsea, VT: Chelsea Green Publishing Company.

VanCleave, J. (1996). *Rocks and minerals: Mind-boggling experiments you can turn into science fair projects.* New York: John Wiley.

Williamson, T. (1985). *Understanding the earth.* Parsippany, NJ: Silver Burdett.

Winner, P. (1986). *Earthquakes.* Parsippany, NJ: Silver Burdett.

Resource Books

Butzow, C. M., & Butzow, J. W. (1989). *Science through children's literature: An integrated approach*. Englewood, CO: Teacher Ideas Press. (volcano, rock, and soil topics on pp. 123–138)

Butzow, C. M., & Butzow, J. W. (1994). *Intermediate science through children's literature: Over land and sea*. Englewood, CO: Teacher Ideas Press. (geological topics on pp. 62–88)

Cordel, B., & Hillen, J. (1996). *Primarily earth*. Fresno, CA: AIMS Education Foundation.

Cuff, K., Sneider, C., Bergman, L., Gould, A., & Seltzer, J. (1996). *Stories in stone*. Berkeley, CA: Great Explorations in Math and Science.

Ecklund, L., Mercier, S., & Wiebe, A. (Eds.). (1987). *Down to earth*. Fresno, CA: AIMS Education Foundation.

Fredericks, A. D., Meinbach, A. M., & Rothlein, L. (1993). *Thematic units: An integrated approach to teaching science and social studies*. New York: HarperCollins. (the changing earth topics on pp. 202–209)

Gosnell, K. (1994). *Geology: Thematic unit*. Huntington Beach, CA: Teacher Created Materials.

Hale, J. (1992). *Rocks and soil: Thematic unit*. Huntington Beach, CA: Teacher Created Materials.

Shaw, D. G., & Dybdahl, C. S. (1996). *Integrating science and language arts: A sourcebook for K–6 teachers*. Boston: Allyn & Bacon. (rock cycle topic on pp. 78–82; rock topics on pp. 111–130)

Sneider, C., & Barrett, K. (1989). *River cutters*. Berkeley, CA: Great Explorations in Math and Science.

WATER, AIR, AND WEATHER

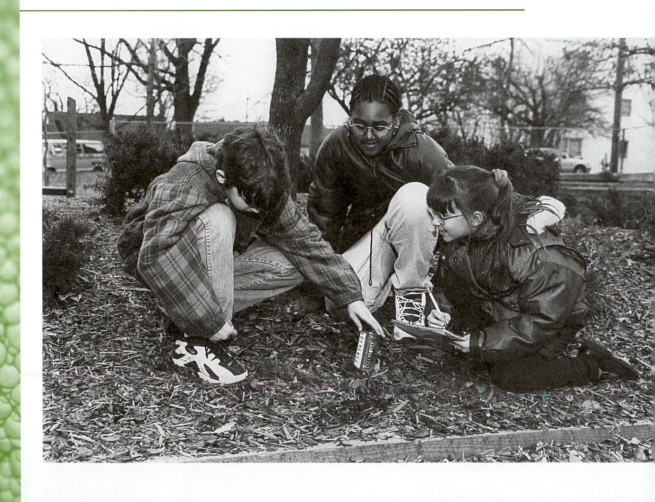

It's easy to take clean air and water for granted, and why not? For many of us, all we need do is breathe easily and turn on a faucet. But experiences of recent years with pollution and water shortages are making people lose their complacency. Let's examine some properties of water and air, the importance of a clean supply of both, and some concepts basic to understanding weather, organized under three headings: water, air and its properties, and weather.

Benchmarks and Standards

Weather, air, and water are popular topics in the elementary grades. Students frequently complete daily weather logs and journal descriptions of the changing weather patterns, often including pictures of what they see. Representative benchmarks and standards related to water, air, and weather include the following:

Sample Benchmarks (AAAS, 1993)

- Water left in an open container disappears, but water in a closed container does not disappear. (By Grades K–2, p. 67)
- Some events in nature have a repeating pattern. The weather changes day to day, but things such as temperature and rain (or snow) tend to be high, low, or medium in the same months every year. (By Grades K–2, p. 67)

Sample Standards (NRC, 1996)

- Weather changes from day to day and over the seasons. Weather can be described in measurable quantities such as temperature, wind direction and speed, and precipitation. (By Grades K–4, p. 134)
- The atmosphere is a mixture of nitrogen, oxygen, and trace gases that include water vapor. (By Grades 5–8, p. 160)

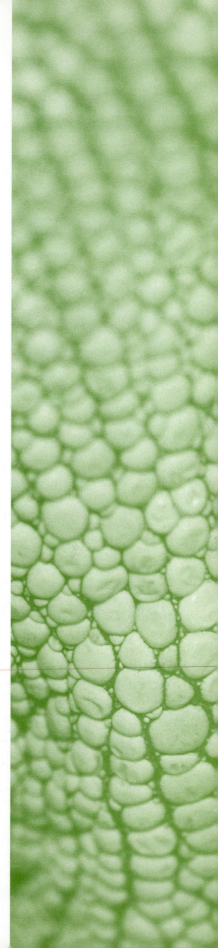

WATER Inquiry

How Water and Other Liquids Stick Together ——————

Invitation

Suppose you fill a glass with water to the very top. What do you think will happen if you add more water? How high can you fill a container of water before it spills?

Exploration

1. Fill a small container to the top with water.
2. Gently drop paper clips into the container one at a time as shown.
3. Watch how the water "heaps" higher in the container. Count the number of clips it takes for the water to spill. Make a record.

MATERIALS

- Three small plastic vials
- Spoon
- Three matched medicine droppers
- Newspaper
- Water
- Liquid soap or detergent
- Paper clips
- Rubbing alcohol
- Safety goggles
- Paper cup
- Meterstick or yardstick
- Partner

Teaching Tips

Any liquid has the property of cohesion, which is the tendency for its molecules to stick together. The cohesion of water is strong, compared with that of some other liquids. This is why water forms a bulge that rises above the rim of an overly full glass. Soap weakens the cohesive power of water, so the bulge of slightly soapy water is noticeably lower. That of alcohol is lower still; its cohesion is relatively weak. This is one reason why it evaporates so quickly.

Caution: Wear safety goggles while you are doing the steps in the Concept Invention and Concept Application.

Concept Invention

1. How high can you heap other liquids? Try soapy water and alcohol. How do these liquids compare with water? Put the three containers side by side and see. How many paper clips does it take for soapy water and alcohol to spill?
2. How large are the drops of different liquids? Take up plain water in one medicine dropper and alcohol in another. Hold up the droppers side by side. Slowly squeeze each bulb until a drop forms at each open end. How do the drop sizes compare? Try soapy water, too.
3. Which liquid—plain water, soapy water, or alcohol—has the largest drops? Which liquid has the smallest drops? Here is another way to find out. Put 100 drops of each liquid into separate, matched, small containers. Compare how high each liquid is inside.
4. What kinds of drop prints do different liquids make on newspaper? Hold a meterstick or yardstick upright over newspaper. Squeeze a drop of water from a medicine dropper held near and about halfway up the stick. What does the drop

print look like on the newspaper? How large is it? Let a drop fall from the top of the stick. How does the print look now? Try drops of soapy water and alcohol, too.

5. Can you match up a liquid with its drop print? Can you tell from how high each drop fell? Ask a partner to make drop prints as you did. Do not watch as the prints are made.

Adapting for Students with Exceptionalities

Make sure to have a lot of paper towels on hand to clean up spills. Also consider students wearing lab coats. Used lab coats can be donated by a local hospital or hospital laundry supply company. (See Mastropieri & Scruggs, 2004, chapter on science and social studies for a discussion on adapting science activities, including preparing for skills.)

Concept Application

Some liquids seem to stick together more strongly than others. What other liquids can you test? How do you think they will compare with your first liquids? Record your hypothesis and observations. Was your hypothesis correct?

How to Measure Volume with Water

Invitation

Rocks and other solid objects have many different shapes. Sometimes it is hard to tell which of two different-shaped objects is larger—that is, takes up more space. (The amount of space an object takes up is its *volume*.) How can you compare the volumes of small solid objects?

MATERIALS

- Five small different-shaped rocks
- Ruler
- Oil-based modeling clay
- Large clear jar with straight sides
- Small lead fishing sinker
- Water
- Masking tape and pencil
- Fork or spoon
- Variety of small objects

Exploration

This investigation may help some children learn to conserve volume as measured by displaced water; that is, the space an object takes up is determined by its overall surface, rather than shape, weight, or number of parts.

1. Fasten a strip of masking tape on a jar the long way.
2. Half-fill the jar with water.
3. Put one rock into the jar. Mark the water level on the tape with a pencil.
4. Remove the rock with a fork or spoon.
5. Put a second rock into the jar. Compare the new water level with the pencil mark. Remove the rock.

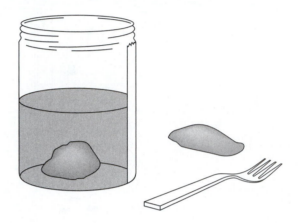

Concept Invention

1. How can you put the rocks in order from smallest to largest?
2. Make a clay ball the size of some rock. Where will the water level be if you put it into the jar? Mark the tape to show your estimate, and then test your hypothesis.
3. Suppose you form the same clay ball into another shape. Where do you think the water level will be? Try many different shapes.
4. Suppose you break the same clay piece into two parts. Where do you think the water level will be? What happens to the water level when you break the clay into more than two parts?
5. Will a heavy clay ball make the water level rise higher than a lighter one? Make two clay balls the same size, but have a lead weight in the middle of one ball. Try each ball and find out.
6. How much larger is one rock compared with another? With a ruler and pencil, make evenly spaced marks on the jar's tape strip. Call each pencil mark 1 "unit." Compare the difference in water-level units before and after a rock is put into the jar. How much difference in units is there between your smallest and largest rock?

Concept Application

The volumes of different-shaped solid objects may be compared by the water each displaces. Get other small objects and record them. How well can you predict the volume of each in units? Experiment and check your predictions.

Things That Float in Water

Invitation

Can you tell, just by looking at an object, if it will float in water? What kinds of objects float? What kinds of objects sink? How can you find out which small objects will float?

Exploration

1. Half-fill a plastic bowl with water.
2. Empty the bag of small objects onto your desk. Put those you think will float into one group. Put those you think will sink into another group.
3. Place all the objects from one group into the water. Observe what happens, and then remove the objects. Do the same thing with the other group of objects.

Concept Invention

1. How many objects did what you thought? What are the objects like that floated? What are the objects like that sank?
2. What can you do to sink the objects that floated?
3. What can you do to float the objects that sank?
4. In what ways can you get a piece of foil to float? In what ways can you get a piece of foil to sink? Can you make a foil boat? How many washers can your foil boat carry? What can you do to make it carry more washers?
5. How can you get a piece of clay to float? Can you make a clay boat the same size as your foil boat? Which do you think will carry more washers?
6. Can you make two foil boats that will carry, from the first try, exactly the same weight? Can you make two clay boats that will carry the same weight from the first try?

> **Teaching Tips**
>
> Children can develop some understanding in this investigation about the buoyancy of different objects in water and how the density of water affects buoyancy. You might also want children to explore liquids other than water. A bag of small objects to test for floating might include a wooden checker, pencil, key, marble, plastic objects, pieces of leather, rubber eraser, and small toy figures. The children can bring in many more. Uniform objects other than large washers may be used to measure the weight-carrying capacity of children's boats. Identical marbles, pennies, or small pieces of ceramic tile work well. To avoid rust, be sure all steel washers are dried before they are stored.

MATERIALS

- Plastic bowl
- Water
- Salt
- Bag of small objects to test
- Ruler
- Oil-based modeling clay
- Spoon
- Large washers
- Paper towels
- Aluminum foil (15 centimeters, or 6 inches, square)

Scaffolding for English Learners

The floating and sinking activity is a common elementary science activity that is not language/vocabulary intensive. It presents an opportunity for English learners to show that they understand a science concept despite language problems. Activities such as this help differentiate true learning disabilities from language disabilities. Many English learners are inappropriately identified as students with special needs due to language difficulties. (See Baca, Baca, & deValenzuela, 2004, for a discussion of the current status of bilingual special education.)

Concept Application

Objects that are light for their size float and adding salt to the water makes floating easier. How do your boats work in saltwater? Can they carry more weight? What can you get to float in saltwater that cannot float in freshwater? List the items. Can you find anything that will float in freshwater and sink in saltwater? List these items, too.

Water Pressure ————

MATERIALS

- Tall, empty milk carton
- Nail or sharp pencil
- Sink
- Water

Invitation

What happens to water pressure with depth?

Exploration

1. Punch a nail hole in the carton's side, halfway up, from the inside out.
2. Punch another hole above it and a third hole below it, from the inside out.
3. Place the carton in a sink. Cover all three holes tightly with three fingers. Fill the carton with water. Keep it in the sink.
4. If you take away your fingers, what do you think will happen?
5. Remove your fingers quickly from the three holes.

Teaching Tips Sometimes the torn edges of the holes will impede the flow of water. Punching the holes from the inside out makes this less likely.

Concept Invention

1. Explain what happened.
2. In what part of the carton was the water pressure the greatest?

Concept Application

Do you think that water pressure will be greater in the bottom of the Pacific or Atlantic Ocean or in one of the Great Lakes? Explain your answer.

High Water ————

MATERIALS

- Rubber tube (1 meter, or 1 yard, long)
- Container of water
- Funnel that fits the tube
- Sink

Invitation

How high can water flow, compared to its origin?

Exploration

1. Stick the funnel end tightly into a tube end. Do this activity in a sink.
2. Hold up the funnel. Have someone pour water into it.
3. When water comes out of the tube, pinch it off.
4. Have someone fill the funnel with water. Keep the tube end pinched off. How high will you be able to hold the tube end and still have water come out? Can you hold it higher than the funnel? What if you hold the tube end the same level or lower than the funnel?
5. Let go of the tube end.

Concept Invention

1. Try holding it at different heights.
2. What did you find?

Concept Application

Do you think that water flow will be greater from a hillside reservoir or from a water tower high above a city? In a tall building, would the water faucets in the sinks on the first floor work differently from the faucets on the top floor, if plumbers did not compensate for the height of the building? How would plumbers make this compensation? What if the building was higher than the water reservoir? Explain your ideas.

The Filtering of Polluted Water

Invitation

Most cities have water treatment plants to clean, or purify, their drinking water. The unclean water is first pumped to a large settling tank, where it stays for a while. Some of the dirt and other polluting particles in the water settle to the bottom. The cleaner water on top then goes into a filtering tank, which has thick layers of sand and gravel. Sometimes a layer of charcoal is put between these layers. As the water filters through, still more polluting materials are left behind. It's not easy to clean polluted water, even by filtering. How can you clean polluted water by filtering?

MATERIALS

- Cut-off pint milk carton
- Clean sand
- Charcoal briquette
- Cotton
- Small glass jar
- Nail
- Jar of soil water
- Small paper bag
- Rock
- Clean tap water

Exploration

1. Punch some holes with a nail in the bottom of a cut-off milk carton.
2. Spread some cotton inside on the carton bottom. Add some clean sand.
3. Put crushed charcoal on top of the sand. (To crush charcoal, put a briquette into a small bag and pound it with a rock.) Then add another layer of sand.
4. Place the filter on top of a small glass jar.
5. Pour some clean tap water into your filter. (This will pack the materials more tightly together.)
6. Prepare a jar of soil water. To do this, put a handful of soil into a jar of water and mix. Let the water settle for a half hour.
7. Pour some soil water from the top of the jar into the filter. Watch the filtered water trickle into the small jar, as illustrated.

 Teaching Tips | Caution the children not to drink their filtered water. They should know that a chemical is added to filtered water in city water plants to kill germs that survive filtering. Try having a contest to determine the best filter. Children may need to be reminded that everyone should filter samples of the same polluted water.

Concept Invention

1. How clean is the filtered water compared to the soil water?
2. How clean would the water get with fewer filtering materials? How clean would the water get with just one filtering material?
3. Will your filter remove ink or food coloring?
4. Does the order in which you place your filter materials matter?

Concept Application

Some water pollutants may be removed by filtering the water through layers of different permeable materials. Would more or other materials work better? How else could you improve your filter? Record your experiments.

WATER CONCEPTS

Our need for water commands our attention in both direct and indirect ways. Water is vital to life. Water transports chemicals to body cells, removes waste materials, and performs other vital bodily functions. Although humans may survive for weeks without food, they need water within a few days. Bathing, cooking, and recreational activities also require water.

Agriculture consumes enormous volumes of water for irrigating plants in rain-poor regions. Industry, too, is a huge user of water. The manufacture of paper, steel, rubber, chemicals, and other products continually requires more water. Even our future energy resources depend, in part, on having adequate water. For example, coal in the western United States would be most efficiently transported if crushed and sent through pipes after being mixed with water. The extraction of oil from shale rock also requires much water. But there is not enough water in the right places to meet all such needs. Because water has so many uses, it is important to understand its properties. Let's look at some now.

Water Properties —————

Water is an excellent solvent. In fact, more substances dissolve in water than in any other common liquid. Some other properties of water basic to our discussion are its molecular attraction, how it exerts pressure, and how it flows.

Molecules and Water

You may recall that the attractive force between molecules is called *cohesion*. In a solid, the spaces between molecules are relatively small, so a solid material sticks together, or coheres, well enough to maintain its own shape. Molecules of a liquid are farther apart; their weaker cohesion causes them to slide about and assume the shape of their container. The cohesion of gas molecules is weaker still because these molecules are even farther apart.

Cohesion of water molecules is central to the process of evaporation. Heat energy must overcome water's cohesive force, as well as the force of air pressing down. If this could not happen, evaporation could not take place. The sun, of course, is the earth's chief source of heat energy. When we spread out a water puddle to make it dry faster, the sun's energy overcomes the cohesive force of more water molecules at one time. So, the rate of evaporation increases.

Pressure

The weight of water gives it pressure. That is to say, as water depth is greater so is its pressure. This is one reason why a dam is built with a thicker base than top. At any depth, the pressure is exerted in all directions and planes.

Pressure is also involved when something floats. For an object to float, opposing balanced forces work against each other. Gravity pulls down on the object, and the water pushes up on it. The key to floating is the object's size relative to its weight or density. If it is light for its size, it has relatively high volume; in other words, it presents a large surface area for the water to push against. This is why a ship made of steel floats. The water displaced by an object that is light for its size pushes up as forcefully as gravity pulls down.

An object floats higher in the ocean than in freshwater because ocean water has more minerals dissolved in it, especially salt. Therefore, a cup of ocean water weighs more than a cup of freshwater. Having more weight, it pushes back with greater force on any object that displaces it. This pushing force allows a ship to carry a heavier cargo in saltwater than in freshwater.

Water Flow

Gravity is the force that moves water in nature. Water cannot flow higher than its source unless some other force is more powerful. To store their water supplies, some towns and small cities pump water into large tanks mounted on towers. Water then flows by gravity through all pipes connected to the towns' tanks.

In some places, buildings are constructed that are taller than the tower. Pumps are installed in the buildings so that water can reach the higher floors. Sometimes a tank is located on the roof of a tall building so that water is available above the normal water source levels. Special plumbing is also required so that water pressure is not extreme at the lower floors, compared with the upper floors.

Clean, Adequate Water

Will there be enough water for enough people in enough places in the foreseeable future? A dependable answer to this question seems impossible now. But we can survey what it takes to get a clean and adequate supply of water, beginning with some sources of water.

Sources

A look at a globe tells us the earth has no shortage of water. About 71% of the earth's crust is covered with it. Most, though, is in the oceans and is too salty for either land plants or animals to drink. So, our immediate sources of freshwater are found elsewhere, such as in lakes, rivers, reservoirs, and beneath the land surface as groundwater.

Groundwater comes from rainwater that is absorbed into the soil and porous rock. It continues to sink until it reaches a layer of solid, nonporous rock. As more rainwater soaks into the ground, more of the below-surface section becomes saturated. The upper limit of the saturated section is called the *water table*. The water table profile often corresponds roughly to that of the earth's surface. Where the earth's surface dips below the water table, we see a lake or spring. Groundwater does not always come from rainwater sinking from directly above. Groundwater may percolate through ground and porous rock diagonally or horizontally for some distance before it stops.

To construct a water well, a hole is drilled or dug to some depth below the water table. This depth helps ensure a steady supply of water should the water table lower during dry spells. Ocean water is the main source of evaporating water on the earth. So, the oceans are the basic source for freshwater. When ocean water evaporates, the salt is left behind. Air currents carry the water vapor far inland. There it condenses and falls as rain, hail, or snow.

Over the long run, the water cycle gives what should be a steady supply of groundwater and other water. But several factors today make finding usable freshwater difficult in many places. Increased uses for water, as mentioned earlier, are one reason; another reason is pollution.

Pollution

Many cities continue to dump partly treated or raw sewage into nearby rivers or lakes, from which drinking water is often drawn. As a result, purification of water is getting more difficult and more expensive. Factories, too, often discharge wastes into accessible waters. Another major source of pollution is agriculture. Chemical fertilizers and pesticides wash off the land into streams and bays.

An overload of fertilizers or sewage in a lake or other body of water causes an abnormally large population of algae to grow. The algae block sunlight from reaching aquatic plants under the water's surface; so, the plants, as well as the animals that feed on them, die. Dead material piles up on the lake bottom. The overcrowded algae also die in time, and the decomposers take over. Eventually, the oxygen supply in the water is largely depleted, and the decomposers die, too. They are replaced by bacteria that can live without oxygen. What was once a source of clean water and a complex community of living things is a silted, near-dead, putrescent swamp. A reversal can occur through natural changes of the land surface and a gradual succession of ever higher forms of life, but this may take centuries or longer.

In recent years, much publicity has been given to a particularly ominous threat to the nation's water supply: hazardous waste dumps. At such sites, poisonous chemicals may leak from storage containers and percolate down through the ground, contaminating groundwater, nearby streams, and lakes. Drinking or swimming in the water, and eating fish whose organs have accumulated the poisons, have been linked to severe health problems, including brain damage, cancer, and birth defects.

Acid Rain

Many waste products are discharged into the air, as well as on the ground and into bodies of water. These, too, may end up polluting our water and other natural resources. The burning of fossil fuels in factories, power plants, and automobiles releases sulfur and nitrogen oxides into the atmosphere. When water vapor is also present, these gases are converted into sulfuric acid and nitric acid. The rain that falls from a polluted region can be as acidic as vinegar.

Acid rain, including acid sleet, hail, and snow, is contaminating water supplies, killing trees and fish stocks, and corroding water systems. Its effects are easily noticeable in areas that have large concentrations of coal-burning power plants, heavy industry, and automobiles. But even more damage may result far beyond these places. Winds aloft, especially the prevailing westerlies in the United States, sweep the pollutants into large, distant regions. The northeastern United States and adjacent Canadian areas have been most affected.

Some progress has been made in reducing pollutants through the use of chemical filters in industry and pollution control devices for automobile exhaust systems. But large-scale improvements in industrial pollution bear a daunting price tag. Especially nettlesome is the answer to the question: Who pays? When suspected sources of pollution are hundreds of kilometers away and thousands of jobs or millions of utility bills are affected, an acceptable answer becomes highly complicated.

Conservation

It seems inevitable that people will need to change certain water-use habits. Many habits were fostered when regional populations were small, pollution was less severe, water uses were fewer, and resources were more abundant. Conservation, or the wise use, of water resources is becoming more common because more people are aware of the consequences if it is not practiced.

Stricter laws to protect water supplies are continually enacted. More attention is being given to the recycling of industrial wastes and the safe storage of long-lasting, harmful chemicals. Bare slopes are being planted to protect watersheds. Fertilizers and pesticides are being used under more controlled conditions in agriculture. People are learning to use less water in more situations without wasting it. An important by-product of water conservation is energy conservation. A significant amount of the nation's energy is used in pumping water and heating it.

Future Water Supply

It's possible that even increased conservation measures will fail to save enough water to meet our future water needs. Where will we get more usable water? Just as some scientists are looking for ways to directly tap the sun's energy, others are investigating methods for directly converting ocean water to freshwater.

One way to remove salt from ocean water is to distill it. The water is heated, changed to a vapor, and condensed, much like in the water cycle. Another method freezes ocean water. The ice that forms at the surface is mostly freshwater. It is removed and melted. Many other methods are now being used and explored, such as reverse osmosis. At present, all are too expensive for widespread use. If more economical means can be found, the direct conversion of ocean water to freshwater could bring major changes in many dry regions of the world and in the world's food supply.

AIR AND ITS PROPERTIES Inquiry

Where Air Can Be

Invitation

Air is found everywhere on the earth. Air can go into tiny places. But can air get inside everything? What things do you think have some air inside? What things do not have air inside? How can you find out what things have some air inside?

Exploration

1. Put a piece of brick into a bowl of water.
2. Watch for tiny bubbles on the brick. These are air bubbles. This shows some air was inside the brick.
3. Put a coin into the water. You will probably see no bubbles. This shows the coin probably had no air inside.

MATERIALS

- Plastic bowl half-filled with water
- Orange peel
- Sand
- Coin
- Several kinds of stones
- Cracker
- Piece of brick
- Leather
- Soft wood
- Several kinds of fabrics

Teaching Tips

Some soft materials show dramatically that they contain air if squeezed under water. Soft pine, balsa wood, and leather are examples. Pliers or tongs may serve as squeezers, if needed. The spaces between sand or soil particles commonly contain much air. Surface air bubbles may easily be seen if water is poured into a small jar with sand inside. (Although water also usually contains air, the volume is small compared with that found in the spaces between sand particles.)

Concept Invention

1. Does a piece of cloth have air in it? Do some kinds of cloth have more air in them than others?
2. Does leather have air in it?
3. Can a soft piece of wood have air in it?
4. Does a cracker have air in it?
5. Does an orange peel have air in it?
6. Can a stone have air in it? Try several different kinds.
7. Does sand have air in it? How can you find out?

Concept Application

Air can be found almost everywhere. Most porous materials contain some air. What else do you think might have air in it? What else might not have air in it? Record your predictions and check for accuracy.

Soap Bubbles

Invitation

Have you ever blown soap bubbles? If so, how big was your biggest bubble? How small was your smallest bubble? How can you blow soap bubbles? What is it like inside a bubble?

Exploration

1. Cut the straw end into four parts. Use the end that bends.
2. Push back the four parts as shown in the drawing.
3. Bend the straw into a J shape.
4. Dip the cut end into the bubble liquid.
5. Put the other straw end into your mouth and blow gently.
6. Place a mixture of dish soap (32–64 ounces), glycerin (10 tablespoons), and water in a child's plastic pool. Place a Hula-Hoop on the center of the bottom of the pool. Set a small wooden box or stool inside the Hula-Hoop (above the water line).
7. Place a student on the stool and then quickly pick the Hula-Hoop straight up from the bottom of the pool to above the student's head. A bubble will form and surround the student. Larger amounts of glycerin or dish soap or both will make longer lasting bubbles.

MATERIALS

- Paper cup of bubble liquid
- Soda can with ends removed
- Bendable plastic straw
- Paper cup half-full of water
- Small piece of cardboard
- Liquid detergent or soap
- Scissors
- Glycerin
- Thin wire (15 centimeters, or 6 inches, long)
- Spoon
- Child's plastic swimming pool
- Hula-Hoop
- Small wooden box or stool
- Water

Concept Invention

1. What different kinds of bubbles can you blow? How big a bubble can you make? How small a bubble can you make?
2. How many bubbles can you blow with one dip of your pipe? How few?

Teaching Tips

Use either a commercial bubble-blowing liquid or prepare your own from liquid detergent. Many teachers have gotten excellent results from Dawn® or Joy® liquid dish detergent. Both products contain a high glycerin content. A water mix of 1 part detergent to 16 parts water works well. Add some glycerin (sold at drugstores) for even bigger bubbles. Mix the solution thoroughly.

This investigation is done best outdoors. However, when students try to steer their bubbles in a certain direction by waving a piece of cardboard (Concept Invention step 5), a near-windless condition is needed. On a windy day, this activity can be done indoors in a more limited way. Children can discover that a bubble stays up best if the cardboard or hand is waved rapidly from side to side over the bubble. This movement decreases the air pressure over the bubble and so the surrounding air rushes in, holding up the bubble. Likewise, for lateral motion, a bubble will "follow" a waved cardboard.

3. What do you see when you look at a bubble? What do you see when you look through the large bubble around you?
4. What will happen if you catch a bubble in your hand? What will happen if your hand is soapy?
5. How can you make a bubble floating in air stay up? Move to your left or right? (*Hint:* How might a piece of cardboard help you?)
6. Bend pieces of wire into loops and other shapes. Dip them into the liquid and blow. What kinds of bubbles do they make?
7. Make extra-large bubbles. Take a soda can that has no top or bottom. Dip one end into bubble liquid. How big a bubble can you make?

Concept Application

A soap bubble is made up of air inside and soap outside. Big bubbles have more air inside than small ones. Moving air can make soap bubbles move. Test the relative effectiveness of several commercial preparations or your own bubble preparations. Which one makes the biggest bubbles? Which one makes bubbles that last the longest? Can you make a better bubble liquid? Mix a capful of liquid detergent or soap in a half-cup of water. How does it work? Will adding some glycerin make bigger bubbles? How much works best? Record your ideas and results.

Adapting for Students with Exceptionalities

Be sure students do not taste the soap mixture or inhale on the straws. To make larger bubbles, use a bent coat hanger or length of string. Some students may want to explore bubbles from the inside through the use of a small plastic swimming pool with bubble solution and a milk crate inside and a Hula-Hoop to make the bubbles (see *http://bubbles.org/*).

Parachutes

MATERIALS

- Thin plastic (dry cleaners bag)
- Sticky tape
- Thin cotton cloth
- Scissors
- String
- Modeling clay

Invitation

How does a parachute help someone who jumps from an airplane? What makes a parachute fall slowly? You can learn more about real parachutes by making small ones. How can you make a small parachute?

Exploration

1. Cut a square the size of a handkerchief from thin plastic.
2. Cut a small hole in the center of the plastic.
3. Cut four strings the same length.
4. Tie one string end to each corner of the plastic.
5. Tie the other string ends together in a knot.
6. Shape a small ball of clay around the knot as illustrated.

Small hole

Clay

Teaching Tips Learning about parachutes allows children to manipulate several variables thoughtfully. In doing so, they learn to think of air as a tangible, material substance. The thin plastic clothes bags that dry cleaners use are excellent material for chutes. (Remind children that a plastic bag should never be placed over the head.)

Concept Invention

1. Try out your parachute on the playground. Drop it from the top of the play slide. Then roll it up loosely and throw it into the air. Does rolling make it work better?
2. Suppose you cover the hole with sticky tape. What difference might this make?
3. Suppose you make the hole larger. What difference might this make?
4. Suppose you add more clay to the ball. What difference might this make?
5. How can you make a parachute that will fall more slowly than the one you have now?
6. How can you get a small and a large parachute to fall equally fast?
7. What is the smallest parachute you can make that will work correctly?
8. What other materials can you use to make parachutes?

Concept Application

A parachute is built to catch the air as it falls. It can be changed to fall faster or slower. Can you construct a parachute with improved performance? Can you predict the effect of wind drift on your parachute? Describe your improved parachute and how it performed.

Air and Space

Invitation

How can you show that air takes up space?

Exploration

1. Fill the bowl three-fourths full with water.
2. Hold a glass with the open end down. Push it straight down into the water.
3. Put a second glass in the water sideways so that it fills with water.
4. Now tip the first glass. Try to "pour" the air up from the first glass into the second glass, as illustrated.

MATERIALS

- Deep, large clear bowl
- Water
- Two small clear glasses
- Paper towels

Teaching Tips

If no air bubbles are lost in the process, the air may be transferred from one glass to the next indefinitely. Because air is less dense than water, the air-filled glass will always need to be below the water-filled glass during the transfer.

Concept Invention

1. What happens to the water in the higher glass?
2. What happens in the lower glass?
3. How can you get the air back into the first glass?

Concept Application

Suppose you put a crushed paper towel in the bottom of a glass. How could you put the open glass underwater without getting the towel wet? Explain your answer.

Balloon Buoyancy

MATERIALS

- Two matched balloons
- Meterstick or yardstick
- Scissors
- Sticky tape
- String
- Paper clip

Invitation

If you have two balanced balloons, will adding air to one balloon cause a change in the balance?

Exploration

1. Hang a meterstick evenly from a doorway or other place. Use a string and tape.
2. Attach a string loosely to each of the two deflated balloons.
3. Tape each string to an end of the stick. Be sure the stick is level after the balloons are hung. If not, place a partly open paper clip on the stick where needed to balance it.

Teaching Tips

Be sure the balloon strings are always affixed to the stick ends to help ensure balance.

You will find that the air within the high-pressure balloon is denser than the air within the low-pressure balloon, causing the balloons to become unbalanced.

Concept Invention

1. What will happen if you blow up one balloon and rehang it?
2. What will happen if the balloon is later deflated and rehung?

Concept Application

In what ways can you make the stick level again? (The strings must stay at the ends of the stick.) Describe your experiment.

Air Needed for Burning

Invitation

What are some ways you can stop a candle from burning? How important is air for a candle to keep burning? How long do you think a candle will burn inside a closed jar?

Exploration

1. Stick some clay to the middle of a pie pan.
2. Stand a candle upright in the clay.
3. Put on safety goggles. Light the candle. Put the used match in the pan.
4. Pick up your next-to-smallest jar. Put it upside down over the candle as shown.
5. Look at a clock that has a second hand. How long does it take for the candle to go out? Record this time.
6. Remove the jar. Move a wad of several paper towels in and out of the jar a few times. This will clear out the bad air inside.

Concept Invention

1. How long will the candle burn a second time? How long will the candle burn a third time? Be sure to remove the bad air after each trial. Record the trial times and the average time in a chart such as the following:

Jar Size	Time for Each			Average Time	Predicted Time
Smallest					
Next Smallest	30	34	32	32	
Next to Largest					
Largest					

MATERIALS

- Small candles of different sizes
- Matches
- Safety goggles
- Modeling clay
- Four different–sized, wide-mouthed glass jars
- Clock or watch with second hand
- Metal pie pan
- Pencil and paper
- Paper towels
- Graph paper
- Measuring cup
- Pairs of matched jars of different shapes

Children should wear safety goggles when working with lighted candles. Also check that all children have long hair tied back and loose sleeves pushed up and out of the way. Note that some schools restrict the use of matches or an open flame to responsible adults.

A candle flame dies out in a closed container after it uses a certain percentage of the oxygen in the air. The flame burns longer in a large jar than in a small one because of the larger oxygen supply. Provide at least four different sizes of wide-mouthed glass jars with straight sides for the investigation. You might try half-pint, pint, quart, and half-gallon sizes, or 200-, 400-, 800-, and 1600-milliliter sizes. The exact capacities are not critical.

If you wish to stress the graphing activity, you might begin with it and continue through the sequence. If you think your students are not ready for it, omit this activity. If many points are plotted on this graph, the line drawn between them will resemble a curve rather than a straight line. Use this finding to demonstrate that using more data allows more accurate predictions.

2. How long do you think the candle will burn in the smallest jar? How long do you think the candle will burn in the next-to-largest jar? Write your predicted times on the chart. Use three trials for each jar. Record the trial times and the average times on your chart. Compare the average and predicted times.

3. How much larger than the other jars is your largest jar? Compare your jars and then study your chart. How long do you think the candle will burn in the largest jar?

4. You can make better predictions. Get different jars. Use a measuring cup to discover how much water each jar holds. Find out burning times for the smallest and largest jars. Then make a graph. Mark the average burning times of the smallest and largest jars. Draw a light line in between.

5. How closely can you predict the burning times for other jars? Find the jar size column on the bottom of the graph. Follow the column up until you reach the drawn line. Then, look straight across to the left at the burning time. How will recording more jar times make it easier to predict more accurately?

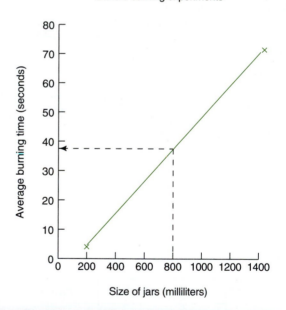

Candle burning experiments

6. What difference will it make in burning times if you change the candle? For example, does candle size make a difference? Does the flame's closeness to the jar top make a difference? Will two candles die out twice as fast as one?

Concept Application

A flame needs air to burn. The time that a flame burns depends, in part, on how much air it has. Does the shape of the jar make a difference in burning times?

Compare pairs of matched jars with different shapes and find out. How can you make a candle burn longer in a small jar than in a larger jar? Can you think of several ways?

AIR AND ITS PROPERTIES CONCEPTS

Air has many of the properties of water and may contain much water in gaseous form. However, air also has some unique properties. To better understand some of its specific features, let's first take an overall look at where our immediate air supply comes from: the atmosphere.

The Atmosphere

Space exploration has made us more aware of how dependent we are on our atmospheric environment. Without an air supply, humans cannot survive for more than minutes. Although we may travel in comfort thousands of kilometers across the earth's surface, an ascent of only 5 kilometers (3 miles) into the sky may require special oxygen apparatus.

How far out does the atmosphere extend? No one knows exactly, but meteorologists have identified four roughly separable layers of differing properties: troposphere, stratosphere, ionosphere, and exosphere (INQ Figure 11–1).

Troposphere

The *troposphere* extends to a height ranging from 8 kilometers (5 miles) at the poles to about 16 kilometers (10 miles) at the equator. This is the region where practically all weather takes place.

Why the difference in altitudes? Tropospheric air is coldest at the poles and so weighs more per unit than warmer, equatorial air. Also, the earth spins on its axis. The fastest speed of rotation, about 1600 kilometers (1000 miles) per hour, is at the equator. This offsets the earth's gravitational pull to some extent. The speed of rotation decreases as distance to the poles decreases, just as a person who runs on an inside track can slowly jog along, while someone on an outside track must run swiftly just to keep abreast. As the rotational speed slows, gravity has an increasing effect. In the troposphere, stable air temperature steadily decreases with altitude.

INQ Figure 11–1   **The atmosphere has several layers.**

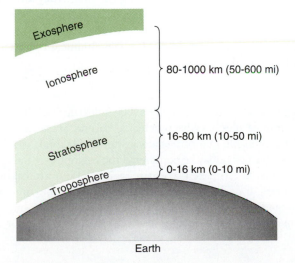

Stratosphere

Just above the troposphere is the *stratosphere*, which reaches to about 80 kilometers (50 miles). This is the layer airlines use on some routes for long-range cruising. The cold, thin air is remarkably clear and turbulence free because vertical movements of warmed air and atmospheric dust particles are largely confined to the layer below. Air travelers may note some pale clouds of ice crystals above cruising altitude, but these are infrequent.

Between the lower reaches of the stratosphere and the troposphere are found winds that vary greatly in force and direction. Most interesting are the *jet streams*, rivers of high-velocity air several kilometers high and more than 150 kilometers wide. They range to thousands of kilometers in length and tend to flow from west to east. A pilot may increase the speed of a plane several hundred kilometers per hour by locating and staying within a jet stream.

In the stratosphere, at an altitude of 16 to 48 kilometers (10 to 30 miles), is a layer of ozone that absorbs much of the sun's harmful ultraviolet radiation. The layer is largely composed of molecules that have three atoms of oxygen, rather than the usual two. Certain chemicals released into the atmosphere, called *chlorofluorocarbons* (CFCs), collect unevenly in the ozone layer and destroy the ozone molecules. This destruction greatly reduces the layer's capacity to block ultraviolet rays, and so more get through to the earth's surface at various places.

Excess ultraviolet radiation increases the risk of skin cancer, eye damage, and immune system impairment. It can also reduce crop yields and disrupt ocean food chains. International agreements in force require the phasing out of CFCs that were once widely used in refrigerants, air conditioners, industrial cleaning solvents, and the manufacture of some plastics. Less harmful but more expensive chemicals have generally replaced CFCs.

Ionosphere

Beyond a height of about 80 kilometers (50 miles), the stratosphere gradually blends into the *ionosphere*. In this region are *ions*, or electrically charged particles formed when high-energy solar and cosmic rays hit air molecules. These harmful rays are largely absorbed at and below this level. Auroras are sometimes visible. Meteors burn to ashes from friction as they strike scattered air molecules.

The ionosphere is an invaluable aid to radio communication on the earth. The earth's surface is curved, but radio waves travel in straight lines. How can straight radio waves be made to travel from city to city on the curved earth? One way of overcoming this problem has been to transmit radio waves to the ionosphere, where they are reflected downward to other points on the earth. Because solar "storms" frequently disturb the ionosphere and disrupt communication, this reflection has not proved to be a completely satisfactory solution. Radio and television signals reflected from communications satellites are turning out to be a better solution to this problem.

Exosphere

The *exosphere* begins at about 1000 kilometers (600 miles) up and extends to an undetermined distance. A few air molecules have been detected beyond where the ionosphere adjoins the exosphere, and it is probable that others are scattered thousands of kilometers beyond. For practical purposes, this region may be considered the beginning of interplanetary space.

Although scientists estimate the entire weight of our atmosphere at an enormous 4.5 quadrillion metric tons, more than half of all air molecules are concentrated below a height of 5.6 kilometers (3.5 miles). The combination of this enormous pressure and the unimaginably small size of air molecules results in the presence of air in practically everything on or near the earth's surface. Air is found in most soils, water, and even in some rocks. Consider now more effects of this pressure.

Air Pressure ─────────

Because the average weight of air is about 1 kilogram per square centimeter (14.7 pounds per square inch) at sea level, tons of air press against us right now. Why, then, are we not crushed? There are two basic reasons. Like water pressure, air at a given level presses with equal force in all directions. Because every force has a counteractive force, the pressure is neutralized. Counteractive pressure also takes place in our bodies. Air molecules are so tiny that they dissolve in our bloodstreams, besides occupying space in our lungs and other body cavities.

Unlike free air, the air in our bodies lags somewhat in building up or reducing counteractive back pressure as atmospheric pressure changes. Have you noticed that your ears "pop" while rising quickly in an elevator of a tall building? This happens because air pressure in the inner ear tends to remain the same while the outside air pressure decreases with increased altitude. The result is an uncomfortable outward pushing sensation behind the eardrums. A slow elevator gives more opportunity for inner ear pressure to be adjusted through the eustachian tube, which connects the inner ear to the nasal passages and mouth.

A similar but much more dangerous situation is faced by deep-sea divers. As they descend into the water, air is pumped under increasing pressure into the diving helmet and suit to counteract increasing water pressure. After working for 20 to 30 minutes, a diver's circulatory system contains an abnormal amount of air. If the diver ascends rapidly to the surface, a region of much lower air pressure, air in the blood may expand and form bubbles. The presence of bubbles in the blood causes a very painful and possibly fatal condition known as "the bends."

The lag in adjusting to outside atmospheric pressure may also help explain why some persons complain of aches and pains just before rainy weather. Outside air pressure usually lessens before a storm. If the body's blood pressure remains the same, the blood will now press outward a little more forcibly than usual against body joints and tissues. It is possible that the slight extra pressure may cause discomfort.

Makeup of Air ─────────

So many references are made to the earth's "ocean of air" that it is easy for us to get the impression that pure air is a uniform compound, such as pure water. Actually, the air we breathe is a mixture of several separate and distinct gases; the three most important to survival are oxygen, nitrogen, and carbon dioxide.

Oxygen makes up about 21% of the air, and nitrogen 78%. Oxygen is essential to us because it combines readily with sugars in our body cells and releases heat energy. Oxygen is also essential to burning.

Nitrogen is essential to survival because it is necessary for plant growth. It also dilutes the oxygen we breathe. Continual breathing of pure oxygen speeds up metabolic processes to the point where the body cannot get rid of waste products fast enough to survive. The small amount of carbon dioxide in the air, about 3/100 of 1%, is needed for photosynthesis in green plants. Besides these gases, the air contains less than 1% of such gases as argon, krypton, helium, neon, radon, and xenon. All these atmospheric gases are remarkably well mixed by winds up to a height of 8 to 10 kilometers (5 to 6 miles).

But this is not all we breathe. As hay fever sufferers know, other substances are mixed in the air. Besides the troublesome pollens are dust, smoke, salt particles, water vapor, chemicals, spores, bacteria, and viruses.

The Reality of Air

Because pure air has no taste, color, or odor, its study for children, especially primary students, has an elusive quality not present in many other areas. So, it is usually good to begin with activities that bring out the tangibility of air. Like other material objects such as automobiles, houses, books, and people, air is a real thing. Children can feel it and see it move things in the form of wind. A blown-up balloon or a soap bubble shows that air takes up space. A slowly falling parachute demonstrates that air resists motion. A can that is crushed when some inside air is removed shows that air has weight. Sipping liquid through a straw shows this, too. Because many children are confused about how a straw works, consider it for a moment.

When we sip some air out of a straw, the air pressure in the straw is reduced. Because the atmosphere now has more relative pressure, it presses down on the liquid's surface and pushes it up inside the straw's space once occupied by the air.

If you are skeptical, try the following experiments. Place two straws in your mouth, but leave one outside a full soda bottle or water glass. You will find it now practically impossible to drink the liquid. Why? Air traveling inward through the outside straw restores the pressure in your mouth and drinking straw to normal. The pressure of the surrounding air is no longer greater than that in the straw and so cannot push down on the liquid and force it up into the straw; air in the straw is pushing back equally hard. For the second experiment, fill a flask with water and seal it tightly with a one-hole stopper containing a glass tube. No matter how hard you sip, no water goes up the tube. No air is pressing down on the water. With a two-hole stopper, though, normal drinking is possible. Air pressure is exerted through the second hole.

As with drinking straws, the events we associate with "suction" are really a result of removing or reducing air pressure from one part of a device. Air pressure on all other parts then pushes and performs the work. In vacuum cleaners, for example, the motor whirls a reversed fan that reduces air pressure at the cleaning nozzle. The surrounding air then pushes dirt particles into the nozzle. A suction cup works in a similar way. By pressing down on the pliable rubber cup, you force out most of the air that is inside. Air from all other sides pushes against the cup's exterior and holds it fast to whatever surface it has been pressed.

Origins of Our Atmosphere

Most scientists agree that the earth formed about 5 billion years ago. By about 4.4 billion years ago, the earth had an atmosphere that could hold a thin layer of gas known as the earth's primeval atmosphere. Outgassing, or the release of embedded gases from rocks through volcanic activity, allowed gases such as carbon dioxide, nitrogen, water vapor, and smaller amounts of ammonia, methane, and sulfur dioxide to accumulate in the atmosphere.

As the earth cooled for the next half billion years, the water vapor condensed into clouds. These clouds soon provided the first rains, streams, rivers, and seas, thus beginning the water cycle here on earth. The accumulation of water caused a reduction of carbon dioxide in the atmosphere as it dissolved into newly created ocean waters.

Almost 2 billion years ago, oxygen, produced through photosynthetic action in the oceans, began to significantly accumulate in the atmosphere, reaching its current level of almost 1% by volume. Carbon dioxide was reduced to less than 1% as we currently find in the layers of air that we call the troposphere and stratosphere—from the earth's surface to 80 kilometers (50 miles) above the earth.

WEATHER Inquiry

Heating Soil and Water

Invitation

How fast does soil heat and cool, compared to water?

Exploration

1. Fill one jar with soil and the other with water.
2. Leave the jars in a shady place for 1 hour.
3. Touch the soil and water surfaces to see if both are about the same temperature. If not, wait a while. If they are, then put both jars in the sun for 1 hour.
4. Touch both surfaces again.

Concept Invention

1. Which feels warmer, the soil or water surface?
2. Which will cool faster if you put both back in the shade?

Concept Application

How does this activity help you understand the unequal heating of the earth's surface as the cause of winds?

> **MATERIALS**
> - Two matched glass jars
> - Sunny and shady areas
> - Soil
> - Water

Evaporation

Invitation

Many persons hang their wet laundry on a clothesline. After a while, the laundry is dry. What do you think happens to the water? When water disappears into the air, we say it evaporated. You can find out more about evaporation by drying wet paper towels. How can you get a paper towel to dry? How long will it take?

Exploration

1. Put a paper towel underwater to soak it.
2. Bunch the wet towel in your fist. Squeeze out all the water you can.
3. Open the towel and lay it on a pie plate, as illustrated.

> **MATERIALS**
> - Plastic bowl of water
> - Piece of cardboard
> - Paper towels
> - Two aluminum pie plates
> - Sunny and shady areas
> - Paper clips

Teaching Tips

This inquiry gives children several chances to manipulate conditions that affect the evaporation rate of water. The Concept Invention activities encourage them to manipulate these conditions creatively. Step 3 calls for fanning one wet towel with cardboard to simulate a windy condition. Clipping the towel to the pie plate with several paper clips will keep it from blowing off the plate.

4. Leave the plate on your desk. Check the time.
5. Every so often, feel the towel to see if it is dry. Check the time again when it is all dry.

Concept Invention

1. Suppose you put one wet towel where it is shady and cool, and another where it is sunny and warmer. Which wet towel do you think will dry first?
2. What can you do to show that a dried-out towel is completely "dry"? How many of your classmates agree with you?
3. Suppose, to make it windy, you fan one wet towel with cardboard. You do not fan a second wet towel. Which towel do you think will dry first?
4. Suppose you spread out one wet towel and leave another bunched like a ball. Which towel do you think will dry first?
5. Suppose you leave one wet towel on top of a plate. You leave a second wet towel under another plate. Which towel do you think will dry first?
6. Play a game with a friend. Who can dry a wet paper towel faster? How can you make the game fair?
7. What is the longest you can keep a wet paper towel from drying?

Concept Application

Wind, heat, and an uncovered and spread-out condition all help a wet paper towel dry faster. Could you find a way to predict the drying times in each of the activities? Could you calculate the drying rate of a wet towel or sponge by using a beam balance? Will half of a wet towel have half the evaporation rate of a whole towel? Try to answer these questions by designing appropriate experiments.

Relative Humidity

Invitation

Can you remember times when the air has felt very dry or very humid? The amount of moisture, or water vapor, in the air often changes. Warm air can hold more moisture without raining than cold air. The percent of moisture now in the air compared with the percent it can hold at the current temperature is the *relative humidity*. You can make an instrument to measure the relative humidity. It is called a *hygrometer*. How can you make a hygrometer?

Exploration

1. Fasten two thermometers to the sides of an empty milk carton. Use rubber bands to hold them in place.
2. Use a pencil to punch a hole in the carton under one thermometer.
3. Put about 2.5 centimeters (1 inch) of water into the carton. Close the top with a paper clip. This will keep the water from evaporating quickly.
4. Wet a strip of cotton cloth with water.
5. Stick one end of the strip through the punched hole into the water inside. Fasten the other end to the bulb of the thermometer above, as shown.

MATERIALS

- Two matched Fahrenheit thermometers
- Cardboard
- Narrow cotton cloth strip or thick cotton shoelace
- Two rubber bands
- Empty quart milk carton with top still on
- Paper clip
- Pencil
- Water
- Ruler
- Clock
- Shady area

— Water inside

6. To use your hygrometer, fan the thermometers with a piece of cardboard for 3 minutes in a shady place. Read the temperatures of each thermometer.

7. Use the relative humidity table to find the percent of moisture in the air. At the left, mark the wet bulb temperature lightly with pencil. At the top, lightly mark the dry bulb temperature. Move one finger across the row and another down the column from the marked spots. Notice the percent of relative humidity where your two fingers meet.

 Teaching Tips When no difference appears between the wet and dry bulb temperatures, the relative humidity is 100%. This condition is unlikely to be recorded outdoors unless there is dense fog or rain. Children may notice a marked difference between indoor and outdoor readings. This is most likely in winter. As the room is heated, the air in it is able to hold more moisture, so the relative humidity goes down.

Dry bulb temperature (°F)

Wet bulb temperature (°F)	56	58	60	62	64	66	68	70	71	72	73	74	75	76	77	78	79	80	82	84
38	7	2																		
40	15	11	7																	
42	25	19	14	9	7															
44	34	29	22	17	13	8	4													
46	45	38	30	24	18	14	10	6	4	3	1									
48	55	47	40	33	26	21	16	12	10	9	7	5	4	3	1					
50	66	56	48	41	34	29	23	19	17	15	13	11	9	8	6	5	4	3		
52	77	67	57	50	43	36	31	25	23	21	19	17	15	13	12	10	9	7	5	3
54	88	78	68	59	51	44	38	33	30	28	25	23	21	19	17	16	14	12	10	7
56		89	79	68	60	53	46	40	37	34	32	29	27	25	23	21	19	18	14	12
58			89	79	70	61	54	48	45	42	39	36	34	31	29	27	25	23	20	16
60				90	79	71	62	55	52	49	46	43	40	38	35	33	31	29	25	21
62					90	80	71	64	60	57	53	50	47	44	42	39	37	35	30	26
64						90	80	72	68	65	61	58	54	51	48	46	43	41	36	32
66							90	81	77	73	69	65	62	59	56	53	50	47	42	37
68								90	86	82	78	74	70	66	63	60	57	54	48	43
70									95	91	86	82	78	74	71	67	64	61	55	49
72											95	91	86	82	79	75	71	68	61	56
74													96	91	87	83	79	75	69	62
76															96	91	87	83	76	69
78																	96	91	84	76
80																			92	84
82																				92

Percent of relative humidity

Concept Invention

1. What is the relative humidity now?
2. How, if at all, might relative humidity change from day to day? How, if at all, does it change?
3. How well can you use your senses to tell if the air is drier or moister from day to day? Use your hygrometer to check how well you do.
4. How does the relative humidity outdoors compare with that indoors?
5. What would you expect the relative humidity to be outdoors on a rainy day? Measure it in some partly sheltered place and see.

Scaffolding for English Learners

Having a teacher-learner alongside of English learners will assist in student development of a difficult concept such as relative humidity. Following this procedure helps maintain the balance between teacher direction and student initiative during the activity. (See Fradd, Lee, Sutman, & Saxton, 2001, for a discussion of teachers and students learning together and the effect of this approach on English language learners.)

Concept Application

A hygrometer can be used to measure the relative humidity. This is the percent of moisture that air holds, compared with the percent it can hold at a given temperature. How do your relative humidity measurements compare with those of the local weather bureau? Develop a chart and compare readings for a 2-week period.

Water Vapor

MATERIALS

- Clean, shiny can
- Water
- Thermometer
- Ice cubes

Invitation

How can you collect and see water vapor in the air?

Exploration

1. Half-fill the can with water. Add five or six ice cubes.
2. Put a thermometer inside the can of ice and water.
3. Watch for tiny drops on the can's sides. When they first appear, record the water temperature. (This is called the *dew point*. It tells the temperature at which water vapor changes from a gas to a liquid and forms drops, or *condenses*, on objects.)

Concept Invention

1. At what temperature was the dew point?
2. Will the dew-point temperature be different in a smaller or larger container?
3. Can an ice-water mixture get colder than the dew point?

Concept Application

How, if at all, will the dew-point temperature change from day to day? Explain your answer.

Air Pressure Changes ———

Invitation

How can you measure changes in air pressure?

Exploration

1. Make a barometer. Cut out a large part of a balloon. Stretch it tightly over the jar opening. Use a rubber band to hold it fast.
2. Pinch one straw end flat. Cut a point with scissors at this end.
3. Glue the straw's other end to the center of the stretched balloon.
4. Use two thumbtacks to fasten a file card to a wall. Place the barometer by it. Have the straw pointer centered on the card and almost touching.
5. Make a mark on the card where the straw points each day for 1 week.

MATERIALS

- Glass jar
- Balloon
- Rubber band
- Scissors
- Straw
- File card
- Glue
- Two thumbtacks

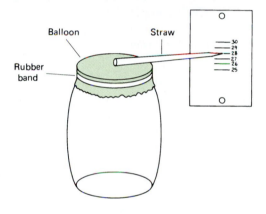

Concept Invention

1. On what day was the air pressure the highest? On what day was the air pressure the lowest?
2. When, if at all, was there no change in air pressure?

Adapting for Students with Exceptionalities

Comprehending air pressure and other weather concepts will be especially difficult for students with exceptionalities. Expand on students' prior knowledge to assist with concept development. (See Mastropieri & Scruggs, 2004, chapter on science and social studies for a discussion on activities related to weather.)

Concept Application

Do you notice any weather changes associated with your barometric pressure readings? Chart the current weather and readings for a 1-month period. Note any associations between the pressure and weather.

Teaching Tips

As air pressure outside the jar increases, it pushes down harder on the balloon diaphragm; this makes the straw pointer go up. As air pressure outside the jar decreases, the higher air pressure inside the jar pushes up on the diaphragm; this makes the straw pointer go down. The movement can be increased a bit by gluing a piece of matchstick under the straw at the jar rim. You might challenge students to calibrate their barometers. They can note the daily barometric pressure in the newspaper or call the weather bureau. After a week or so of recording the official pressure next to their own recordings, they may be able to predict roughly the official pressure from their own barometers. Place this kind of barometer where it will have the least change of temperature. Otherwise, the air in the jar may expand and contract so much that the effects of changing air pressure will be obscured.

WEATHER CONCEPTS

Weather is the condition of the lower atmosphere at a given time and place. If you have been rained on while expecting a sunny afternoon, you know how quickly weather can change. Weather changes happen because changes in temperature, moisture, pressure, and other variables alter the way air "behaves." We examine some of these variables in this section.

Causes of Winds

At early morning off an African coast, hundreds of fishing boats point out to sea as a fresh land breeze fills their colorful lateen sails. The boats return in the afternoon with sails taut from a sea breeze blowing in the opposite direction. You have probably experienced a similar shift of winds at the seashore or by a large lake. How does this happen? (See INQ Figure 11–2.)

Temperature Differences

You may recall from Inquiry Unit 2 on heat energy that warmed air expands and is pushed up by denser, colder air that rushes in and replaces it. The unequal heating and cooling of the earth's surface cause winds. During the day, solar radiation is absorbed by the sea and the land. The land heats up much faster. One reason is that sunlight penetrates only a short distance below the land's surface, but penetrates more deeply into water. Another reason is that water has a higher heat capacity.

After a short period of sunlight, air immediately above the earth is heated by the ground and begins expanding. Cooler, heavier air from the sea rushes in and pushes the lighter air upward. The reverse occurs at night and until the following morning. During this period, the land cools quickly and stays cool while the sea remains relatively warmer. As air warmed by contact with the water expands, it is pushed upward by cooler air rushing in from the cooler land.

INQ Figure 11–2   Winds are caused by the unequal heating and cooling of the earth's surface.

Day   Night

These air movements are not confined to land and sea settings. The same basic air movements take place between any surfaces that have a temperature difference. As temperature differences increase, the resulting wind force increases. This is one reason why a large fire is so destructive; it creates a powerful, localized wind that fans and spreads the flames.

Prevailing Winds

The world's prevailing winds are caused by the same unequal heating of the earth's surface on a grand scale. But the earth's rotation adds a factor. If the earth did not rotate, heavy, cold air at the poles would simply flow due south and north, and push up warmed, expanding equatorial air. The rotation results in a wind deflection (named the *Coriolis effect*) to the right in the Northern Hemisphere and to the left in the Southern Hemisphere. With a globe and some chalk, you can see why this happens. Rotate the globe from west to east. While it is moving, draw a line from the North Pole due south toward the equator. Notice that the line curves to the right. Draw a line from the South Pole, and the curve is reversed.

Winds Aloft

Detailed understanding of wind patterns requires much more background than can be given here. For example, we have briefly discussed jet streams. Other winds, however, are also aloft. It is possible for an airplane pilot to meet a wind blowing from one direction at one altitude and another blowing from another direction higher up. You will not want to explore this subject in detail at the elementary level. Still, it will be worthwhile to help children learn that wind direction aloft may differ from surface wind direction.

To calculate winds aloft, meteorologists use measuring instruments to observe small, helium-filled balloons as they rise to various altitudes. A cruder method is to observe cloud movements with a *nephoscope*, a circular mirror marked with the points of a compass. Properly aligned, this instrument can show children the direction of cloud movement as the cloud reflection moves across the mirror.

Air Temperature —————

In parts of southern California and in Mexico, it is sometimes possible in winter to observe snowy mountain peaks while lying on a warm, sunny beach. Children are curious about conditions like this (e.g., "Aren't the mountain peaks closer to the sun?"). Most adults know that air is colder at higher altitudes. But why does this occur?

Temperature and Altitude

One reason why air is colder at higher altitudes is the varying distance of air molecules from the earth's surface. Air molecules closest to the earth are warmed more easily by conduction and heat waves radiated from the earth's surface than those farther away.

Second, as we get closer to sea level, more and more molecules are piled up. This increased weight compresses the air. With reduced space for movement, more energy is exchanged among molecules as they collide. So, the heat energy in the denser molecule "population" is concentrated into a relatively low, dense layer.

Third, as warmed air is pushed up, it expands and cools when it meets lower air pressure with the increased altitude. Whatever heat energy is contained in the original air parcel is dissipated throughout an ever-larger volume.

The combined effect of these causes makes pushed-up air cool about 2°C for each 300 meters (3.5°F for each 1000 feet). As pushed-down air is compressed, the opposite happens.

Temperature and Pollution

The atmosphere is a gigantic greenhouse that slows the loss of heat received from solar radiation. Fortunately, the earth loses and gains about the same amount of heat each day. A narrow temperature range enables life as we know it to continue. Since the Industrial Revolution, though, conditions have been developing that may upset this delicate balance.

Most scientists think the lower atmosphere is gradually becoming slightly warmer because of increased levels of carbon dioxide from the burning of fuels such as coal and oil. As light waves from the sun warm the earth's surface, heat waves going from the surface into the atmosphere are partly blocked by carbon dioxide. Some of the heat energy cannot escape into space. This causes the atmosphere to lose slightly less heat than it gains from solar radiation. Recent data seem to support a global warming trend.

Yet, a few scientists say it is also possible that the trend may be reversing. To them, data suggest that the earth's atmosphere is cooling very gradually. In recent years, there has been a large increase in air pollution throughout the world. The greater number of suspended pollutants in the air may be causing more and more sunlight to be reflected away from the earth before it reaches the earth's surface. If true, this could overcome the effect of the increased carbon dioxide.

Although not everyone agrees about what is happening to the air temperature, a definite trend in either direction could bring trouble. An average increase of a few degrees could turn huge, fertile land areas into semideserts, and an average temperature drop of 4° to 5°C could launch another Ice Age.

Evaporation and Humidity ─────────────

Many children understand in a limited way the concepts of evaporation and humidity but may not understand how the two are related. This section can help deal with these concepts.

Evaporation

In an earlier inquiry, you saw that heat and atmospheric pressure affect an evaporating liquid. Increased heat energy increases the speed of molecules. Additional speed enables molecules to overcome the cohesive forces of nearby molecules, and greater numbers leave the liquid's surface than before. Any decrease of atmospheric pressure also affects evaporation because it tends to "take the lid off." The counterforce of air molecules pressing down on the surface of an evaporating liquid becomes weaker, and more evaporation takes place. This is a reason why mountain climbers must be so careful with dehydration.

It is easy to see why increasing a liquid's surface area increases the rate of evaporation. There is greater exposure to the air above and a higher probability of more molecules escaping. This is why you have to add water more often to an open rectangular aquarium than to an open fish bowl of equal volume.

The wind, too, speeds up evaporation. When air just above the surface of an evaporating fluid becomes saturated, the wind blows it away and replaces it with drier air.

Humidity

Another factor influencing evaporation is *humidity*, which is the amount of moisture already present in the air. On humid days, we feel sticky and uncomfortable because our perspiration evaporates very slowly. We may use a fan to feel more comfortable. Moving air from a fan cools us because it speeds up evaporation of perspiration from the skin.

Without an evaporating liquid, a fan has no cooling effect at all. You can see this by putting a thermometer in front of a whirling electric fan. There is no difference in the before and after readings. But dampen some cotton and stick it to the thermometer bulb, and the rapidly evaporating water will cause a noticeable drop in temperature.

The moisture content of air changes considerably from time to time. The capacity of air to hold moisture depends on its temperature, so warm air holds more moisture than cooler air. The percentage of moisture in air at a certain temperature, compared with all it could hold at that temperature, is called its *relative humidity*. During a period of low relative humidity, our skin moisture evaporates more quickly than it can be effectively replaced. This results in dry, chapped skin.

One reason why we have more colds in winter may be directly related to the relative humidity of the air in our homes. The cool air of winter holds comparatively little moisture. As heaters warm it, the air expands and becomes even drier. Unless the home heating system is equipped to give additional moisture, the air becomes increasingly dry. The protective mucous film that coats the delicate nasal membrane evaporates, and we become more open to infections that begin in the nasal cavities.

Relative humidity is often measured with a wet-and-dry bulb thermometer apparatus called a *hygrometer*. Two identical thermometers are placed next to each other. The bulb of one instrument is enclosed in a wet cotton wick that is immersed in water. The wet-bulb thermometer is fanned rapidly until its reading steadies at some lower point. As water evaporates from the wick, it is continually replaced by water traveling upward through the wick by capillary action. Any difference in thermometer readings can be translated into the percentage of relative humidity by consulting a reference table.

Condensation

Dew

Many mornings, we see dewdrops glistening on lawns, parked automobiles, spider webs, and other surfaces. When the ground cools during the night, its temperature may fall below that of the surrounding air. As the surrounding air loses heat energy, the air's molecules slow down. Water molecules in the air slow enough to be attracted to, and condense on, cool nearby surfaces. The same thing happens when water droplets form on a cold soda bottle or cold water pipe.

Remember, relative humidity varies with air temperature. Any parcel of air containing some water vapor becomes saturated if cooled enough. The loss of heat energy slows molecular speed and reduces the range of molecular movement. The attractions of water molecules for one another now draw them together into visible drops.

Dew Point

The temperature at which condensation takes place is called the *dew point*. In very humid air, as in a steamy shower room, water vapor condenses on walls and mirrors although they may be only several degrees cooler than the air. Comparatively dry desert air may have to be cooled much more before reaching its dew point.

Fog

We may see fog when the surface temperature is low enough to cool air that is a short distance above the ground to its dew point. In this case, water vapor condenses on tiny specks of airborne dust and this water remains suspended.

Sometimes fog results from the unequal cooling of land and water. Such fog is common over a lake in summer. Cool air from the land flows over warm, moist air just above the lake. As the warmer air cools to its dew point, condensation occurs and we see fog. Fog can be considered a low cloud.

Clouds and Cloud Types

Clouds at higher altitudes are formed in several ways, but all involve a parcel of air that is cooled to its saturation, or dew, point. In one method, wind may blow moist air up a mountain slope. As the air rises, it expands because of decreasing air pressure, cools, and condenses on airborne dust particles. If the dew point is below freezing, tiny ice crystals may form.

Sometimes air is pushed aloft when two huge air masses merge. The cooler, heavier air mass will push under the warmer, lighter mass. Again, expansion, cooling, and condensation take place.

A third method of cloud formation happens when heat from the ground develops convection currents. The affected air near the ground is heated and is pushed up by heavier, cooler surrounding air. The rising air finally cools and its moisture condenses.

When enough moisture is present, the tiny, constantly moving droplets within a cloud collide from time to time and combine to form larger drops. These large drops may fall as rain. In freezing temperatures, ice crystals collect and fall as snow.

Knowing the air temperature and its dew point can enable you or upper-grade students to roughly calculate cloud heights in the following manner. Suppose the outdoor air temperature is now 88°F. Stir a thermometer around in a metal can of ice and water. At the exact instant water droplets occur on the can, read the temperature of the immersed thermometer. This is the dew point. Say it reads 74°F, which makes a difference of 14°F between the two figures. Rising air cools at about 3.5°F for each 1000 feet of altitude. Fourteen (14) divided by 3.5 results in a quotient of 4. Multiply this figure by 1000. The bases of nearby clouds should be about 4000 feet above you. (With metric measures, use 2°C for 3.5°F and 300 meters for 1000 feet.)

Although experts have invented more than 200 cloud classifications, young children can be taught to recognize three basic cloud forms. *Cirrus clouds* are high, wispy formations of ice crystals. *Cumulus clouds* are white, fluffy, and usually associated with clear visibility and fair weather. *Stratus clouds* are lower, darker formations that appear as a dense layer. These clouds may blanket the entire sky and precipitate rain within a short time (see INQ Figure 11–3).

Water Cycle

You can see that condensation is the opposite of evaporation. Together, they form the water cycle. Powered by the sun, an immense but finite volume of water over the earth constantly evaporates, condenses, and falls without apparent end.

Air Masses and Cyclones ———

At one time, it was thought that air pressure over any one certain point was always the same. We now know otherwise. Huge masses of air continually move over the earth, bringing changes in pressure and weather.

Air Masses

An *air mass* is a huge volume of air that picks up distinctive temperature and humidity conditions from the surface underneath. These conditions are fairly uniform throughout the mass, which may cover thousands of square kilometers.

INQ Figure 11–3   **Three basic cloud forms: (A) cirrus, (B) cumulus, and (C) stratus.**

A

B

C

An ocean air mass is typically moist. Air over land is drier. Air near the polar regions is cold, whereas that near the equator is warm. So, four kinds of air masses are possible: cold and dry, cold and moist, warm and dry, and warm and moist. INQ Figure 11–4 shows the origins of four kinds of air masses that often move into the continental United States.

Cold air is heavier than the same volume of warm air. Dry air is heavier than the same volume of moist air. Just as water flows from a high point to a lower one, air flows from a region of relatively high pressure to one of lower pressure. But because of the earth's rotation, the flow is not in a straight line.

Cyclones and Anticyclones

The Coriolis effect causes air masses and the general circulation of air to move in gigantic spirals called cyclones and anticyclones. (Cyclones should not be confused with *tornadoes*, which are small, violent, twisting air currents that come from a mixture of superheated and cold air.) A *cyclone* is a large area of relative lower pressure with the point of lowest pressure in the center; it is also called a low. An *anticyclone* is a large area of relatively high pressure with the highest pressure in the center; it is also called a high.

In the Northern Hemisphere, air movements spiral counterclockwise toward the center of a low. In a high, they spiral clockwise, away from the center of highest pressure. These movements are reversed in the Southern Hemisphere. Highs and lows may move hundreds of kilometers a day. A typical pattern of movement in the United States is from west to east. Lows often bring bad weather. This is so because cold or dry heavier air moves in and

INQ Figure 11–4   **Four common kinds of air masses.**

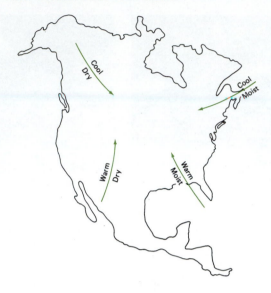

pushes up warm or moist lighter air. The moisture condenses when the air rises to its dew-point altitude and falls as rain or snow.

Highs usually bring more pleasant weather. As cool or dry heavier air spirals downward from the center of a high, it warms about 2°C for each 300 meters (3.5°F for each 1000 feet) loss of altitude. As it warms, the mass of air is able to hold more and more moisture without it condensing. The result is usually clear, sunny weather.

Measuring Pressure

Highs and lows are detected by noting changes in cloud, temperature, and wind patterns. The most important changes observed, however, are those in air pressure. An instrument used for measuring air pressure is the *barometer*. There are two kinds.

In a *mercurial barometer*, a glass tube about 90 centimeters (36 inches) long and closed at one end is filled with mercury and inverted into a dish of mercury. While some of the liquid runs out, a column of about 76 centimeters (30 inches) remains. This height tells the force of air pressing on the liquid's surface. As air pressure increases, the column rises higher into the vacuum above. The reverse takes place with reduced pressure. Because mercurial barometers are easily broken and cumbersome, most weather observers use an *aneroid barometer* (INQ Figure 11–5). It consists of a thin, flexible, metal box from which almost all air has been removed. As air presses on it with varying degrees of force, the box moves in and out accordingly. A cleverly linked leverage system transfers these movements to a movable needle on a dial.

Because air pressure also changes with altitude, aneroid barometers are used in many airplanes to indicate altitude. This is done by merely changing the dial to read in a unit of height rather than one of pressure. Such a barometer is called an *altimeter*.

INQ Figure 11–5   **Aneroid barometer.**

References

American Association for the Advancement of Science (AAAS). (1993). *Benchmarks for science literacy*. New York: Oxford University Press.

Baca, L. M., Baca, E., & deValenzuela, J. S. (2004). Background and rationale for bilingual special education. In L. M. Baca & H. T. Cervantes (Eds.), *The bilingual special education interface* (pp. 1–23). Upper Saddle River, NJ: Merrill/Prentice Hall.

Fradd, S. H., Lee, O., Sutman, F. X., & Saxton, M. K. (2001). Promoting science literacy with English language learners through instructional materials development: A case study. *Bilingual Research Journal, 25*(4), 417–434. Retrieved November 13, 2004, from *http://brj.asu.edu/content/vol25_no4/pdf/ar5.pdf*

Mastropieri, M., & Scruggs, T. E. (2004). *The inclusive classroom: Strategies for effective instruction* (4th ed.). Upper Saddle River, NJ: Merrill/Prentice Hall.

National Research Council (NRC). (1996). *National science education standards*. Washington, DC: National Academy Press.

Selected Trade Books: Water, Air, and Weather

For Younger Children

Aardema, V. (1981). *Bringing the rain to Kapiti Plain*. New York: Puffin Books.

Ardley, N. (1983). *Working with water*. Danbury, CT: Watts.

Bang, M. (1997). *Common ground: The water, earth, and air we share*. New York: Scholastic.

Barrett, J. (1982). *Cloudy with a chance of meatballs*. New York: Aladdin Paperbacks.

Berger, M., & Berger, G. (1993). *How's the weather? A look at weather and how it changes*. Nashville, TN: Ideals Children's Books.

Branley, F. (1986). *Sunshine makes the seasons*. New York: HarperTrophy.

Branley, F. (1987). *Air is all around you*. New York: HarperTrophy.

Branley, F. (1999). *Flash, crash, rumble, and roll*. New York: HarperCollins.

Carle, E. (1996). *Little cloud*. New York: Philomel.

Cole, J. (1986). *The magic school bus at the waterworks*. New York: Scholastic.

Cole, J. (1996). *The magic school bus wet all over: A book about the water cycle*. New York: Scholastic.

Cole, J. (2000). *The magic school bus kicks up a storm: A book about weather*. New York: Scholastic.

DeWitt, L. (1993). *What will the weather be?* New York: HarperTrophy.

Dorros, A. (1990). *Feel the wind*. New York: HarperTrophy.

Gibbons, G. (1987). *Weather forecasting*. New York: Macmillan.

Greene, C. (1991). *Caring for our air*. Springfield, NJ: Enslow.

Greene, C. (1991). *Caring for our water*. Springfield, NJ: Enslow.

Kalan, R. (1991). *Rain*. New York: Morrow.

Kirkpatrick, R. K. (1985). *Look at weather*. Austin, TX: Raintree.

Leutscher, A. (1983). *Water*. New York: Dutton.

Llewellyn, C. (1991). *First look in the air*. Milwaukee, WI: Gareth Stevens.

Lloyd, D. (1983). *Air*. New York: Dial Books.

Locker, T. (1997). *Water dance*. Orlando, FL: Harcourt Brace.

Locker, T. (2003). *Cloud dance*. San Diego, CA: Voyager.

Maki, C. (1993). *Snowflakes, sugar, and salt*. Minneapolis: Lerner.

Markle, S. (1993). *A rainy day*. New York: Orchard Books.

Martin, C. (1987). *I can be a weather forecaster*. Danbury, CT: Childrens Press.

Miller, D. (2003). *Arctic lights, arctic nights*. New York: Walker and Company.

Morrison, G. (2002). *Pond*. New York: Houghton/Mifflin, Walter Lorraine Books.

Otto, C. (1992). *That sky, that rain*. New York: Harper.

Palazzo, J. (1982). *What makes the weather?* New York: Troll Associates.

Pluckrose, H. (1987). *Think about floating and sinking*. Danbury, CT: Watts.

Schnur, S. (2000). *Spring thaw*. New York: Viking Books.

Seixas, J. S. (1987). *Water—what it is, what it does*. New York: Greenwillow Books.

Smeltzer, P., & Smeltzer, V. (1983). *Thank you for a drink of water*. Palm Beach, FL: Winston.

Swallow, S. (1991). *Air*. Danbury, CT: Watts.

Taylor, K. (1992). *Flying start science series: Water; light; action; structure*. New York: John Wiley.

Webb, A. (1987). *Water*. Danbury, CT: Watts.

Webster, V. (1982). *Weather experiments*. Danbury, CT: Childrens Press.

Wilder, L. (1995). *Winter days in the big woods*. New York: HarperCollins.

For Older Children

Arnov, B. (1980). *Water: Experiments to understand it*. New York: Lothrop, Lee & Shepard Books.

Branley, F. M. (1982). *Water for the world*. New York: Harper & Row.

Bright, M. (1991). *Polluting the oceans*. Danbury, CT: Watts.

Cosner, S. (1982). *Be your own weather forecaster*. Parsippany, NJ: Julian Messner.

De Bruin, J. (1983). *Young scientists explore the weather*. Torrance, CA: Good Apple.

Dickinson, J. (1983). *Wonders of water*. New York: Troll Associates.

Elson, D. (1997). *Weather explained*. New York: Henry Holt.

Flint, D. (1991). *Weather and climate*. Danbury, CT: Watts.

Ford, A. (1982). *Weather watch*. New York: Lothrop, Lee & Shepard Books.

Frevert, P. (1981). *Why does the weather change?* Chicago: Creative Education.

Gallant, R. A. (1987). *Rainbows, mirages, and sundogs*. New York: Macmillan.

Jeffries, L. (1983). *Air, air, air*. New York: Troll Associates.

Kiefer, I. (1981). *Poisoned land: The problem of hazardous waste*. New York: Atheneum.

McKinney, B. (1998). *A drop around the world*. Nevada City, CA: Dawn.

Mebane, R., & Rybolt, T. (1995). *Water & other liquids*. New York: Twenty-First Century Books.

Miller, C., & Berry, L. (1987). *Acid rain*. Parsippany, NJ: Julian Messner.

Murata, M. (1993). *Science is all around you: Water and light*. Minneapolis: Lerner.

Pollard, M. (1987). *Air, water, and weather*. New York: Facts on File.

Pratt, K. (1994). *A swim through the sea*. Nevada City, CA: Dawn.

Pratt-Serfini, K. J. (2001). *Salamander rain: A lake and pond journal*. Nevada City, CA: Dawn.

Riley, P. D. (1986). *Air and gases*. New York: David & Charles.

Seabrooke, S. (2004). *The world almanac for kids 2005*. New York: World Almanac.

Seymour, P. (1985). *How the weather works*. New York: Macmillan.

Smith, H. (1983). *Amazing air*. New York: Lothrop, Lee & Shepard Books.

Snodgrass, M. E. (1991). *Environmental awareness: Water pollution*. Marco, FL: Bancroft Sage.

Sorensen, V. (1956). *Miracles on maple hill*. Orlando, FL: Harcourt Brace.

Steele, P. (1991). *Wind: Causes and effects*. Danbury, CT: Watts.

Walpole, B. (1987). *Water*. Danbury, CT: Watts.

Ward, A. (1986). *Experimenting with surface tension and bubbles*. New York: David & Charles.

Wick, W. (1997). *A drop of water*. New York: Scholastic.

Wu, N. (1991). *Planet earth: Life in the oceans*. Boston: Little, Brown.

Resource Books

Agler, L. (1986). *Liquid explorations*. Berkeley, CA: Great Explorations in Math and Science.

Barber, J. (1986). *Bubble·ology*. Berkeley, CA: Great Explorations in Math and Science.

Barber, J., & Willard, C. (1994). *Bubble festival*. Berkeley, CA: Great Explorations in Math and Science.

Benjamin, R. F., Wilson, J., & Youngs, D. (2001). *Spills and ripples*. Fresno, CA: AIMS Education Foundation. (water activities)

Butzow, C. M., & Butzow, J. W. (1989). *Science through children's literature: An integrated approach*. Englewood, CO: Teacher Ideas Press. (water topics on pp. 150–157; weather topics on pp. 200–205)

Butzow, C. M., & Butzow, J. W. (1994). *Intermediate science through children's literature: Over land and sea*. Englewood, CO: Teacher Ideas Press. (weather topics on pp. 24–36; ocean and lake topics on pp. 131–169)

Deery, R. (1985). *Tornadoes and hurricanes*. Torrance, CA: Good Apple.

Fredericks, A. D., Meinbach, A. M., & Rothlein, L. (1993). *Thematic units: An integrated approach to teaching science and social studies*. New York: HarperCollins. (weather topics on pp. 153–160)

Graube, I. (1990). *Seasons thematic unit*. Huntington Beach, CA: Teacher Created Materials.

Halverson, C., Beals, K., & Strang, C. (2001). *Ocean currents*. Berkeley, CA: Great Explorations in Math and Science. (ocean, water, and wind activities)

LeCroy, B., & Holder, B. (1994). *Bookwebs: A brainstorm of ideas for the primary classroom*. Englewood, CO: Teacher Ideas Press. (air activities on pp. 97–98)

Lyons, W. (1997). *The handy weather answer book*. Detroit, MI: Visible Ink Press.

Malnor, B., & Malnor, C. (1998). *A teacher's guide to a drop around the world*. Nevada City, CA: Dawn.

Malnor, B., & Malnor, C. (1998). *A teacher's guide to a swim through the sea*. Nevada City, CA: Dawn.

Shaw, D. G., & Dybdahl, C. S. (1996). *Integrating science and language arts: A sourcebook for K–6 teachers*. Boston: Allyn & Bacon. (water cycle topic on pp. 73–78)

Watercourse & Council for Environmental Education. (1995). *Project WET*. Bozeman, MT: Author.

Western Regional Environmental Education Council. (1992). *Aquatic Project WILD*. Boulder, CO: Author.

Wiebe, A. (1990). *Soap film and bubbles*. Fresno, CA: AIMS Education Foundation.

Wiebe, A. (2002). *Weather sense: Moisture*. Fresno, CA: AIMS Education Foundation. (weather activities)

Wiebe, A. (2002). *Weather sense: Temperature, air pressure, and wind*. Fresno, CA: AIMS Education Foundation. (weather activities)

Williams, J. (1992). *USA Today: The weather book*. New York: Vintage Books.

THE EARTH IN SPACE

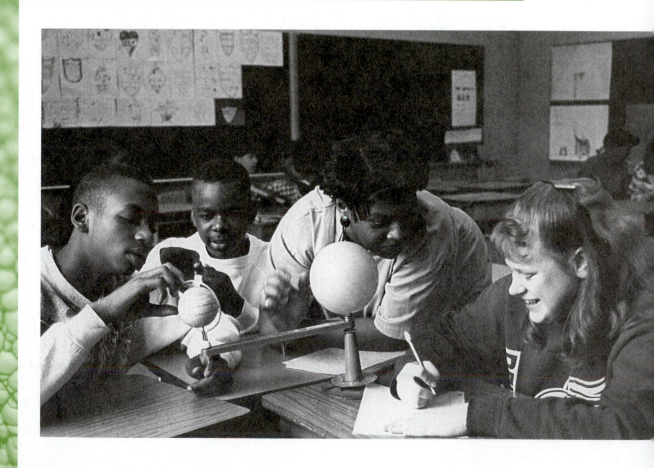

"The sky's the limit." "What goes up must come down." Even young children today smile at these clichés. Television, magazines, and space missions have given children a beyond-the-earth outlook unknown to most previous generations.

Outside school, however, few children learn the basic ideas and physical laws that give meaning to the motions of objects in space. We concentrate on several of these ideas and laws in this section as we examine how the earth's motions in space cause time and seasonal changes; how the relative motions of sun, earth, and moon bring about moon phases, eclipses, and tides; how size and distance are measured in the solar system and beyond; and how gravity and the laws of motion affect the movements of planets, satellites, and rockets.

Benchmarks and Standards

A child who observes the sun, moon, stars, and planets will begin to find patterns in their behavior. Seasons, tides, phases of the moon, and day and night are all relevant topics as indicated in the sample standards and benchmarks.

Sample Benchmarks (AAAS, 1993)

- Like all planets, the earth is approximately spherical in shape. The rotation of the earth on its axis every 24 hours produces the night-and-day cycle. (By Grades 3–5, p. 68)
- We live on a relatively small planet, the third from the sun. (By Grades 6–8, p. 68)

Sample Standards (NRC, 1996)

- Objects in the sky have patterns of movement. The sun, for example, appears to move across the sky in the same way every day, but its path changes slowly over the seasons. (By Grades K–4, p. 134)
- Most objects in the solar system are in regular and predictable motion. Those motions explain such phenomena as the day, the year, phases of the moon, and eclipses. (By Grades 5–8, p. 160)

TIME AND THE SEASONS Inquiry

The Way the Earth Rotates

MATERIALS

- Globe
- Sunny area
- Small nail with large head
- Hammer
- Sticky tape
- Stick (1 meter, or 1 yard, long)
- Directional compass
- Pebble
- Clock

Invitation

Each day, the sun seems to follow a pattern in the sky. It seems to rise in one direction, move across the sky, and then set in the opposite direction. But the sun is relatively still. We know that it only seems to move because the earth rotates. In which direction does the earth rotate? You can find out for yourself by using a globe and then the earth itself.

Exploration

1. Get a small nail. Push the nail point through the sticky side of a small piece of tape. Fasten the nail head down to the place on the globe where you live.
2. Take the globe, hammer, and stick outdoors to a sunny area. Pound the stick upright into the ground.
3. Notice the shadow made by the stick. Position the globe so that the nail is upright and makes a shadow exactly in the same direction. (You may have to slip a book under the globe's base to keep the nail upright.)
4. Rotate the globe from west to east as shown.

Teaching Tips

Some children may need to be shown directions outdoors and on the globe. You might help them understand that north always runs from where they are to the North Pole and that south runs from there to the South Pole.

For the best shadow, the stick needs to be reasonably upright. A plumb bob made of string tied to a piece of chalk can help children align the stick if needed. You may substitute a tetherball pole for the stick. The nail, too, should be upright. If needed, a book or other object can be slipped under the globe base to make the nail vertical. If you can borrow some globes from other teachers, you might want to do this as a small-group activity.

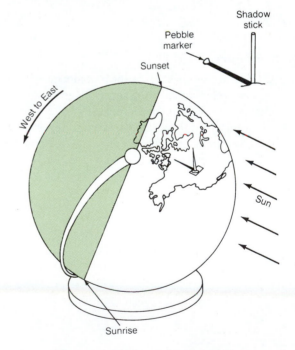

Concept Invention

1. What happens to the nail shadow if you rotate the globe a little from west to east? Make a record of the direction and length of the shadow.
2. What happens to the nail shadow if you rotate the globe a little from east to west? Make a record.

3. Put a pebble marker at the tip of your stick's shadow. Look at the shadow again 5 minutes later. In which direction did the shadow move?
4. In which direction does the earth rotate?

Concept Application

Daily shadows on the earth move from west to east. Shadow movement shows that the earth rotates the same way. Notice other shadows around you. How does their direction compare to the direction of the stick's shadow? Where will their shadows be in 1 hour? in 3 hours? Check your predictions and record what you find.

A Shadow Clock

Invitation

Before people had clocks, one way they told time was by watching shadows on sunny days. You can do that, too. But now you can use a clock to check how well you can keep time using shadows.

MATERIALS

• Large blank file card

• Pencil

• Nail

• Clock or watch

• Sunny area

Exploration

1. Lay the card in a sunny place. Put the nail, pointing up, in the center of the card. Trace a small circle around the nail head. If the nail falls over, be sure to replace it inside the circle.
2. Each hour you can, trace the nail shadow with a pencil and then check a clock. Record the hour by the tip of the pencil tracing as illustrated. It is all right to carry your shadow clock back and forth, but always put it back in the same way and place.
3. Plan to check your shadow clock on the next sunny day.

Teaching Tips
It is essential that children align their shadow clocks exactly the same way each time. Otherwise, their pencil recordings may not coincide with additional shadows. A chalk outline or piece of tape to align an edge can be a helpful reminder. Within a week, or sooner, children will detect a difference in the shadow alignments. This difference happens because the tilted earth continues to move around the sun. The same event is responsible for the changes of seasons.

Concept Invention

1. Check the shadow clock each hour, or when you can. Notice where the shadow is. How well can you keep time by the hour?
2. Can you tell the right time on the half hour? Can you tell when it is 15 minutes before the hour? Can you tell when it is 15 minutes after the hour?
3. Will your shadow clock keep the right time for a week or longer?
4. Do the nail shadows slowly change? If so, how do they change?

Concept Application

It is possible to keep track of the time in a general way with a shadow clock; however, it gets less accurate as time goes on. Compare a shadow clock and other types of clocks (such as analog, digital, or atomic clocks). What are some advantages and disadvantages of each?

Direct Sun ————

MATERIALS

- Cardboard
- Ruler
- Two matched thermometers
- Black paper
- Stapler
- Scissors
- Books

Invitation

How warm is slanted versus direct sunshine?

Exploration

1. Cut two same-sized pieces of cardboard.
2. Staple black paper to each piece. Staple a pocket for each thermometer as shown. Slip a thermometer into each pocket.

Sunlight

Teaching Tips

Your students may be unsure about how high they must prop up the direct sunlight thermometer. You might have them tape a nail head down to the cardboard. They then can tilt the cardboard until the nail no longer makes a shadow, indicating relatively vertical sunlight.

3. Lay one thermometer flat in the sun. It will get slanted sunshine. Prop up the other thermometer with some books so that the sun strikes it directly.
4. Look at each thermometer carefully. Be sure the temperature in neither thermometer rises so high that the thermometer breaks. After a few minutes, take out the thermometers and check the temperatures.

Concept Invention

1. Which thermometer has the higher temperature?
2. Which seems to give more heat-slanted or direct sunshine?

Adapting for Students with Exceptionalities

When experimentation involves measuring devices such as thermometers, it may be helpful to purchase large, specially made measuring instruments for adapting activities.

Concept Application

Check how far North America is from the sun during winter and summer. Also check the tilt of the earth's axis for North America during winter and summer. What does this say about direct and slanted sunlight?

Why the Earth Has Seasons

Invitation

Suppose you could see the earth from outer space as it circles the sun each year. This would help you understand why the earth has seasons. But you might have to wait a long time to do that. You can use a globe and light to find out now. How can a model earth (globe) and sun (lighted bulb) be used to show seasons?

Exploration

1. Get a tilted globe. The earth rotates on a make-believe pole. The pole's north end always points toward the North Star as the earth circles the sun. (That is why globes are tilted.)
2. Label one wall "north." (You will need to keep the globe tilted toward that wall.)
3. Tape a nail head down to the place on the globe where you live.
4. Set up the globe and lamp as shown in the illustration. Darken the room.

MATERIALS

- Tilted globe
- Unshaded table lamp
- Small nail with large head
- Pencil and paper
- Sticky tape
- Ruler

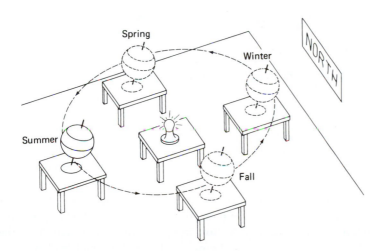

5. Begin at the summer position. Center the nail in the "sunshine" and point the North Pole toward north. Look at the nail shadow where you live. Measure and record how long it is. Notice how much daylight there is east and west of where you live.
6. Repeat step 5 at each of the other three positions.

Teaching Tips
If four globes are available, all four can be set up and used at the same time with four groups of students. Each group can rotate to a new position after a few minutes for observation and measurement. The best place from which to observe the amount of daylight and darkness at one's latitude is just above the globe's North Pole.

Concept Invention

1. During which season do you see the shortest shadow where you live? During which season do you see the longest shadow where you live? (A short shadow shows strong, direct sunshine. A long shadow shows weak, slanted sunshine.)
2. When is the longest period of sunshine where you live? When is the shortest period of sunshine? (The longer the sun shines, the warmer it gets where you live.)

Concept Application

The earth's tilted axis and revolution about the sun cause seasonal changes. During which seasons will the periods of daylight and darkness be about the same? Where and when north of you is it possible to have 24 hours of darkness or 24 hours of daylight? When and where can this happen south of you?

TIME AND THE SEASONS CONCEPTS

Because the earth is so large, compared to the size of a person, it is difficult at first to visualize the earth's motions in space. One remedy is to make the earth small compared to a person. That is what a globe model of the earth does.

Globe and Shadows

If you put a globe in the sun, the sunlight shines on one-half of the globe, as it does on one-half of the earth. If you position your town or city so that it is facing directly upward, and north on the globe faces north, the globe will face the sun as the earth does.

How will you know this is so? You can test it. Stick a small nail through a piece of sticky tape and fasten the nail head to your town on the globe. Be sure the nail is vertical. (You may have to prop up the globe base with a book or two.) Then look at the nail's shadow. You'll find it identical in direction and proportional to shadows of other objects around you. Leave the globe in place during the day, and the nail shadow will move and change length as other shadows do as the earth rotates. Or, if you want a preview of what shadows the earth objects will make, you can rotate the globe and watch the nail's shadow.

Rotation and Time

Most upper-grade students know the earth rotates, but few can tell in which direction. The sun rises in a generally eastern direction and sets in a generally western direction, with opposite shadows. Therefore, it is a west-to-east rotation.

INQ Figure 12–1 shows how people on the East Coast of the United States move into the sunlight. To them, it looks as though the sun is rising from the horizon and climbing higher as time goes by. Six hours from the time they first observe "sunrise," the sun is closest to being directly overhead. This is *midday*, or the exact middle of the daylight period. Gradually, they continue to rotate counterclockwise. Shadows grow longer. Around 6:00 P.M., it is almost twilight, and the sun appears to sink into the western horizon. The next 12 hours they spend in darkness, until once again the sun appears to rise. A complete rotation takes 24 hours, or one complete day. Of course, most of the time people in New York (or elsewhere) do not have equal parts of daylight and darkness. You know that summer days are longer than winter days, for example. We shall discuss why shortly.

INQ Figure 12–1 The apparent motion of the sun is caused by the earth's rotation.

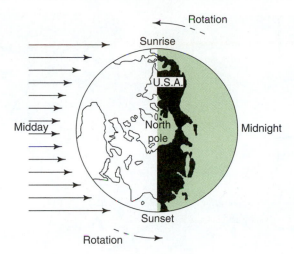

Expect some trouble with the term *day* because it has two meanings: the hours during which it is light, and the time for one complete rotation. You might use the terms *complete day* and *daylight* to distinguish the two.

Time Zones

It would be extremely inconvenient to judge time by where the sun is overhead. Every location a few kilometers east or west of another location would have a different noon-time as the sun reached its midday position, for example. Although this was not a problem in the days of slow-moving transportation, it became intolerable when railroads were established.

The problem was solved in 1833 by creating four standard time zones in the United States. INQ Figure 12–2 shows those in use today in the continental United States. We set our watches ahead going eastward and back going westward. The entire globe is now divided into 24 time zones, 15° apart. (The 15° separations came from dividing 360° by 24 hours, because the earth is a near sphere.)

The practical effect of having the same time zone for three cities hundreds of kilometers apart is shown in INQ Figure 12–3. Notice that only one city can experience midday at a given moment, although it is noon at all three cities.

Seasons

People in New York on December 21 experience about 9 hours of daylight and 15 hours of darkness. Six months later, the reverse happens. An even greater difference is found at a higher latitude, such as near Seattle, Washington (50th parallel). To see why, first examine INQ Figure 12–4. Notice that the earth's axis is tilted 23° from the plane of the earth's orbit around the sun. As the earth revolves about the sun, its axis continues to point in the same direction—toward the North Star. Check the winter position. Because of the tilt, the Northern Hemisphere is in darkness longer than it is in daylight. You can see this by checking the length of the parallels of latitude shown. In the summer position, you see the reverse. Now the same latitude is exposed to sunlight for a much longer period. At the "in between" periods of spring and fall, day and night periods are more nearly equal.

INQ Figure 12–2   The continental United States has four time zones.

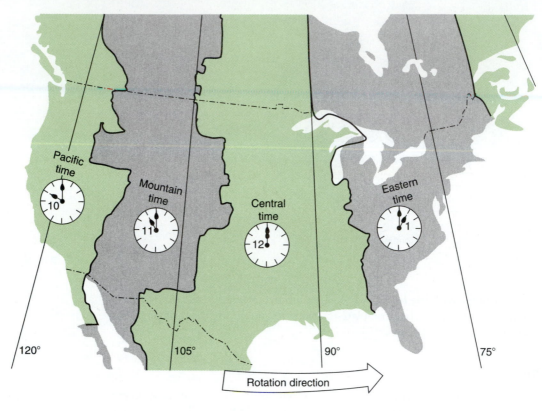

INQ Figure 12–3   Midday at one city and noon at three cities in the same time zone (not to scale).

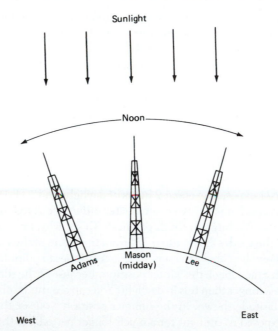

INQ Figure 12–4   The seasons. Outside figures as viewed from above. Notice the unequal periods of daylight at the 50th parallel except on March 21 (spring equinox) and September 23 (fall equinox).

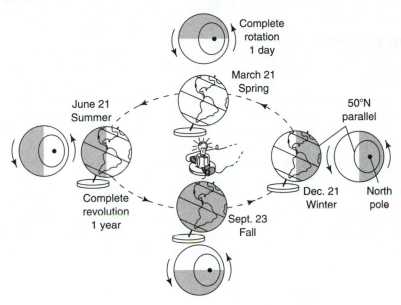

Also observe that the Southern Hemisphere has conditions opposite those in the Northern Hemisphere. While New York shivers in December, the beaches in sunny Rio de Janeiro are crowded with swimmers and sunbathers enjoying their summer.

Besides the increased length of the days, there is another reason why summers are warmer than winters. The sun's rays are more nearly overhead during summer than at other times. Note the words "more nearly overhead." Because the earth's axis is tilted, at noon the sun can never be completely vertical (at a 90° angle) north of the Tropic of Cancer or south of the Tropic of Capricorn.

If you ask children to explain why it is warmer in summer than it is in winter, don't be surprised if one replies, "The earth is closer to the sun." This answer is entirely logical even though it is wrong. In fact, the opposite is true. The earth's path (orbit) around the sun is a slightly elongated circle, or ellipse, as are nearly all the orbits of celestial bodies. In winter, we are almost 5 million kilometers (3 million miles) closer to the sun than in summer. But because this distance is small compared with the average distance, about 150 million kilometers (93 million miles), the effect is negligible.

MOON, EARTH, AND SUN INTERACTION Inquiry

Moon Phases ─────

MATERIALS

- White ball (tennis or volleyball)
- Bright window
- Daytime moon

Invitation

Have you ever watched the moon over 1 or 2 weeks? If so, you know its shape seems to go through changes, or phases. You can predict what phase will show when you understand why the moon's appearance changes. Working with a moon model can help. A ball can be the moon, and your head can be the earth. Light from a bright window can be the sun. How can a model be used to show moon phases?

Exploration

1. Close all the classroom shades or curtains except for one bright window.
2. Hold the ball above eye level and face the window, as illustrated. See the dark or shadowy side of the model. This is a new moon. (A real new moon cannot be seen from the earth.)

3. Turn the model moon to the left. Stop when you are sideways to the window. This is a first-quarter moon. The moon has gone one-quarter, or one-fourth, of the way around the earth.
4. Make another quarter turn to the left. Stop when your back is to the window. Now the entire moon facing you is lighted by the sun. This is a full moon.
5. Move a quarter turn left until you are sideways to the window. This is a last-quarter moon. Compare it with the first-quarter moon. Notice that the opposite part is lighted now.
6. Move the last quarter turn to your left. This is the new moon again. From one new moon to the next takes about 4 weeks.

Teaching Tips

If a bright window is unavailable, use the light from a filmstrip projector in a dark room. To do Concept Invention step 2, a daytime moon must be visible. Consult the detailed weather section of your local newspaper for moonrise and moonset times during a period when a daytime moon is visible.

Concept Invention

1. The illustration shows eight moon phases out of order. Using your moon model, can you figure out the correct order? Start with the new moon.

2. Go outside in the sun. Point your model toward the real moon. Notice where the sun shines on the real moon. Notice where it shines on the model. How does the real-moon phase compare to the model phase?

3. How can you move your model in the sun to make other phases? (Never look at the sun; it may harm your eyes.)

Scaffolding for English Learners

Remember not to focus on language errors that may impede concept development. For example, if the student says, "The new moon appear invisible" instead of "The new moon appears invisible," then the scientific concept is still understood despite the error in language. These language errors will be resolved naturally as the English learner progresses with language development. (See Ovando, Collier, & Combs, 2003, for a discussion of the role of error correction with English learners.)

Concept Application

Moon phases appear because one-half of the moon is lighted by sunshine as it revolves around the earth. Observe the moon now and then for a few days. Notice how its appearance changes. Keep a record. Can you predict what it will look like in 1 week? Can you predict what it will look like in 2 weeks? Draw what you think and then find out if you were correct.

An Earth–Moon Model

Invitation

Astronauts have walked on the moon several times, so it is easy to think that the moon is close to the earth, even though it is far away. One way to show its distance is to make a scale model.

Exploration

1. You will need a large ball for the earth and a smaller one for the moon. The earth is about four times as wide as the moon. Measure the width of a ball by putting it between two books. Use a ruler to find the distance between the books. A basketball is about four times wider than a tennis ball.

2. The moon is about 30 earth widths away, or 10 times farther away than the distance around the earth. Wrap a string 10 times around the basketball. Cut off what is left.

MATERIALS

- Basketball
- String
- Tennis ball
- Two books
- Ruler
- Scissors
- Clay

3. Stretch the string between the "earth" and the "moon" as illustrated. This scale model shows sizes and distance compared to the real earth.

Teaching Tips

The sequence is designed to help children gain an understanding of proportion without its mathematics. After these experiences, most children should have a realistic scaled view of the earth–moon system. If you want, you might proceed directly with figures they can scale: the earth's diameter, 12,800 kilometers (8000 miles); the moon's diameter, 3200 kilometers (2000 miles); and average distance between them, 384,000 kilometers (240,000 miles).

Concept Invention

1. How can you make a scale model that is half this size?
2. Suppose you had a ball 10 centimeters (4 inches) wide to use as the earth. How large would the moon need to be? How far apart should the earth and the moon be?
3. Suppose you had a ball 5 centimeters (2 inches) wide to use as the moon. How large would the earth need to be? How far apart should the earth and the moon be?

Concept Application

Relative sizes and distance in the earth–moon system may be shown in a scale model. Suppose you wanted your whole model to be no longer than a meterstick or yardstick. How large would you make your earth and moon? How far apart would you place them?

Eclipses of the Sun and Moon

Invitation

Sometimes the earth, moon, and sun are in a straight line in space. Then, something interesting may happen: The moon may block off, or eclipse, the sunlight, or the earth may block, or eclipse, the moon. You can learn how eclipses work with a model of the sun, moon, and earth. How can you use the following items—volleyball, tennis ball, and projector—to demonstrate eclipses?

Exploration

1. Set up the materials as shown. Put a basketball or volleyball on a table. This will be the "earth."
2. Use sticky tape to fasten a short string to a tennis ball. This will be the "moon."
3. Darken the room. Turn on the projector "sun." Point it toward the earth.
4. Holding the string, move the moon around the earth. Notice the shadows made by the moon and the earth.

MATERIALS

- Volleyball or basketball
- Filmstrip projector
- Tennis ball
- Sticky tape
- String
- Table
- Two large index cards

Concept Invention

1. At what position does the moon make a shadow on the earth? (This is an eclipse of the sun.)
2. How much of the earth is covered by the moon's shadow?
3. At what position does the earth make a shadow on the moon? (This is an eclipse of the moon.)
4. How much of the moon is covered by the earth's shadow?

Teaching Tips

Some students may wonder why a solar eclipse and a lunar eclipse do not occur every month. You might help them understand that the plane of the moon's orbit around the earth is somewhat tilted. Also, the two bodies are relatively much farther apart than in the model, so usually the moon's shadow misses the earth, and the earth's shadow misses the moon. The distance between the two bodies also means that the moon's shadow on earth in solar eclipses is much smaller than found in the inquiry. Remember that you should never look at the sun during a solar eclipse. The sun can quickly injure eyes.

Adapting for Students with Exceptionalities

When involving exceptional students in complex activities such as eclipses, use a variety of visual diagrams and pictures to supplement the activity and make the information understandable. For example, in the Concept Application, show students several eclipse pictures along with the basketball and tennis ball manipulations.

Concept Application

A lunar eclipse happens when the earth's shadow falls on the moon. A solar eclipse happens when the moon's shadow falls on the earth. Would more people on the earth be able to see a sun eclipse or a moon eclipse? Explain your answer. Move the moon around the earth again, but now have it go just above or below the earth. Do you see eclipses now? Explain why or why not.

MOON, EARTH, AND SUN INTERACTION CONCEPTS

Why does the moon seem to change its shape? Why do the oceans have tides? What causes eclipses? Children are curious about these things. This section presents some ways the sun, earth, and moon interact. We consider moon phases first.

Moon Phases

You know that the moon, like our earth, receives and reflects light from the hot, glowing sun. Also, the moon revolves around the earth in about 28 days. Study INQ Figure 12–5 for a moment. The drawings on the right show the earth and moon as seen from far out in space. The drawings of the moon on the left illustrate how it appears to us on the earth as it goes through each of eight different positions or phases.

Suppose we are standing on the earth in the right-hand part of this illustration. Look at position 1. This is the new moon position. The moon's face is now dark to us. Slowly, the moon moves on in its orbit. At position 2, we see a new crescent moon; at position 3,

INQ Figure 12–5   Moon phases as seen from the earth (left); the earth and moon as seen from far out in space (right).

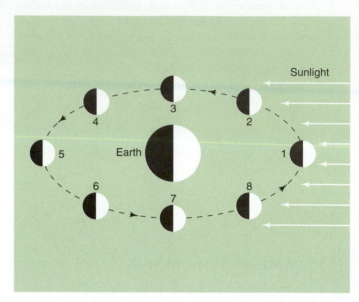

a first-quarter moon. At position 4, we see a new gibbous moon; one side is now almost fully illuminated. At position 5, the moon is full. The other positions reverse the sequence of phases from old gibbous, last quarter, old crescent, to new moon.

As the moon moves from the new to full positions, more and more of it appears to be shining; it is said to be *waxing*. But from full- to new-moon positions, less and less of its lighted part is visible from earth, so it is said to be *waning*. Compare the moon phases you actually see with those in INQ Figure 12–5.

Tides

The interaction of sun, moon, and earth also results in tides. How do tides happen? The law of universal gravitation, first formulated by the great 18th-century philosopher and scientist Sir Isaac Newton, provides much of the answer. Briefly stated, every object in the universe attracts each other; the force of this attraction depends on the mass of each object and the distance between them. (*Mass* is the amount of matter that makes up the object.)

As shown in INQ Figure 12–6, the mutual attraction between earth and moon causes the ocean to bulge at position 1. This is a direct high tide. An indirect high tide appears at position 3 because it is most distant from the moon; gravitational attraction is weakest here. Also, the land surface is pulled slightly away from this region. Positions 2 and 4 have low tides because these are areas of weak attraction that furnish the extra water making up the high tides.

INQ Figure 12–6

Mutual attraction between earth and moon causes ocean tides.

What causes the tides to rise and fall? Put yourself in position 1. As you rotate on the earth toward position 2, the tide will seem to *ebb*, or fall. You experience a low tide. Moving from position 2 into 3, you gradually come into the bulge. It seems as though the tide is "coming in." You experience a high tide. Rotating onward, you have another low tide before once again arriving at the direct high-tide area. In other words, the oceans tend to bulge continually in the moon's direction and opposite point, as the earth

INQ Figure 12–7   The sun also affects tidal flows.

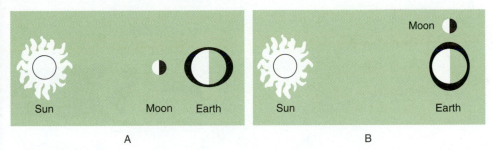

rotates. The continual bulges create the illusion that the tides are moving in and out independently.

Because the earth's rotation takes about 24 hours, high tides happen about every 12 hours. Therefore, we have one direct high tide and one indirect high tide simultaneously. Six hours elapse between low and high tides. Actually, these times are a little longer because the moon itself moves some distance in its orbit while the earth rotates. Because the tidal bulge moves in alignment with the moon as it advances, the earth must rotate an extra 52 minutes each 24 hours before it is again in the direct high-tide zone.

Twice monthly, unusually high and low tidal ranges occur called *spring tides*. High tides are very high and low tides are very low. (Incidentally, there is no connection between spring tides and the season. Perhaps the name arose because these tides appear to "spring up" so fast.) A week later, there is much less variation from high to low tides. Tides during this period are called *neap tides*.

INQ Figure 12–7 shows how these tides take place. When the sun and moon are aligned (A), the sun's added gravitational attraction causes very high spring tides. This happens during the time when the moon is in either the full- or new-moon phase. Because the sun is so far away, its tremendous mass adds only one-third to the force of gravitational attraction. When the sun and moon pull at right angles (B), we have neap tides. This happens when the moon is in its first- and last-quarter phases.

Interestingly, besides water tides, there are also huge atmospheric tides and tiny land tides. All happen through the same interaction of sun, moon, and earth. Accurate measurements show that some land portions of the earth rise and fall more than 30 centimeters (1 foot) with the tides.

Eclipses

Causes of eclipses are seen in INQ Figure 12–8. Both earth and moon cast conelike shadows. When the moon is in position 1, the tip of its shadow barely reaches the earth. Persons in this small, shadowy area see a solar eclipse. A total eclipse is never more than 272 kilometers (170 miles) across. Sunlight is cut off except for a whitish halo, called the *corona*. The shadow moves quickly over the ground because both the earth and the moon are in motion. Sunlight is never blocked for more than 8 minutes.

In position 2, the moon is eclipsed when it revolves into the earth's large shadow. Practically everyone on the earth's dark side can see a lunar eclipse, which may last for 2 hours before the moon revolves out of the earth's shadow. Several partial lunar and solar eclipses occur each year.

Notice that eclipses happen in the full- and new-moon positions. Why, then, don't they occur every few weeks? The reason is that the moon's plane of orbit is tilted about 5°

INQ Figure 12–8   Cause of solar (1) and lunar (2) eclipses.

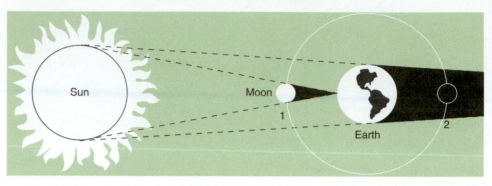

from the earth's orbital plane around the sun. This tilt usually causes the moon to pass above and below positions required for eclipses.

A 5° tilt would be only a minor deviation from the earth's orbital plane in INQ Figure 12–8, hardly enough to make a difference. In proper scale, however, this small deviation is quite significant. With a scale of 2.5 centimeters to 1600 kilometers (1 inch to 1000 miles), the earth's diameter is 20 centimeters (8 inches), and the moon's diameter is 5 centimeters (2 inches). Their distance apart is 6 meters (20 feet). The sun's diameter and distance at this scale are even more surprising. Imagine a sun model 22 meters (72 feet) across, 2.4 kilometers (1.5 miles) away!

The Earth–Moon System

We usually think of the moon revolving around the earth, but strictly speaking, this is not quite the case. The gravitational attraction of these two objects is such that they are locked together in a revolving system that has a common center of mass (barycenter). To see why this is so, look at INQ Figure 12–9. The large ball of clay represents the earth, and the small one is the moon. A short wire joins the two to simulate their gravitational attraction. If you suspend system A from the middle with a string, the much heavier earth goes down and the moon goes up. The same thing would happen if a heavy adult and a small child got on a seesaw with the fulcrum in the middle.

In system B, the balance is improved, but much the same thing happens. In system C, though, a balance is found. If you spin each model system with a twisted string, systems A and B will wobble and sway unevenly; but system C will revolve uniformly and simulate the motion of the earth–moon system. In any spinning system such as this, there is a tendency for the two objects to fly apart. The gravitational attraction between the two prevents this from happening.

In system D, the side of the earth facing the moon is strongly attracted to the moon. The water moves more easily than the solid earth, so it flows strongly toward the near side and becomes a high tide. The earth's opposite side is attracted less because it is farther away. So, the tendency of this far side of the spinning system to fly apart is countered only weakly by the weakened gravitational pull. The result is an indirect high tide.

Our model is imperfect in several ways. The earth's mass is about 80 times greater than the moon's. Also, the distance scale is wrong. If we were to use the proper scale, our short wire connector would need to be at least several feet long.

INQ Figure 12–9 The earth-moon system has a common point of balance, or center of mass, called the barycenter (distance not to scale).

The Moon's Orbit

From an earth reference position, it is natural to regard the moon as revolving in a circular path around the earth (or, more accurately, the barycenter). But motion is relative to the observer. If we could see the moon's path from far out in space, it would not look circular. Instead, it would weave in and out in a shallow, alternating pattern along the earth's orbit. (See INQ Figure 12–10.) Because the sun is in motion, a similar pathway is woven by the earth. Is it wrong, then, to say that the moon revolves around the earth and the earth around the sun? No, it is just another way of looking at the same set of facts.

Solar Wind

One interesting interaction between the earth and the sun is the stream of ionized particles ejected at high speeds from the surface of the sun known as *solar wind*. Most of the current information we have about solar wind comes from the Solar and Heliospheric Observatory (SOHO) project. The International Solar Terrestrial Physics (ISTP) science

INQ Figure 12–10 The earth and moon orbits drawn to scale.

initiative is a collaborative effort by U.S., European, and Japanese space agencies to obtain coordinated, simultaneous investigations of the sun–earth space environment over an extended period of time. SOHO, one component of the ISTP program, includes a cooperative venture between the European Space Agency (ESA) and the National Aeronautics and Space Administration (NASA). Launched on December 2, 1995, the SOHO spacecraft is specifically designed to study the internal structure of the sun, the sun's outer atmosphere, and the origins of the solar wind that blows continuously outward throughout our solar system. SOHO will help scientists understand the interactions between the sun and the earth's environment.

According to SOHO scientists, solar wind is a stream of particles, primarily ionized hydrogen (electrons and protons), with a component of helium and trace amounts of heavy ions, flowing outward from the sun at speeds as high as 900 kilometers (559 miles) per second. SOHO scientists view solar wind as essentially the hot solar corona expanding into interplanetary and interstellar space. Solar wind has been detected from the sun outward past the orbit of Neptune. The stream of particles comes in two varieties. Low-speed solar wind moves about 1.5 million kilometers (932,056 miles) per hour, and high-speed solar wind moves at speeds as high as 3 million kilometers (1,864,114 miles) per hour.

As solar wind flows past the earth, it changes the shape and structure of the earth's magnetic field. Changes in solar wind can disrupt telecommunications, interfere with electrical power systems, and even damage satellites. To find out more information about SOHO, to see the current solar wind speed and other real-time data, to receive free materials, or to see related lesson plans, check the SOHO website (*http://sohowww.nascom.nasa.gov/*).

SOLAR SYSTEM AND BEYOND Inquiry

Size and Distance in the Solar System

Invitation

The solar system is huge. You cannot make a model that shows both size and distance at the same time. It would be too big to fit in the classroom or playground. But you can make a scale model of part of the system—the sun and the earth. It can help you understand more about distance and size in the solar system.

Exploration

1. Make a clay ball 1 centimeter (3/8 inch) wide for the earth.
2. The sun is 108 times wider than the earth, so cut out a circle 108 centimeters (43 inches) wide from yellow construction paper. (You may need to tape some sheets together.)
3. The sun is about 150 million kilometers (93 million miles) from the earth, so the two models will need to be about 116 meters (383 feet) apart.
4. Practice taking giant steps. Try to make each step 1 meter (or 1 yard) long. Then, step off the sun–earth distance on the playground.
5. Have someone hold up the model sun at one end. Hold up your tiny model earth, stuck on a pin, at the other end. Notice how far away the sun is.

> ### MATERIALS
> - Yellow construction paper
> - Clay
> - Meterstick or yardstick
> - Straight pin
> - Sticky tape
> - Playground
> - Scissors

> **Teaching Tips**
> A large circle may be drawn with a pencil tied to a string. Its radius with the current sun model would be 54 centimeters (21 inches). Many children will enjoy being challenged to extend their solar system model on a local map. Pluto will need to be placed several kilometers or miles away!

Concept Invention

1. The planet Jupiter is five times farther away from the sun than the earth. How far away (meters or feet) would Jupiter be with your model?

2. Uranus is almost 18 times farther from the sun than the earth. How far away would Uranus be with your model?

3. Pluto, the farthest planet, is more than 39 times farther away. How far would Pluto be with your model?

4. The largest of the solar system's nine planets is Jupiter. It is 11 times wider than the earth. How large would Jupiter be with your model?

5. The smallest planet is Pluto. It is only about one-third as wide as the earth. How large would it be with your model?

Concept Application

The large distances among planets in the solar system make it difficult to scale planet sizes and distances together in a model. Explain what would happen if you were to try to make a model of the entire solar system.

Constellations

MATERIALS

- Cardboard box
- Aluminum foil
- Scissors
- Black thread
- Black paint or paper
- Sticky tape
- Partner

Invitation

Most people have seen the group, or constellation, of stars called the Big Dipper. The stars make a pattern that looks like an old-fashioned water dipper. There are many more constellations of stars. But although they seem to make a pattern, they may be very different in size and millions of kilometers from each other. Seen from another angle, they may not look at all like constellations. You can find out more about what constellations are like by making a model.

Exploration

1. Cut off the top and one side of a cardboard box.
2. Cover the side and back inside with black paint or paper.
3. Snip different-sized pieces of black thread to hold your "stars."
4. Make different-sized stars from pieces of foil. Wrap each piece around a thread end. Squeeze each into a ball shape.
5. Ask someone to use tape and hang your stars in some pattern different from the one shown in the illustration. (Notice that, in the front view, this constellation looks like a **W**, but from the side looks like an upside-down **V**. If the box's side was as long as the playground, you could put the stars even farther apart. Then you would see no pattern at all from the side.)

It is essential that children first view the constellation model directly from the front and from some distance. Otherwise, the activity may be less effective. The foil balls may be suspended quickly, and shifted as needed, by affixing each thread end to the box top inside with a bit of tape.

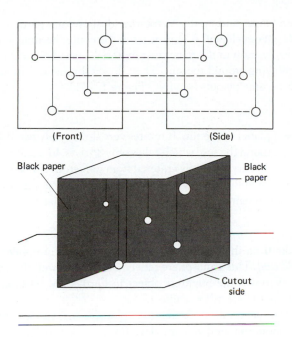

Concept Invention

1. Look at the constellation your partner has made from the front view from 15 steps away. Can you draw its shape?
2. At what distances from you are the stars? Which is the closest or next closest? Record what you think from left to right.
3. What do you think the constellation looks like from the side? Draw what you think.
4. Ask your partner to twist the box around very slightly. How, if at all, does this help you tell distances and the side pattern? How many more times must you twist the box around to tell?
5. Play a game with your partner. Each person hangs a different constellation. How many stars can you order properly by distance from you? How many side patterns can you tell from front patterns?

Concept Application

Stars of a constellation share a common direction, but they may vary greatly in size and distance from each other. Check the night sky on a clear day and record the location of stars from one constellation. Describe and name your constellation (such as the Big Dipper was named). Can your classmates locate your constellation on subsequent clear nights?

SOLAR SYSTEM AND BEYOND CONCEPTS

Planets ——————

The earth is one of nine planets revolving around a medium-sized star, the sun. How did the solar system begin? Scientists are not sure. One prominent theory holds that the sun and planets may have been formed from an enormous swirling cloud of dust and gases. Slowly, gravitational attraction caused these materials to come closer together. The speed of rotation increased more and more. As rotating dust and gas particles rubbed together, much friction and heat developed. A large mass in the center became so hot that it formed into the sun. Gradually, most of the remaining materials spread out as a result of their spinning and began revolving around the sun. They slowly shrank and cooled into nine separate masses, which became planets (see INQ Figure 12–11).

Mercury

Mercury is the closest planet to the sun. It rotates very slowly, only two thirds around to one complete revolution around the sun, which takes only 88 days. Its small mass results in a very weak surface gravity. Mercury is heavily cratered from numerous collisions with meteoroids.

Mercury was explored in three flybys by the *Mariner 10* spacecraft in 1974 and 1975. During these missions, scientists found evidence there of a polar ice cap.

Venus

Venus, next in order from the sun, is enveloped in a dense atmosphere of mostly carbon dioxide and sulfuric acid. This atmosphere reflects sunlight so well that, except for the sun and Earth's moon, Venus is the brightest object in Earth's sky. Its surface temperature is very high as a result of the greenhouse effect.

NASA's *Magellan* spacecraft used radar to explore Venus's surface during its orbit from 1990 to 1994. Astronomers found volcanic lava flows, "venusquake" faults, and other features on the surface. *Mariner 2, 5,* and *10* and the *Pioneer* Venus spacecraft have all made missions to Venus.

Mars

After Earth is Mars. It has an unusual reddish appearance and polar ice caps that advance and recede with the seasons. It is more like Earth than the other planets, but its very thin

INQ Figure 12–11   **The solar system (not to scale).**

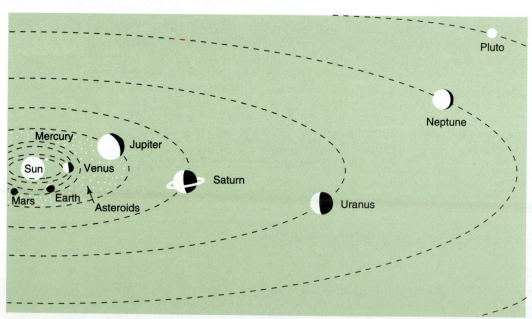

atmosphere and severe weather make it unlikely that living things are on this planet. Two tiny natural satellites, or moons, revolve speedily around Mars. *Mariner 4, 6,* and *7,* in the 1960s, explored the planet. In the 1970s, *Mariner 9* and the *Viking* missions allowed two landers to explore the planet further. Unfortunately, the landers did not find evidence of life.

On July 4, 1997, the Mars *Pathfinder* mission landed on the planet and left a mobile robot rover to explore the surface. In 1999, a polar lander was launched. The spirit and opportunity rovers have now visited Mars. A Mars Global Surveyor is scheduled to create high-resolution maps of the planet's surface. Other orbiters and landers were launched in 2001, 2003, and 2005, including a reconnaissance orbiter. Further information can be found on the Mars Exploration Program web page. New images and updated information are also available for viewing on the Internet from NASA's Jet Propulsion Laboratory's web pages.

Jupiter

Jupiter is a giant ball of hydrogen and helium gas and the largest outer planet. It is almost big enough to form into a star. In fact, Jupiter's diameter is 11 times greater than that of Earth. The Great Red Spot on Jupiter appears to be a storm that is almost three times the size of planet Earth.

NASA's *Pioneer 10* and *11* and *Voyager 1* and *2* spacecrafts explored Jupiter. It was also studied by the Jupiter-orbiting *Galileo* spacecraft.

Saturn, Uranus, Neptune, Pluto

Saturn, the second biggest planet in our solar system, is conspicuous because of its many rings. They are believed to be composed of ice and rock particles that can be as big as a house. Saturn was explored by NASA's *Pioneer 11* in the 1970s and by the *Voyager 1* and *2* spacecrafts in the 1980s. The *Cassini* spacecraft, launched in 1997, arrived at Saturn in 2004.

Uranus is about three and one half times Earth's diameter. This planet rotates on its side. The *Voyager 2* spacecraft flew by Uranus in 1986.

Neptune is the furthest of the giant outer planets in the solar system. Neptune's Great Dark Spot is a storm that is similar to Jupiter's Great Red Spot. The *Voyager 2* spacecraft flew by Neptune in 1989.

Pluto is so small and distant that it was not discovered until 1930. Its "moon," Charon, is about half the diameter and mass of Pluto. Its orbital plane is tilted sharply from those of other planets, and its orbit is so elliptical that at times the planet is closer to the sun than Neptune. Pluto is the only planet that has not been visited by spacecraft, although NASA has a mission called "New Horizons" that will be launched in 2006.

New Information on the Planets

Ancient sky-watchers were so puzzled by the changing appearance of the planets that they named them "wanderers." Long ago, all such objects were thought to be stars, which ordinarily seem fixed in space. We realize now that their differences in brightness and position from time to time occur because they revolve at different distances and speeds in their orbits around the sun.

Today, astronomers are finding new planets and are discovering more about distant bodies through the use of the Hubble Space Telescope and other space probes. For an up-to-date account of new findings, children can log on to NASA's web pages on the Internet (see the Companion Website for specific addresses). NASA's Office of Space Science Solar System Exploration Education and Outreach Forum is available to the public; it contains educational and informational resources that pertain to solar system exploration. This office provides information about the planets and other bodies contained in our solar system.

Comets, Meteors, and the Asteroid Belt

Comets are huge, unstable bodies apparently composed of gases, dust, ice, and small rocks. A few are briefly visible as they occasionally sweep near the sun and far out again in immense, highly elliptical orbits. They have so little mass that the pressure of sunlight causes a long streamer, or "tail," to flow from the comet head always in a direction opposite the sun. Like the planets, comets may have originated from the gases and dust of the solar nebula over 4 billion years ago.

Most children have seen "shooting stars." These are fragments of rock and metal, probably from broken-up asteroids and parts of comets that hurtle through interplanetary space at high speeds. Although most are no larger than a grain of sand, some weigh tons. It is estimated that billions of such *meteors*, as they are called, plunge daily into the earth's atmosphere and burn up from the heat of air friction. The few that do penetrate to the earth's surface in solid form other than dust are called *meteorites*.

Is there any danger of being struck by a meteorite? Not much. Only a few instances of anyone ever being injured are recorded. One such event happened in 1954. An Alabama woman was grazed by a 3.7-kilogram (10-pound) meteorite that crashed through her home's roof. In 1982, a 2.2-kilogram (6-pound) meteorite smashed through the roof of a home in Connecticut; no one was injured.

NASA is planning a mission to the asteroid belt that will be launched in 2005 and will reach the asteroid belt in 2008. The name of the mission is "Dawn" and it involves a new solar-electric propulsion system.

Sizes and Distances

By far the most difficult ideas in astronomy for children to grasp are the distances and sizes of objects in space. It would be helpful to their thinking if a large section of the playground could be used for scaled distance activities. Yet, even a very large area can be inadequate to demonstrate both distance and size on the same scale. At 2.54 centimeters to 12,000 kilometers (1 inch to 8000 miles), for example, Pluto would need to be located about 11 kilometers (7 miles) away!

Distances are even more astounding as we move beyond the solar system. Now, the kilometer or mile is too tiny a unit of measurement for practical purposes. You will want to acquaint students with the *light-year*, defined as the distance a beam of light travels in 1 year. At 300,000 kilometers (186,000 miles) per second, this is almost 9.5 trillion kilometers (6 trillion miles). The *parsec*, or the distance to a star that shows a parallax of 1 second of arc, is another unit of astronomical measurement that advanced students may be able to understand.

The Asteroid Belt

Between Mars and the next planet, Jupiter, is an unusually large gap containing several thousand irregularly shaped chunks of stone and metal called *asteroids* (tiny "stars") made of rock and metal that is mostly nickel and iron. Some astronomers think these may be the remains of a planet that came too close to huge Jupiter and disintegrated under its powerful gravitational attraction. Ranging from about 1.6 to 800 kilometers (1 to 500 miles) in diameter, they are invisible to the unaided eye.

Flybys of asteroids were completed in 1991 and 1993 by the *Galileo* spacecraft. In 1996, the *Near Earth Asteroid Rendezvous (NEAR)* spacecraft also explored the asteroid belt.

The Stars

When we view the stars, some seem to group into patterns, or constellations. People commonly think such stars are about the same in size and distance from the earth. But the only thing stars in a constellation typically share is a common direction. If we could view constellations from other angles (we can, very slightly, as the earth orbits the sun), most constellation patterns would disappear.

The light from our nearest star, the sun, takes about 8 minutes to reach the earth. In contrast, a distance of 4.3 light-years separates us from the next nearest star, Proxima Centauri. These stars have more than 100 billion companions clustered in an immense aggregation of stars and filmy clouds of gas and dust called the Milky Way galaxy. The shape of our galaxy is like a pocket watch, with a thickened center, standing on end (INQ Figure 12–12). It is thought to be about 100,000 light-years long and 12,000 light-years thick. The galaxy seems to be rotating slowly about its center, where the stars are most thickly concentrated.

Our galaxy is but one of millions more strewn throughout space at incomprehensible distances, containing further stars beyond reliable calculation.

Stellar Types and Evolution

The stars we see range in size from the small, dim, *white dwarf* with a diameter that is much smaller than the sun, to the very large, very bright star known as a red *supergiant*, with a diameter hundreds of times larger than the sun. Stars change in size as part of an evolutionary process. All stars begin as a mass of cool gas. Gravity will cause the gas to contract. Eventually a high temperature and pressure condition causes a nuclear fusion chain reaction, which gives off energy, and the gas becomes a star. When the star's core runs out of hydrogen gas to transform into helium gas, it undergoes a change that puts it into a new phase of its evolution. What happens next depends on the mass of the star.

If the star was similar in mass to our sun, it will swell in size and become a large, bright red giant star. The red giant will continue nuclear fusion until all of its helium gas becomes carbon. It then shrinks in size and becomes a dim white dwarf star.

If a star is a lot more massive than the sun, it expands to a much greater size and is called a red supergiant, with brightness thousands of times greater than that of our sun. As a massive red supergiant star enters the late stage of its evolution, it explodes in a tremendous

INQ Figure 12–12 The Milky Way galaxy.

burst called a *supernova* that is visible in distant galaxies. This star will eventually contract to become a *neutron star* with an astounding density of 100 million tons per cubic centimeter (0.061 cubic inch).

If the collapsing star of a supernova has a great enough mass, then even the star's huge density cannot hold gravity back, and the supernova creates a new form that contracts forever. Eventually the gravitational force becomes so great that light cannot escape and the star disappears forever into a collapsing *black hole*.

GRAVITY AND THE LAWS OF MOTION **Inquiry**

The Sun's Gravity

Invitation

Why doesn't the sun's gravity pull in the near planets?

Exploration

1. Tie one end of the string tightly to the ball. Slide the other end through the hole of a sewing spool.
2. You will be the "sun." The ball "planet" will revolve around you on the string. Hold the spool in one hand. Whirl the planet by moving the spool around. Hold the string with your other hand to keep it from slipping through the spool, as shown. (You could mark the string below the spool to easily see any slip.)
3. Feel how the ball pulls on the string. Have someone count the number of times your planet circles the sun in 15 seconds. Try to keep the string length above the spool the same.

> **MATERIALS**
>
> - Strong string (2 meters, or 6 feet, long)
> - Partner
> - Rubber ball
> - Watch with second hand
> - Sewing thread spool
> - Outdoor place

Concept Invention

1. Try it a second time. Keep the string length the same as before, but now pull harder on the string below the spool. This increases the pull of "gravity" on your planet.
2. If the planet is to stay at the same distance, what must happen to its speed?

Concept Application

Have someone count again the number of orbits your planet makes in 15 seconds. Describe how the first and second counts compare. What do you think makes it possible for the closer planets not to be pulled into the sun?

Rockets

Invitation

What makes a rocket work?

Exploration

1. Thread one end of the string through a straw. Fasten that end low on a table leg. Fasten the other end high on a wall. The string should be tight.
2. Blow up the balloon. Fold over the small, open end and fasten it with a paper clip.
3. Use tape to fasten the balloon to the straw as shown.
4. Hold the balloon near the floor end of the string. Quickly remove the paper clip and let go.

MATERIALS

- Sausage-shaped balloon
- Sticky tape
- String (6 meters, or 20 feet, long)
- Paper clip
- Soda straw
- Five pennies

eaching ips

When air rushes out of the balloon, there is an equal and opposite push inside, so the balloon moves. In a rocket engine, burned fuel forms hot gases that push out through the open back of the engine. An equal and opposite push inside moves the rocket forward.

Concept Invention

1. What happens to the balloon?
2. How can you explain what happens?

Concept Application

Have a contest with teams of classmates to see whose balloon rocket can lift the most weight to a "space station." Tie one end of each string to a light fixture or other high place. Use sticky tape to fasten pennyweights to each balloon. Make some fair rules: The lower end of each string and rocket must touch the floor when the rocket is released. Each team gets two turns; the first is for practice. Observe carefully what the best rockets look like during the first trial and record this data. Also draw how your "improved" rocket will look. Use this information to prepare for the second trial. No team can change its rocket once the second trials begin. To win, here are some things to consider.

- How much air should be in the balloon? (If it breaks, you're out of the contest.)
- How long should the straw be?
- How should the straw be attached to the balloon?
- Should the string be upright or at a slant?
- What kind of string is best?
- How many pennies should be stuck on the balloon?
- Where is it best to put the pennies for balance?

GRAVITY AND THE LAWS OF MOTION CONCEPTS

Nobody knows what caused the planets to begin moving, but the reason they keep moving is readily understandable: There is almost nothing in space to stop them. But why do they circle the sun? You have already been introduced to Newton's law of gravitation. Equally important to understand is Newton's law of inertia. Briefly stated, any object at rest or in motion remains at rest or continues in motion in a straight line unless acted on by some outside force.

Anyone who has ever tried to push a heavy, stalled automobile knows how hard it is to move a heavy body at rest. It has much inertia. Anyone who has ever tried to stop a heavy, rolling automobile by pushing against it knows how difficult this is. A body in motion has the inertia of motion (momentum). The more momentum it has, the harder it is to stop it.

Causes of Orbits

INQ Figure 12–13 shows how the laws of gravitation and inertia combine to keep objects in orbit. Although a natural satellite, our moon, is shown in this case, the same laws operate with all bodies that orbit other bodies in space.

If the moon were unaffected by our earth's powerful gravitational force, it would follow a straight path owing to its inertial momentum. Because it is affected, the moon follows a path that is a result of each factor countering the other.

A common example of this countering effect happens when a ball rolls swiftly off a table. Instead of falling straight down, the ball's inertia of momentum keeps it going nearly sideways for an instant until gravity forces it to the floor. The resultant path of its fall is an arc.

In our illustration, gravity and inertia are equally powerful. If this were not so, the moon would either be drawn into the earth or pull away from it. This is what happens to an artificial satellite that moves too slowly or too quickly. Clearly, getting a space satellite into a sustained orbit is tricky business. Its velocity and angle of entry into orbit must be

INQ Figure 12–13   **A balance between gravity and inertia keeps a satellite in orbit.**

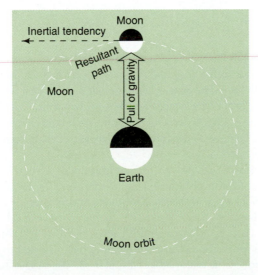

calculated closely. Because perfection in these matters is nearly impossible, most orbits are markedly elongated (elliptical).

Because gravity weakens with distance, the speed of the orbiting body must be slower as the distance from its parent body increases. This is necessary to maintain balance of the two forces. At 35,680 kilometers (22,300 miles) from the earth, for example, the proper orbital speed for a satellite results in one complete orbit each 24 hours. Because this is the period of the earth's rotation, a satellite positioned above the equator always stays in the same relative position. With several of these satellites properly spaced, television and radio signals are relayed to any place on earth.

Zero Gravity

When astronauts circle the earth in a spaceship, they have no sensation of weight; the pull of gravity is balanced exactly by the counteracting inertia of motion. We sometimes experience this weightless, or *zero gravity*, condition on the earth for an instant when an elevator starts rapidly downward or an automobile goes too fast over the crown of a steep hill.

In one science lesson not long ago, a bright child asked her teacher an astute question: "If we would be weightless in an orbiting satellite, why wouldn't we be weightless on the moon?" The teacher had her reconsider the law of gravitation, especially the part that says ". . . this attraction depends on the mass of each object and the distance between them."

Because the moon has a much smaller mass than the earth, its surface gravity is only about one sixth that of the earth's. An 81-kilogram (180-pound) astronaut weighs a mere 13.5 kilograms (30 pounds) on the moon. However, the moon's mass is almost infinitely greater than that of a space vehicle. The tiny mass of a space vehicle has practically no gravity at all.

Because prolonged periods of weightlessness seem detrimental to astronauts' health, attempts are being made to design space vehicles that create a gravitylike condition. This may be done by rotating the vehicle at a carefully calculated speed. The astronauts' inertia gives them a feeling of gravity as they are slightly pressed against the spaceship's interior. An analogy is the small ball that remains stationary on the rim of a roulette wheel until it stops turning.

Rockets

Through the ages, people have always yearned to explore what mysteries lie beyond the earth. Until recently, our technology had not been as advanced as our ambitions. Early devices and inventions designed for space travel included hitching a flock of geese to a wicker basket, hand-cranking propellers attached to hot-air balloons, and festooning a box with crude rockets containing gunpowder. Occasionally, such contraptions were personally occupied by their daring inventors—and some did depart from this earth, although not in the manner intended.

Because space is a near vacuum, no engine that draws oxygen from the air to burn its fuel can serve in a propulsion system. Instead, rocket engines are used; these carry their own oxygen supply. Rockets work because for every action there is an equal and opposite reaction (another of Newton's laws of motion). When a rocket pushes hot gases out of its combustion chamber (action), the gases push back (reaction) and thrust the rocket ahead.

Most rockets today are composed of multiple stages fastened together in a cluster or a tandem arrangement. The main rocket propels all the stages to a point where the rocket's fuel is expended and then it drops off. The remaining stages reach even higher velocities as the process continues, lightening the load each time. The speed of the last stage represents the accumulated sum of speeds attained by each stage. Perhaps future rockets will be efficient enough to reduce or eliminate the necessity for current cumbersome staging techniques.

Problems in Space Travel

Although modern rocketry provides the means to reach beyond the earth, travel for astronauts poses some difficult problems. As the rocket blasts off in a terrifying surge of power, the rapid acceleration pins the astronauts' bodies to the seats with crushing force.

Once beyond the earth's atmosphere, they need oxygen and sufficient pressure to keep their bodies working normally. They need some means of temperature control. Without air conduction of heat energy, the side of the spaceship facing the sun gets very hot, and the dark side gets freezing cold. Because of their weightless condition, the astronauts may eat and drink from plastic squeeze bottles.

To prevent the space vehicle from being burned to a cinder as it reenters the atmosphere, the angle and speed of reentry must be exactly right. These are only some of the problems of space travel.

With so many difficulties, why do people venture into space? Although our curiosity is one answer, of course, there are many advantages for continued space efforts. Some benefits are improved communications, surveys of earth resources, long-range weather forecasting and possible weather control, astronomers' observation posts beyond the annoying interference of the earth's atmosphere, possible answers to how the universe was formed, and improved mapping and navigation. All these benefits may help us understand and solve problems here on the earth.

Eventually will come the most important reason of all. Someday, perhaps 3 to 5 billion years from now, the sun's nuclear fuel will be largely depleted. The sun should gradually expand and engulf the inner planets in an unimaginable inferno of extinction before it finally collapses and dies out. Perhaps by then our descendants will have found a comfortable haven among the stars.

References

American Association for the Advancement of Science (AAAS). (1993). *Benchmarks for science literacy.* New York: Oxford University Press.

National Research Council (NRC). (1996). *National science education standards.* Washington, DC: National Academy Press.

Ovando, C. J., Collier, V. P., & Combs, M. C. (2003). *Bilingual and ESL classrooms: Teaching in multicultural contexts.* Boston: McGraw-Hill.

Selected Trade Books: The Earth in Space

For Younger Children

Bendick, J. (1991). *Artificial satellites: Helpers in space.* Brookfield, CT: Millbrook Press.

Bendick, J. (1991). *Comets and meteors: Visitors from space.* Brookfield, CT: Millbrook Press.

Branley, F. M. (1987). *Rockets and satellites.* New York: Harper & Row.

Branley, F. M. (1991). *The big dipper.* New York: HarperCollins.

Branley, F. M. (1998). *The planets in our solar system.* New York: HarperTrophy.

Branley, F. M. (1999). *The moon seems to change.* Topeka, KS: Econo-Clad Books.

Branley, F. M. (1999). *What makes day and night.* Topeka, KS: Econo-Clad Books.

Branley, F. M. (2000). *The International Space Station*. New York: HarperCollins.

Branley, F. M. (2000). *The sun, our nearest star*. New York: HarperCollins.

Coffelt, N. (1999). *Dogs in space*. Topeka, KS: Econo-Clad Books.

Cole, J. (1990). *The magic school bus lost in the solar system*. New York: Scholastic.

Cole, J. (1996). *The magic school bus out of this world: A book about space rocks*. New York: Scholastic.

Cole, J. (1999). *The magic school bus sees stars: A book about stars*. New York: Scholastic.

Donnelly, J. (1989). *Moonwalk: The first trip to the moon*. New York: Random House.

Fradin, D. (1984). *Spacelab*. Danbury, CT: Childrens Press.

Friskey, M. (1982). *Space shuttles*. Danbury, CT: Childrens Press.

Gorey, E., & Neumeyer, P. (1982). *Why we have day and night*. Santa Barbara, CA: Capra Press.

Hamer, M. (1983). *Night sky*. Danbury, CT: Watts.

Hasen, R. (1998). *Astronauts today*. New York: Random House.

Hort, L. (1991). *How many stars in the sky?* New York: Morrow.

Jackson, K. (1985). *The planets*. New York: Troll Associates.

Jay, M. (1987). *Planets*. Danbury, CT: Watts.

Lyon, G. (1990). *Come a tide*. New York: Orchard Books.

Polacco, P. (1996). *Meteor*. Ossining, NY: Paper Star.

Simon, S. (2004). *Space travelers*. San Francisco, CA: Seastar Publishing Co.

Stearns, C. (1998). *Where did all the water go?* Centreville, MD: Tidewater.

Weimer, T. E. (1993). *Space songs for children*. Pittsburgh, PA: Pearce-Evetts.

For Older Children

Adams, R. (1983). *Our wonderful solar system*. New York: Troll Associates.

Adler, I. (1980). *The stars: Decoding their messages*. New York: Thomas Y. Crowell.

Alexander, K. (1990). *The kid's book of space flight*. Philadelphia, PA: Running Press.

Asimov, I. (1990). *Projects in astronomy*. Milwaukee, WI: Gareth Stevens.

Asimov, I. (1991). *Ancient astronomy*. New York: Dell.

Becklake, S. (1998). *Space, stars, planets, and spacecraft*. Hillsdale, NJ: DK Publishing.

Bendick, J. (1982). *Space travel*. Danbury, CT: Watts.

Berger, M. (1983). *Bright stars, red giants, and white dwarfs*. New York: G. P. Putnam.

Branley, F. (1987). *Star guide*. New York: Harper & Row.

Buchanan, D. (1999). *Female firsts in their fields: Air and space*. Broomall, PA: Chelsea House.

Burnham, R. (2000). *The Readers' Digest children's atlas of the universe*. Pleasantville, NY: Reader's Digest Children's Books.

Cabellero, J. A. (1987). *Aerospace projects for young children*. Atlanta: Humanics.

Couper, H., & Henbest, N. (1987). *The moon*. Danbury, CT: Watts.

Dickinson, T. (1998). *Nightwatch: A practical guide to viewing the universe*. Willowdale, Ontario: Firefly Books.

Fichter, G. S. (1982). *Comets and meteors*. Danbury, CT: Watts.

Furniss, T. (1987). *Let's look at outer space*. Danbury, CT: Watts.

Gallant, R. A. (1983). *Once around the galaxy*. Danbury, CT: Watts.

Gardner, R. (1988). *Projects in space science*. Parsippany, NJ: Julian Messner.

Harris, A., & Weissman, P. (1990). *The great voyager adventure: A guided tour through the solar system*. Parsippany, NJ: Julian Messner.

Harris, R. (1999). *I can read about the sun and other stars*. Topeka, KS: Econo-Clad Books.

Kelch, J. (1990). *Small worlds: Exploring the 60 moons of our solar system*. Parsippany, NJ: Julian Messner.

Koppes, S. N. (2003). *Killer rocks from outer space: Asteroids, comets, and meteorites*. Minneapolis, MN: Carolrhoda Books/Lerner.

Lauber, P. (1982). *Journey to the planets*. New York: Crown.

Lewellen, J. (1981). *Moon, sun, and stars*. Danbury, CT: Childrens Press.

Myring, L. (1982). *Sun, moon, and planets*. Toronto, Ontario: EDC Press.

Richard, G. (1987). *Spacecraft*. Danbury, CT: Watts.

Ride, S., & O'Shaughnessy, T. (2003). *Exploring our solar system*. New York: Crown Books for Young Readers.

Ridpath, I. (1991). *Space*. Danbury, CT: Watts.

Riley, P. D. (1986). *The earth and space*. New York: David & Charles.

Shepherd, D. (1995). *Auroras: Light shows in the night sky*. Danbury, CT: Watts.

Simon, S. (1982). *The long journey from space*. New York: Crown.

Simon, S. (1984). *The moon*. Portland, OR: Four Winds.

Simon, S. (1999). *Comets, meteors, and asteroids*. Topeka, KS: Econo-Clad Books.

Vogt, G. (1982). *Mars and the inner planets*. Danbury, CT: Watts.

Vogt, G. (1987). *Space laboratories*. Danbury, CT: Watts.

Wood, R. (1991). *Thirty-nine easy astronomy experiments*. Silver Springs, MD: Tab Books.

Resource Books

AIMS Project Team. (1998). *Gravity rules!* Fresno, CA: AIMS Education Foundation.

Beals, K., Erickson, J., & Sneider, C. (2000). *Messages from space*. Berkeley, CA: Great Explorations in Math and Science. (solar system and beyond)

Butzow, C. M., & Butzow, J. W. (1989). *Science through children's literature: An integrated approach*. Englewood, CO: Teacher Ideas Press. (astronomy and outer space topics on pp. 158–168)

Engelbert, P., & Dupuis, D. (1998). *The handy space answer book*. Detroit, MI: Visible Ink Press.

Fredericks, A. D., Meinbach, A. M., & Rothlein, L. (1993). *Thematic units: An integrated approach to teaching science and social studies*. New York: HarperCollins. (earth, sun, and moon topics on pp. 161–167; space exploration on pp. 210–217)

Glaser, D., Willard, C., Beals, K., & Pompea, S. (2002). *Living with a star*. Berkeley, CA: Great Explorations in Math and Science.

Gould, A., Willard, C., & Pompea, S. (2000). *The real reasons for the seasons*. Berkeley, CA: Great Explorations in Math and Science.

Shaw, D. G., & Dybdahl, C. S. (1996). *Integrating science and language arts: A sourcebook for K–6 teachers*. Boston: Allyn & Bacon. (rocket and space travel topics on pp. 213–230)

Sneider, C. I., & Bergman, L. (Eds.). (1999). *Earth, moon, and stars*. Berkeley, CA: Great Explorations in Math and Science.

Sneider, C. I., & Bergman, L. (Eds.). (1999). *Experimenting with model rockets*. Berkeley, CA: Great Explorations in Math and Science.

Sutter, D., Gould, A., & Sneider, C. (1999). *Moons of Jupiter*. Berkeley, CA: Great Explorations in Math and Science. (reenact Galileo's telescopic study)

Wiebe, A., Cordel, B., & Hillen, J. (1994). *Out of this world*. Fresno, CA: AIMS Education Foundation.

Young, R. (2000). *Astronomy thematic unit*. Huntington Beach, CA: Teacher Created Materials.

General Sources of Activities

American Association for the Advancement of Science, & Walthall, B. (Ed.). (1995). *IdeAAAS: Sourcebook for science, mathematics, & technology education.* Washington, DC: Learning Team.

American Chemical Society. (2001). *The best of wonderscience* (Vol. 2). Belmont, CA: Wadsworth.

Cothron, J., Giese, R., & Rezba, R. (2002). *Science experiments by the hundreds* (2nd ed.). Dubuque, IA: Kendall/Hunt.

DeVito, A. *Creative sciencing.* Minneapolis, MN: Sagebrush Educational Resources.

Freidl, A., & Koontz, T. (2004). *Teaching science to children: An inquiry approach.* New York: McGraw-Hill Higher Education.

Sewall, S. (1990). *Hooked on science: Ready-to-use discovery activities for grades 4–8.* West Nyack, NY: Center for Applied Research in Education.

Stringer, J. (Ed.). (1996). *Science and technology ideas for the under 85.* Hatfield, Herts., UK: Association for Science Education.

Stringer, J. (Ed.). (1998). *More science and technology ideas for the under 85.* Hatfield, Herts., UK: Association for Science Education.

Strongin, H. (1991). *Science on a shoestring.* Reading, MA: Addison-Wesley.

Van Cleave, J. P. (1989–1999). *Science for every kid* (5 volumes: biology, chemistry, earth, astronomy, physics). New York: John Wiley.

Others

Also visit the AIMS Education Foundation (*http://www.aimsedu.org/*), Great Explorations in Math and Science (*http://www.lhs.berkeley.edu/GEMS/ gems.html*), National Science Teachers Association (*www.nsta.org*), and the Association for Science Education (*http://www.ase.org.uk/*) for new activity books and ideas.

Teacher Periodicals

Discover, 114 Fifth Ave., New York, NY 10011. (monthly; interesting, up-to-date information about developments in science; *http://www.discover.com/*)

Journal of Elementary Science Education, (*http://static.highbeam.com/j/journalofelementaryscience.education/*) (practical and theoretical articles related to elementary science teaching and learning)

Journal of Science Teacher Education, contact Jon Pederson, Association for the Education of Teachers in Science Executive Secretary, University of Oklahoma, Norman, OK 73070; *pedersenj@ou.edu.* (practical and scholarly articles related to teacher preservice, teacher in-service, and science teaching)

School Science and Mathematics, *http://oreganstate.edu/pubs/ssm/* (monthly; nine issues a year; includes articles on methods and research)

Science, American Association for the Advancement of Science. (accurate, up-to-date nontechnical information about developments in science; *http://www.scienceonline.org/*)

Science Activities, Heldref Publications, 1319 Eighteenth Street, NW, Washington, DC 20036-1802. (10 issues a year; useful activities for teachers of the upper grades and beyond; *http://www.heldref.org*)

Science and Children, National Science Teachers Association, 1840 Wilson Blvd., Arlington, VA 22201-3000. (monthly; eight issues a year; articles of interest and practical value to elementary school teachers; *www.nsta.org/*)

Science Education, John Wiley and Sons, Inc., 605 Third Ave., New York, NY 10158. For individual subscriptions contact Jon Pederson, Association for the Education of Teachers in Science Executive Secretary, University of Oklahoma, Norman, OK 73070; *pedersenj@ou.edu.* (reports of research and essays on the teaching of elementary and secondary school science)

Science News. (weekly; brief, easy-to-read reports on current findings of scientific research; *http://www.sciencenews.org/*)

CHILDREN'S PERIODICALS

National Geographic Kids Magazine, National Geographic Society, 1145 17th St. NW, Washington, DC 20036. (monthly; articles on environmental features of interest to children; *http://www.nationalgeographic.com/world/*)

Odyssey, Cobblestone Publishing Company, 30 Grove St., Suite C, Peterborough, NH 03458. (bimonthly; full-color astronomy and space magazine for children 7–13; *http://www.odysseymagazine.com/*)

Ranger Rick Nature Magazine, National Wildlife Federation, 11100 Wildlife Center Drive, Reston, VA 20190–5362. (monthly; for children of elementary school age; interesting stories and pictures on natural subjects, including ecology; *Your Big Backyard* is for preschool and primary-level children; *http://www.nwf.org/kidzone/*)

3–2–1 Contact, Sesame Workshop, P.O. Box 2933, Boulder, CO 80322. (10 issues a year; experiments, puzzles, projects, and articles for children 8–14; *http://www.sesameworkshop.org/*)

Wonderscience, American Chemical Society, 1155 16th St., NW, Washington, DC 20036. (science activities for children; also includes *Best of Wonderscience; http://www.chemistry.org/portal/a/c/s/1/acsdisplay.html?DOC= education%5curriculum%5cwondsci.html* and *http://www. chemistry.org/portal/a/c/s/1/wondernetdisplay.html?DOC= wondernet\topics_list\index.html*)

PROFESSIONAL TEXTS

Abruscato, J. (2004). *Teaching children science: A discovery approach* (6th ed.). Needham Heights, MA: Allyn & Bacon/Pearson Education. (methods, activities, and content for elementary school science)

Barba, R. H. (1998). *Science in the multicultural classroom: A guide to teaching and learning* (2nd ed.). Needham Heights, MA: Allyn & Bacon. (elementary science methods)

Carin, A., & Bass, J. (2005). *Teaching science as inquiry* (10th ed.). Upper Saddle River, NJ: Merrill/Prentice Hall. (methods and activities, with emphasis on discovery teaching)

Ebenezer, J., & Conner, S. (1998). *Learning to teach science: A model for the 21st century.* Upper Saddle River, NJ: Merrill/Prentice Hall. (methods and activities, with emphasis on discovery teaching)

Esler, W. K., & Esler, M. K. (2000). *Teaching elementary science* (8th ed.). Belmont, CA: Wadsworth. (methods and subject matter; exemplifies and applies three kinds of lessons)

Gabel, D. (1993). *Introductory science skills.* Prospect Heights, IL: Waveland Press. (a laboratory approach to learning science and mathematics skills and basic chemistry)

Harlan, J., & Rivkin, M. (2004). *Science experiences for the early childhood years: An integrated affective approach* (8th ed.). Upper Saddle River, NJ: Merrill/Prentice Hall. (everyday science activities for younger children)

Howe, A. C. (2002). *Engaging children in science* (3rd ed.). Upper Saddle River, NJ: Merrill/Prentice Hall. (elementary science methods)

Krajcik, J., Czerniak, C., & Berger, C. (1999). *Teaching children science: A project-based approach.* New York: McGraw-Hill.

Lind, K. K. (1999). *Exploring science in early childhood: A developmental approach* (3rd ed.). Albany, NY: Delmar. (elementary science methods)

Martin, D. J. (2003). *Elementary science methods: A constructivist approach* (3rd ed.). Albany, NY: Delmar. (elementary science methods)

Martin, R. E., Jr., Sexton, C., & Gerlovich, J. (2005). *Teaching science for all children: Inquiry lessons for constructing understanding* (3rd ed.). Needham Heights, MA: Allyn & Bacon. (methods and content of elementary school science)

Rezba, R., Sprague, C., Fiel, R. L., & Funk, H. J. (2002). *Learning and assessing science process skills* (4th ed.). Dubuque, IA: Kendall Hunt. (process skill development and assessment)

Tolman, M. N. (2001). *Discovering elementary science: Method, content, and problem-solving activities* (3rd ed.). Needham Heights, MA: Allyn & Bacon. (elementary science methods and content)

Victor, E., & Kellough, R. (2000). *Science K-8: An integrated approach* (10th ed.). Upper Saddle River, NJ: Merrill/Prentice Hall. (methods, content, and activities; features an extensive scope of subject matter in outline form)

AGENCIES AND SOCIETIES

The Association for Science Teacher Education (ASTE), contact Walter S. Smith and Caryl Kelley Smith, ASTE Executive Secretaries, Department of Biology, Ball State University, Muncie, IN 47306-0440, *wsmith@bsu.edu* (WSS) or *eelslake1@aol.com* (CKS and WSS) (*http://theASTE.org*).

Computer Learning Foundation, P.O. Box 60007, Palo Alto, CA 94306-0007 (*http://www.computerlearning.org/*).

Foundation for Science and Disability, E. C. Keller, Jr., Treasurer, 236 Grand St., Morgantown, WV 26506-6057 (*http://www.as.wvu.edu/~scidis/organizations/FSD_brochure.html*).

The Franklin Institute Science Museum, 222 North 20th Street, Philadelphia, PA 19103, (215) 448-1200 (*http://www.fi.edu/*).

International Council of Associations for Science Education (ICASE), Jack B. Holbrook, Executive Secretary, ICASE, P.O. Box 6138, Limassol, Cyprus.

National Audubon Society, 700 Broadway, New York, NY 10003, (212) 979-3000, fax (212) 979-3188 (*http://www.audubon.org/*).

National Energy Foundation, 3676 California Ave. Suite A117, Salt Lake City, UT 84104 (*http://www.nefl.org/*).

National Science Foundation, 4201 Wilson Blvd., Arlington, VA 22230 (*http://nsf.gov/*).

National Science Teachers Association, 1840 Wilson Boulevard, Arlington, VA 22201-3000, (703) 243-7100 (*http://www.nsta.org/*).

National Weather Service, 1325 East West Highway, Silver Spring, MD 20910 (*http://www.nws.noaa.gov/*).

Office of Indian Education Programs, Bureau of Indian Affairs (*http://oiep.bia.edu/*).

Society for Advancement of Chicanos and Native Americans in Science (SACNAS), P.O. Box 8526, Santa Cruz, CA 95061, (831) 459–0170 (*http://www.sacnas.org/*).

Technical Education Resource Center, 2067 Massachusetts Ave., Cambridge, MA 02140, (617) 547-0430, fax (617) 349-3535 (*http://www.terc.edu/*).

U.S. Environmental Protection Agency, Ariel Rios Bldg., 1200 Pennsylvania Ave. NW, Washington, DC 20460, (202) 272-0167 (*http://www.epa.gov/*).

U.S. Geological Survey, Information Services (*http://www.usgs.gov/*).

SCIENCE CURRICULUM PROJECTS

ACTIVITIES FOR INTEGRATING MATHEMATICS AND SCIENCE (AIMS)

Grades K–8. This program, developed at Fresno (California) Pacific College, was originally funded by the National Science Foundation to train a group of teachers in the rationale and methods for integrating science and mathematics in grades 5–8. The classroom testing of written materials produced such positive results that a full-fledged writing project was launched to develop additional teaching booklets. Materials are now available for K–8.

The rationale for AIMS includes these points: (a) Mathematics and science are integrated outside the classroom and so should also be integrated inside it; (b) as in the real world, a whole series of mathematics skills and science processes should be interwoven in a single activity to create a continuum of experience; (c) the materials should present questions that relate to the students' world and arouse their curiosity; (d) the materials should change students from observers to participants in the learning process; and (e) the investigations should be enjoyable because learning is more effective when the process is enjoyed.

For more information, write to AIMS Education Foundation, 1595 S. Chestnut Ave., Fresno, CA 93702-4706 (*http://www.aimsedu.org/*), 888-733-2467.

FULL OPTION SCIENCE SYSTEM (FOSS)

Grades K–6. The FOSS program is designed to serve both regular and most special education students in a wide cross section of schools. Developed at the Lawrence Hall of Science, in Berkeley, California, the program features several modules at each grade level that include science lesson plans in the earth, life, and physical sciences and extension activities in language, computer, and mathematics applications.

The laboratory equipment includes several package options, from complete kits to individual items. Materials assembly directions show how teacher and students can gather and construct equipment for many activities. A correlation table tells how to integrate activities with other programs and state department of education guidelines for science.

Much care is taken to have a suitable match between activities and students' ability to think at different ages. Further work has made the program easy to instruct and manage. Provisions for preparation time, ease of giving out and retrieving materials, cleanup, storage, and resupply have continually guided program developers.

The commercial distributor of FOSS is Delta Education, 80 Northwest Blvd., P.O. Box 3000, Nashua, NH 03061-3000, 800-258-1302 (*http://www.delta-ed.com/*, *http://www.lawrencehallofscience.org/foss/*).

GREAT EXPLORATIONS IN MATH AND SCIENCE (GEMS)

Grades Preschool–9. Gems is a growing resource for activity-based science and mathematics. Developed at the University of California at Berkeley's Lawrence Hall of Science and tested in thousands of classrooms nationwide, more than 50 GEMS teacher's guides and handbooks offer a wide spectrum of learning opportunities from preschool and kindergarten through 10th grade. GEMS guides can be integrated into your curriculum or stand on their own as a stimulating way to involve students. The GEMS series interweaves a number of educational ideas and goals. GEMS guides encompass important learning objectives, summarized on the front page of each guide, under the headings of skills, concepts, science themes, mathematics strands, and the nature of science and mathematics. Taken together, these headings help provide a summary of the unit objectives. These objectives can be directly and flexibly related to science and mathematics curricula, local and district guidelines, state frameworks, benchmarks, and the national standards. For more on flexible ways to build your own curricula using GEMS, contact the University of California, GEMS, Lawrence Hall of Science #5200, Berkeley, CA 94720-5200 (*http://lhsgems.org/gems.html*).

NATIONAL GEOGRAPHIC KIDS NETWORK

Grades 4–6. The National Geographic Kids Network is a program that has children gather data on real science problems and then use a computer network to share their data with a scientist and children in other locations. The developer is the Technical Education Resource Center (TERC) in partnership with the National Geographic Society, which publishes and distributes the program.

Each instructional unit is 6 weeks long and focuses on a central science problem. Children learn to ask questions and gather data in scientifically acceptable ways. The data are transmitted to an interested scientist who analyzes the data, answers children's questions, and then sends back an overview of all the collected information from cooperating schools. Curriculum materials include children's handbooks that have background information on the topic of study, teacher guides, and computer software. The software is made up of a word-processing program, data charts, and a computer map of North America, all of which are used to ready and transmit data. For details, write National Geographic Society, 1145 17th St. NW, Washington, DC 20036-4688 (*http://www. nationalgeographic.com/kids/*), 800-647-5463.

OUTDOOR BIOLOGY INSTRUCTIONAL STRATEGIES (OBIS)

Ages 10–15. Developed at the Lawrence Hall of Science, University of California (Berkeley), OBIS is designed for use with community youth organizations and schools that want to offer outdoor laboratory experiences. Four activity packets offer a broad selection of interesting, firsthand activities for studying ecological relationships in different environments: desert, seashore, forest, pond and stream, city lots, and local parks. Each activity card consists of background information for the leader, description of materials needed and any advance preparation required, a lesson plan, and several follow-up suggestions. Each activity can be used alone or as part of a developmental sequence. For more information see *http://www.lawrencehallofscience.org/OBIS/OBISpubs.html*, University of California, OBIS, Lawrence Hall of Science #5200, Berkeley, CA 94720-5200.

SCIENCE FOR LIFE AND LIVING

Grades K–6. The full name for this curriculum is "Teaching Relevant Activities for Concepts and Skills." The developer is the BSCS Group, a nonprofit foundation for science education.

After readiness activities at the kindergarten level, these concepts and skills form the main curriculum structure: order and organization (grade 1); change and measurement (grade 2); patterns and prediction (grade 3); systems and analysis (grade 4); energy and investigation (grade 5); and balance and decisions (grade 6). Children build their own understanding of an integrated world of science, technology, and health as they work through activities that bring out the concepts and skills.

Each complete lesson contains five consecutive phases: (a) An engagement activity begins the lesson. Children connect what they know to the current material and reveal their prior knowledge, including misconceptions. (b) Exploration follows, in which students explore the materials or environment and form a common base of experience. (c) An explanation phase gives students a chance to describe what they are learning and gives the teacher an opportunity to state the intended learning. (d) Elaboration then provides activities that extend understandings and give further chances to practice skills. (e) The last phase, evaluation, allows students and teacher to assess what has been learned.

Published materials are available from the Kendall/Hunt Publishing Company, 4050 Westmark Drive, P.O. Box 1840, Dubuque, IA 52004-1840 (*http://www. kendallhunt.com/*).

SCIENCE AND TECHNOLOGY FOR CHILDREN (STC)

Grades 1–6. The developer of the STC curriculum project is the National Science Resources Center, established in 1985 by the National Academy of Sciences and the Smithsonian Institution to improve the teaching of science and mathematics in the nation's schools. The project's mission is to increase significantly the number of schools that offer hands-on science programs to children and to interest more females and minority members in science.

Teaching units include such titles as Weather (grade K–1), The Life Cycle of Butterflies (grade 2), Plant Growth and Development (grade 3), Electric Circuits (grade 4), Microworlds (grade 5), and Magnets and Motors (grade 6). They are designed to focus on easy-to-use materials and integrate science with other areas of the curriculum. Each unit includes a teacher's guide; pupil activity booklet; description of needed materials; and annotated lists of recommended trade books, computer software, and audiovisual materials.

The developers sought to make the management of materials and activities as practical as possible. In the field testing of units, evaluation procedures monitored how well the units worked under a wide variety of classroom conditions.

For details, contact the National Science Resources Center, 901 D St. SW, Suite 704B, Washington, DC 20024 (*http://www.nsrconline.org/*).

SCIENCE CURRICULUM IMPROVEMENT STUDY (SCIS)

Grades K–6. SCIS is organized on a base of powerful and modern science concepts. Each of 12 instructional units features a central concept, with supporting subconcepts and process skills integrated into the activities.

Lessons have three parts: exploration, invention, and discovery. In the exploratory part, children are given objects to observe or manipulate. At times, these observations are guided by the teacher; otherwise, the children observe and manipulate the objects as they wish.

Explorations allow firsthand contact with the material under study and provide a basis for children to use language. At the same time, the need arises for an explanation to make sense out of what has been observed. This is taken up in the second part of the lesson sequence. After discussion, the teacher gives a definition and a word for the new concept.

This "invention" of a concept sets up the third part of the lesson. Now, children are given a variety of further experiences within which they discover many applications of the concept. These extend and reinforce their knowledge and skills.

An updated version of this program, SCIS3, is available from Delta Education, 80 Northwest Blvd., P.O. Box 3000, Nashua, NH 03061-3000 (*http://www.delta-ed.com/*).

SCIENCE IN A NUTSHELL

Grades K–8. Real fun with real science. Discover how exciting real science can be with Delta's Science in a Nutshell mini-kit series. Introduce or enhance specific science content areas in the classroom, at home, in a resource room, or in an after-school program. Clearly written, hands-on activities challenge young scientists aged 6–12 to investigate their world. Mini-kits are suitable for use with individuals or with small groups of two to three. Contact Delta Education, 80 Northwest Blvd., P.O. Box 3000, Nashua, NH 03061-3000 (*http://www.delta-ed.com/*).

WONDERSCIENCE

Wonderscience offers hands-on science activities for elementary school teachers and students. The *Best of WonderScience* was developed as a joint effort of the American Chemical Society (ACS), and the American Institute of Physics. The ACS is at toll-free 1-800-227-5558 (*http://www.chemistry.org/portal/a/c/s/1/acsdisplay.html?DOC=education%5curriculum%5cwondsci.html*).

COMMERCIAL SCIENCE SUPPLIERS

The following classifications of suppliers may not be entirely accurate, because suppliers often change offerings with business conditions. A current catalog should reveal the full scope of materials for sale in each case. Use school stationery when requesting free elementary-level catalogs. An annual, comprehensive listing of suppliers accompanies each January issue of *Science and Children*.

GENERAL SUPPLIES

Wisconsin Fast Plants Program, University of Wisconsin-Madison, Science House, 1630 Linden Drive, Madison, WI 53706, 1-800-462-7417 (*http://www.fastplants.org/ _home_flash.html*), info@fastplants.org.

Carolina Biological Supply Company, 2700 York Road, Burlington, NC 27215 (*http://www.carolina.com/*, carolina@carolina.com, 800-334-3551.

Delta Education, 80 Northwest Blvd., P.O. Box 3000, Nashua, NH 03061-3000 (*http://www.delta-ed.com/*).

Edmund Scientific Company, 60 Pearce Ave, Tonawanda, NY 14150, 1-800-728-6999 (*http://www.edsci.com/*).

Frey Scientific Company, P.O. Box 8101, 100 Paragon Parkway, Mansfield, OH 44903, 1-800-225-3739 (*http://www.freyscientific.com/*).

Ward's Natural Science Establishment, 5100 West Henrietta Road, P.O. Box 92912, Rochester, NY 14692-9012, 800-962-2660, (*http://www.wardsci.com/*).

BALANCES

Ohaus Scale Corporation, 19A Chapin Road, P.O. Box 2033, Pine Brook, NJ 07058, 800-672-7722 ext. 7804 (*http://www.ohaus.com/*).

MICROSCOPES AND MICROPROJECTORS

Brock Optical, 1959 Barber Road, Sarasota, FL 34240, 941-342-7727 (*http://www.magiscope.com/*).

Leica Microsystems, Inc., 90 Boroline Rd., Allendale, NJ 07401, 201-236-5900 (*http://www.discovermicroscopy.com/ website/sc_ead1.nsf*).

Ken-A-Vision Manufacturing Company, 5615 Raytown Road, Raytown, MO 64133 (*http://www.ken-a-vision.com/*) 800-501-7366, info@ken-a-vision.com.

Swift Optics, 1190 North 4th St., San Jose, CA 95112, 800-523-4544 (*http://www.swift-optics.com/*).

AQUARIA, TERRARIA, CAGES

Carolina Biological Supply Company, 2700 York Road, Burlington, NC 27215 (*http://www.carolina.com/*), carolina@carolina.com, 800-334-3551.

Delta Education, 80 Northwest Blvd., P.O. Box 3000, Nashua, NH 03061-3000 (*http://www.delta-ed.com/*).

Frey Scientific Company, P.O. Box 8101, 100 Paragon Parkway, Mansfield, OH 44903, 1-800-225-3739 (*http://www.freyscientific.com/*).

KITS AND MODELS

Delta Education, 80 Northwest Blvd., P.O. Box 3000, Nashua, NH 03061-3000 (*http://www.delta-ed.com/*).

SOFTWARE

Scholastic Software & Multimedia, 2931 East McCarty Street, Jefferson City, MO 65101, 1-800-724-6527 (*http://scholastic.com/*).

Sunburst Technology, Inc., 1550 Executive Drive, Elgin, IL 60123, 1-800-321-7511 (*http://store.sunburst.com/*).

APPENDIX D

ENVIRONMENTS AND NUTRITION FOR CLASSROOM ANIMALS

Animal[1]	Environment	Nutrition[2]
Ants	Glass terrarium or large jar with dirt (covered with black paper)	Small food scraps or dead insects
Birds	Bird cage (ensure cage is large enough for bird to move freely)	Birdseed (nutritional mix from pet store—not wild bird seed)
Butterflies and Moths	Butterfly "tent" (sold in kits) or large jar with wire screen on top with small branches	Sugar water solution
Caterpillars	Medium-sized jar with holes in lid; includes a small branch	Leaves (preferably near to where they were found)
Chameleons and Lizards	Aquarium with screened top; dirt, stones, and branches on bottom	Mealworms or live insects
Fish	Aquarium with gravel and filter (dechlorinate water before use)	Fish food from pet store (do not overfeed); brine shrimp
Frogs and Toads	Aquarium with shallow water and rocks to climb out of the water	Mealworms, small caterpillars, or live insects
Fruit Flies	Small jars with fine mesh covering	A small amount of overly ripe fruit
Guinea Pigs and Rats	Large animal cage with secure openings and an exercise wheel	Guinea pig food; small amounts of fresh fruit and vegetables
Hamsters, Gerbils, and Mice	Medium or large animal cage with secure openings and an exercise wheel	Hamster or gerbil food; small amounts of fresh fruit and vegetables
Mealworms	Wide jar or plastic bucket with screen or mesh cover	Oatmeal and small slices of fresh apple
Newts and Salamanders	Aquarium with shallow water and rocks rising above water line	Mealworms and live insects
Rabbits	Large animal cage (rabbits will chew on cage, so avoid wood)	Rabbit pellets, fresh vegetables (avoid too much lettuce)
Snakes	Terrarium with secure openings; heating device (contact pet shop)	Live mice or insects (contact pet shop for specifics)
Spiders	Glass jar covered with screen	Live insects
Tadpoles	Aquarium 1/4 filled with water and rocks above the water line	Small insects or finely chopped meat
Turtles (land)	Terrarium with nonpoisonous plants and water pool	Mealworms, insects, earthworms; finely chopped vegetables
Turtles (aquatic)	Aquarium that is mostly water covered, but with small land area	Mealworms, insects, earthworms; finely chopped vegetables

[1]Contact the National Science Teachers Association (1840 Wilson Blvd., Arlington, VA 22201-3000 for the Guidelines for Responsible Use of Animals in the Classroom.

[2]All animals require plenty of fresh water. To remove the chlorine from water, leave it standing overnight.

SUMMARY OF CHILDREN'S THINKING

Thought Process	Intuitive Thought[1]	Concrete Operations	Formal Operations
Cause and Effect	Logic often contradictory, unpredictable. Events may occur by magic or for human convenience.	Contradictions avoided. Physical objects are linked to show cause and effect. Commonsense explanations may be wrong but logical.	Can separate logic from content. Systematic control of variables possible, as well as hypothetical "thought experiments," to test ideas.
Relative Thinking	Egocentric perceptions and language. Little grasp of how vertebrates interrelate. Physical properties viewed in absolute, not relative, ways.	Perceptions of position and objects more objective. Aware of others' views. Some understanding of interrelated variables, when connected to concrete objects and pictures.	Understand relative position and motion. Can define and explain abstract concepts with other concepts or analogies. May temporarily show some egocentricity in propositions.
Classifying and Ordering	Sort one property at a time. Little or no class inclusion. Trial-and-error ordering in early part of stage.	Understand class inclusion principle. More consistent seriation with diverse objects. Can follow successive steps, less discrete thinking.	Can recombine groups into fewer, more abstract categories. Can form hierarchical systems.
Conservative Thinking	Mostly do not conserve. Perceptions dominate thinking. Center attention on one variable and do not compensate. Little or no reverse thinking.	Can reverse thinking, consider several variables and compensate. Conserve most of the Piagetian test concepts.	Conserve all of the Piagetian test concepts, with displaced and solid volume usually last.

Table based on a format suggested by Robert Mele.
[1]Intuitive thought is the last period of the preoperational stage.

STATE EDUCATION AGENCIES

Alabama
Alabama State Dept. of Education
Gordon Persons Bldg.
Montgomery, AL 36130
(*http://www.alsde.edu/*)

Alaska
State of Alaska
Dept. of Education
801 W. 10th St., Ste. 200
Juneau, AK 99801-1894
(*http://www.educ.state.ak.us/*)

Arizona
Arizona Dept. of Education
1535 W. Jefferson St.,
Phoenix, AZ 85007
(*http://www.ade.state.az.us/*)

Arkansas
Arkansas Dept. of Education
4 State Capitol Mall
Little Rock, AR 72201
(*http://arkedu.state.ar.us/*)

Bureau of Indian Affairs
Dept. of Interior, BIA
1849 C St., NW
Mail Stop 3525, Code 521, MIB
Washington, DC 20240
(*http://www.doi.gov/bureau-indian-affairs.html*)

California
State Dept. of Education
1430 N. Street
Sacramento, CA 95814
(*http://www.cde.ca.gov/*)

Colorado
Colorado Dept. of Education
201 E. Colfax Ave.
Denver, CO, 80203
(*http://www.cde.state.co.us/index_home.htm*)

Connecticut
State Dept. of Education
165 Capitol Ave.
Hartford, CT 06145
(*http://www.state.ct.us/sde/*)

Delaware
State Dept. of Public Instruction
Townsend Bldg.
401 Federal St., Suite 2
Dover, DE 19901
(*http://www.doe.state.de.us/*)

District of Columbia
Education Program
D.C. Public Schools
415 12th St., NW, Rm. 1004
Washington, DC 20004
(*http://www.k12.dc.us/dcps/home.html*)

Department of Defense
4040 N. Fairfax Dr.
Arlington, VA 22203
(*http://www.dodea.edu/*)

Florida
Florida Dept. of Education
Florida Education Center, Ste. 522
Tallahassee, FL 32399
(*http://www.fldoe.org*)

Georgia
Georgia Dept. of Education
1862 Twin Towers East
Atlanta, GA 30334
(*http://www.doe.k12.ga.us/index.asp*)

Hawaii
Education Program
1390 Miller St.
Honolulu, HI 96804
(*http://doe.k12.hi.us/*)

Idaho
Idaho State Dept. of Education
650 W. State St.
P.O. Box 83720
Boise, ID 83720-0027
(*http://www.sde.state.id.us/Dept/*)

Illinois
Illinois State Board of Education
100 N. First St.
Springfield, IL 62777-0001
(*http://www.isbe.state.il.us/*)

Indiana
Indiana Dept. of Education
Rm. 229 State House
Indianapolis, IN 46204-2798
(*http://www.doe.state.in.us/*)

Iowa
State of Iowa
Department of Education
Grimes State Office Building
Des Moines, IA 50319-0146
(*http://www.state.ia.us/educate/index.html*)

Kansas
Kansas Dept. of Education
120 S.E. 10th St.
Topeka, KS 66612-1103
(*http://www.ksbe.state.ks.us/*)

Kentucky
Kentucky Dept. of Education
Capitol Plaza Tower
500 Mero St.
Frankfort, KY 40601
(*http://www.education.ky.gov*)

Louisiana
State Dept. of Education
P.O. Box 94064
Baton Rouge, LA 70804-9064
(*http://www.louisianaschools.net/lde/
    index.html*)

Maine
Maine State Dept. of Education
State House Station #23
Augusta, ME 04333
(*http://www.state.me.us/education/
    homepage.htm*)

Maryland
Maryland State Dept. of Education
200 W. Baltimore St.
Baltimore, MD 21201-2595
(*http://www.marylandpublicschools.
    org/msde*)

Massachusetts
Massachusetts Dept. of Education
350 Main St.
Malden, MA 02148-5023
(*http://www.doe.mass.edu/*)

Michigan
Michigan Dept. of Education
P.O. Box 30008
Lansing, MI 48909
(*http://www.michigan.gov/mde*)

Minnesota
Minnesota Dept. of Education
1500 Highway 36 West
St. Paul, MN 55113
(*http://education.state.mn.us/html/mde_
    home.htm*)

Mississippi
State Dept. of Education
Walter Sillers Bldg., Ste. 501
P.O. Box 771
Jackson, MS 39205-0771
(*http://www.mde.k12.ms.us/*)

Missouri
Missouri Dept. of Education
Dept. of Elementary & Secondary
    Education
P.O. Box 480
Jefferson, MO 65102
(*http://www.dese.state.mo.us/*)

Montana
Office of Public Instruction
State Capitol Bldg.
Helena, MT 59620
(*http://www.opi.state.mt.us/*)

Nebraska
Nebraska Dept. of Education
301 Centennial Mall South
P.O. Box 94987
Lincoln, NE 68509-4987
(*http://www.nde.state.ne.us/*)

Nevada
Nevada Dept. of Education
Capitol Complex
Carson City, NV 89710
(*http://www.doe.nv.gov/*)

New Hampshire
New Hampshire Dept. of Education
1010 Pleasant St.
Concord, NH 03301
(*http://www.ed.state.nh.us/*)

New Jersey
New Jersey Dept. of Education
Division of Standards and Assessment
CN 500
Trenton, NJ 08625-0500
(*http://www.state.nj.us/education/*)

New Mexico
State of New Mexico
Dept. of Education
300 Don Gaspar
Santa Fe, NM 87501-2786
(*http://sde.state.nm.us/*)

New York
New York State Education Dept.
Bureau of Professional Career
    Opportunity Programs
Empire State Plaza
Cultural Education Center, Rm. 5C64
Albany, NY 12230
(*http://www.nysed.gov/*)

North Carolina
Dept. of Public Instruction
116 W. Edenton St.
Raleigh, NC 27603-1712
(*http://www.dpi.state.nc.us/*)

North Dakota
Dept. of Public Instruction
600 E. Boulevard Ave., Department 201
Bismark, ND 58505
(*http://www.dpi.state.nd.us/*)

Ohio
Ohio Dept. of Education
65 S. Front St.
Columbus, OH 43266-0208
(*http://www.ode.state.oh.us/*)

Oklahoma
State Dept. of Education
2500 N. Lincoln Blvd.
Oklahoma City, OK 73105-4599
(*http://sde.state.ok.us/*)

Oregon
Oregon Dept. of Education
700 Pringle Pkwy., S.S.
Salem, OR 97310
(*http://www.ode.state.or.us/*)

Pennsylvania
Pennsylvania Dept. of Education
8th Floor, 333 Market Street
Harrisburg, PA 17126-0333
(*http://www.pde.state.pa.us*)

Puerto Rico
Office of Education
Office 809
Dept. of Education
Hato Rey, PR 00919
(*http://www.eduportal.de.gobierno.pr/
    EDUportal/*)

Rhode Island
Rhode Island Dept. of Education
255 Westminster St.
Providence, RI 02903
(*http://www.ridoe.net/*)

South Carolina
South Carolina Dept. of Education
Curriculum Section
801 Rutledge Bldg.
Columbia, SC 29201
(*http://www.myscschools.com/*)

South Dakota
Dept. of Education and Cultural
   Affairs
700 Governors Dr.
Pierre, SD 57501-2291
(*http://www.state.sd.us/deca/*)

Tennessee
Tennessee Dept. of Education
4th Floor Northwing
Cordell Hull Bldg.
Nashville, TN 37243-0388
(*http://www.state.tn.us/education/*)

Texas
Texas Education Agency
1701 N. Congress
Austin, TX 78701
(*http://www.tea.state.tx.us/*)

Utah
Utah Dept. of Education
250 East 500 South
Salt Lake City, UT 84111
(*http://www.usoe.k12.ut.us/*)

Vermont
Vermont State Dept. of Education
120 State St.
Montpelier, VT 05602
(*http://www.state.vt.us/educ/*)

Virgin Islands
Dept. of Education
No. 44-46 Kongens Gade
Charlotte Amalie,
U.S. Virgin Islands 00802
(*http://www.usvi.org/education/*)

Virginia
Virginia Dept. of Education
P.O. Box 2120
Richmond, VA 23218-2120
(*http://www.pen.k12.va.us/*)

Washington
Office of Superintendent of Public
   Instruction
P.O. Box 47200
Olympia, WA 98504-7200
(*http://www.k12.wa.us/*)

West Virginia
West Virginia Dept. of Education
1900 Kanawha Blvd. East
Charleston, WV 25305
(*http://wvde.state.wv.us/*)

Wisconsin
Dept. of Public Education
125 S. Webster St.
P.O. Box 7841
Madison, WI 53707-7841
(*http://www.dpi.state.wi.us/*)

Wyoming
State Dept. of Education
241 Hathaway Bldg.
Cheyenne, WY 82002-0050
(*http://www.k12.wy.us/*)

INDEX

Page numbers for appendices are in italics.

Aardema, V., 365
Aaseng, N., 261
Absorbed sounds, 85–86
    reverberation and, 86
Acid rain, 340–341
Adams, R., 400
Adamsczyk, P., 116, 151
Adkins, J., 180
Adler, D., 116
Adler, D. A., 295
Adler, I., 116, 400
Agencies and societies, *3–4*
    state education agencies, *13–15*
Agler, L., 366
AIMS (Activities for Integrating Mathematics
        and Science), *5*
Air, and its properties
    activities, 342–349
    concepts, 349–351
    makeup of air, 351–352
    reality of air, 352
Air masses, 362–363
Air pressure, 351
    measuring, 364
Air temperature, 359
    and altitude, 359
    and pollution, 360
Albert, E., 63
Alexander, K., 400
Allington, R. L., 93
Allison, L., 295
Amaral, O. M., 113, 115
Amphibians, 234
    cold-blooded, 234
    frogs, 234
    reproduction, 235
    salamanders, 235
    toads, 234–235
Animal(s)
    ecosystems, 253–261
    habitats and their dwellers, 257–258
Animal classification
    activity, 218
    concepts, 218–220
    extensions, 220
    invertebrates. *See* Animals without
            backbones
    vertebrates. *See* Animals with backbones
Animals with backbones, 219
    activities, 221–225

amphibians. *See* Amphibians
birds. *See* Birds
concepts, 225–240
fish. *See* Fishes
mammals. *See* Mammals
reptiles. *See* Reptiles
Animals without backbones
    activities, 241–246
    brine shrimp, 244–245, 250, 251–252
    concepts, 246–252
    crayfish, 250–251
    earthworms, 252
    insects. *See* Insects
    snails, 245–246, 252
Aquariums, 237–240
Archambault, J., 35
Archimedes, 164
Ardley, N., 36, 63, 93, 151, 365
Arnold, N., 295
Arnov, B., 365
Asimov, I., 36, 400
Asteroid belt, 392
Atmosphere, 349
    exosphere, 350–351
    ionosphere, 350
    origins of, 352
    stratosphere, 350
    troposphere, 349
Aulenbach, N. H., 327
Axles. *See* Wheels and axles

Baca, E., 335, 365
Baca, L. M., 335, 365
Bailey, M. W., 151
Baines, R., 35, 180
Bains, R., 151
Bang, M., 365
Barber, J., 198, 214, 263, 366
Barkin, C., 180
Barrett, J., 365
Barrett, K., 262, 328
Barrett, N. S., 180
Barrett, S., 93
Bartch, M., 36, 64
Barton, B., 180
Barton, H. A., 327
Bates, J., 215
Batteries, 123
    connecting, 132–133
    current electricity, 149–150

Baylor, B., 327
Beals, K., 151, 262, 366, 400
Beaty, W., 35
Becklake, S., 400
Behm, B., 295
Bell, electric, 143
Bendick, J., 63, 399, 400
Benjamin, R. F., 366
Berg, C., 262
Berger, G., 295, 365
Berger, M., 36, 93, 151, 261, 295, 365, 400
Bergman, L., 328, 401
Berquist, L., 164, 180
Berry, L., 366
Bibliography, professional, *1–4*
Biotic potential, 259
Birch, B., 93, 151
Birds, 229
    beaks, 230, 231f
    chick, caring for, 232
    chick hatching, 231–232
    feet, 230, 231f
    flight adaptations, 230
    food, 229
    heat loss, 229–230
    reproduction, 231
    senses, 230
Bishop, P. R., 295
Blobaum, C., 327
Block and tackle pulleys, 172
Bones. *See* Skeletal system
Booth, E., 327
Borton, P., 115
Brain, 278
Bramwell, M., 327
Brandt, K., 93, 151
Branley, F., 115, 327, 365, 400
Branley, F. M., 327, 365, 399, 400
Branzei, S., 262
Breathing. *See* Respiratory system
Breeden, R., 261
Bright, M., 262, 365
Brine shrimp, 244–245, 250, 251–252
British thermal units (BTUs), 52
Brockel, R., 35
Broekel, R., 93
Brown, M. G., 180
Brown, R., 214
Brown, W. F., 180
Bruchac, J., 261

Brynie, F. H., 295
Buchanan, D., 400
Buds, 203–204
Bulbs, 123–124
Burnett, R., 198, 214, 262
Burnham, R., 400
Burton, J., 215
Busby, P., 180
Busch, P., 214
Butler, D., 327
Butterflies, 249, 250f
Butzow, C. M., 36, 64, 93, 151, 181, 215,
    262, 296, 328, 366, 400
Butzow, J., 215
Butzow, J. W., 36, 64, 93, 151, 181, 215, 262,
    296, 328, 366, 400
Buxton, C., 261

Cabellero, J. A., 400
Calories, 52
Carbohydrates, 292–293
Carbon dioxide-oxygen cycle, 260
Cardiopulmonary system
    circulatory system. See Circulatory system
    respiratory system. See Respiratory system
    and vital signs, 286–287
Carle, E., 35, 93, 261, 295, 365
Carratello, J., 220, 261
Carratello, P., 220, 261
Carroll, J., 35
Catherall, E., 36, 93, 116
Catlin, D., 180
Cave, V., 115
Challand, H., 151, 214, 327
Challand, H. J., 115
Challoner, J., 36
Chemical weathering, 307
Chicks
    caring for, 232
    hatching, 231–232
Children's thinking, 12
Circuit breakers, 140–141
Circuits
    closed and open, 120–125
    hazards, 140
    overloaded, 140
    series and parallel, 126–134
    short, 140
Circulatory system
    activity, 281–282
    concepts, 285, 286–287
Classroom animals
    environments and nutrition, 10–11
    mammals. See Classroom mammals
    snakes, 233–234
Classroom mammals, 227–228
    breeding, 229
    cage, 228
    food, 228
    handling, 228

Clemence, J., 151
Closed and open circuits
    activities, 120–123
    concepts, 123–125
Clouds, 362
Cobb, V., 63, 93, 151
Cochrane, J., 215
Coffelt, N., 400
Cohesion, 43–44
Coldrey, J., 215
Cole, J., 35, 63, 93, 151, 214, 295, 327,
    365, 400
Collier, V. P., 6, 35, 92, 180, 379, 399
Collins, D., 35
Color
    activities, 23–26
    concepts, 26–27
    digital camera pictures, 28–29
    mixing colors, 27–28
Combs, M. C., 6, 35, 92, 180, 379, 399
Comets, 392
Commercial science suppliers, 9
Condensation
    activity, 356
    dew, 361
    dew point, 361
    fog, 361–362
Conduction, 60
Conduction, convection and radiation
    activities, 54–59
    concepts, 59–61
Conductors, electrical, 138–139
Conservation
    of soil, 312–313
    of water, 341
Contraction. See Expansion and contraction
Convection, 60–61. See also Conduction,
    convection and radiation
Conway, L., 215
Cooper, M., 36
Cordel, B., 36, 64, 93, 181, 215, 262, 263,
    296, 328, 401
Corfield, B., 93
Corfield, R. B., 151
Cosner, S., 365
Couper, H., 400
Cousins, L., 261
Cowles, K., 93
Crayfish, 250–251
Crenson, V., 36, 262
Crews, D., 35
Crump, D., 261
Crump, M., 262
Cuff, K., 328
Curren, P., 151
Current electricity, 149–150
Cyclones and anticyclones, 363–364

Dalby, D. K., 27, 35
Daley, M. J., 63

Darwin, C., 214
Davidson, S., 295
Davis, K., 93
Day, J., 261
Dean, A., 262
De Bruin, J., 36, 151, 295, 365
Deery, R., 366
Density and light speeds, 20–21
deValenzuela, J. S., 335, 365
Dew, 361
DeWeese, B., 180
Dewey, J. O., 261
DeWitt, L., 365
Dew point, 361
Dickinson, J., 365
Dickinson, T., 400
Diet. See Food and nutrition
Digestive system
    activity, 288
    concepts, 288–289
Digital camera pictures, 28–29
Diller, H., 93
Dispezio, M., 36
Donnelly, J., 400
Dorros, A., 327, 365
Downs, R., 164, 180
Downs, S. F., 327
Dreyer, E., 261
Duerling, C. K., 63
Dunham, M., 36
Dupuis, D., 400
Dybdahl, C. S., 36, 116, 151, 181, 215, 263,
    296, 328, 366, 401

Earle, S. A., 262
Earthbooks Staff, 262
Earth-moon system, 384, 385f
Earthquakes and faults, 316, 317f
Earth's magnetism, 111
Earth's rotation
    activities, 370–374
    concepts, 374–377
Earth's surface
    building up of, 314–317
    earthquakes and faults, 316, 317f
    erosion. See Weathering and erosion
    magma, 315–316
    plate theory, 316
    rocks. See Rocks
    sample unit, 48f–52f
    soil. See Soil
    weathering. See Weathering and erosion
Earthworms, 252
Echoes, 81–82, 84–85
Echols, J. C., 215, 262, 263
Ecklund, L., 296, 328
Eclipses
    activity, 380–381
    concepts, 383–384

Ecosystems
    adaptations, 259
    animal life, 253–261
    biotic potential, 259
    carbon dioxide-oxygen cycle, 260
    material cycles, 261
    nitrogen cycle, 260
    plant life, 194–198
    pollution, 259
    and their energy, 258
    water cycle, 260–261
Ehlert, L., 35
Electrical connections, 125
Electrical flow
    activities, 135–138
    concepts, 138–141
Electric bell, 143
Electricity
    conductors, 138–139
    flow of. See Electrical flow
    generating, 146–150
    resistance, 139–140
    static, 146–147, 149
    voltage, 133–134
Electric motor, 144
Electromagnetic waves, 150
Electromagnets
    activities, 142
    concepts, 143–145
Elementary Science Study (ESS), 5–6
Elson, D., 365
Energy
    changing forms of, 59–60
    circuits. See Circuits
    electrical. See Electricity
    heat. See Heat energy
    sound. See Sound
Engelbert, P., 400
Erickson, G. L., 59, 63
Erickson, J., 151, 400
Erickson, S., 181
Erosion. See Weathering and erosion
Evaporation
    activity, 353–354
    concept of, 360
Exosphere, 350–351
Expansion and contraction
    activities, 40–42
    cohesion, 43–44
    concepts, 42–44
    molecules, 42–43
    plastics, 44
    water, 43
    weathering and erosion, 302, 307–308
Eyeglasses, 33–34
Eyes
    activities, 30–32
    concepts, 32–33
    iris, 32–33
    lenses, 33

nervous system, as part of, 271, 279
    reptiles, 233
    retina, 33
    sight, sense of, 279

Fahnestock clips, 124
Farndon, J., 36
Fathman, A. K., 10, 35, 81, 92, 295
Fats, 290–291
Fiarotta, N., 36
Fiarotta, P., 36
Fichter, G. S., 262
Fife, J., 133, 150
Fishes, 235
    aquariums, 237–240
    body, 236
    breathing, 235–236
    reproduction, 237, 238f
    senses, 237
Fitzpatrick, J., 116
Fixed pulleys, 171–172
Fleischman, P., 93
Fleisher, P., 180
Fleming, D., 261
Flint, D., 365
Flowers, 204–205, 207–208
Fog, 361–362
Food and nutrition
    activities, 290–292
    carbohydrates, 292–293
    classroom animals, 10–11
    concepts, 292–296
    fats, 290–291, 293
    healthy diet, choosing, 294
    minerals, 293
    proteins, 293
    vitamins, 293
    water, 294
Food chains, 253, 258
Food guide pyramid, 294f
Food tube, 289
Ford, A., 365
Fordor, R. V., 327
Fossils, 322, 326
Fowler, A., 35, 63, 115, 261
Fradd, S. H., 356, 365
Fradin, D., 400
Frances-Law, P., 116, 151
Fredericks, A. D., 215, 263, 296, 328,
    366, 400
Freedman, R., 261
Freeman, M., 115, 116
Frevert, P., 365
Frichter, G. S., 400
Friction
    activity, 177–178
    concept, 179
Friedhoffer, B., 180
Friedhoffer, R., 116, 151
Friedman, J. T., 93

Friskey, M., 400
Fritz, J., 151
Frogs, 234
Full Option Science System (FOSS), 6
Fungi. See Molds and fungi
Furniss, T., 400
Fuses, 140–141

Gabb, M., 295
Galan, M., 262
Gallant, R. A., 215, 262, 327, 365, 400
Galperin, A., 295
Gardner, R., 180, 400
Garrison, L., 113, 115
Gears, 169
Generating electricity
    activities, 146–148
    concepts, 148–150
Geographic poles, 111–112
George, J. C., 63
George, T. C., 261
Gertz, S., 36, 44, 63, 64
Gibbins, G., 214
Gibbons, G., 180, 365
Gibson, G., 93, 115
Glacial erosion, 305–306, 308
Glaser, D., 400
Glaser, L., 261
Glass, A., 180
Glover, D., 35, 115, 151
Gold-Dworkin, H., 35
Goldfluss, K., 181
Goodman, S. E., 214
Goor, N., 35
Goor, R., 35
Gorey, E., 400
Gosnell, K., 151, 328
Gould, A., 36, 328, 400, 401
Grafton, A., 327
Graube, I., 366
Gravity
    concepts, 397–398
    sun's gravity, 395
    zero gravity, 398
Great Explorations in Math and Science
    (GEMS), 6
Greene, C., 365
Greenway, S., 261
Grimshaw, C., 93
Guthridge, S., 93
Gutnik, M. J., 151

Haab, S., 63
Habitats
    animal life, 257–258
    ecosystems. See Ecosystems
    plant life, 197
Hale, J., 328
Halverson, C., 366
Hamer, M., 400

Hampton, E., 51, 63
Hansard, P., 262
Hardy, G. R., 316, 327
Harlow, R., 295
Harris, A., 400
Harris, R., 296, 400
Harris, S., 327
Hart, J. E., 121, 150
Hasen, R., 400
Hausherr, R., 295
Hawcock, D., 295
Hawthorne, C., 36
Healthy diet, choosing, 294
Hearing, sense of, 279
Hearing ranges, 92
Hearing sounds, 93–94
Heart. *See* Circulatory system
Heat capacity, 52
Heat conservation, 52–53
Heat energy
    activities, 49–51
    concepts, 52–53
    conduction, 60. *See also* Conduction,
        convection and radiation
    contraction. *See* Expansion and contraction
    convection, 60–61. *See also* Conduction,
        convection and radiation
    expansion. *See* Expansion and contraction
    matter, states of. *See* Matter, states of
    radiation, 59. *See also* Conduction,
        convection and radiation
    solar energy, 61–62
    temperature and, 49–51
Heat loss and gain, 47–48
Heat quantity, 52
Hecht, J., 36
Heiligman, D., 261
Heinz, B. J., 262
Heller, R., 214
Hellman, H., 180
Henbest, N., 400
Hewitt, P. G., 180
Hewitt, S., 36
Hickman, P., 262
Hill, J., 36
Hillen, J., 36, 64, 93, 181, 215, 263, 296,
    328, 401
Hillerman, A., 63
Hiscock, B., 327
Hoban, T., 35
Hodge, D., 180
Hogner, D. C., 215
Holder, B., 93, 215, 263, 366
Holley, B., 215
Hooper, M., 327
Hoover, E., 36, 64, 93, 214, 215, 263
Hoover, R., 295
Horowitz, R., 262
Hort, L., 400
Hosoume, K., 198, 214, 263

Hostetler, M., 262
Hubbard, P., 35
Hughes, A. E., 93
Hulls, J., 180
Human body
    circulatory system. *See* Circulatory system
    digestive system. *See* Digestive system
    eyes. *See* Eyes
    muscle system. *See* Muscle system
    nervous system. *See* Nervous system
    respiratory system. *See* Respiratory system
    skeletal system. *See* Skeletal system
Humidity
    activity, 354–356
    concept of, 360–361
Hunt, J., 214
Hvass, U., 295

Igneous rocks, 322, 323t–324t
Imes, R., 262
Inclined planes
    activities, 154–155
    concepts, 155–156
    wedges, 156–157
Ingoglia, G., 327
Insects, 246–247
    adult insects, 247–248
    butterflies, 249, 250f
    legs, 247
    life cycles, 248
    mealworms, 241–242, 250
    moths, 249, 250f
    skeleton, 247
    survival features, 248
Intestines, 289
Invertebrates. *See* Animals without backbones
Iona, M., 35
Ionosphere, 350
Iris, 32–33

Jackson, D., 36
Jackson, K., 400
James, E., 180
Janulewicz, M., 295
Jasmine, G., 296
Jay, M., 400
Jefferies, D., 214, 296
Jeffries, L., 365
Jenkins, S., 262
Jennings, T., 36, 93, 115
Johnson, J., 262
Johnstone, L., 116
Joints, movable, 269
Joyce, W., 44, 63
Jupiter, 391
Jupo, F., 180

Kalan, R., 365
Kaner, E., 93
Kaplan, S., 63

Kaufman, K., 262
Keeler, P., 180
Kelch, J., 400
Kessler, C., 10, 35, 81, 92, 295
Ketteman, H., 63
Kettlekamp, L., 93
Kiefer, I., 365
Kiley, D., 180
Kim, S., 63
Kindersley, D., 295
Kirkpatrick, R. K., 115, 214, 365
Klein, A. E., 295
Klentschy, M., 113, 115
Knapp, B., 63
Knight, D. C., 93, 115
Knutson, R., 295
Kohn, B., 93
Kopp, J., 215
Koppes, S. N., 400
Kruger, C., 151
Kuchalla, S., 214

Lambert, M., 215
Lampton, C., 180, 327
Land. *See* Earth's surface
Langley, A., 63
Laplante, B., 59, 63, 92, 109, 115, 295
Lasky, K., 180
Lauber, P., 180, 214, 261, 327, 400
Lawson, R., 151
Learning
    concept of, 279
    practice and, 273–275
Leary, C., 36
Leaves, 201–203
    vegetative reproduction, 193
LeCroy, B., 93, 215, 263, 366
Lee, J. D., 93
Lee, O., 121, 150, 356, 365
LeJars, D., 36
Lenses, 21–22
    eyes, 33
Leon, D., 262
Lerner, C., 262
Leutscher, A., 215, 327, 365
Levers
    activities, 158–162
    application of, 164
    classes of, 163
    concepts, 162–164
    mobiles, 161–162, 164
    parts of, 162–163
Levine, E., 327
Levine, S., 116, 327
Levy, M., 327
Lewellen, J., 400
Lewis, T., 327
Light pathways
    activities, 6–13
    concepts, 15–17

Light refraction
 activities, 18–19
 concepts, 19–22
Light speeds, 20–21
Lillegard, D., 151
Lindop, L., 327
Livingston, M., 35
Lizards, 233
Llewellyn, C., 63, 261, 365
Lloyd, D., 365
Locker, T., 365
Lodestones, 100–101
Loudness, 70–71
Lunar eclipse, 380–381, 383–384
Lye, K., 327
Lyon, G., 400
Lyons, W., 366

Macaulay, D., 35
Machines, simple. *See* Simple machines
Mackie, D., 151
MacPherson, R., 262
Maestro, B., 63
Maestro, G., 63
Magma, 315–316
Magnetic domains, 114
Magnetic fields
 activities, 106–108
 inferring, 108
Magnetic poles
 activities, 109–110
 concepts, 110–112
 geographic poles, 111–112
Magnetic theory
 activities, 113–114
 concepts, 114
Magnetic transparency, 108
Magnets
 activities, 98–100
 caring for, 114, 115f
 concepts, 100–101
 electromagnets. *See* Electromagnets
 fields of force. *See* Magnetic fields
 lodestones, 100–101
 making, 102–105
 manufactured magnets, 101
 permanent, 104–105
 superconducting, 105
 temporary, 104
 what magnets attract, 100
Maki, C., 365
Malnor, B., 215, 366
Malnor, C., 215, 366
Mammals, 225–226
 classroom mammals, 227–229
 internal development, 226
 teeth, 226–227
 warm-blooded, 226
Mant, J., 151
Marcus, E., 215, 327

Markle, S., 261, 365
Markowsky, J., 263
Mars, 390–391
Martin, B., 35
Martin, C., 365
Mason, C., 262, 263
Mastro, J., 261
Mastropieri, M., 73, 92, 180, 214, 223, 246,
 261, 295, 327, 365
Math, I., 151
Mathers, D., 93
Matter, states of
 activities, 45–46
 concepts, 46–48
 heat loss and gain, 47–48
 pressure and, 46–47
 temperature, 46
Mayer, G., 295
Mayle, P., 295
Maynard, T., 262
McKinney, B., 365
McNulty, F., 327
Mealworms, 241–242, 250
Mebane, R., 366
Mebane, R. C., 64
Meinbach, A. M., 215, 296, 328, 366, 400
Melton, L., 63
Mercer, A. R., 12, 35, 115, 150, 180, 295
Mercer, C. D., 12, 35, 115, 150, 180, 295
Mercier, S., 36, 64, 93, 214, 215, 296, 328
Mercury, 390
Merrell, J., 181
Merrians, D., 327
Metamorphic rocks, 322, 325t
Meteors, 392
Miller, C., 366
Miller, D., 365
Miller, D. S., 261
Miner, O. I., 214
Minerals, 293
Mintzes, J. J., 295
Mirrors, 16–17
Mitchell, D., 215
Mobiles, 161–162, 164
Molds and fungi
 activity, 213
 concepts, 214
Molecules
 expansion and contraction, 42–43
 and sound, 70
 and water, 332–333, 338
Moncure, J. B., 93, 214
Moon
 earth-moon system, 384, 385f
 orbit of, 385
 phases of. *See* Moon phases
 and tides, 382–383
Moon, B., 36
Moon, C., 36
Moon phases

activity, 378–379
 concepts, 381–382
Morgan, A., 93
Morgan, B., 295
Morgan, G., 295
Morgan, S., 93
Morrison, G., 365
Morton, J., 36, 64, 93, 116, 151, 181
Moss, M., 214
Moths, 249, 250f
Motion
 activity, 174
 types of, 178
Motor, electric, 144
Mouth, 288–289
Movable pulleys, 171–172
Munsch, R., 36
Murata, M., 36, 366
Murphy, B., 295
Muscle system
 activities, 266–267
 concepts, 269–270
 makeup of muscles, 269–270
 muscles, 269
 tendons, 269
Myring, L., 400

Nankivell-Aston, S., 36
National Geographic Kids Network, 6
Neptune, 391
Nervous system
 activities, 271–278
 brain, 278
 concepts, 278–280
 nerves, 278
 reflexes, 272–273, 278
 senses, 279–280
Neumeyer, P., 400
Newman, F. R., 93
Nixon, H. H., 327
Nixon, J. L., 327
Nutrition. *See* Food and nutrition

Oleksy, W., 63
Oliver, S., 93
Open circuits. *See* Closed and open circuits
Oppenheim, J., 261
Orbits
 causes of, 397–398
 moon's orbit, 385
Orr, R., 214
O'Shaughnessy, T., 400
Otto, C., 365
Outdoor Biology Instructional Sequence
 (OBIS), 6–7
Ovando, C. J., 4, 35, 92, 180, 379, 399
Overloaded circuits, 140

Palazzo, J., 365
Palotta, J., 261

Pandell, K., 261
Parallel circuits. *See* Series and parallel circuits
Parizeau, N., 262
Parker, S., 151, 295
Parnall, P., 93
Patent, D., 215, 261, 262, 295
Pellant, C., 327
Pendulums, 175–176
Penn, L., 214, 215, 261, 295
Penny, M., 261, 262
Perception
    activities, 28–30
    concepts, 34–35
    sight, sense of, 279
Perham, M., 93
Periodicals, 1–2
Petersen, D., 63
Pettigrew, M., 93
Pfeffer, W., 214
Pfeiffer, W., 93
Pfloog, J., 261
Pipe, J., 180
Pitch changes
    activities, 87–90
    concepts, 90–92
Planes. *See* Inclined planes
Planets, 389–391
Plant life
    adaptation and survival, 209–212
    buds, 203–204
    environmental conditions, 194–198
    flowers, 204–205, 207–208
    fungi. *See* Molds and fungi
    growth conditions, 196–197
    habitats, 197
    leaves, 201–203
    life cycles, 208
    molds. *See* Molds and fungi
    parts and functions, 199–208
    pollination, 208
    reproduction. *See* Vegetative reproduction
    roots, 199–200, 205, 206f
    seeds. *See* Seeds
    stems, 205
    terrarium investigations, 198
    tropisms, 210–212
Plastics, 44
Pluckrose, H., 365
Pluto, 391
Podendorf, I., 115, 327
Polacco, P., 400
Pollard, M., 366
Pollination, 208
Pollution, 259
    air temperature and, 360
    water. *See* Water pollution
    weathering and erosion, 307
Pompea, S., 400
Portman, D., 36, 44, 63, 64
Posada, M., 214, 261

Power plants, 150
Power pulleys, 172–173
Pratt, K., 215, 366
Pratt-Serfini, K. J., 366
Prevailing winds, 359
Priestly, A., 261
Pringle, L., 262
Projects, 5–8
Proteins, 293
Pulleys
    activities, 170–171
    block and tackle, 172
    concepts, 171–173
    fixed, 171–172
    movable, 171–172
    power, 172–173

Quinn, M. E., 10, 35, 81, 92, 295

Radiation, 59. *See also* Conduction,
        convection and radiation
    solar. *See* Solar energy
Ramsay, H., 93
Rayner, C., 295
Reed-Jones, C., 262
Reflections, 16
    sound, 81–82, 86
Reflexes
    activity, 272–273
    concept, 278
Refraction. *See* Light refraction
Relays, electromagnetic, 144–145
Reproduction
    amphibians, 235
    birds, 231
    fishes, 237, 238f
    plants. *See* Vegetative reproduction
    reptiles, 232–233
Reptiles, 232
    cold-blooded, 232
    eyes, 233
    lizards, 233
    reproduction, 232–233
    snakes in the classroom, 233–234
Resistance, electrical, 139–140
Respiratory system
    activities, 282–284
    concepts, 285–287
Retina, 33
Reverberation, 86
Richard, G., 400
Richardson, J., 93
Richmond, B., 215
Rickard, G., 327
Ride, S., 400
Ridpath, I., 400
Riley, P., 93, 366, 400
Robbins, K., 180
Roberts, A., 327
Rock cycle, 326

Rockets
    activity, 396
    concepts, 398
Rocks
    erosion. *See* Weathering and erosion
    formation, 318–326
    fossils, 322, 326
    igneous, 322, 323t–324t
    metamorphic, 322, 325t
    sedimentary, 321–322, 324t–325t
Rockwell, A., 180, 261
Rockwell, H., 180
Rodriguez, R., 51, 63
Roots, 199–200, 205, 206f
    vegetative reproduction, 191–192
Rosenblum, R., 327
Ross, M. E., 262, 327
Rotation of earth. *See* Earth's rotation
Rothlein, L., 215, 296, 328, 366, 400
Rowan, J., 93
Rubino, A. M., 61, 63
Russell, C., 36
Ruthland, J., 327
Rutland, J., 295
Rybolt, T., 366
Rybolt, T. R., 64
Rydell, W., 327
Ryden, H., 215
Rye, J., 93

Sabin, F., 262
Sabin, L., 215
Salamanders, 235
Sanders, J., 262
Santrey, L., 63, 116
Sattler, H. R., 295
Saturn, 392
Sauvain, P. A., 180
Savage, S., 261
Saxton, M. K., 356, 365
Sayer, A. P., 262
Schneider, H., 115
Schneider, N., 115
Schnur, S., 365
Schories, P., 214
Schwartz, L., 327
Science: A Process Approach, 7
Science Curriculum Improvement Study
        (SCIS), 8
Science curriculum projects, 5–8
*Science for Living: Integrated Science,
        Technology, and Health*, 7
Science in a Nutshell, 8
Scott, J. M., 64
Screws, 157
Scruggs, T. E., 73, 92, 180, 214, 223, 246,
        261, 295, 327, 365
Seabrooke, S., 366
Searle, B., 36, 64
Seasons. *See* Time and seasons

Sedimentary rocks, 321–322, 324t–325t
Seeds
   activities, 184–187
   concepts, 187–190
   growth stages, 185–186, 187–188
   parts of, 184, 187
   soil, 189
   sprouting, 189
   survival conditions, 188
   travel, 188
Seifer, M., 151
Seixas, J. S., 365
Selden, P., 327
Selsam, M. E., 214
Seltzer, J., 328
Senses
   birds, 230
   fishes, 237
   human nervous system, 279–280
Serfozo, M., 36
Series and parallel circuits
   activities, 126–131
   concepts, 132–134
Seymour, P., 366
Shadows, 15–16
Shank, M., 63, 110, 115, 195, 214, 218, 261
Shaw, D. G., 36, 116, 151, 181, 215, 263,
     296, 328, 366, 401
Shepherd, D., 36, 400
Short circuits, 140
Showers, P., 295
Sight, sense of, 279
Sill, C., 262
Sill, J., 262
Silver, B., 262
Silverstein, S., 214
Sima, P., 181
Simon, H., 36
Simon, S., 36, 93, 295, 327, 400
Simple machines
   inclined planes, 154–157
   levers, 157, 158–164
   motion and friction, 174–179
   pulleys, 170–173
   screws, 157
   wheels and axles, 165–169
Sipier, P., 327
Skeletal system
   activities, 266–267
   composition of bones, 268
   concepts, 268–269
   groups of bones, 268
   joints, movable, 269
Skin sensitivity, 276–277, 280
Smell, sense of, 279–280
Smeltzer, P., 365
Smeltzer, V., 365
Smith, H., 366
Smith, K. B., 36
Smith, S., 50, 63

Smith, S. J., 110, 115, 195, 214, 218, 261
Smith, W., 327
Snails, 245–246, 252
Sneider, C., 328, 400, 401
Sneider, C. I., 36, 401
Snodgrass, M. E., 366
Societies and agencies, 3–4
   state education agencies, 13–15
Soil
   activities, 310–312
   concepts, 312–313
   erosion. See Weathering and erosion
Soil conservation, 312–313
Solar eclipse, 380–381, 383–384
Solar energy
   heat energy, 61–62
   heating homes with, 62–63
Solar system
   activities, 387–389
   concepts, 389–394
Solar wind, 385–386
Sonic booms, 79
Sootin, H., 116
Sorensen, V., 366
Sound
   absorbed and reflected, 80–84
   echoes, 81–82, 84–85
   hearing, 93–94
   located, 94
   loudness, 70–71
   molecules and, 70
   pitch. See Pitch changes
   reflected and absorbed, 80–84
   reverberation, 86
   speeds of, 78–79
   travel. See Sound travel
   vibrations. See Sound vibrations
Sound reflection, 81–82
   reverberation and, 86
Sound travel
   activities, 74–78
   concepts, 78–79
Sound vibrations
   activities, 68–70
   concepts, 70–73
   forced vibrations, 72
   properties of objects and, 73
   sympathetic vibrations, 72–73
Sound waves, 71–72
Spier, P., 93
Sproule, A., 295
Sprouting seeds, 189
Sraquis, M., 36, 44, 63, 64
Stars, 392–394
State education agencies, 13–15
Static electricity, 146–147, 149
Stearns, C., 400
Steele, P., 366
Stems, 205
   vegetative reproduction, 192–193

Stille, D. R., 63
Stinson, K., 36
Stoker, W., 151
Stomach, 289
Stone, L. M., 262
Strang, C., 366
Stratosphere, 350
Suess, Dr., 36
Sullivan, E. P., 93
Summers, M., 151
Sun's gravity, 395
Superconducting magnets, 105
Suppliers, 9
Surface of earth. See Earth's surface
Sussman, A., 327
Sutman, F. X., 356, 365
Sutter, D., 401
Sutton, F., 262
Suzuki, D., 295
Swallow, S., 365
Swinburne, S. R., 262
Switches
   activity, 122–123
   concept, 123
   two-, three-, and four-way, 125
Symmetry, 17
Sympathetic sound vibrations, 72–73

Tagholm, S., 262
Taste, sense of, 280
Tatham, B., 262
Taylor, B., 36, 93, 151, 180, 214
Taylor, K., 36, 215, 365
Taylor, R., 295
Telephones, 143–144
Temperature
   air. See Air temperature
   heat energy and, 49–51
   matter, states of, 46
   skin sensitivity, 277–278
   winds, causes of, 358–359
Tendons, 269
Terrarium investigations, 198
Thermal equilibrium, 53
Thermodynamics, 53
Thinking, children's, 12
Thomas, P., 262
Tides, 382–383
Time and seasons
   activities, 370–374
   concepts, 374–377
Time zones, 375, 376f
Toads, 234–235
Tolman, M., 36, 64, 93, 116, 151, 181, 316
Tolman, M. N., 327
Tompert, A., 180
Tongue, 280
Touch, sense of
   activities, 275–278
   concept, 280

Tresselt, A., 214
Tropisms, 210–212
Troposphere, 349
Turnbull, A., 50, 63, 110, 115, 195, 214, 218, 261
Turnbull, R., 50, 63, 110, 115, 195, 214, 218, 261

Uranus, 391
Urquhart, J. C., 262

VanCleave, J., 180, 296, 327
Vegetative reproduction
    activities, 190–191
    concepts, 191–193
    leaves, 193
    roots, 191–192
    stems, 192–193
    why study, 193
Venus, 390
Vertebrates. See Animals with backbones
Victor, E., 116
Vital signs, 286–287
Vitamins, 293
Vogt, G., 151, 400
Voltage, 133–134

Wade, H., 63, 93, 115, 151, 180
Wagner, B. V., 215
Walker, R., 295
Walker, S. M., 262
Walpole, B., 36, 295, 366
Ward, A., 36, 93, 115, 116, 151, 366
Ward, Alan, 151
Ward, B., 93
Ward, B. R., 295
Water
    activities, 332–338
    clean, adequate water, 339–341
    concepts, 338–341
    conservation, 341
    and erosion, 308
    expansion and contraction, 43
    future supply of, 341
    molecules and, 332–333, 338

nutrition and, 294
pollution. See Water pollution
properties of, 338–339
sources of, 339–340
Water cycle, 362
Water flow, 339
Water pollution, 340
    acid rain, 340–341
    filtering polluted water, 337–338
Water pressure, 336, 339
Weather
    activities, 353–357
    concepts, 358–366
Weathering and erosion
    activities, 300–306
    chemical weathering, 307
    concepts, 306–309
    expansion and contraction, 302, 307–308
    glacial erosion, 305–306, 308
    interplanetary weathering, 308–309
    plant actions, 306–307
    running water, 308
    wind erosion, 304–305, 308
Webb, A., 93, 365
Webster, V., 214, 365
Wedges, 156–157
Weimer, T. E., 400
Weiss, H., 180
Weissman, P., 400
Wells, R., 180
Whalley, M., 115
Wheels and axles
    activities, 165–168
    belts and chains, 169
    concepts, 168–169
    gears, 169
Whyman, K., 36, 64, 151
Wick, W., 366
Wiebe, A., 263, 296, 328, 366, 401
Wilcox, C., 151
Wilder, L., 365
Wildsmith, B., 262
Wilkin, F., 180
Wilkins, M. J., 36
Willard, C., 366, 400

Williams, J., 366
Williams, L., 327
Williamson, T., 327
Wilson, J., 20, 35, 215, 366
Wilson, R., 295
Wind erosion, 304–305, 308
Winds
    causes of, 358–359
    prevailing, 359
    solar wind, 385–386
Winds aloft, 359
Winer, Y., 262
Winkelman, G., 181
Winkleman, G., 116, 151, 215
Winner, P., 327
Wire clips, 124
Wires, 124
    connecting, 132
Witmer, L., 262
Wold, M. L., 295
Wolf, D., 295
Wonderscience, 8
Wong, O., 295
Wood, N., 93
Wood, R., 64, 400
Wood, R. W., 93, 115, 116, 151
Wood, Robert W., 151
Woodruff, J., 116
Wozmek, F., 262
Wu, N., 261, 366
Wyatt, V., 295
Wyler, R., 93, 180, 327

Yamashita, K., 262
Young, E., 36
Young, R., 401
Youngs, D., 151, 263, 366
Yount, L., 64

Zemlicka, S., 262
Zero gravity, 398
Zim, H. S., 295
Zoehfeld, K., 327
Zubrowski, B., 151
Zuchora-Walske, C., 262